JOINT TAX PROGRAM OF
THE ORGANIZATION OF AMERICAN STATES
AND THE INTER-AMERICAN DEVELOPMENT BANK

FISCAL SURVEY OF COLOMBIA

A Report Prepared under the Direction of The Joint Tax Program

FISCAL MISSION TO COLOMBIA

Milton C. Taylor, Mission Chief
(Michigan State University)

Raymond L. Richman, Senior Economist
(University of Pittsburgh)

with the collaboration of:

Carlos Casas Morales   Alvaro López Toro   Eduardo Wiesner Durán
Jorge Franco Holguín   Bernardo Rueda Osorio   Richard C. Williams

PUBLISHED FOR THE JOINT TAX PROGRAM
BY THE JOHNS HOPKINS PRESS
BALTIMORE, MARYLAND

© 1965 The Johns Hopkins Press, Baltimore, Maryland 21218

Printed in the United States of America

Library of Congress Catalog Card No. 64-25074

JOINT TAX PROGRAM OAS/IDB

Committee of Alternates

Alvaro Magaña (OAS)
James A. Lynn (IDB)

Editor of the Fiscal Survey

Marto Ballesteros
(Chief, Public Finance Unit, Department of Economic Affairs, Pan American Union)

Preface

THE JOINT TAX PROGRAM of the Organization of American States (OAS), the Inter-American Development Bank (IDB), and the United Nations Economic Commission for Latin America (ECLA) was organized a few months before the August, 1961, Conference of Punta del Este, with the objective of uniting the efforts of these three organizations for the purpose of contributing to strengthening the taxation systems of Latin America.

The Charter of Punta del Este gave special emphasis to the programming of development, economic integration, the solution of the problems of basic products, and the adoption of structural reforms. Among the structural reforms fiscal reform has an important role, and the charter indicates that it should be oriented to achieve a more equitable income distribution, to increase public revenues, to create conditions favorable to a more efficient utilization of financial resources together with other measures that contribute to maintaining the stability propitious to development.

Fiscal reform, which is the result of a frequently slow process—from the creation of a climate favorable for the adoption of appropriate measures to the point of preparation of legal texts—has been the ultimate objective of the Joint Tax Program. In order to contribute to this objective, two closely related activities have been undertaken during the last two years, which have already shown positive results in various countries.

The first activity involved two conferences: the first, on Tax Administration, took place in Buenos Aires, Argentina, in October, 1961; and the second, on Fiscal Policy, took place in Santiago, Chile, in December, 1962.

The Santiago Conference produced a document of extraordinary importance, namely, the Summary and Conclusions which established the general guidelines for the tax reforms that should be undertaken by the countries of Latin America to accelerate their development. In accordance with original plans, the participation of ECLA in the activities of the Joint Tax Program ended with the realization of these two conferences.

The program's second type of activity is concerned with the preparation of detailed studies of the fiscal systems of the individual Latin American countries. Through these surveys it is hoped to point out salient characteristics and problems, thus permitting the formulation of concrete proposals for reform. The examination of the effects of a tax system on the over-all economy, the effectiveness of incentive programs, and the analysis of other fiscal policy problems provides the information necessary for the formulation of reform measures oriented to the achievement of a more equitable distribution of income and an acceleration of the development process.

The agencies sponsoring the Joint Tax Program are pleased to present the second volume of these studies, which covers Colombia, to those interested in fiscal reform in Latin America.

A distinguishing feature of these studies is that they not only display adequate comprehensiveness and technical competence but, also, that they are oriented to the objectives of the Charter of Punta del Este and to the guidelines offered by the Santiago Conference. The specific recommendations contained in this work are the joint product of the members of the Fiscal Mission and the Public Finance Unit of the Pan American Union, who sought to apply these general principles to the particular fiscal problems existing in Colombia.

This study has greatly benefited from the interest and co-operation of Colombian authorities. Special recognition is owed to the Honorable Carlos Sanz de Santamaría, Minister of Finance and Public Credit, and Dr. Hernando Gómez Otalora, General Secretary of the Ministry of Finance. A number of tax reforms, introduced after the field work for this survey was completed and briefly described in the text and Appendix to Chapter 1, give eloquent testimony of the Colombian authorities' interest in the subject. Other officials whose assistance was invaluable are Dr. Juan Rafael Bravo, Director of National Taxes, Hernando Zuleta, Director of the Budget Division, and Jesús Antonio Lombo, Chief of the Collection Subdivision.

The Fiscal Mission was headed by Professor Milton C. Taylor of Michigan State University; closely collaborating with him was Professor Raymond L. Richman of the University of Pittsburgh. Heavy reliance was placed on local experts in the integration of the Mission's staff. Research on individual chapters was undertaken by Jorge Franco Holguín, Alvaro López Toro, Bernardo Rueda Osorio, Eduardo Wiesner Durán, and Richard C. Williams. Other contributions were made by Hector Julio Becerra, Carlos Casas Morales, Benllini Galindo, Fernando Gaviria C., José Vincente Malo R., Jaime Sabogal, Luis Guillermo Soto and Eduardo Suarez Glaser. Research assistance was provided by Luis Carlos Parra, Ernesto Vélez Koppel, Enrique Paredes Suárez, Wilma Lucía Cabanillas, Eduardo Nelson Polo, and Francisco E. Thoumi.

The representative of the Inter-American Development Bank, Dr. James A. Lynn, has collaborated in setting the general directions of the program and in the specific orientation of the tax studies.

Washington, D.C.   ALVARO MAGAÑA,
May, 1964   *Executive Director*
                                                      OAS/IDB Joint Tax Program

Contents

LIST OF TABLES

CHAPTER 1

The Fiscal Problems
and Proposals for Reform

INTRODUCTION

COLOMBIA IS A COUNTRY of paradoxes. While Bogotá is called the "Athens of Latin America" because of the high culture of its ruling classes, and bookstores abound in the city streets, over one-third of the population is illiterate. The country is unusually well endowed with natural resources, has a relatively large land area and a population of 15.6 million, but the per capita income is only the eighth highest in Latin America. Colombia is relatively underpopulated, with the same population as the Netherlands and thirty-five times its area, but there are millions of landless *campesinos*. Living in Bogotá, and walking the paths of the wealthy, it is difficult for a foreigner (and also for many Bogotanians) to believe that most Colombians are desperately poor. This is because Bogotá and the other main cities are like islands in a sea of poverty.

But if Colombia is atypical in some respects, it also represents in microcosm the economic and social ills of Latin America. There is an endemic balance-of-payments problem, stemming from a coffee-dominated, one-crop agriculture, with export earnings largely dependent on the whims of the coffee market. There is, also, the vicious circle of trade imbalance, devaluation and inflationary pressure. Compounding these problems is a fiscal and monetary system that has fed the

inflationary pressures within recent years with large-scale deficits and imprudent monetary management. Familiar, too, is a dissipation of resources through a maldistribution of wealth, excessive speculation instead of real investment, the flight of capital, and wasteful consumption expenditures on the part of the wealthy. Perhaps these problems are not as severe as in some other Latin American countries, but this is small solace to millions of Colombians who view their problems without geographic perspective.

Despite all these handicaps, Colombia has been moving ahead, but in a minimal and uncertain way that reflects the basic economic problems. In the eleven years from 1951 to 1961 inclusive, the average annual increase in the real gross internal product was 4.6 per cent. With an average increase in population of 2.9 per cent per annum, this results in an average annual per capita improvement of only 1.7 per cent. Nor is the growth rate consistent, the real gross internal product, for example, rising by 7.0 per cent in 1959 but only by 4.1 per cent in 1960.

Quite obviously, Colombia needs a sustained and higher rate of growth, but it also needs a better distribution of the gains. While in most countries of Latin America one must simply assume by casual observation and various clues that the distribution of income is markedly unequal, it is possible as a result of this study to offer more tangible if not definitive information. In order to calculate the incidence of the tax burden it was first necessary to determine the distribution of income for the labor force. It was found that 11.06 per cent of the persons in the labor force in 1961, earning less than $1,000, received only 1.92 per cent of the national income, and that 64.54 per cent received 26.16 per cent of the income.[1] At the other end of the scale, .91 per cent of the labor force received 12.44 per cent of the income, and 2.15 per cent received 18.95 per cent of the income. Expressed in quartiles of the labor force, the lowest quartile received 5 per cent of the income while the upper quartile received 65 per cent. By anyone's standards, this is a maldistribution of income.

When the United States and nineteen Latin American republics signed the Punta del Este Charter establishing the Alliance for Progress, there was good reason for emphasizing the importance of fiscal reform and self-help measures. It is the revenue system that must provide the public investment needs to achieve a per capita growth rate of 2.5 per cent per annum. It is a rational tax system that will encourage private savings and investment. It is the revenue system that will provide adequate budgetary resources to contain inflationary pressures and the funds needed for public health, housing, and education. It is the revenue system that should play a leading role in promoting a better distribution of income and wealth. Clearly, without a productive, equitable, and rational tax system, the objectives of the Alliance for Progress in Colombia are unattainable.

Giving emphasis to the need for tax reform does not minimize the importance of expenditure policy. Revenues and expenditures are two sides of the same coin, for what can be gained in revenue can be dissipated in imprudent expenditures. For this reason, a considerable part of the ensuing pages of this chapter are concerned with expenditure analysis.

Revenues in General

Colombia in 1962 imposed some thirty different taxes, not counting fees, contractual and proprietary income, and occasional receipts. This total considers the income and complementary tax system and the vast number of stamp taxes as single levies. Included among the fees are charges on banks and corporations, special assessments, highway tolls, and licenses for fishing and mining. Altogether, fifty-six different accounts, including taxes, fees, and fines, are maintained by the Comptroller General. Contractual and occasional income add an additional fifty-five accounts.[2] Among the contractual receipts are mining and petroleum royalties, while occasional income includes coinage profits and a special contribution of $.04 per gallon of gasoline from Ecopetrol to subsidize the departments. With this multiplicity of revenues, receipts, and accounts, it is apparent that simplification and consolidation would result in economies of collection and accounting. In general, the imposition of surcharges for one purpose or another, additional fees, and special earmarked taxes results in more costly administration as well as increased compliance burdens for taxpayers. These problems are discussed at greater length in the chapters analyzing the various individual taxes.

From 1950 to 1962, the income and complementary taxes and other direct taxes grew in relative importance, the former increasing from 42.7 per cent of current revenues of the national government to 48.9 per cent, and other direct taxes (property, death and gift, etc.) increasing from 2.7 per cent to 7.2 per cent. Customs duties rose from 18.3 to 24.3 per cent, but this increase is somewhat misleading since the tariff reforms effective in 1951 raised customs duties to 32.2 per cent of current revenues in 1951.

---

[1] All amounts expressed in value and prefixed by "$" refer to Colombian pesos. During 1963 the official rate of exchange was $9.00 per U.S. dollar, and the free market rate was approximately $10.00 per U.S. dollar.

[2] *Informe Financiero de la Contraloría General, 1962,* pp. 354–56.

Other indirect taxes declined sharply in relative importance from 22.8 per cent in 1950 to 10.0 per cent in 1962. This decrease undoubtedly was due principally to the impact of inflation, since these taxes are principally specific rather than *ad valorem,* and thus they decrease as a percentage of the value of the taxed items under inflationary conditions. Only successive tariff revisions have prevented a similar decline in customs revenues.

Until recent years, total revenues of the national government have tended to increase slightly faster than the growth in the gross domestic product. From 1950 to 1959 total revenues increased from 6.3 per cent of the gross domestic product to 8.2 per cent. (See Table 1–2.) However, as a result of the tax reforms of 1960, which weakened the yield of the income taxes, and the relative decrease of indirect taxes, total revenues fell to 6.3 per cent of the gross domestic product in 1962, exactly the ratio which existed in 1950.

Direct taxes have tended to be elastic with respect to changes in the gross domestic product, rising from 2.9 per cent in 1950 to 4.2 per cent in 1960 but declining to 3.5 per cent as a result of the effects of the 1960 tax reform. Indirect taxes have tended to

fall as a percentage of the gross domestic product, but they show no consistent relationship due to successive tariff reforms and alterations in the level of the excises from time to time. Total indirect taxes fell from 2.6 per cent of the gross domestic product in 1950 to 2.2 per cent in 1962.

Fees and fines, contractual income, and occasional receipts (shown in Table 1–2 as "Other Revenues") have also decreased, but they show considerable variation, rising and falling within a range of .48 to 1.30 per cent of the gross domestic product. In the absence of converting specific indirect taxes and fees and fines to an *ad valorem* basis, their rates should be adjusted every year or two in order to maintain their yields.

In the case of the municipalities, tax and non-tax revenues have grown faster than the gross domestic product. Municipal revenues increased from 1.53 per cent of the gross domestic product in 1950 to 3.18 per cent in 1960. Non-tax income grew from .70 to 1.92 per cent of the gross domestic product from 1950 to 1960, reflecting the growth of municipal enterprises, while tax revenues increased from .83 to 1.26 per cent.

The departments show a substantially different pattern. Relying almost exclusively on excise taxes for their revenues, departmental

TABLE 1–1

Ordinary Revenues of the National Government, Various Years, 1950 to 1962

(Millions of Pesos)

	1950	Per Cent	1955	Per Cent	1960	Per Cent	1962	Per Cent
Income and complementary taxes	$210.9	42.7	$ 500.0	44.2	$1,032.7	48.4	$1,047.4	48.9
Other direct taxes	13.3	2.7	56.1	5.0	79.1	3.7	153.6	7.2
Total direct taxes	224.2	45.4	556.1	49.2	1,111.8	52.1	1,201.0	56.1
Customs and surcharges	90.6	18.3	268.6	23.7	567.7	26.6	521.0	24.3
Other indirect taxes	112.5	22.8	215.6	19.1	249.8	11.7	215.0	10.0
Total indirect taxes	203.1	41.1	484.2	42.8	817.5	38.3	736.0	34.3
Fees and fines	29.8	6.0	38.6	3.4	100.7	4.7	74.2	3.5
Contractual income	24.8	5.0	26.5	2.3	80.2	3.8	85.6	4.0
Occasional income	12.2	2.5	26.4 [a]	2.3	22.1	1.0	46.2	2.1
Total ordinary revenues	$494.1	100.0	$1,131.8 [a]	100.0	$2,132.3	99.9	$2,143.0	100.0

[a] Excluding $310.8 million resulting from the sale of stock of the *Paz del Río* Steel Plant to the Central Bank.

Sources: Anuario General de Estadística, 1960, and *Informe Financiero de la Contraloría General,* 1955 and 1962.

tax revenues declined slightly with respect to the gross domestic product, falling from 1.44 per cent of the gross domestic product in 1950 to 1.43 per cent in 1962 after having been as high as 1.89 per cent in 1958. Non-tax revenues, mainly profits from liquor monopolies and proprietary incomes, dropped sharply from 1.14 per cent of the gross domestic product in 1950 to .89 per cent in 1960.

In 1950 the total tax revenues of all levels of government amounted to 7.7 per cent of the gross domestic product. This percentage increased to 10.0 per cent by 1960. Non-tax revenues, including fees and fines, rose from 2.7 per cent of the gross domestic product in 1950 to 3.6 per cent in 1960. Total current revenues, therefore, rose from 10.4 per cent of the gross domestic product in 1950 to 13.6 per cent in 1960.

TABLE 1–2

Revenue Yields of the National Government in Relation to the Gross Domestic Product, 1950 to 1962

(Millions of Pesos)

	Gross Domestic Product (GDP)	Total Ordinary Revenues	Percentage of GDP	Direct Taxes	Percentage of GDP	Indirect Taxes	Percentage of GDP	Other Revenues	Percentage of GDP
1950	$ 7,860.5	$ 494.2	6.29	$ 224.2	2.85	$203.2	2.59	$ 66.9	.85
1951	8,940.9	669.1	7.48	290.1	3.24	296.4	3.32	82.6	.92
1952	9,650.9	703.7	7.29	327.5	3.39	282.4	2.93	93.7	.97
1953	10,734.7	839.6	7.82	341.0	3.18	358.8	3.34	139.8	1.30
1954	12,758.8	1,042.9	8.17	452.3	3.55	455.0	3.57	135.6	1.06
1955	13,249.8	1,131.7[a]	8.54	556.1	4.20	484.2	3.65	91.5	.69
1956	14,862.8	1,137.8	7.66	610.6	4.11	455.6	3.07	71.6	.48
1957	17,810.6	1,227.1	6.89	600.7	3.37	438.9	2.46	187.5	1.05
1958	20,682.5	1,636.6	7.91	762.3	3.69	668.2	3.23	206.1	1.00
1959	23,472.1	1,916.1	8.16	947.1	4.04	664.1	2.83	304.8	1.30
1960	26,417.6	2,132.3	8.07	1,111.9	4.21	817.5	3.09	203.0	.77
1961	30,067.0	2,130.7	7.09	1,139.6	3.79	847.3	2.82	212.5	.71
1962	34,220.5	2,143.0	6.26	1,201.0	3.51	736.0	2.15	206.0	.60

[a] Excluding $310.8 million resulting from the sale of stock of the *Paz del Río* Steel Plant to the Central Bank.

Sources: Anuario General de Estadística, 1960, and *Informe Financiero de Contraloría General,* 1961 and 1962.

TABLE 1–3

Revenues of the Municipalities and Departments in Relation to the Gross Domestic Product, 1950 to 1960

(Millions of Pesos)

	Gross Domestic Product (GDP)	Municipalities				Departments			
		Taxes	Percentage of GDP	Non-Tax Income[a]	Percentage of GDP	Taxes	Percentage of GDP	Non-Tax Revenues	Percentage of GDP
1950	$ 7,860.5	$ 65.3	.83	$ 55.1	.70	$112.8	1.44	$ 89.4	1.14
1951	8,940.9	79.9	.89	65.4	.73	119.5	1.34	100.6	1.13
1952	9,650.9	120.4	1.25	121.8	1.26	138.4	1.43	112.9	1.17
1953	10,734.7	112.5	1.05	100.2	.93	146.8	1.37	126.7	1.18
1954	12,758.8	139.8	1.10	151.3	1.19	178.8	1.40	148.1	1.16
1955	13,249.8	157.4	1.19	182.1	1.37	229.7	1.73	153.6	1.16
1956	14,862.8	186.4	1.25	216.2	1.45	259.6	1.75	151.4	1.02
1957	17,810.6	167.3	.94	283.6	1.59	316.9	1.78	162.5	.91
1958	20,682.5	211.3	1.02	347.1	1.68	335.8	1.62	185.1	.89
1959	23,472.1	266.3	1.13	425.5	1.81	356.0	1.52	209.1	.89
1960	26,417.6	332.9	1.26	508.2	1.92	377.3	1.43	234.7	.89

[a] Primarily sales of services and income of municipal enterprises.

Source: Dirección Nacional de Presupuesto.

The Burden of Taxation

Chapter 11 of this study presents an effort to calculate the distribution of the tax burden for all levels of government. Even though the income and complementary taxes are paid by the upper 10 per cent of income receivers and the tax system must be progressive with respect to these taxpayers, the quartile results show only a mild progression for the total tax system. The lowest 25 per cent of income receivers had an effective tax burden of 10.93 per cent, while the upper quartile had a burden of 12.66 per cent. If anything, the techniques used exaggerated the burden in the upper quartile. Thus, it can be concluded that the distribution of income after taxes is more or less the same as before taxes. The policy conclusion for tax purposes from this evidence is obvious: for the economic, social, and political good of Colombia, everything possible must be done to use the tax system for promoting a more equitable distribution of income. And since the income and complementary tax system has failed in large part to have an impact on income distribution, it is appropriate to examine the way in which other taxes can be contrived so that their impact will be progressive.

Particular Revenue Sources [3]

1) *The Income and Complementary Taxes.* Colombia has a unique and enlightened combination of three direct taxes on income and wealth: a net income tax, an excess profits tax, and a net wealth tax. But marring and complicating these three taxes are five others that are superimposed in the nature of surtaxes, three of them being earmarked. The tax on excess profits is justified because of the prevalence of monopoly and the distortions caused by chronic inflationary pressures and devaluation, both of which create

windfall profits. There is also ample justification for the net wealth tax because of its relationship to capacity to pay, and its incentive effects on activating wealth into more productive use. Not the least of the advantages in using this trinity of an income tax, excess profits tax, and net wealth tax is their interlocking relationship, in which each one buttresses the others in terms of compliance and enforcement.

Notwithstanding that the income and complementary taxes constitute a desirable grouping of direct taxes, grave faults exist in the system. With the exception of the tax on absenteeism, the other four surtaxes complicate the system and prevent an orderly budgetary system through earmarking. Assessments from the income and complementary taxes have risen by over 500 per cent from 1950 to 1962, and even if this increase is corrected for price level changes, the rise is still over 100 per cent. But there has been a marked change in the rate of increase since 1960. Although assessments increased in absolute terms by 3.0 per cent from 1960 to 1961, total assessments as a percentage of the national income fell from 5.22 to 4.76 per cent. If the national income increased at the same rate in 1962 as it did in the previous year, total assessments as a percentage of the national income decreased again to 4.13 per cent. This is the revenue price Colombia paid for the income tax reforms in 1960, when substantial tax relief was given to the middle income groups and the net wealth tax was removed from corporations.[4]

The number of taxpayers filing returns shows a vigorous growth similar to the increase in assessments, increasing from 78,692 in 1950 to 486,113 in 1962 for natural persons and from 1,067 to 15,481 for juridical persons during the same span of years. The government has also made progress in shifting the burden of taxation from juridical

---

[3] The ensuing pages represent merely a digest of the more important characteristics of the revenue system. For this reason, there are a great number of unsubstantiated statements, the evidence for which is presented in subsequent chapters.

[4] Law 21 of August 20, 1963, which imposed a 20 per cent surtax applicable to the income and complementary tax liabilities for 1962 and 1963, will increase the yields of these taxes substantially, but only for a two-year period. The first impact of this surtax was experienced in the fourth quarter of 1963, when the yield of the income and complementary taxes increased by about $200 million.

to natural persons, the proportion of total assessments attributable to natural persons increasing from 38.31 to 54.37 per cent from 1950 to 1962. But there is a marked concentration of assessments among a relatively small number of taxpayers. The largest single taxpayer in Colombia accounted for 3.69 per cent of total assessments for national government purposes in 1962; 92 taxpayers (nearly all corporations) accounted for about one-third of all assessments, and 961 taxpayers out of 501,594, or only .19 per cent, accounted for over one-half of all assessments.

Business savings in Colombia are an important component of total private savings, and a large part of private savings for the fulfillment of the development plan are expected to originate in business savings. Nevertheless, corporate growth is inhibited by a progressive income tax schedule and by unneutrality of tax treatment as compared with limited liability companies. The progressive corporate income tax, together with a structurally imperfect excess profits tax, provides a curious mixture of incentives and disincentives, the former penalizing large firms and the latter discriminating against small firms. Evident of the tax discrimination against the corporate sector is that corporations in 1959 paid 37.91 per cent of total national direct taxes but contributed only 10.40 per cent to the net private product. By comparison, it is estimated that the agricultural sector contributed 14.29 per cent of the national direct taxes in 1959, although this sector in the same year contributed 42.54 per cent of the net private product. Although serious tax unneutralities exist among corporations, other legal entities, and individual proprietorships, and some of these can and should be corrected, the integration of the corporate and individual income tax appears undesirable on equity grounds because of an exaggerated concentration of corporate ownership. In 1959 only 411 shareholders owned 55.93 per cent of all Colombian corporations.

Direct taxes on individuals have increased from $78.4 million in 1950 to $600.0 million in 1960, an increase of over sevenfold,

but during the latter year direct taxes paid by individuals represented only 2.95 per cent of income received by individuals—hardly an oppressive burden. Among the more important factors that militate against an effective income tax as applied to individuals are an unduly low initial marginal tax rate; an excessive number of exemptions, deductions, and exclusions; the splitting of earned income up to $60,000 between husband and wife; and the failure to tax capital gains effectively.

Several other faults of the income and complementary tax system may be noted briefly: (1) depreciation is excessively rigid; (2) percentage depletion is undesirable because it represents a concealed and overly generous subsidy; (3) the absence of a loss carry-over militates against risky investment; and (4) tax incentives are excessive.

Special mention should be made of the administration of the income and complementary taxes. A limited inquiry into evasion indicates that self-employed professional workers in Bogotá probably only report about one-half of their taxable income. At the same time, administrative procedures are inefficient, auditing is weak, and the application of penalties is anemic.

2) *Death and Gift Taxation.* Colombian legislation on death and gift taxation includes levies on estates, bequests, and *inter-vivos* gifts. There is a progressive schedule of rates for the estate tax as well as separate schedules for the inheritance and gift tax levies. But the rates are extremely moderate both in their level and degree of progression. The estate tax rates only extend from 1 to 7 per cent on taxable estates over $2,000,000, while the inheritance tax rates range from 1 to 8 per cent for the closest degree of affinity and from 12 to 26 per cent for the furthest degree of affinity.

In 1962 death and gift tax assessments represented only 6.0 per cent of total assessments for direct taxes of the national government. And when compared to the national income, death and gift taxes show a declining relationship from 1956 to 1958 and, again, from 1959 to 1961. This is very undesirable in a country with a conspicuously unequal distribution of income and wealth.

Law 21 of August 20, 1963, increased the rates of the existing taxes on estates, inheritances, and gifts by 30 per cent. Despite this increase the rate structure still remains moderate. Moreover, the death and gift taxes have several structural faults. The estate tax is eroded by a provision that permits a reduction of the estate tax by 5 per cent for each child in excess of five, to a maximum of 25 per cent; and the yield of the gift tax is relatively low, accounting for less than 5 per cent of total assessments of death and gift taxes for most years.

Tax administration of death and gift taxes is probably weaker than in any other area of taxation. In the first instance, it is corrupted by a requirement that one of the two appraisers must be appointed by the heirs. Although there are only about seven thousand estate assessments per annum, there is a backlog of pending estate proceedings of nearly three times this number, some extending back for forty years. Undervaluation of real estate assets is commonplace, other assets are hidden, and in the case of still other assets, there is no incentive for the heirs to settle the estate because they can enjoy the income even if the title is not transferred. Gift taxation is inhibited by fraudulent transactions and several other forms of evasion.

3) *The Taxation of the Agricultural Industry*. Agriculture is Colombia's most important industry, but it is beset by numerous and severe problems involving land tenure, production, and marketing as well as taxation. It is important to have an understanding of these non-fiscal problems, because tax reform should play a role in their resolution. Among the more important non-fiscal problems in agriculture are a maldistribution of land, with the result that 3.6 per cent of the landowners occupy 64 per cent of the land, while 56 per cent occupy 4.0 per cent; inefficiency and underutilization of the land held in very large units (*latifundia*) together

with subsistence farming on the many minuscule land holdings (*minifundia*); inefficient, unsanitary, and costly marketing; inadequate and misallocated agricultural credit; and undue concentration in the production of a few crops, notably coffee, which represents one-fourth of all farm production and 70 to 75 per cent of all exports.

Although the taxation of the agricultural industry should contribute to the resolution of these problems, it is currently an ineffective instrument for this purpose. The contribution of the agricultural industry to governmental revenue is greatly out of proportion to the industry's importance. As noted previously, it is estimated that the agricultural sector contributed 14.29 per cent of the national direct taxes in 1959, although this sector in the same year contributed 42.54 per cent of the net private product. The land tax system has been characterized by relatively low rates, general underassessment practices, factors giving rise to a new decree affecting assessments enacted in 1963 (see the appendix to this chapter). Income tax evasion is undoubtedly extensive, resulting from inadequate (and sometimes nonexistent) accounting records and weak enforcement. A tax on underutilized agricultural land enacted in 1957 still remains a dead letter because of the inability to classify land for the purpose of levying the tax.

4) *The Taxation of Urban Real Property*. Although the urban real property tax is principally a source of revenue for the municipalities, two of the departments, the national government, and three regional development agencies also derive revenue from the tax. This fractioning of the base, together with an overly generous exemption policy, general underassessment, and tax delinquency, has relegated the tax to a rather minor role as a source of revenue. The tax produced $158 million for the municipalities in 1961, which represents only about 50 per cent of their tax revenues and only about 14 per cent of their over-all revenues. Moreover, there are indications that the urban real property tax is becoming weaker, as property tax

collections as a percentage of total municipal revenues and, also, as a percentage of the national income have decreased since 1959.

The failure of the property tax as a strong and dependable source of municipal revenue has set off a chain of undesirable results. Transfer expenditures from the national government are necessary to balance municipal budgets. Because effective tax rates are relatively low, the burden of taxation does not depress land prices through the process of tax capitalization. As a result, land prices are relatively high, and urban land speculation is used as a principal hedge against inflation.

5) *Revenues from Foreign Commerce.* As a source of receipts for the national government, revenues from foreign commerce are next in importance to the income and complementary taxes, amounting in 1961 to $695.2 million or 31.61 per cent of the ordinary revenues of the national government. Of the total revenues from foreign commerce, import duties accounted for 81.21 per cent, while the other receipts included consular fees and charges, navigation and shipping fees, profits on foreign exchange dealings with importers and exporters, and stamp taxes.[5] As a result of currency depreciation and of periodic prohibitions of certain heavily taxed imports, severe fluctuations in the relative importance of customs duties as a source of revenue have occurred over the years.

The tariff list is characterized by very high duties on luxury items and high protective tariffs. There are multiple duties on single items in the tariff list, and both specific and *ad valorem* duties invariably are applied. In addition, controls over foreign trade are exercised by means of import and export prohibitions, quotas, advance licensing requirements, and various foreign exchange and administrative regulations. Duties and

controls are used for a variety of purposes: to provide revenues, to protect and develop domestic industry, to conserve foreign exchange, and to promote price stability. But there are conflicts among these goals, and the various devices used to attain the goals are often used unwisely.

Protective tariffs, coupled with high domestic prices of some protected goods, create problems of distributing equitably the burden of development. The protective tariffs are also so high, as a rule, that they virtually eliminate foreign competition, which results in some evidence (presented later) of restrictive practices and monopoly pricing. There is also reason to question the advisability of prohibiting certain imports in order to conserve foreign exchange. In the case of automobiles, for example, import prohibitions provide windfall profits for a few (including the diplomatic corps and technical assistants) without resolving the fundamental problem of balance-of-payments disequilibrium.

Total exemptions from duties are excessive, amounting to 21.96 per cent of total imports in 1961. The bulk of these exemptions are government or government-related imports, but there are also an increasing number of exemptions being granted as a development incentive for private enterprise. The justification for many of these developmental exemptions appears weak.

The administration of foreign trade policy is exceedingly complex, unwieldy, and wasteful. There are several agencies, not counting legislative committees, which make and administer tariff and foreign trade policies. Nevertheless, despite this bureaucratic overhead, there is an appreciable amount of smuggling, some of it open to the degree of being blatant.

6) *Internal Indirect Taxes.* Each of the three levels of government in Colombia levy internal indirect taxes, but they are relatively important as a source of revenue only at the departmental level. In 1961 internal indirect taxes were 8.0 per cent of total national tax revenues, while they represented 93.98 per

---

[5] As part of the devaluation of December, 1962, Colombia adopted an exchange rate differential on coffee and petroleum export earnings. Under this system exporters are required to sell their foreign exchange earnings for $7.30 per U.S. dollar, while the government realizes a profit by selling the earnings for $9.00 per U.S. dollar. During 1963, this tax increased government revenues by $469.3 million.

cent of departmental tax revenues and 28.54 per cent of municipal tax collections.

Most of the indirect taxes are regressive, while others are a nuisance and obstruct business, are difficult to administer, and are capricious with respect to their burden. At the national level, there is an excessive use of stamps and stamped paper, and the charges for these are not related to the cost of the services involved. With the consumption and production taxes, there is also an excessive use made of earmarking. The remaining taxes used at the national level—taxes on liquor and tobacco products, public shows, gambling, cotton and cotton yarns, matches, playing cards, and lotteries—are largely regressive in their incidence.

Most of the departmental indirect taxes are levied on tobacco and liquor products, and the revenue productivity of these taxes is impaired by the use of specific rather than *ad valorem* levies. Two other departmental indirect taxes are very regressive in their impact; namely, taxes on lotteries and livestock-slaughtering. One of the best indirect taxes, on gasoline, is also one of the least exploited, with the tax representing only 3.2 per cent of the retail price of a gallon of regular gasoline.

The most important municipal indirect tax, which is superior to the others used, is a tax on industry and commerce, but the levy is marred by the use of multiple bases comprising rents, sales, and installed horsepower. A tax on entertainment and public shows is appropriate for use at the municipal level, but this levy is shared with the national government. The other two indirect taxes used by the municipalities—on weights and measures and on the slaughtering of small animals—are archaic and regressive.

7) *The Autonomous Agencies.* Constituting almost a fourth level of government in Colombia, the autonomous agencies have grown from a mere handful at the end of World War II until there are now about fifty major ones in operation. These agencies were created primarily to undertake activities in agricultural and industrial development, hous-

ing, and public works, although their activities are no longer confined to these areas. Reflecting their importance, the combined budgets of the autonomous agencies reached a total of $2,706.7 million in 1962, not counting contributions and aids received from the national government. This amount was 81.79 per cent of the national government's budget for the same year. Increasingly, autonomous agencies are used as a vehicle of investment by the national government. In 1962, 33.06 per cent of the total of direct and indirect investment of the national government was made through autonomous agencies.

On balance, the autonomous agencies operate at a deficit. Noted above is a total budget of $2,706.7 million for 1962. In addition to this amount, the agencies received $603.2 million in contributions and aids from the national government.

The size and importance of autonomous agencies in the public sector pose difficult problems of co-ordinating government activities so that they are unified and consistent. There is nothing inherently wrong with an extensive use of autonomous agencies, and there may even be some considerable merit. But this presupposes that their operations and activities are closely integrated with those of the national government and that they are subject to the control and supervision of the government. Such is not always the case in Colombia.

EXPENDITURE ANALYSIS

Investment Expenditures of the National Government

National government investment expenditures from 1950 to 1962, measured in 1958 prices, increased from $254.3 million to $1,332.1 million or by 523 per cent. As a proportion of the total national budget, investment expenditures increased from 22.2 per cent in 1950 to 40.7 per cent in 1962, while consumption expenditures declined as a proportion of total expenditures from 48.5 to 32.3 per cent. (See Table 1–4.)

A declining proportion of the national government's investment expenditures is spent directly, while a rising percentage is spent indirectly through other governments and autonomous agencies. In 1950 investment expenditures of the national government were nearly two-thirds direct and one-third indirect by transfers to other governments and to autonomous agencies, while in 1962 the proportion of direct investment had decreased to 53.9 per cent.

The functional allocation of investment expenditures is shown in Table 1–5. Transportation represented 88.0 per cent of the direct investment expenditures made by the national government in 1962 and 40.7 per cent of the indirect expenditures of the autonomous agencies. Two of the largest of these agencies are the national railways and the ports authority. Agriculture is second among direct government expenditures, representing 9.5 per cent of investment expendi-

tures, and is also important among autonomous agency investment, amounting to 19.4 per cent of their total. Energy and fuel accounted for 32.1 per cent of the total investment of the autonomous agencies.

The extent of government participation in development is indicated by the fact that the government's investment in development enterprises by the end of 1962 totaled $959.9 million, and its investments in other national enterprises amounted to an additional $4,514.5 million.[6] In order of investment magnitude, the most important quasi-public institutions are the Institute for Water and Electrical Development, the Institute for Municipal Development, the Colombian Airports Enterprise, the Cotton Institute, the Industrial Development Institute, several other development institutes, a number of banks, a steel mill, a housing fund, a tourist hotel, and a nuclear materials institute. Among the wholly national enterprises, also in order of magni-

[6] *Informe Financiero de 1962*, II, 16.

TABLE 1–4

Distribution of the National Government's Expenditures by Economic Classification, 1950, 1956, and 1962
(Millions of 1958 Pesos)

	1950	Percentage of Total	1956	Percentage of Total	1962	Percentage of Total
Consumption	$ 556.3	48.5	$ 817.0	45.7	$1,060.5	32.3
Personnel	411.4	35.9	544.0	30.4	814.4	24.8
Goods and services	144.9	12.6	273.0	15.3	246.0	7.5
Transfer expenditures	191.9	16.7	218.1	12.2	595.0	18.2
Social security	23.6	2.1	26.8	1.5	107.1	3.3
Other public entities (not for investment purposes)	157.8	13.7	155.6	8.7	397.9	12.2
Private	6.8	0.6	24.8	1.4	72.9	2.2
International	3.7	0.3	10.9	0.6	17.1	0.5
Debt service	144.6	12.6	132.7	7.4	286.5	8.8
Investment	254.3	22.2	620.0	34.7	1,332.1	40.7
Direct	167.6	14.6	417.2	23.3	717.7	21.9
Indirect	86.7	7.6	202.8	11.4	614.4	18.8
TOTALS	$1,147.1	100.0	$1,787.8	100.0	$3,274.1	100.0

Source: *Análisis Económico del Presupuesto, 1962*, pp. 78f.

TABLE 1–5

National Government Expenditures for Economic Development, Selected Years, 1950 to 1962

(Millions of Pesos)

	1950	1955	1960	1961	1962
Direct investment	$ 57.9	$274.1	$414.8	$403.0	$ 606.9
Agriculture	4.6	7.5	43.2	45.4	57.8
Mining (except coal)	.6	—	—	1.0	.5
Energy and fuel	.2	.2	.3	—	10.5
Industry	—	—	4.9	—	—
Transportation	51.9	258.1	363.8	350.3	534.1
Communications	.6	8.3	2.6	6.3	4.0
Indirect investment of the autonomous agencies	23.7	73.5	116.4	197.8	230.8
Agriculture	—	—	3.7	13.7	44.7
Energy and fuel	11.8	10.0	44.4	53.1	74.1
Industries	.2	4.5	2.8	16.8	18.0
Transportation	11.7	59.0	65.5	114.2	94.0
Total development expenditures	81.6	347.6	531.2	600.8	837.7
Non-development investment a	34.2	202.2	279.6	347.3	596.8
TOTALS	$115.8	$549.8	$810.8	$948.1	$1,434.5

a Total investment expenditures less development expenditures.

Source: Análisis Económico del Presupuesto, 1962, pp. 15–16.

tude, are the Colombian Petroleum Enterprise, the National Railways Enterprise, the Land Credit Fund, the Fund for Agricultural, Industrial, and Mining Credit, the Ports Authority, the National Telecommunications Enterprise, salt mines, a military factory, universities, and geodetic, health, and welfare institutes.

At the beginning of 1950, investments in these institutions and agencies totalled only $480.4 million.[7] Over the thirteen-year period to 1962, government investment in its own decentralized institutions and quasi-public enterprises increased more than ten times. Even allowing for price changes, this growth demonstrates the emphasis on development in government expenditures.

The bulk of the national government's investment expenditures were financed from ordinary revenues during the period from 1950 to 1962. Only in 1962 did the increase in net debt exceed the total investment figure. (See Table 1–6.) Over the entire period, total

[7] Informe Financiero de 1962, II, 60.

TABLE 1–6

National Government Investment Expenditures and Net Borrowing, 1950 to 1962

(Millions of Pesos)

	Increase in Net Debt a	Total Investment	Development Expenditures d
1950	$ −0.4	$ 115.2	$ 81.0
1951	3.0	208.1	148.7
1952	31.9	188.6	111.5
1953	16.5	265.1	165.2
1954	130.7	381.6	252.8
1955	−97.5	549.8 c	347.6 c
1956	141.3	470.5	293.7
1957	374.7	439.0	325.3
1958	253.8	411.8	321.8
1959	−13.5	663.7	474.0
1960	104.6	810.8	531.2
1961	697.4	948.1	600.8
1962	2,282.2	1,434.6	837.8
	$3,924.7	$6,886.8	$4,491.7 b

a The change in the balance of internal and external debt, excluding accrued interest.
b Total does not add due to rounding.
c This amount is apparently understated because it does not include the substantial increase in the budget during 1955 of $1,003.8 million.
d Direct investment and investment through autonomous agencies.

Source: Dirección Nacional del Presupuesto.

national government investment was $6,886.8 million, while the net increase in debt amounted to $3,924.7 million. The investment in so-called development expenditures, either direct or channelled through autonomous agencies, amounted to $4,491.7 million, which also exceeded the net increase in debt. Therefore, government policy with respect to financing investment, with the exception of 1962, was consistent with sound financial practices.

Total Expenditures

National government expenditures in current prices increased by 551.5 per cent between 1950 and 1962 but only by 172.8 per cent expressed in constant prices. On a per capita basis the increase in real terms was 92.3 per cent. (See Table 1–7.) In relation to the gross domestic product, national government expenditures increased from 6.6 per cent in 1950 to 17.1 per cent in 1955 but decreased to 11.6 per cent in 1961 and to 9.9 per cent in 1962. Including the departments and municipalities, expenditures as a percentage of the gross domestic product increased from 11.2 per cent in 1950 to 22.8

per cent in 1955 but then declined to 14.2 per cent in 1960. (See Table 1–8.)

Since government expenditures include a large proportion of transfer items, a more realistic indication of their impact on the economy is the amount expended on goods and services in relation to the gross domestic product. This relationship, shown in Table 1–9, indicates that the amount spent on goods and services as a percentage of the gross domestic product remained within a narrow range of 3.12 to 4.75 per cent for the national government and 5.66 to 7.35 per cent for all governments, including the autonomous agencies. In 1961 these percentages were 3.59 per cent for the national government's expenditures on goods and services and 5.87 per cent for all government expenditures on goods and services. There was no increase and actually a slight decrease in these ratios from 1950 to 1961.

Taking all levels of government into consideration, development expenditures increased in importance from 25.0 per cent of total budgeted expenditures in 1950 to 27.4 per cent in 1960. Education and cultural expenditures also increased from 8.3 to 11.4 per cent. (See Table 1–10.) Health and welfare

TABLE 1–7

Expenditures of the National Government in Current and Constant Prices, and on a Per Capita Basis, 1950 to 1962

(Millions of Pesos)

	Expenditures	Expenditures in 1958 Prices [a]	Index	Population (Millions)	Expenditures Per Capita in 1958 Prices	Index
1950	$ 519.7	$ 971.4	100.0	11.0	$ 88.31	100.0
1951	690.5	1,170.3	120.5	11.4	102.66	116.3
1952	732.7	1,223.2	125.9	11.8	103.66	117.4
1953	930.7	1,482.0	152.6	12.1	122.48	138.7
1954	1,109.8	1,587.7	163.4	12.4	128.04	145.0
1955	2,259.7	3,237.4	333.3	12.8	252.92	286.4
1956	1,356.8	1,801.9	185.5	13.2	136.51	154.6
1957	1,322.4	1,499.3	154.3	13.6	110.24	124.8
1958	1,673.3	1,673.3	172.3	14.0	119.52	135.3
1959	1,833.4	1,728.0	177.9	14.4	120.00	135.9
1960	2,294.4	2,000.3	205.9	14.8	135.16	153.1
1961	3,495.2	2,809.6	289.2	15.2	184.84	209.3
1962	3,386.0	2,649.5 [b]	272.8	15.6	169.84	192.3

[a] Adjusted by the price index implicit in the gross domestic product.
[b] Estimated.

Sources: *Análisis Económico del Presupuesto, 1962*, and *Cuentas Nacionales, 1961*.

TABLE 1-8

Government Expenditures in Relation to the Gross Domestic Product, 1950 to 1962

(Millions of Pesos)

	Gross Domestic Product	National Government Expenditures	Percentage of the Gross Domestic Product	All Government Expenditures [a]	Percentage of the Gross Domestic Product
1950	$ 7,860.5	$ 519.7	6.6	$ 877.7	11.2
1951	8,940.9	690.5	7.7	1,062.6	11.9
1952	9,650.9	732.7	7.6	1,218.4	12.6
1953	10,734.7	930.7	8.7	1,461.4	13.6
1954	12,758.8	1,109.8	8.7	1,752.3	13.7
1955	13,249.8	2,259.7	17.1	3,024.0	22.8
1956	14,862.8	1,356.8	9.1	2,252.4	15.2
1957	17,810.6	1,322.4	7.4	2,290.5	12.9
1958	20,682.5	1,673.3	8.1	2,799.9	13.5
1959	23,472.1	1,833.4	7.8	3,141.5	13.4
1960	26,417.6	2,294.4	8.7	3,744.9	14.2
1961	30,067.0	3,495.2	11.6	n.a.	n.a.
1962	34,220.0 [b]	3,386.0	9.9 [b]	n.a.	n.a.

[a] National government, departments, and municipalities, excluding intergovernmental transfers.
[b] Estimated.

Sources: Análisis Económico del Presupuesto, 1962, and Cuentas Nacionales, 1961.

TABLE 1-9

Government Expenditures on Goods and Services in Relation to the Gross Domestic Product, 1950 to 1961

(Millions of 1958 Pesos)

	Gross Domestic Product	National Government Expenditures on Goods and Services	Percentage of the Gross Domestic Product	All Government Expenditures [a]	Percentage of the Gross Domestic Product
1950	$14,688.8	$556.2	3.79	$ 867.6	5.91
1951	15,146.6	602.2	3.98	977.9	6.46
1952	16,102.0	669.8	4.16	1,043.1	6.48
1953	17,081.0	810.8	4.75	1,254.6	7.35
1954	18,262.3	785.0	4.30	1,304.9	7.14
1955	18,976.1	810.1	4.27	1,361.7	7.18
1956	19,745.7	816.0	4.13	1,328.9	6.73
1957	20,186.2	783.7	3.88	1,188.3	5.89
1958	20,682.5	760.2	3.68	1,231.5	5.95
1959	22,128.6	689.7	3.12	1,253.2	5.66
1960	23,041.8	869.8	3.77	1,333.4	5.79
1961	24,179.0	867.4	3.59	1,418.7	5.87

[a] Includes government enterprises and autonomous agencies.

Sources: Análisis Económico del Presupuesto de Colombia, 1962, p. 13, and Cuentas Nacionales, 1961.

expenditures decreased in relative importance, as did the service requirements of the public debt, while defense and "other" expenditures increased slightly.

Expressed in per capita terms and adjusted for price changes, per capita expenditures increased from $166.7 in 1950 to $242.7 in 1960 or by 45.6 per cent. Economic development expenditures, measured in 1958 prices, increased from $41.7 to $66.4 per

capita or by 59.2 per cent, while per capita educational expenditures increased from $13.8 to $27.6 or by 100 per cent.

Although the category of "other" expenses in Table 1-10 showed an increase, the consumption expenditures of the national government have been decreasing in relative importance. (See Table 1-11.) When consumption expenditures were adjusted by a price index, they showed an increase of

TABLE 1-10

Functional Distribution of Government Expenditures, 1950 and 1960[a]

(Millions of Pesos)

1950	National Government	Departments	Municipalities	Total	Percentage of Total	Per Capita Expenditures	Per Capita Expenditures in 1958 Prices	Index of Per Capita Change in 1958 Prices
Total expenditures	$ 584.6	$227.8	$169.2	$ 981.6	100.0	$ 89.2	$166.7	100.0
Economic development	183.2	31.3	30.6	245.1	25.0	22.3	41.7	100.0
Education and culture	27.5	46.1	8.2	81.8	8.3	7.4	13.8	100.0
Health and welfare	70.0	26.9	20.8	117.7	12.0	10.7	20.0	100.0
Public debt	65.5	21.1	35.8	122.4	12.5	11.1	20.7	100.0
National defense	83.2	—	—	83.2	8.5	7.6	14.2	100.0
Other	155.2	102.4	73.8	331.4	33.8	30.1	56.3	100.0
1960 Total Expenditures	$2,294.4	$858.8	$966.5	$4,119.7	100.0	$278.4	$242.7	145.6
Economic development	658.8	193.1	276.3	1,128.2	27.4	76.2	66.4	159.2
Education and culture	184.5	227.6	56.5	468.6	11.4	31.7	27.6	200.0
Health and welfare	183.8	95.7	77.7	357.2	8.7	24.1	21.0	105.0
Public debt	229.0	55.9	23.5	308.4	7.5	20.8	18.1	87.4
National defense	357.4	—	—	357.4	8.7	24.1	21.0	147.9
Other	680.9	286.5	532.5	1,499.9	36.4	101.3	88.3	156.8

[a] Totals may not add because of rounding.

Sources: *Dirección Nacional del Presupuesto* and *Anuario General de Estadística, 1960.*

TABLE 1-11

Per Capita Consumption Expenditures of the National Government, 1950 to 1962

(Millions of Pesos)

	Consumption Expenditures	Consumption Expenditures in 1958 Prices [a]	Index of Total Consumption Expenditures in 1958 Prices	Population (Millions)	Per Capita Consumption Expenditures in 1958 Prices [a]	Index of Per Capita Consumption Expenditures in 1958 Prices
1950	$252.0	$471.0	100.0	11.0	$42.82	100.0
1951	289.7	491.0	104.2	11.4	43.07	100.6
1952	342.3	571.5	121.3	11.8	48.43	113.1
1953	431.4	686.9	145.8	12.1	56.77	132.6
1954	509.5	728.9	154.8	12.4	58.78	137.3
1955	555.0	795.1	168.8	12.8	62.12	145.1
1956	620.1	823.5	174.8	13.2	62.39	145.7
1957	643.5	729.6	154.9	13.6	53.65	125.3
1958	760.2	760.2	161.4	14.0	54.30	126.8
1959	742.9	700.2	148.7	14.4	48.63	113.6
1960	931.1	811.8	172.4	14.8	54.85	128.1
1961	921.3	740.6	157.2	15.2	48.72	113.8
1962	1,230.6	962.9 [b]	204.4	15.6	61.72	144.1

[a] Using the implicit deflator of the gross domestic product.
[b] Estimated.

Sources: *Dirección Nacional del Presupuesto; Cuentas Nacionales, 1961;* and *Departamento Administrativo Nacional de Estadística.*

104.4 per cent measured in constant prices and 44.1 per cent on a per capita basis. Referring back to Table 1-7, total expenditures of the national government, adjusted similarly, showed an increase of 172.8 per cent and 92.3 per cent on a per capita basis.

FISCAL POLICY PERFORMANCE

In the thirteen years from 1950 to 1962 inclusive, the deficits of the national government on an accrual-accounting basis totalled $3,814.2 million of which $2,397.5 million occurred in the last two years of the period. After an extreme deficit of $1,124.6 million in 1955, Colombia struggled back to a point where even modest surpluses were achieved in 1959 and 1960. But in 1961 and 1962 the country plunged back into sizable deficits. The deficit in 1962 of $1,236.7 million represented 36.5 per cent of budgeted expenditures.[8]

[8] Although the final figures were not available when this study was completed, it was apparent that the deficit was substantially narrowed in 1963 as a result of the exchange rate differential on coffee and petroleum export earnings, the 20 per cent surtax on income and complementary taxes, and a curtailment of expenditures in the latter six months of 1963, particularly investment expenditures.

Table 1-12 shows the revenues and expenditures of the national government on a accrual basis from 1950 to 1962. Treasury resources, which are "surpluses" resulting from operations in preceding years, are included among total revenues, but anticipated borrowings are excluded. Total expenditures include the entire debt service. Revenues and expenditures, thus defined, result in the balances shown in Column 3 of Table 1-12. In Column 5 the balances are shown for current expenditures, i.e., assuming that no debt amortization had taken place. It should be noted that Table 1-12 excludes expenditures that took place with funds allocated in previous years but includes expenditures which are budgeted in the current year but whose actual expenditures will take place in subsequent years.

As compared to this statement of revenues and expenditures on an accrual basis, Table 1-13 represents a simplified version of a cash budget. The data in Table 1-13 have been adjusted by excluding treasury resources and unexpended funds from the current budget and by adding expenditures included but not spent in previous budgets. Column 6 shows the balances including current debt

TABLE 1-12

Revenues and Expenditures of the National Government on an Accrual Basis, 1950 to 1962[a]

(Millions of Pesos)

	(1) Total Revenues Including Treasury Resources	(2) Total Expenditures	(3) Balance Including Debt Amortization	(4) Debt Amortization	(5) Balance Less Debt Amortization
1950	$ 522.3	$ 519.6	$ 2.7	$ 20.0	$ 22.7
1951	672.9	690.5	−17.6	25.4	7.8
1952	725.1	732.7	−7.6	31.6	24.0
1953	844.9	930.7	−85.8	34.8	−51.0
1954	1,061.9	1,109.8	−47.9	27.5	−20.4
1955	1,135.1	2,259.7	−1,124.6	31.8	−1,092.7
1956	1,149.6	1,356.8	−207.2	39.4	−167.8
1957	1,229.6	1,322.4	−92.8	54.9	−38.0
1958	1,656.6	1,673.3	−16.7	84.8	68.1
1959	1,968.9	1,833.4	135.5	237.3	372.9
1960	2,339.8	2,294.4	45.4	106.6	152.0
1961	2,334.3	3,495.1	−1,160.3	120.1	−1,040.7
1962	2,149.3	3,386.0	−1,236.7	156.4	−1,080.3
	$17,790.3	$21,604.6	$−3,814.2	$970.7	$−2,843.5

[a] Totals may not add due to rounding.

Sources: *Departamento Administrativo Nacional de Estadística*, and *Informe Financiero de la Contraloría General*, various years.

TABLE 1–13

Revenues and Expenditures of the National Government on a Cash Basis, 1950 to 1962[a]

(Millions of Pesos)

	(1) Ordinary Revenues	(2) Budgeted Expenditures	(3) Plus Previous Years' Accruals	(4) Minus Deferred Expenditures	(5) Actual Expenditures Including Debt Amortization	(6) Balance Including Debt Amortization	(7) Balance Excluding Debt Amortization
1950	$ 494.2	$ 519.7	$ 40.2	$ 35.0	$ 524.9	$ −30.7	$ −10.7
1951	669.1	690.5	29.8	152.7	567.6	101.5	126.9
1952	703.7	732.7	121.5	121.2	733.0	−29.3	2.3
1953	839.6	930.7	102.4	178.3	854.8	−15.2	19.6
1954	1,042.9	1,109.8	138.5	182.7	1,065.6	−22.7	4.8
1955	1,442.5	2,259.7	134.0	254.4	2,139.3	−696.8	−664.9
1956	1,137.8	1,356.8	186.3	157.3	1,385.9	−248.1	−208.7
1957	1,227.1	1,322.4	179.2	205.0	1,296.6	−69.5	−14.6
1958	1,636.6	1,673.3	201.2	256.9	1,617.6	19.0	103.8
1959	1,916.1	1,833.4	244.7	216.5	1,861.6	54.5	291.8
1960	2,132.3	2,294.4	188.3	388.4	2,094.3	38.0	144.6
1961	2,130.7	3,495.2	287.0	669.1	3,113.1	−982.4	−862.3
1962	2,143.0	3,386.0	497.9	659.1	3,224.8	−1,081.8	−862.4
	$17,515.6	$21,604.6	$2,351.0	$476.6	$20,479.0	$ −2,963.5	$ −1,992.8

[a] Totals may not add due to rounding.

Sources: Anuario General de Estadística, 1960, and *Informe Financiero de la Contraloría General,* various years.

amortization, while Column 7 shows the balance on current account.

Both ways of viewing the government's fiscal operations have their usefulness. Table 1–12 shows the results of the official budget, but Table 1–13 shows actual receipts and expenditures and is therefore more meaningful for economic planning. From an economist's point of view, what is desired in budget reporting, either planned or realized, is a clear portrayal of the impact of government receipts and expenditures on the economy during a given period of time. Items inserted in the budget in one year may not be spent until some years in the future, while government spending in one year may include items which had been authorized in preceding years. To show clearly the impact of actual government receipts and expenditures, a cash budget is of great importance. A budget should show the cash revenues anticipated during the year as well as expected cash expenditures. At the end of the period, the realized revenues and expenditures should be calculated. It is customary, but not obligatory, to exclude increases and

amortizations of debt from the cash budget, but debt transactions should be clearly differentiated. The amount of new debt to be incurred, its sources, and the amount to be amortized should be determined only after examining the cash budget and after considering the likely impact of debt operations on the economy in view of existing economic conditions.

The cash budgets in Table 1–13 show deficits in all but four years of the entire period. (Column 6.) However, the cash budgets, excluding debt amortization, indicate a surplus in a majority of the years on current operations. (Column 7.) On a cash basis, the deficit including debt amortization was $1,081.8 million in 1962 as compared to the deficit of $1,236.7 million on an accrual basis. Thus, either on a cash or on an accrual basis, the deficit in 1962 was substantial.

At the beginning of 1950 the public debt of the national government amounted to $512.1 million, while by the end of 1962 it had risen to $4,601.9 million, an increase of $4,089.8 million. The accrual budget shown in Table 1–12, however, indicates that the net deficit for the period from 1950 to 1962 amounted to $3,814.2 million. The difference between these amounts represents the larger nominal cost of servicing the external debt as a result of successive devaluations in 1949, 1957, and 1962.[9]

Debt Management

Debt management provides considerable latitude for the exercise of policy decisions. It is possible to avoid net repayments of debt in years when it is economically undesirable by offsetting amortizations with new loans. Or it is possible to accelerate debt repayment by buying bonds in the open market regardless of whether they are due. The choice of one policy or the other should depend on domestic economic conditions as well as balance-of-payments considerations.

It should also be borne in mind that different sources of borrowing have different inflationary effects. Borrowing from the Central Bank is the most inflationary, since the reserves of the banking system are increased, which makes possible an expansion of bank loans. Borrowing from commercial banks is less inflationary, since bank reserves are not affected and the capacity of the banks to lend is not increased. Borrowing from individuals is similarly less inflationary. Borrowing from abroad to finance internal purchases would be highly inflationary, but since, at least in Colombia, such borrowing is used to finance external purchases, it is either neutral with respect to its price effects or it may relieve domestic inflationary pressures. Debt management also may be used to counter inflationary tendencies. A governmental surplus realized by borrowing can extract money from the banking system,

which reduces bank reserves and restricts or reduces bank credit. It is only when borrowing is associated with equivalent government spending that it has an inflationary impact on the economy.

It follows that the main function of debt management is economic and not fiscal. Deficits should be deliberate, not accidental. They can stimulate the economy when the economy needs stimulation. But when a stimulus is not needed, and when economic conditions are inflationary and a deficit is unavoidable, borrowing should be done in the least inflationary way, and it should be co-ordinated closely with appropriate monetary policies.

The funded national government debt on December 31, 1962, amounted to $4,430.0 million, consisting of $2,728.3 million in internal debt and $1,701.7 million in foreign debt. In 1962, the internal debt increased by $1,506.5 million, of which only $370 million was financed by a public issue of bonds; the balance, i.e., $1,214.3 million was borrowed directly from the Central Bank. A small amount was borrowed from the Departments of Cauca and Magdalena, and $81.5 million of internal debt was amortized. It is hardly necessary to call attention to the inflationary nature of this large amount of borrowing from the Central Bank. On December 31, 1962, the Central Bank held $1,658.1 million of national government debt, not counting negotiable bonds. The bank's balance sheet showed that it owned a total of $2,143.0 million of government obligations, including negotiable bonds. Clearly, no internal market other than the Central Bank exists for government bonds and short-term obligations.

If the devaluation of 1957 was considered necessary because of the unexpected fall in the international price of coffee, the devaluations, including negotiable bonds. Clearly, no to coffee. Rather, it can be traced to several causes: the aforementioned deficits, the method of financing the deficits, the inability or unwillingness of the Central Bank to control the money supply, the flight of capital,

[9] In Colombia, deficits have an accounting rather than an economic meaning. Government officials often pride themselves on the existence of a "balanced" budget, even though the planned budget requires borrowing in excess of amortization of debt. If the realized budget has not required *unanticipated* borrowing, it is likewise "in balance." Or, they may speak of a "surplus" if revenues exceed projections, even though an increase in the public debt results from the year's activities.

and the failure to reduce imports and/or increase exports. In the face of inflationary conditions and a serious balance-of-payments problem, deficits could well prove disastrous unless the Central Bank acts to prevent a secondary increase in the money supply by increasing reserve requirements. Instead, the Central Bank permitted commercial bank demand deposits to increase from $2.49 billion in December, 1960, to $4.05 billion in December, 1962, an increase of 62.7 per cent. It is not surprising, therefore, that Colombians moved into foreign assets in the face of such inflationary policies.

With the sole exception of cotton, no significant increase in exports has occurred during recent years. On the other hand, the import substitution program has resulted in the premature establishment of an excessive number of firms devoted to the production (or more correctly, assembly) of luxury consumer goods, which continue to require large amounts of imported intermediate goods. (This problem is analyzed in Chapter 9 on Tariffs and Development.)

One lesson to be learned by experience is that the government and the Central Bank should take action to develop a domestic market for government obligations. A deficit by itself is neither good nor bad; it depends on the economic conditions of the country. With large-scale unemployment, a deficit should not be excessively inflationary. But without a secondary market for government obligations, deficits realized under inflationary economic conditions aggravate inflationary pressures. Among the possible actions that may be taken to prevent excessive inflationary pressures and to create a market for government obligations are the following:

1) All borrowing from the Central Bank should be in the form of negotiable instruments with the bank authorized to sell them.

2) The Central Bank, together with the Minister of Finance and the Planning Council, could be given the authority to require that a certain percentage of the assets of commercial and savings banks, insurance companies, and public and private social security systems is to be held in the form of government obligations.[10]

3) The Central Bank should exercise control over the legal reserve ratios of the commercial and savings banks. The Central Bank imposed a temporary limit on credit expansion by the commercial banks in 1963, but it was tardy in doing so. In the absence of a market for government obligations, the bank should move quickly to restrict a secondary expansion of the money supply.

4) As pointed out later in this study, the inflationary problem is aggravated by foreign exchange difficulties. Utilization of foreign exchange for travel and for other purposes should be subject to higher taxes, if only to compensate for the relative changes in the domestic prices of luxury goods due to tariffs.

Magnitude of the Public Debt

At the end of 1962, the debt of the national government amounted to $4,430.0 million or approximately 13 per cent of the gross domestic product and 206.6 per cent of ordinary revenues during the year. (See Table 1–14.) However, the debt is understated, because the external debt is payable in foreign currency and successive devaluations have resulted in an increase in the debt's peso equivalent. Thus, the devaluation of the peso in December, 1962, from $6.70 to the U.S. dollar to $9.00 to the U.S. dollar increased the peso equivalent of the external debt by $629 million.

Nevertheless, the magnitude of the external debt does not create a serious burden, although, of course, the service requirements of the external debt constitute a drain on foreign exchange. In 1962, the service requirements of the external debt amounted to U.S. $18.7 million. Exports of goods and services in 1961 amounted to $3,993.5 million[11] or approximately U.S. $596 million. Therefore, foreign debt service does not appear to be a serious problem, although it

---

[10] Law 21 of August 20, 1963, decreed measures along the lines here suggested. See Appendix to this chapter.
[11] Data for 1962 are not available.

contributes to the balance-of-payments problem. The total proportion of the debt to the gross domestic product and to ordinary revenues is by no means large, although Table 1–14 shows that it has been increasing. These proportions registered a decline from 1950 to 1955 and only experienced substantial increases with the deficit budgets of 1961 and 1962.

Data with respect to the debt of the departments and municipalities are not available for 1962. At the end of 1961, however, the combined debt of the departments and municipalities was $843.8 million (Table 1–15), and the combined debt for all levels of government was $2,991.6 million. The external

debt of the departments and municipalities in 1961 was $313.4 million. Again, although the service requirements of this debt aggravate the balance-of-payments problem, it is a relatively small contributor to the total demand for foreign exchange.

FISCAL POLICY GOALS

After documenting the faults of the revenue system, it is appropriate before summarizing the recommendations to offer a few comments on the objectives of a desirable revenue system. Actually, most of these goals are quite obvious, and are generally

TABLE 1–14

National Government Debt in Relation to the Gross Domestic Product and Total Revenues, 1950 to 1962

(Millions of Pesos)

	Internal National Government Debt	External National Government Debt	Total Debt	Gross Domestic Product	Percentage of Total Debt to the Gross Domestic Product	Ordinary Revenues	Percentage of Total Debt to Ordinary Revenues
1950	$ 360.2	$ 144.5	$ 504.7	$ 7,860.5	6.4	$ 494.3	102.1
1951	340.4	167.4	507.8	8,940.9	5.7	669.1	75.9
1952	351.7	188.0	539.7	9,650.9	5.6	703.7	76.7
1953	374.1	182.1	556.2	10,734.7	5.1	839.6	66.2
1954	487.0	199.9	686.9	12,758.8	5.4	1,042.9	65.9
1955	388.3	201.2	589.5	13,249.8	4.4	1,442.5	40.9
1956	495.5	235.3	730.8	14,862.8	4.9	1,137.8	64.2
1957	588.4	517.1	1,105.5	17,810.6	6.2	1,227.0	90.1
1958	650.3	709.0	1,359.3	20,682.5	6.6	1,636.6	83.1
1959	707.7	638.1	1,345.8	23,472.1	5.7	1,916.1	70.2
1960	806.8	643.6	1,450.4	26,417.6	5.5	2,132.3	68.0
1961	1,221.8	926.0	2,147.8	30,067.0	7.1	2,130.7	100.8
1962	2,728.3	1,701.7	4,430.0	34,216.2 [a]	12.9	2,143.0	206.7

[a] Estimated. Source: Dirección Nacional de Presupuesto.

TABLE 1–15

Public Debt of the Various Levels of Government, 1950 and 1961

(Millions of Pesos)

	Debt as of December 31, 1950			Debt as of December 31, 1961		
	External	Internal	Total	External	Internal	Total
National government	$144.5	$360.2	$504.7	$ 926.0	$1,221.8	$2,147.8
Departments	43.7	54.9	98.7	84.3	142.4	226.7
Municipalities	20.8	104.2	125.0	229.1	388.0	617.1
TOTALS	$209.0	$519.3	$728.4	$1,239.4	$1,752.2	$2,991.6

Source: Dirección Nacional de Presupuesto.

accepted. Disagreement arises only with respect to their interpretation. Eight propositions may be advanced in terms of a general framework for the recommendations:

1) Colombia is in urgent need of additional governmental revenues at all three levels of government. This additional revenue is needed to contain inflationary pressures, to finance the investment goals of the development program, and to provide for rising governmental consumption expenditures.

2) There is no technical or economic problem that constitutes an insurmountable obstacle to increasing revenues appreciably, even to the degree of balancing the national government budget. If there is a problem, it is political and not economic.

3) It is more important in terms of economic development in Colombia to develop a productive revenue system than to have generally low tax rates for the purpose of promoting private savings and investment. In other words, private enterprise will thrive better under conditions of relative price stability and where public investment needs are satisfied than in a fiscally starved and inflation-ridden community where the tax burdens are low.

4) Apart from sacrificing the general revenue productivity of the tax system, everything possible should be done to develop a revenue system that is conducive to private savings and investment.

5) Emphasis should be given in tax reform to the promotion of a more equitable distribution of income and wealth, using both direct and indirect taxes for this purpose.

6) Tax reform should be co-ordinated with and should facilitate broad development goals, such as the reduction of luxury consumption spending, the increase in exports, and the promotion of a more effective use of resources.

7) The improvement of tax administration is important and should be emphasized, but it should not be viewed as a substitute for structural changes in the tax system.

8) Recognition should be given to the traditional canons of taxation, such as neu-

trality, simplicity, administrative feasibility, and flexibility.

One additional step, in terms of guidelines, is to relate these broad goals to specific sources of revenue. In general, direct taxes should be emphasized. In Colombia's case, this means a strengthening and rationalization of the income and complementary taxes, death and gift taxes, and the real property tax. At the same time, however, there is a presumption in the use of direct taxes in favor of *ad personam* instead of *ad rem* taxes, and the application of a progressive income tax on corporations is to be avoided. Indirect taxes, in principle, do not rate a high score, but they may make an important contribution through their revenue productivity and by influencing the allocation of resources. Their desirability may also be increased by efforts to make them progressive in their incidence.

PRINCIPAL RECOMMENDATIONS

Each of the analytical chapters of this survey is policy-oriented. As a result, numerous reforms are advanced for the improvement of the revenue system. In each case, these reforms are explained and defended, and a summary of recommendations usually is included at the end of the chapter. Therefore, there is need at this point only to list briefly the more important proposed reforms.

1) *The Income and Complementary Taxes.* The system of taxing corporations should be rationalized by: (1) the adoption of an income tax with only two rates, 24 per cent up to $100,000 of net profits and 40 per cent on profits over $100,000; and (2) the retention of the excess profits tax but without a deduction for the income tax and with new schedules for both the determination of excess profits and for excess profits tax rates. Limited liability companies should be taxed as corporations, with the same income tax rates, and pay the excess profits tax or any other tax borne by corporations. Taxes on partnerships should be increased to 6 per cent on

the first $100,000 of taxable income and 12 per cent on the remainder.

Several reforms should be instituted to strengthen the revenue productivity and the progressivity of the income tax on individuals: (1) The rates should be increased from a range of .50 to 51.00 per cent to 2.00 to 62.00 per cent. (2) The base of the tax should be broadened by a severe reduction or elimination of many of the exemptions and deductions (but not the personal exemptions). (3) The exemption applicable to the imputed rent of owner-occupied residences should be eliminated, and the applicable rate to determine the amount to be included in gross income should be a flat 10 per cent of cadastral value. (4) The splitting between spouses of earned income up to $60,000 should be eliminated. (5) Bearer shares should be eliminated or their use made more onerous. (6) All capital gains realized on real and personal property should be taxed under the income tax regardless of the length of ownership and with the application of an averaging device.

The adoption of other recommendations would serve to encourage investment on the part of business firms: (1) the allowance of any business expense for foreign firms provided that the expense is allocable by customary accounting practices to income earned in Colombia; (2) the removal of limitations on the deductibility of salaries; (3) a more generous depreciation policy; and (4) a loss carry-over provision. On the other hand, depletion should be based on cost and not on a percentage basis, while the whole area of tax incentives should be curbed and limited to areas of high priority that promise significant increases in investment and employment.

The administration of the income and complementary taxes may be improved by a number of reforms, but by far the most important is the introduction of withholding on wages, salaries, interest, and dividends. At the same time, all other taxpayers should be placed on current payment on the basis of four quarterly installments. Other important

administrative reforms are needed: for all taxpayers to calculate their own tax liabilities; the elimination of all assessment notices, except in the case of additional assessments; the extension of the statute of limitations to four years; and the rigorous application of penalties.

2) *Death and Gift Taxes.* Colombian death and gift taxes need substantial changes in both structure and administration. An improvement would result by making the rate structure more progressive, and by removing the provision permitting the reduction of the estate tax by 5 per cent for each child in excess of five, to a maximum of 25 per cent. Among the more important administrative reforms that are necessary are the appraisal of estates by the Division of Natural Taxes without participation on the part of nongovernmental experts; the institution of provisional assessments on the basis of the latest income and net wealth tax returns of the deceased; and the allocation of more staff resources and the institution of organizational reforms.

3) *The Taxation of the Agricultural Industry.* A presumptive income tax should be adopted in agriculture because of the general undertaxation of the agricultural industry and the inability effectively to apply the regular income tax to this sector. Presumptive income should be determined by applying a rate of 10 per cent to the assessed value of property. This amount would be added to the taxpayer's net taxable income from other sources, if any, and the resulting total would be taxed according to the current income tax rate schedule. Losses on non-farm operations should not be deductible from the presumptive agricultural income.

To improve the real property tax, the reassessment project of the Geographic Institute should be completed in the shortest possible time by the allocation of additional government funds and by a lowering of assessment standards so that the assessment procedure is less meticulous. To discourage *latifundia* and to encourage a better utilization of land, the property tax rate should be made progressive within the range of four to eight mills.

4) *Urban Real Property Taxation.* The strengthening of the urban real property tax involves reforms in both structure and administration, both of which are essential for a rehabilitation of the tax. The national government and the departments should relinquish their use of the tax in favor of the municipalities. Property tax incentives to encourage housing and industry should be abandoned. The rate structure should be strengthened by consolidating the existing rates and by eliminating earmarking, by giving the smaller municipalities more taxing authority, and by applying a special surtax to luxury-type residential housing.

National government assistance is mandatory for an improvement of assessment and collection procedures. To attain realistic assessment levels, the Geographic Institute should be provided with additional resources. To prevent the erosion of the tax base through inflation, an annual adjustment should be made of the assessed values of all properties. The collection problem should be resolved by the provision of technical assistance by the national government, by the application of adequate penalties on delinquent accounts, and by the prompt sale of properties on which taxes are delinquent.

5) *Revenues from Foreign Commerce.* For purposes of simplification and rationalization, the various duties and fees need to be consolidated. Among the charges that should be eliminated are consular fees, development taxes, stamp taxes, and tonnage fees. *Ad valorem* instead of specific duties should be used. Exemptions from customs duties need to be curbed. With respect to private firms, exemptions should be given only when goods will be incorporated into exports or when no claims on foreign exchange are involved. For the income tax exemption on exports, the rule presuming that the income originating from exports is equal to 40 per cent of the value of the exported goods should be changed to an exemption of that proportion of income that foreign sales are of total sales.

Vehicles and household furnishings imported by personnel of diplomatic and technical assistance missions should be subject to import duties when they are sold within the country.

Several faults need to be corrected in the broad area of tariffs and development policy: (1) Encouragement of industrial development through tariff protection should be restricted to those industries that can be expected to use a significant proportion of domestic materials. (2) The level of protective tariffs should be moderate, and import restrictions either should not be used or be used very infrequently. (3) An excessive number of firms are being encouraged in mass production industries, which prevents a realization of economies of scale. (4) Increased public resources should be devoted to import substitution and export development in the agricultural sector.

Several changes also need to be introduced for purposes of achieving more equity, conserving foreign exchange, and obtaining additional revenues: (1) Foreign remittances should be taxed, except where the taxpayer can show exchange earnings in excess of remittances. (2) Additional taxes on foreign travel should be levied. (3) Duties should be increased on raw materials and intermediate goods incorporated in consumer durable goods and on taxis, jeeps, and automobile parts. (4) Duties on automobiles should be based on c.i.f. value, which is their f.o.b. value at the port of embarkation plus freight, insurance, and other transportation costs.

An improvement in tariff administration would result if the number of agencies were reduced. In particular, the intervention of foreign consulates and the Central Bank is unnecessary. The government should also attempt to reduce large-scale contraband activity by agreements with neighboring countries and by firm action against vendors and their suppliers.

6) *Internal Indirect Taxes.* At the national governmental level, several activities (as detailed in Chapter 10 on Internal Indirect Taxes) should be freed completely of stamp

taxes on the grounds that they hinder business and are a nuisance, while for other activities, the charge made should be related to the cost of providing the service. The earmarking of revenues also should be eliminated. Wherever possible, *ad valorem* rather than specific taxes should be used.

The national government also should relinquish some of its indirect taxes to the departments and municipalities in order to eliminate two levels of government taxing the same base and to provide additional revenues for the departments and municipalities. The taxes on distilled liquor, tobacco products, and gambling should be given to the departments, while taxes on public shows and admissions should be transferred to the municipalities.

To compensate for this loss of revenue and to provide additional receipts, the national government should adopt a broad-based system of selective excises on luxury and semi-luxury goods with rates varying from 5 to 20 per cent. It has been estimated that this system of excises would produce annually about $650 million.

Departmental indirect taxes should be improved by converting the levies on tobacco and liquor products from specific to *ad valorem* duties and by eliminating the tax on livestock-slaughtering. Gasoline taxes should be raised by $.50 per gallon, with the revenues used for highway purposes. Another levy that should be exploited more effectively at the departmental level is the tax on vehicle registrations, which should be based on the value of the vehicles at a rate of about 3 per cent applicable throughout Colombia.

At the municipal level, the taxes on weights and measures and on slaughtering should be eliminated, as they are essentially regressive and arbitrary levies. To compensate for this loss of revenue, the municipalities should receive the exclusive right to tax public shows and to retain any tax levied on entertainment. The municipalities should rationalize and develop the tax on industry and commerce by using the single base of gross sales rather than the combination of gross sales and rent.

Also, the same tax rate should be applicable to both industry and commerce.

7) *The Autonomous Agencies.* The trend toward an increasing reliance on autonomous agencies should be restricted by a realization that these agencies are a mixed blessing. One of the principal problems in the use of autonomous agencies is the lack of co-ordination between the activities of the government and the agencies. To achieve greater co-ordination, all autonomous agencies, including financial institutions and the National Federation of Coffee Growers, should be brought within the control of the national government. The best means of achieving this control is to require all autonomous agencies to submit their budgets for review and approval by the national government. The agencies should also submit their accounts for auditing by the Comptroller General.

EFFECTS OF THE RECOMMENDATIONS

Revenue estimating is circumscribed by a number of considerations, yet something can be said that may be helpful. The government of Colombia, faced with an urgent need for additional revenues, should select a given number of recommendations for implementation, basing the tax reforms on priorities with respect to such issues as revenue productivity, equity, and political feasibility.

Two questions arise with respect to this advice. The first is whether there is sufficient tax capacity in Colombia to provide the financial resources that are needed. This question has a simple and incontrovertible answer. It was noted earlier that the combination of tax and non-tax revenues in 1960 for all levels of government in Colombia represented 13.6 per cent of the gross internal product. Under these circumstances, nothing but inertia should prevent the government from eventually raising this ratio to at least 20 per cent.

Second, do the recommendations themselves provide the additional financial resources that are needed by the government?

The best way to answer this is to single out a few of the major proposals and to indicate their expected revenue yields. As shown below, only five major recommendations are expected to yield additional revenues of $1,305 million.

	Estimated Additional Revenues (Millions)
National system of internal excises on luxury and semi-luxury goods	$ 650
Withholding and current payment of the income tax	400
Conversion of customs duties from specific to *ad valorem* and an increase in rates to compensate for the devaluation of 1962	100
Elimination of the exemption from the foreign exchange tax applicable to importers	45
Increases in the vehicle registration tax	110
	$1,305

Turning to the issue of equity and the effect of the recommendations, those proposals that would have a progressive effect on the incidence of taxation are the following: (1) an increase in individual income tax rates; (2) the elimination of the provision permitting the splitting of earned income up to $60,000; (3) the effective taxation of capital gains; (4) the taxation of agricultural income on a presumptive basis; (5) a progressive rate schedule for rural real property; (6) a special surtax on luxury-type residential housing; and (7) the adoption of a national system of internal excises on luxury and semi-luxury goods.

On the other hand, there are other proposals that would provide positive inducements to private saving and investment: (1) a reduction in the progressivity of the corporate income tax; (2) a more generous depreciation policy; (3) a loss carry-over provision; and (4) the removal of limitations on the deductibility of business salaries. With these inducements, provided in an atmosphere of political and economic stability, private enterprise should be able to fulfill its role in Colombia's development.

With deliberate intent, the burden of the recommendations falls mainly on income receivers in the upper 25 per cent of the labor force. It should be recalled, however, that in Colombia these are the persons who receive 65 per cent of the income.

APPENDIX TO CHAPTER 1

After the field work for this fiscal survey was completed in July, 1963, it became apparent that the fiscal outlook would be improved considerably in 1963 for three reasons: (1) the revenues accruing from the exchange differential enacted in December, 1962, on coffee and petroleum export earnings; (2) the curtailment of government outlays, especially investment expenditures; and (3) the institution of certain tax reforms under Law 21 of August 20, 1963. In general, however, these changes, desirable as they may be under the circumstances, do not render the analyses and recommendations of this survey invalid.

The process of tax reforms originated with Law 21 of August 20, 1963. This law introduced some reforms outright and, at the same time, gave the executive branch extraordinary powers to decree reforms in a number of areas.

The principal structural changes introduced by Law 21 were as follows:

1) *Income tax.*

   a) Extraordinary tax for 1963 and 1964: Article 6 establishes a non-deductible extraordinary tax payable by every natural or juridical person in 1963 and 1964. The tax liability will be 20 per cent of the total income and complementary taxes paid on 1962, and due on 1963, incomes.

b) Deduction of livestock losses:

Article 9 establishes that as of January 1, 1963, losses arising from livestock operations will not be deductible from income from other sources, although these losses may be carried forward to be deducted from future income from livestock operations.

2) *Estate, inheritance, and gift taxes.*

Article 7 of the Law increases by 30 per cent the rates of estate, inheritance, and gift taxes. The increase is immediately applicable for the first two but deferred to January 1, 1965, in the case of gift taxes.

3) *Import registrations and licenses.*

Article 10 authorizes the offices of the Exchange Registry and the National Superintendent of Imports to change from $5 to $100 the fee for registration and license forms, the revenues to be used to finance the operation of the offices.

4) *Development bonds.*

Article 11 grants the national government authority to issue development bonds paying 8 per cent interest to which banks will be required to subscribe up to 5 per cent of their demand as well as time deposits payable in thirty days or less.

The principal structural reforms decreed by virtue of the extraordinary powers granted the President by the Congress (Article 1 of Law 21) were the following:

1) *Valuation of rural real estate.*

Decree 2895 of November 26, 1963, establishes that the cadastral values of rural property will be taken as the tax base for purposes of real estate taxes and as the value to be paid in case of expropriation of the property. Owners who consider the present cadastral assessment of their property to be lower than its commercial value, may request, not later than February 29, 1964, a reassessment by the Geographic Institute.

Owners of property exceeding 100 hectares or presently assessed at over $20,000, are required to make a declaration of the commercial value of their property every two years. The first declaration, which will represent the value of the property as of December 31, 1963, and may not be lower than the present cadastral value or its purchase price, must be made by February 29, 1964.

2) *Sales taxes.*

Decree 3288 of December 30, 1963, establishes a sales tax on finished goods, with rates of 3, 5, 8, and 10 per cent according to the product. Basic food products, school textbooks, drugs, and exports are excluded. The tax will be levied beginning January 1, 1965.

Decree 3289 of December 30, 1963, establishes a 10 per cent tax on the sale of gasoline by producers and importers effective January 8, 1964. Most of the proceeds of this tax are earmarked for highway purposes.

CHAPTER 2

The Income and Complementary Taxes—Statutory Provisions, Revenue Productivity, and Characteristics of Taxpayers

STATUTORY PROVISIONS [1]

COLOMBIA HAS THE distinction of being the first country in the Western Hemisphere to impose a tax on income. Enacted in 1821, this tax was schedular in type, with a rate of 10 per cent on income from investments, business, and property and a rate of 2 to 3 per cent on income from personal services, depending on the level of income. Nearly one hundred years passed before another income tax law was enacted. Once more, this tax was schedular in form, with income from capital taxed at 3 per cent, income from personal services at 1 per cent, and mixed income at 2 per cent. In 1927 the schedular form was abandoned and a progressive tax of from 1 to 8 per cent was levied on all income, regardless of source, after specified deductions.

Colombia's current system of taxing income dates from 1935, when the income tax structure was completely reorganized.

[1] This descriptive information on the income tax and related taxes is based on several sources but principally on a mimeographed study entitled "Taxation in Colombia," prepared by the Harvard Law School International Program in Taxation. This study will appear as a publication in the World Tax Series.

Tax rates were increased, with the new rates rising from 1.5 to 17.0 per cent. It was in 1935, also, that two so-called "complementary" taxes were added—an excess profits tax and a net wealth tax. These two taxes have always been viewed in Colombia as part of the income tax system despite the fact that the net wealth tax, as the name implies, is a levy on wealth. Initially, the excess profits tax had rates rising from 10 per cent on income exceeding 12 per cent of net wealth to 30 per cent on income exceeding 50 per cent of net wealth, while the net wealth tax had rates within a range of .1 to .8 per cent of net wealth.

Numerous changes were introduced to the income tax and complementary taxes from 1935 to 1960, but most of these involved the level of rates. No purpose would be served by detailing all of these changes. Suffice it to say that by 1960 there was a progressive income tax levied on individuals, with rates rising from .5 per cent to 48.0 per cent, a schedule of progressive rates applicable to corporations of from 1.00 to 33.75 per cent, an excess profits tax with rates rising from 18.75 per cent on profits exceeding 12 per cent of net wealth to 51.25 per cent on profits exceeding 50 per cent of net wealth, and a net wealth tax with rates of .15 to 1.50 per cent.

In 1960 a completely revised income tax law was enacted to serve three purposes: (1) to codify the myriad number of existing decrees and laws; (2) to improve administrative efficiency; and (3) to promote a more equitable distribution of the tax burden and the stimulation of investment.[2]

In addition to the basic income tax and the two complementary taxes on excess profits and net wealth, there are currently five other taxes on income and wealth that are collected simultaneously with the income and complementary taxes. As additional income taxes, there are the electric and steel development tax, which is an additional 3 per cent tax imposed on the income of individuals and corporations but not on ordinary partnerships; a housing tax of 6 per cent imposed on partnerships, limited liability companies, and corporations but not on individuals; and a surcharge for absenteeism of 15 per cent of the basic income and complementary taxes imposed on Colombians living abroad. As additional taxes on wealth, there is a tax on underutilized agricultural land of 2 to 10 per cent of the value of rural real estate, and a livestock tax of 1 per cent of the value of livestock imposed on the breeders and raisers of livestock.[3]

These eight taxes are inextricably intertwined in the Colombian income tax structure and, for this reason, they will be reviewed and analyzed as a group. All of these taxes, also, are assessed and collected at the national level, with an absence of sharing or supplementation at the departmental and municipal levels of government.

The Basic Income Tax

Tax Rates. The basic income tax is a unitary progressive tax on net taxable income imposed on all natural and juridical persons except those exempted by law. Currently, the tax rate on individuals is in fifty-six brackets, from .50 per cent on taxable income up to $2,000 to 51.00 per cent on income over $2,000,000.

Tables 2–1 and 2–2 respectively present the income tax rates on individuals during the period from 1953 to 1959 and for the period since 1960. By a comparison of the effective rates on taxable income in these two tables, it may be seen that the tax rate amendments introduced in 1960 resulted in no change in the tax burden of taxable income up to $6,000, a saving in taxes on income from $6,000 to approximately $70,000, and higher tax burdens for taxable incomes over $70,000.

Before presenting information on the tax rates applicable to juridical persons, it is necessary to describe these various entities briefly, for there are a bewildering number of them in Colombia. First, there is the Colombian corporation (*sociedad anónima*), which is the typical association of capital and is the counterpart of the United States corporation. The Colombian corporation is a separate juridical entity, having its own name, domicile, and property. Corporations are subject to the control of the Superintendent of Corporations and are closely supervised, being required, for example, to have an auditor and to maintain a legal reserve. Foreign corporations, partnerships, and other companies or entities are taxed as corporations.[4] Also taxable as corporations are limited stock partnerships (*sociedades en comandita por acciones*), which are limited partnerships with the partnership interests represented by shares of stock.

A second tax distinction is made for general partnerships (*sociedades colectivas*); so-called mining partnerships (*sociedades ordinarias de minas*), which are in substance joint mining ventures; *de facto* or constructive partnerships (*sociedades de hecho*); or-

---

[2] Law No. 81 of December 22, 1960.
[3] Another surtax, a 15 per cent tax on bachelors, was terminated in 1960.

[4] Formerly, a foreign company was classified according to its organizational structure for Colombian taxation, but under the tax revision of 1960 all foreign companies are taxed as share-issuing companies.

TABLE 2–1
Individual Income Tax Rates, 1953 to 1959 [a]

Taxable Income Brackets			Rates (Per Cent)	Taxable Income	Tax	Effective Rates on Taxable Income (Per Cent)
	Up to $	2,000	.50	$ 2,000	$ 10	.50
$ 2,000	to	3,000	1.00	3,000	20	.66
3,000	to	4,000	1.50	4,000	35	.87
4,000	to	5,000	2.00	5,000	55	1.10
5,000	to	6,000	2.50	6,000	80	1.33
6,000	to	7,000	4.75	7,000	127	1.81
7,000	to	8,000	5.00	8,000	177	2.21
8,000	to	9,000	5.50	9,000	232	2.57
9,000	to	10,000	5.75	10,000	290	2.90
10,000	to	12,000	8.75	12,000	465	3.88
12,000	to	13,000	9.75	13,000	562	4.32
13,000	to	14,000	10.00	14,000	662	4.73
14,000	to	15,000	10.25	15,000	765	5.10
15,000	to	16,000	10.50	16,000	870	5.44
16,000	to	17,000	11.00	17,000	980	5.76
17,000	to	18,000	11.25	18,000	1,092	6.07
18,000	to	19,000	11.50	19,000	1,207	6.35
19,000	to	20,000	12.00	20,000	1,327	6.64
20,000	to	21,000	12.25	21,000	1,450	6.90
21,000	to	22,000	12.50	22,000	1,575	7.16
22,000	to	24,000	13.00	24,000	1,835	7.64
24,000	to	26,000	18.25	26,000	2,200	8.46
26,000	to	28,000	19.00	28,000	2,580	9.21
28,000	to	30,000	20.00	30,000	2,980	9.93
30,000	to	35,000	21.00	35,000	4,030	11.51
35,000	to	40,000	22.00	40,000	5,130	12.83
40,000	to	50,000	23.25	50,000	7,455	14.91
50,000	to	60,000	24.50	60,000	9,905	16.51
60,000	to	70,000	25.50	70,000	12,455	17.79
70,000	to	80,000	26.75	80,000	15,130	18.91
80,000	to	90,000	28.00	90,000	17,930	19.92
90,000	to	100,000	29.00	100,000	20,830	20.83
100,000	to	150,000	30.25	150,000	35,955	23.97
150,000	to	200,000	31.25	200,000	51,580	25.79
200,000	to	300,000	32.50	300,000	84,080	28.03
300,000	to	400,000	34.25	400,000	118,330	29.58
400,000	to	500,000	36.50	500,000	154,830	30.97
500,000	to	600,000	39.00	600,000	193,830	32.31
600,000	to	700,000	40.25	700,000	234,080	33.44
700,000	to	800,000	41.25	800,000	275,330	34.42
800,000	to	900,000	42.00	900,000	317,330	35.26
900,000	to	1,000,000	43.00	1,000,000	360,330	36.03
1,000,000	to	1,500,000	43.25	1,500,000	577,830	38.52
1,500,000	to	2,000,000	44.25	2,000,000	799,080	39.95
2,000,000	to	3,000,000	45.25	3,000,000	1,254,080	41.80
3,000,000	to	5,000,000	46.75	5,000,000	2,189,080	43.78
Over		5,000,000	48.00			

[a] Legislative Decree No. 1,615 of 1953.

ganized associations; associations; and foundations. These entities are currently subject to a two-rate tax schedule that is lower than the tax rates applicable to corporations.

Finally, there is a third type of entity that is subject to a three-rate tax schedule that is lower than the one applicable to corpora-

tions but higher than in the case of a general partnership. The first of these is the ordinary limited partnership (*sociedad en comandita simple*); i.e., one other than a limited stock partnership. Second, there is the limited liability company (*sociedad de responsabilidad limitada*). The limited liability company,

TABLE 2–2
Individual Income Tax Rates, 1960 to 1963 ᵃ

Taxable Income Brackets	Rates (Per Cent)	Taxable Income	Tax	Effective Rates on Taxable Income (Per Cent)
Up to $ 2,000	.50	$ 2,000	$ 10	.50
$ 2,000 to 3,000	1.00	3,000	20	.67
3,000 to 4,000	1.50	4,000	35	.88
4,000 to 5,000	2.00	5,000	55	1.10
5,000 to 6,000	2.50	6,000	80	1.33
6,000 to 7,000	3.00	7,000	110	1.57
7,000 to 8,000	3.50	8,000	145	1.81
8,000 to 9,000	4.00	9,000	185	2.06
9,000 to 10,000	4.50	10,000	230	2.30
10,000 to 11,000	5.00	11,000	280	2.55
11,000 to 12,000	6.00	12,000	340	2.83
12,000 to 14,000	7.00	14,000	480	3.43
14,000 to 16,000	8.00	16,000	640	4.00
16,000 to 18,000	9.00	18,000	820	4.56
18,000 to 20,000	10.00	20,000	1,020	5.10
20,000 to 22,000	11.00	22,000	1,240	5.64
22,000 to 24,000	12.00	24,000	1,480	6.17
24,000 to 26,000	13.00	26,000	1,740	6.69
26,000 to 28,000	14.00	28,000	2,020	7.21
28,000 to 30,000	15.00	30,000	2,320	7.73
30,000 to 32,000	16.00	32,000	2,640	8.25
32,000 to 34,000	17.00	34,000	2,980	8.76
34,000 to 36,000	18.00	36,000	3,340	9.28
36,000 to 38,000	19.00	38,000	3,720	9.79
38,000 to 40,000	20.00	40,000	4,120	10.30
40,000 to 42,000	21.00	42,000	4,540	10.81
42,000 to 44,000	22.00	44,000	4,980	11.32
44,000 to 46,000	23.00	46,000	5,440	11.83
46,000 to 48,000	24.00	48,000	5,920	12.33
48,000 to 50,000	25.00	50,000	6,420	12.84
50,000 to 52,000	26.00	52,000	6,940	13.35
52,000 to 54,000	27.00	54,000	7,480	13.85
54,000 to 56,000	28.00	56,000	8,040	14.36
56,000 to 58,000	29.00	58,000	8,620	14.86
58,000 to 60,000	30.00	60,000	9,220	15.37
60,000 to 70,000	31.00	70,000	12,320	17.60
70,000 to 80,000	32.00	80,000	15,520	19.40
80,000 to 90,000	33.00	90,000	18,820	20.91
90,000 to 100,000	34.00	100,000	22,220	22.22
100,000 to 150,000	35.00	150,000	39,720	26.48
150,000 to 200,000	36.00	200,000	57,720	28.86
200,000 to 250,000	37.00	250,000	76,220	30.49
250,000 to 300,000	38.00	300,000	95,220	31.74
300,000 to 400,000	39.00	400,000	134,220	33.56
400,000 to 500,000	40.00	500,000	174,220	34.84
500,000 to 600,000	41.00	600,000	215,220	35.87
600,000 to 700,000	42.00	700,000	257,220	36.75
700,000 to 800,000	43.00	800,000	300,220	37.53
800,000 to 900,000	44.00	900,000	344,220	38.25
900,000 to 1,000,000	45.00	1,000,000	389,220	38.92
1,000,000 to 1,200,000	46.00	1,200,000	481,220	40.10
1,200,000 to 1,400,000	47,00	1,400,000	575,220	41.09
1,400,000 to 1,600,000	48.00	1,600,000	671,220	41.95
1,600,000 to 1,800,000	49.00	1,800,000	769,220	42.73
1,800,000 to 2,000,000	50.00	2,000,000	869,220	43.46
Over 2,000,000	51.00			

ᵃ Law No. 81 of 1960.

which is quite important in Colombia, combines certain features of a corporation and a partnership. It is organized in the same manner as a general partnership but with the additional requirement that the articles of association must indicate that the personal liability of the partners is limited to the capital contributed. The limited liability company offers a number of advantages as compared to a corporation, chiefly, the lower cost of organization and taxation and comparative freedom of operation. Under Colombian law, the limited liability company is an association of persons, not of capital, and it is not subject to the control of the Superintendent of Corporations unless more than one-third of its shares is owned by a corporation.

Before 1960 corporations (and entities taxed as corporations) were taxed progressively through forty-three brackets of taxable income, with rates rising from 1.00 to 31.75 per cent. With the income tax reforms of 1960, these brackets were reduced to three: on net taxable income up to $100,000, the tax rate is 12 per cent; on taxable income from $100,000 to $1,000,000, the rate is 24 per cent; and on taxable income in excess of $1,000,000, the rate is 36 per cent. Tables 2–3 and 2–4 show that the effect of the 1960 rate changes on corporations was quite capricious, at least with respect to raising and lowering the income tax burdens. On net incomes up to $50,000, the effective tax rates on taxable income were increased; from $50,000 to $150,000, they were reduced; from $150,000 to $800,000, they were increased; at the level of $1,000,000, they were reduced; and on all net taxable incomes in excess of $1,000,000, they were increased.

Tax rates were also changed in 1960 for partnerships and limited liability companies, but for these entities the tendency was in the direction of higher tax burdens. Before 1960 both partnerships and limited liability companies were taxed at a flat rate of 3 per cent of net taxable income. Since 1960 partnerships have been taxed at 3 per cent of the first $100,000 of net taxable income and

at a rate of 6 per cent of income in excess of $100,000. Limited liability companies have three rates: 4 per cent of the first $100,000 of taxable income, 8 per cent of income between $100,000 and $300,000, and 12 per cent of income in excess of $300,000.

Net Taxable Income, Deductions, and Exemptions. The fundamental criterion of income is enrichment; that is, anything that adds to a taxpayer's wealth is income unless expressly excluded or exempted. As a result, gross income includes all receipts, ordinary or extraordinary, obtained by the taxpayer during the tax year less the costs incurred in obtaining the receipts. Taxable income includes dividends of corporations, the shares of profit from limited liability companies and partnerships, and the annual rental value of owner-occupied residences. However, a taxpayer whose net wealth does not exceed $48,000 is exempt from tax on $5,000 of dividends received from a share company which declares dividends in Colombia. Also, the rental value of owner-occupied residences is exempt if the value of land and buildings does not exceed $100,000. Excluded from income taxation are insurance compensation for losses, reimbursement of capital, damages for breach of contract (involving only loss of capital), repayments of debts, and the non-Colombian income of non-resident aliens and of foreign corporations. These excluded types of receipts need not be reported in the annual tax return.

In addition to these examples of excluded income, there are certain types of exempt income that must be reported but are not taxable. These include dividends received by corporations from other corporations that are themselves subject to Colombian tax; gifts and inheritances; winnings from lotteries, raffles, and wagers; interest on Colombian national government, departmental, and municipal securities; social security and similar benefits; and certain non-business capital gains.

After deducting these excluded and exempt receipts, taxpayers are allowed to subtract those business costs involved in producing

TABLE 2–3

Statutory and Effective Income Tax Rates for Corporations and Other Entities Taxed
as Corporations, 1953 to 1959[a]

Taxable Income Brackets		Rate (Per Cent)	Taxable Income	Tax	Effective Rates on Taxable Income (Per Cent)
Up to $	2,000	1.00	$ 2,000	$ 20	1.00
$ 2,000 to	3,000	1.50	3,000	35	1.17
3,000 to	4,000	2.00	4,000	55	1.38
4,000 to	5,000	2.50	5,000	80	1.60
5,000 to	6,000	3.00	6,000	110	1.83
6,000 to	7,000	4.75	7,000	157	2.24
7,000 to	8,000	5.00	8,000	207	2.59
8,000 to	9,000	5.50	9,000	262	2.91
9,000 to	10,000	5.75	10,000	320	3.20
10,000 to	12,000	8.75	12,000	495	4.13
12,000 to	13,000	9.75	13,000	592	4.55
13,000 to	15,000	10.00	15,000	792	5.28
15,000 to	16,000	10.50	16,000	897	5.61
16,000 to	18,000	11.00	18,000	1,117	6.21
18,000 to	19,000	11.50	19,000	1,232	6.48
19,000 to	20,000	11.75	20,000	1,350	6.75
20,000 to	21,000	12.00	21,000	1,470	7.00
21,000 to	22,000	12.25	22,000	1,595	7.25
22,000 to	24,000	12.75	24,000	1,850	7.71
24,000 to	26,000	13.00	26,000	2,110	8.12
26,000 to	28,000	13.50	28,000	2,380	8.50
28,000 to	30,000	14.00	30,000	2,660	8.87
30,000 to	35,000	14.25	35,000	3,372	9.63
35,000 to	40,000	15.00	40,000	4,122	10.31
40,000 to	50,000	15.50	50,000	5,672	11.34
50,000 to	60,000	16.25	60,000	7,297	12.16
60,000 to	70,000	17.00	70,000	8,997	12.85
70,000 to	80,000	17.50	80,000	10,747	13.43
80,000 to	90,000	18.50	90,000	12,597	14.00
90,000 to	100,000	19.00	100,000	14,497	14.50
100,000 to	150,000	19.50	150,000	24,247	16.16
150,000 to	200,000	20.00	200,000	34,247	17.12
200,000 to	300,000	20.75	300,000	54,997	18.33
300,000 to	400,000	22.00	400,000	76,997	19.25
400,000 to	500,000	23.25	500,000	100,247	20.05
500,000 to	600,000	24.75	600,000	124,997	20.83
600,000 to	800,000	26.00	800,000	176,997	22.12
800,000 to	1,000,000	26.75	1,000,000	230,497	23.05
1,000,000 to	1,500,000	27.25	1,500,000	366,747	24.45
1,500,000 to	2,000,000	28.00	2,000,000	506,747	25.34
2,000,000 to	3,000,000	29.25	3,000,000	799,247	26.64
3,000,000 to	5,000,000	30.25	5,000,000	1,409,247	28.18
Over	5,000,000	31.75			

[a] Legislative Decree No. 2,317 of 1953.

the income, including depreciation, amortization of intangible assets, depletion, and other allowable deductions. In general, these allowable expenses are in accordance with the usual principles of business accounting, but there are exceptions, as in the nondeductibility of a salary in excess of $6,000 per month for the manager of an enterprise. Special rules also apply to petroleum, mining, agricultural, and other particular activities.

Next, there are "special personal exemptions." For these, a distinction is made among taxpayers depending on their level of income and the number of children they support. Taxpayers with an income of $36,000 or less, regardless of the number of children supported, are entitled to the following personal exemptions: (1) all payments to doc-

TABLE 2–4

Effective Income Tax Rates for Corporations and
Other Entities Taxed as Corporations, 1960 to 1963 ᵃ

Net Taxable Income	Tax	Effective Rates on Taxable Income (Per Cent)
$ 2,000	$ 240	12.00
3,000	360	12.00
4,000	480	12.00
5,000	600	12.00
6,000	720	12.00
7,000	840	12.00
8,000	960	12.00
9,000	1,080	12.00
10,000	1,200	12.00
12,000	1,440	12.00
13,000	1,560	12.00
15,000	1,800	12.00
16,000	1,920	12.00
18,000	2,160	12.00
19,000	2,280	12.00
20,000	2,400	12.00
21,000	2,520	12.00
22,000	2,640	12.00
24,000	2,880	12.00
26,000	3,120	12.00
28,000	3,360	12.00
30,000	3,600	12.00
35,000	4,200	12.00
40,000	4,800	12.00
50,000	6,000	12.00
60,000	7,200	12.00
70,000	8,400	12.00
80,000	9,600	12.00
90,000	10,800	12.00
100,000	12,000	12.00
150,000	24,000	16.00
200,000	36,000	18.00
300,000	60,000	20.00
400,000	84,000	21.00
500,000	108,000	21.60
600,000	132,000	22.00
800,000	180,000	22.50
1,000,000	228,000	22.80
1,500,000	408,000	27.20
2,000,000	588,000	29.40
3,000,000	948,000	31.60
5,000,000	1,668,000	33.36

ᵃ Law No. 81 of 1960.

tors and dentists; (2) all payments to hospitals and clinics in Colombia up to $500 for each case; (3) all payments to educational institutions in Colombia up to $500 for the taxpayer and for each of his dependents; (4) 20 per cent of payments made to professionals other than doctors and dentists; and (5) payments up to $3,600 for rental housing inhabited by the taxpayer. In the event that a taxpayer's net income exceeds $36,000, but he supports five or more children, he is entitled to 50 per cent of the above deductions. Taxpayers with a net income exceeding $36,000 who support less than five children are entitled to deduct only 20 per cent of all fees paid for professional services. For entitlement to the deductions, proof in the form of receipts must be filed with the tax returns.

Finally, there are exemptions for the taxpayer and his dependents. Both husband and wife are given a personal exemption of $2,500. If the husband and wife live together, they may each take the $2,500 allowance, split the aggregate allowance between them, or assign all of it to one or the other. If only one spouse is required to file a return, the entire $5,000 allowance is taken on that return. These options apply to all persons married and living together at the close of the tax year, even though they may have been married during the year. If the return covers a period of eleven months or less, the taxpayer is permitted one-twelfth of the annual allowance for each month or fraction of a month covered by the return.

A dependency allowance of $1,000 is permitted for each child under twenty-one years of age or for any other person whom the taxpayer is obligated to support or educate under requirements of the Civil Law. In all cases, the taxpayer must show, by affidavit of two witnesses, that the claimed dependents are unable to support themselves.

Capital Gains. Although the basic concept of taxable income in Colombia is defined as any increment that adds to a taxpayer's wealth, an anomaly exists in that capital gains were totally exempt until 1960 and are only partially taxed since that date. Capital gains from the sale of securities and other personal property continue to be nontaxable unless the properties are bought and sold as inventory assets in the normal course of business. Under the latter circumstances, the gains are treated as ordinary business income and are added to income from other sources. Gains from the sale of real property bought and sold in the normal course of business are also taxed as ordinary income.

For other real estate sales, the beginning basis for determining the taxable capital gain depends on whether or not the property was owned on December 31, 1960. On purchases made before December 31, 1960, the capital gain is computed from the assessed value as of December 31, 1960, or, at the owner's option, on the basis of his sworn affidavit of value during the period from January 1 to August 31, 1961. On purchases after December 31, 1960, the capital gain is calculated on the basis of cost price.

The taxable gain is also reduced by 10 per cent for each year that the property was held. For purposes of this tax reduction, the duration of ownership is calculated in the following manner: (1) from the date of purchase or acquisition if the property was owned before 1961 and no sworn affidavit of value was made; (2) from January 1, 1961, if a sworn affidavit of value was made; and (3) from the date of acquisition if obtained after December 31, 1960.

Thus, gains from the sale of real property held for ten years or more are exempt. Capital losses, likewise diminished by 10 per cent for each year of tenure, are deductible from gross income.

There is also one final relief clause for low income groups. If the seller's net wealth does not exceed $100,000, gains from the sale of real estate held over two years are exempt.

Exemptions for Incentive and Other Purposes. Income tax exemptions are provided for a long list of governmental and quasi-governmental financial, developmental, industrial, and other enterprises. In addition, income tax exemptions, limitations, or reductions are granted as an incentive to oil companies, certain mining companies, large-scale agricultural improvements, cattle-raisers, rural real estate subdivisions, Colombian airlines, certain investment companies, public utility companies, tourist hotels, certain basic industries, manufacturers using products of the *Paz del Río* steel plant, and to the exporters of products other than coffee, petroleum, bananas, hides, and precious metals.

Other tax incentives are provided in the form of depletion allowances and the amortization of exploration costs in the petroleum and mining industries, special deductions on investments in agriculture, annual accruals to an economic development reserve of up to 5 per cent of net profits for the year, and a newly authorized annual accrual to a reserve for replacement of industrial machinery and equipment.

Classes of Taxpayers and Their Tax Status. Regardless of nationality or citizenship, individuals are taxable upon their net taxable income from all sources if they are resident in Colombia, unless reciprocal exemption is extended. Non-resident individuals are taxable only upon their income from Colombian sources, subject to an additional surcharge in the case of Colombian nationals living abroad. Married persons are taxed separately but, if living together, may split their aggregate *earned* income up to $60,000 on a 50-50 basis.

In addition to the basic income tax, individuals are subject to the excess profits tax, if applicable, the net wealth tax, the electric and steel development tax, the tax on under-utilized agricultural land, and the livestock tax.

Colombian corporations, limited share partnerships, and companies treated as corporations are taxable on Colombian-source income, and since 1960 they are also taxable on dividends, partnership distributions, interest, and rent received from abroad. Foreign companies pay tax only on Colombian-source income, but they are subject to a withholding tax on dividends of 12 per cent or, in the case of a branch, a tax of 6 per cent [5] on income not reinvested in Colombia. Foreign companies, unlike Colombian corporations, are not permitted to exclude inter-corporate dividends from their taxable income.

[5] Effective January 1, 1964, the rate was increased to 12 per cent (Decree 3191 of December 26, 1963).

In addition to the basic income tax, corporations are subject to the excess profits tax, the electric and steel development tax, the housing tax, the tax on underutilized agricultural land, and the livestock tax. Corporations have been exempt from the net wealth tax since 1960.

Individuals holding stock in corporations are, in general, taxable only on their dividends and not on undistributed earnings, but if 75 per cent or more of the shares of a corporation is held by one shareholder, he must pay a tax on his share of the corporation's taxable earnings after deducting the tax paid by the corporation and certain reserves. Dividends paid from surplus or reserves accumulated prior to January 1, 1953, are tax-exempt.

Because the corporate income tax is progressive, there is an encouragement to split a company's activities among a number of subsidiary companies. This tendency is curtailed by a surtax on the normal income and excess profit taxes that, in effect, treats the earnings of a parent and its subsidiaries as if they were derived from a single entity whenever there is at least a 50 per cent common ownership.

Partnerships and companies treated as such are taxed on Colombian-source income and on dividends, partnership distributions, interest, and rent received from abroad. The partners are also taxed upon their respective shares (after tax) of the taxable income of the partnership whether distributed or not. In addition to the basic income tax, partnerships and companies treated as such are subject to the housing tax, the tax on underutilized agricultural land, and the livestock tax. They are not subject to the excess profits tax, the net wealth tax, and the electric and steel development tax.

Limited liability companies are taxable on Colombian-source income and on dividends, partnership distributions, interest, and rent received from abroad. The shareholders of limited liability companies are also taxed upon their respective shares (after tax) of the taxable income of the company. If the limited liability company is owned over 50 per cent by a corporation, limited liability company, or limited partnership, it is treated as a corporation with respect to its own tax liability, and any individual shareholders must pay tax on 50 per cent of their respective shares of the company's taxable income, without deduction for the tax paid by the company. Besides the basic income tax, limited liability companies are subject to the housing tax, the tax on underutilized agricultural land, and the livestock tax.

Assessment and Collection. All individuals, corporations, partnerships, and other juridical entities having a gross income of over $2,500 for the prior year, or gross wealth in Colombia of over $5,000 at the close of the prior year, are required to file tax returns. Individuals having net incomes of over $25,000 or net wealth of over $500,000 and all juridical entities must calculate their own tax liabilities. These taxpayers are permitted to pay their taxes in quarterly installments, and, if their total tax assessment in the previous year was more than $100,000, they may pay in ten equal installments from February to November. All other taxpayers are permitted but are not required to file a self-assessment return, and they have a period of three months after the date of official assessment to pay the tax. Payment may be made through either the 22 regional offices of the Division of National Taxes, the 786 collector's offices throughout the country, or through the commercial banks located in 24 major cities.

The required time for filing returns varies with different classes of taxpayers: (1) Individual taxpayers who are not required to file self-assessments and whose taxable incomes do not exceed $3,000 are required to file returns by February 15. (2) Individual taxpayers who are not required to file self-assessments and whose taxable incomes exceed $3,000 are required to file returns by the last day of February. (3) All juridical persons and entities, provided that they do not have an interest in partnerships, must file by March 15. (4) Returns for taxpayers

with an interest in partnerships and for individuals required to file self-assessments or
filing voluntary self-assessments must be filed
by March 31.

With respect to withholding as an administrative device, there is a 12 per cent tax
on dividends paid or credited by Colombian
corporations to foreign companies.[6] If, however, the foreign company fails to submit
proof that over 50 per cent of its stock is
held by persons who are not Colombian
nationals resident in Colombia, or if it has
no more than thirty shareholders on record, or
if the paid-in capital is not over $30,000,000,
then the tax imposed and withheld is 36 per
cent instead of 12 per cent.[7]

Two further withholding provisions exist:
(1) Interest and dividends on bearer securities
are subject to a 12 per cent withholding of
the tax at source. (2) Payments made to
nonresidents of dividends, profits, interest,
rent, royalties, salaries, and other remunera-
tions for personal services are subject to
withholding at source at the rate of 12 per
cent. These withholding provisions, however,
are merely administrative procedures to facilitate tax collection. They do not relieve the
taxpayer of filing a return and paying any
additional tax due, nor do they prevent a
taxpayer from filing a return and claiming a
refund for overpayment.

Provision was made in 1956 for the withholding of the tax at source on salaries and
wages to commence on January 1, 1957, at
rates of from .50 per cent on salaries of
$5,000 to $10,000 per annum up to 10.00
per cent on salaries over $40,000. Before
this provision went into effect, the withholding rates were reduced by 50 per cent for
the year 1957 on the grounds that taxpayers
would have to pay the full tax on 1956
earnings in the same year that 1957 taxes
were withheld from their wages. Then, due
to adverse public reaction and administrative
difficulties, withholding on wages and salaries
was suspended completely within six months
after its introduction.

A unique feature of the Colombian income
tax law is the option accorded taxpayers to
pay three taxes—the electric and steel development tax, the housing tax, and the livestock tax—either in whole or in part by the
purchase of securities. In practice, taxpayers
generally prefer to purchase securities, for
they can be resold, although at a discount.

The Excess Profits Tax

The excess profits tax, introduced by the
Income Tax Act of 1935, was enacted for
two purposes: (1) to recoup any excessive
profits that may arise by reason of government protection; and (2) to protect consumers and workers on the theory that an
excess profits tax would encourage employers
to either lower prices or raise wages. Both
individuals and corporations are subject to
the tax, as well as other juridical persons
taxed as corporations.[8]

The excess profits tax is administered by
the Division of National Taxes as an integral
part of the general income tax. This integration includes the use of the same tax return
for both the income and excess profits taxes.

In general, partnerships are exempt from
the excess profits tax, and the tax, if applicable, is levied on the partners.[9] Two other
general exemptions are all those persons and
entities exempt from the income tax and
income taxpayers with a net wealth of less
than $100,000. (Previous to the tax revisions
of 1960, the exemption limit was $36,000 of
net wealth.) In addition to these general

---

[6] Before the tax revision of 1960, the withholding rate
was 10 per cent instead of 12 per cent.

[7] Effective January 1, 1964, the number of shareholders
was increased to fifty and the tax rate to 42 per cent
(Decree 3191 of December 26, 1963).

[8] More specifically, the tax applies to corporations and
limited stock partnerships; de facto or constructive partnerships whose articles of association show that they are
intended to operate as corporations; limited liability companies if over 50 per cent of the interest in the company
is held by corporations or by other limited liability companies or limited partnerships; and foreign companies
doing business in Colombia regardless of their corporate
or non-corporate structure.

[9] Exempt are general partnerships, limited partnerships
other than limited stock partnerships, mining partnerships, de facto or constructive partnerships or limited
liability companies not assimilable to corporations, organized co-ownerships, unorganized co-ownerships, associations, and foundations.

exemptions, there are a large number of exemptions that are subject to the restrictions and qualifications of various incentive laws: gold, silver, and platinum mining and certain other mining operations; certain large- and medium-scale agricultural operations; the profits applicable to the initial $5,000 invested in rural subdivision and development operations; fishing companies and co-operatives; residential housing mortgaged by the Military Housing Fund or Territorial Credit Institute; Colombian airlines; tourist hotels; automobile assembly and manufacturing plants; publishing enterprises; certain basic industries and iron and steel fabricators; and governmental and quasi-governmental entities.

In the computation of the excess profits tax, profits are considered to be "excessive" when the taxpayer's net income subject to the excess profits tax exceeds certain percentages of his net wealth. For example, excess profits are those in excess of 12 per cent of net wealth when the latter is over $200,000. But the excess profit tax has certain complications derived from the fact that the total profits subject to the tax constitute a unique tax base. Similarly, the definition of net wealth for purposes of determining excess profits is different from the definition of this term for the net wealth tax. Accordingly, before considering the rates and the computations of the excess profits tax, it is necessary to give attention to the determination of both taxable profits and net wealth for purposes of the excess profits tax.

The Base of the Excess Profits Tax. The base of the excess profits tax is net income derived from capital. As a result, income received from personal services and that part of mixed income attributable to personal services are deductible. Other deductions include: (1) the regular allowances for dependents and personal and special exemptions; (2) the amount of the basic income tax, including the special 6 per cent tax on the distributed earnings of foreign branches but not the 12 per cent withholding tax on dividends paid to foreign companies; (3) the

amount of the net wealth tax; (4) dividends paid by Colombian corporations to foreign companies provided that no dividends are distributed within Colombia; (5) capital gains from the sale of personal property other than those arising in the usual course of business; (6) inheritances, bequests, gifts, gambling gains (as long as these are subject to other taxes), and any other extraordinary receipts not derived from the taxpayer's net wealth; (7) the amount of the year's accrual to the special reserve for replacements; (8) the allowance for depletion after the normal depletion allowance under the income tax has been exhausted; and (9) income from capital invested in gold, silver, or platinum mining.

On the other hand, there are certain types of income that are exempt under the income tax, but which are part of the excess profits tax base. These include intercompany dividends, partnership and similar income, interest on Colombian governmental obligations, and interest on savings bank deposits and Colombian mortgage bank bonds and certificates.

Net Wealth for Excess Profits Tax Purposes. The basis for computing net wealth for purposes of the excess profits tax is the net wealth at the end of the year defined under the net wealth tax less two subtractions. The first is the value of property that is legally or physically incapable of producing income to the taxpayer, while the second is the value of shares that pay dividends subject to the 12 per cent (or higher) withholding tax. This net wealth basis may be higher than the net taxable wealth under the net wealth tax, for the latter is reached after deducting a number of general and special exemptions, which the taxpayer is not required to deduct in computing his excess profits base.

Moreover, the taxpayer is permitted to make a number of other adjustments, each having the result of increasing his net worth and thus reducing the amount of the excess profits tax: (1) When the net value of a tangible asset acquired during the year is less than cost on December 31, it is valued at cost price. (2) When the value of a tax-payer's net wealth in Colombia on December 31 is less than it was at the beginning of the year because of gifts, legal re-exports of capital, or non-deductible losses from income, net wealth for purposes of the excess profits tax is taken at its value at the beginning of the year. (3) When a taxpayer receives the right to income from property for life or for a fixed term, he is permitted to report the full value of the property during the term of his tenure. (4) When a taxpayer reports income from foreign real estate in his basic income tax and excess profits tax returns, he is permitted to include the value of the property in his net wealth base. (5) The value of brood cows under the age of eight years may be included in the excess profits tax base even though it is not in-cludible for purposes of the net wealth tax. (6) Taxpayers may include in their excess profits tax base the par value of shares and bonds of the *Paz del Río* steel plant and the obligations of the Territorial Credit In-stitute. (7) In certain hardship cases, such as a natural catastrophe or a stock market crash, the Division of National Taxes permits the use of a date earlier than December 31 for computation of the excess profits tax base.

On the other hand, there are two required deductions from the net wealth tax base, and these have the effect of deflating the excess profits tax base and thus increasing the tax liability. The first is assets acquired during the year in the form of gifts, in-heritances, and gambling winnings. The value of these must be prorated according to the length of time held. Second, all actual lia-bilities must be deducted from the excess profits base.

Excess Profits Definition and Tax Rates. Profits are considered to be "excessive" when the taxpayer's net income subject to the excess profits tax exceeds the percentages of his net wealth shown in Table 2–5. When the amount of the excess profits has been determined in this manner, it is subject to the tax rates shown in Table 2–6. There is no excess profits tax on taxpayers whose net

wealth for excess profits tax purposes is less than $100,000.

The application of Tables 2–5 and 2–6 may be illustrated under the assumptions that a taxpayer has a net income for excess profits tax purposes of $75,000 and a net wealth for excess profits tax purposes of $150,000. Under these circumstances, the excess profits according to Table 2–5 are those in excess of 30 per cent of $150,000, or $30,000 ($75,000 – $45,000). This amount of excess profits ($30,000) is then subject to the pro-gressive tax rates in Table 2–6. Applying these rates gives a total excess profits tax liability of $8,160.[10]

The Net Wealth Tax

The net wealth tax (*impuesto complemen-tario de patrimonio*), although actually a tax on net worth or net wealth, was adopted in 1935 as an intrinsic part of the income tax system. When it was introduced, it had

[10] Before the tax revision of 1960, the excess profits tax was computed at rates ranging from 18.75 per cent to 51.25 per cent on the part of excess profits exceeding 50 per cent of taxable net wealth.

TABLE 2–5
Determination of Excess Profits

Net Wealth for Excess Profits Tax	Excess Profits Are Those in Excess Of:
$100,000 to $120,000	42 per cent
120,000 to 140,000	36 per cent
140,000 to 160,000	30 per cent
160,000 to 180,000	24 per cent
180,000 to 200,000	18 per cent
Over $200,000	12 per cent

TABLE 2–6
Excess Profits Tax Rates

On that Part of Excess Profits:	Tax Rate (Per Cent)
Up to 6 per cent of net wealth	20
Between 6 and 12 per cent of net wealth	26
Between 12 and 18 per cent of net wealth	32
Between 18 and 24 per cent of net wealth	38
Between 24 and 30 per cent of net wealth	44
Between 30 and 36 per cent of net wealth	50
In excess of 36 per cent of net wealth	56

two declared purposes: (1) to impose a higher rate of tax on unearned income; and (2) to impose a penalty upon landowners who withheld their property from productive use. A major feature of the 1960 revision of the income tax law was the elimination of the net wealth tax on corporations and other legal entities taxed as corporations.

The base of the net wealth tax is defined as the total of all property rights having a monetary value and held within the country on December 31 less the taxpayer's indebtedness on that date. Property rights are considered to have a monetary value if they can be used to obtain income. Thus, with the exception of private automobiles, household and personal effects are excluded from the base of the tax. Also, the net wealth tax is applicable to persons having the right to the use, income, and enjoyment of the property and not merely to persons with the bare legal title.

The application of the net wealth tax is confined to real and tangible personal property located in Colombia. Even in the case of intangible property, the tax is confined to assets having an "economic situs" in the country. As a result, mortgages and chattel liens held by residents of Colombia on real or personal properties located abroad are not taxable. On the other hand, mortgages and chattel liens on property located in Colombia are taxable to foreign creditors.

With respect to intangible property, stock shares of corporations domiciled in Colombia are taxed under the net wealth tax both in the case of residents and non-residents, the latter by way of withholding. But shares of stock and participations in foreign companies are not taxable. Similarly, creditors in Colombia subject to the net wealth tax are taxed on all indebtedness owed to them by debtors resident in Colombia but not on debts owed to them from abroad. Debts owed by Colombians to persons residing abroad are taxed under the net wealth tax on the principal and under the basic income tax on the interest, on the grounds that the economic situs of the debt is in Colombia.

Also taxable are the value of concessions, patents, trademarks, copyrights, brand and company names, and commercial or industrial reputation. These intangibles are considered to have their situs in Colombia to the extent that they relate to business enterprises doing business in Colombia.

For the valuation of assets, the general criterion of value is cost price, which is the cost of acquisition, production, or manufacture less depreciation, but there are a number of exceptions: (1) Colombian currency, bank deposits, and foreign currency are taken at their face or market values as of December 31 of the tax year. (2) Real property is taken at its assessed value on the last day of the tax year. (3) Accounts receivable are taken at their face value but with allowance made for difficulty of collection. (4) Livestock are valued at their retail, cash market value. (5) Shares of stock in corporations or limited stock partnerships are taken at their stock exchange value at the close of the tax year or, in the case of unlisted stocks, by values determined by the Division of National Taxes. (6) Good will is taken at the valuation determined by the Division of National Taxes. (7) Automobiles in private use are valued at cost price in the year of acquisition less 20 per cent depreciation per annum. (8) Inventories of stock in trade or current assets are valued at cost. (9) When a taxpayer has the right of use, enjoyment, and income to real or personal property, the life or fixed term tenant is considered to possess the rights and is taxed on the full value of the assets.

Deductions and Exemptions. Permissible deductions include all debts owed by a taxpayer, both to residents and non-residents. Thus, there is the anomalous situation that tangible and intangible foreign assets are not included in the base of the net worth tax, but foreign indebtedness (for example, borrowing on foreign assets) is deductible. In general, deductions for reserves, such as those established for dividends or tax payments, are not deductible, but an exception is made in the case of reserves for terminal pay.

In addition to property located outside of Colombia, there are a large number of exemptions from the net wealth tax. These may be divided into general and special exemptions. General exemptions include:

1) property that is economically incapable of producing income, as in the case of the organization and installation of a plant, where the costs exceed the gross income;[11]

2) assets originating in the capitalization of payments for personal services, social security benefits, death, illness, or accident compensation, or worker's bonuses;

3) works of art and art collections originating from abroad and books of foreign authors up to a value of $1,000 per item or a total of $10,000, and domestic works of art and art collections and books of Colombian authors without limitation;

4) when particular items of wealth are exempt to general partnerships, limited liability companies, ordinary limited partnerships, mining partnerships, and de facto partnerships, they are also exempt to the partners;

5) furniture and personal and household effects other than jewelry, for which a maximum exemption of $10,000 is permitted;

6) property belonging to tax-exempt persons, and property which produces tax-exempt income (e.g., government bonds, the first $5,000 of savings deposits, etc.);

7) public or private cemeteries, vaults, and mausoleums;

8) Indian reservations;

9) amounts not in excess of $20,000 in corporate or limited partnership stock, provided the taxpayer's net income is not over $48,000;

10) a basic exemption of $20,000 in the case of net wealth not exceeding $200,000;

11) investments in non-profit corporate entities, associations, and foundations;

12) investments in gold, silver, and platinum mines; and

13) shares or bonds in the Paz del Río

Steel Plant, the Territorial Credit Institute, the Livestock Fund, and the securities of other governmental and quasi-governmental entities.

The number of special exemptions is equally extensive:

1) worker's and middle-class houses and apartments, and houses mortgaged by the Military Housing Fund or Territorial Credit Institute;

2) investments in agricultural machinery made after January 1, 1958;

3) livestock kept for breeding and raising purposes;

4) investments made in rural areas for wood lots or permanent reforestation, subject to the approval of the Ministry of Agriculture;

5) investments in petroleum and natural gas operations and in lead, copper, bauxite, sulphur, and tin mines during the period of exploration, certain iron, coal, limestone, and gypsum mines for a five-year period, and gold, silver, and platinum mines;

6) the costs of certain farm improvements, including fences, wells, electric power, dairy equipment, laborers, houses, clearing, irrigation, and drainage, while other large- and medium-scale improvements are permitted a 50 per cent reduction in the net wealth tax until December 31, 1968;

7) the first $5,000 in value of rural lands and improvements subdivided for share croppers or others;

8) assets of companies and co-operatives engaged in the fishing industry until December 31, 1962;

9) the assets of qualified Colombian airlines invested or to be invested in flight equipment or in Latin American international air transport enterprises;

10) the assets of investment management funds invested in Colombian enterprises (although the subscribers must pay the tax on their proportionate shares);

11) mutual investment funds established for the benefit of company employees, as well as the beneficiaries on their holdings of these funds;

[11] However, the mere fact that property does not produce income does not suffice for exclusion. Thus, non-dividend-paying securities and idle land are available, unless the taxpayer can show proof that he is not responsible for the fact that the asset is unproductive of income.

12) the assets of qualified, privately owned public utility companies;

13) investments in tourist hotels (within limitations provided by law) for a ten-year period from the date of construction;

14) investments in motor vehicle assembly or manufacturing plants for ten years or until the tax-free recovery of 150 per cent of paid-in capital;

15) investments in the publishing business (scientific, literary, or textbooks) until 1968;

16) investments in certain basic industries and certain iron and steel fabricators until 1969; and

17) the capital, machinery, and imports of public and private international agencies engaged by contract in social, economic, cultural, or sanitary projects.

Exclusive of the above exemptions, a taxpayer's net wealth as of December 31 of each year is subject to the progressive rates shown in Table 2–7. These rates rise from .1 per cent on the first $20,000 of taxable net wealth to 1.5 per cent on amounts over $800,000.[12] All taxpayers are subject to the same rates, whether individuals, estates, or others liable for the tax. Table 2–7 also shows some representative calculations for the effective rates of the net wealth tax. The

[12] Before the tax revision of 1960, the rates varied from .15 to 1.50 per cent on that part of taxable net wealth exceeding $1,000,000.

table shows, for example, that the effective rate of the net wealth tax on taxable net wealth of $1,000,000 is 1.03 per cent.

The Electric and Steel Development Tax

The electric and steel development tax (*impuesto especial para fomento eléctrico y siderúrgico*) is an additional levy on income, but it is computed on a base which differs from that on which the basic income tax is computed. This tax, introduced in 1960, is actually an amended version of a tax levied in 1946 and earmarked originally for housing and later for the benefit of the *Paz del Río* steel plant. Previous to the tax revision in 1960, the rate of the tax was 4 per cent payable at the taxpayer's option in cash or by purchase of shares in the *Paz del Río* plant. Three amendments to the tax were introduced in 1960: (1) The rate was reduced from 4 to 3 per cent. (2) A ceiling was introduced for the benefit of low income taxpayers, under which the tax may not exceed 40 per cent of the aggregate income and complementary taxes (net wealth and excess profit taxes) for the same year. (3) Two-thirds of the tax must be paid in cash. According to another amendment by an administrative decree of April 9, 1962, taxpayers are required to pay two-thirds of the tax (2 per cent) in cash to be earmarked

TABLE 2–7
Statutory and Effective Rates for the Net Wealth Tax

Brackets of Net Wealth	Statutory Tax Rates (Per Cent)	Amounts of Net Wealth	Total Tax	Effective Rates on Taxable Net Wealth (Per Cent)
Up to $20,000	0.1	$ 20,000	$ 20	0.10
$ 20,000 to 40,000	0.2	40,000	60	0.15
40,000 to 60,000	0.3	60,000	120	0.20
60,000 to 80,000	0.4	80,000	200	0.25
80,000 to 100,000	0.5	100,000	300	0.30
100,000 to 200,000	0.6	200,000	900	0.45
200,000 to 300,000	0.7	300,000	1,600	0.53
300,000 to 400,000	0.9	400,000	2,500	0.63
400,000 to 600,000	1.1	600,000	4,700	0.78
600,000 to 800,000	1.3	800,000	7,300	0.91
Over 800,000	1.5	1,000,000	10,300	1.03
		5,000,000	70,300	1.41
		10,000,000	145,300	1.45

for electrical development, and one-third (1 per cent) in cash or in the form of *Paz del Río* shares.

Taxpayers subject to the electric and steel development tax include individuals, decedent's estates, corporations, limited stock partnerships, limited liability companies, *de facto* partnerships assimilable to corporations, and foreign companies that are taxed as corporations. Electric power companies are exempt from the tax.

Although the net taxable income for purposes of the electric and steel development tax is calculated in the same manner as for the basic income tax, the base of the tax differs from that of the income tax because of the availability of two special deductions. The first of these is an exemption of $5,000, and the second is the deduction of the income tax and excess profits tax.

Taxpayers must pay the entire electric and steel development tax in cash simultaneously with the basic income tax, and are then given a receipt which entitles them to obtain the *Paz del Río* stock from that company to the amount of one-third of their tax payment. If the taxpayer elects not to purchase the shares, the portion of his tax payment which is authorized for that purpose is invested in shares in the name of the government. Under these circumstances, it is only to be expected that practically all taxpayers purchase the steel plant shares, which they may sell later. Also, with this type of arrangement, it is realistic to view the investment in steel plant shares as obligatory in practice.

Like all the taxes that form a part of the Colombian income and complementary tax structure, the electric and steel development tax is paid in the year following the tax year. Accordingly, the tax is allowed as a deduction from the gross income of the year in which it is paid in order to arrive at net taxable income for that year. The shares of the *Paz del Río* plant are exempt from the net wealth tax, and if dividends are ever paid, they will be exempt from the basic income tax. For the net wealth tax base used in the computation of the excess profits tax,

Paz del Río shares are includible at par, but only by taxpayers who purchased the shares in fulfillment of their tax obligations.

The Housing Tax

The tax on corporations for the support of middle and low income housing projects was enacted in 1960. However, the levy was not intended as a net increase in the tax burden on corporations, for it was enacted at a time when corporations were relieved of the net wealth tax and, also, when the tax for the support of the *Paz del Río* Steel Plant was reduced from 4 to 3 per cent.

Taxpayers liable for the housing tax may be divided into two groups depending on the level of their exemptions. Corporations, limited stock partnerships, limited liability companies, *de facto* partnerships assimilable to corporations for tax purposes, and foreign companies of any of the foregoing classes have a basic exemption of $20,000 after deducting the basic income and excess profits taxes of the same tax year. Other entities have a higher basic exemption of $100,000. These include general partnerships, ordinary limited partnerships, limited liability companies, *de facto* partnerships not assimilable to corporations, and all juridical persons engaged in mining. For these firms with the higher $100,000 exemption, only the income tax, and not the excess profits tax, is deductible. Taxpayers engaged in the production of petroleum and derivates are not considered to be engaged in the mining industry and are therefore taxable under the $20,000 or $100,000 limitations, depending on their form of organization.

The rate of the housing tax is 6 per cent of net taxable income, but only 34 per cent of the tax must be paid in cash. According to the law establishing the housing tax, 33 per cent of the tax may be paid by purchasing mortgage certificates of the Central Mortgage Bank and another 33 per cent by the purchase of stock or bonds in non-profit housing associations. Until the latter are formed, 66 per cent of the tax may be paid by the purchase of mortgage certificates of the Central

Mortgage Bank. Taxpayers making payment of the tax by the purchase of mortgage certificates are required to hold them in a custodian account with the bank for five years. As the mortgage certificates were quoted at $86.00 in March, 1963, and they pay a guaranteed return of 7 per cent on their par value of $100, taxpayers have every incentive to purchase securities rather than pay the entire tax in cash.

Surcharge for Absenteeism

The surcharge for absenteeism is levied on the Colombian income of nationals residing abroad continuously for over six months in any tax year or those who complete this continuous period in the tax year or those who are absent for over eight months in the year. Exempt from the surcharge are: (1) career diplomats and consular officers, including their families; (2) persons on official missions; (3) Colombian wives of non-resident aliens; (4) students enrolled in foreign universities; (5) employees of governmental or quasi-governmental entities; (6) employees of private Colombian companies who are required to live abroad, provided that they are not partners or stockholders in the company or relatives of partners or stockholders within the fourth degree of consanguinity or second degree of affinity; (7) members or employees of international bodies of which Colombia is a member; and (8) persons living abroad because of grave illness.

The surcharge for absenteeism is a flat surtax of 15 per cent of the basic income tax and complementary taxes (the net wealth tax and the excess profits tax). Thus, it is a tax on both income and wealth. The tax is collected by means of withholding on payments made abroad.

The Tax on Underutilized Agricultural Land

The tax on underutilized agricultural land was enacted in 1957 as part of the agricultural incentive legislation, its purpose being to foster more intensive use of arable land

resources. This tax is in the nature of a penalty levied on the capital value of land if certain obligations are not fulfilled.

With respect to the obligations, owners and tenants of agricultural land of over 50 hectares are required to utilize their land in the following way: (1) 25 per cent of Type I land and 15 per cent of Type II land must be utilized annually; (2) Type III land must be cleared annually at the rate of 10 hectares per annum on properties of 50 to 200 hectares and 10 per cent of the area annually for larger properties; and (3) Type IV land must be kept in pasture or timberland, or reforested. The government may also increase these obligations by as much as 50 per cent where government irrigation or drainage projects have raised the productive capacity of the land and increased its value. However, pending the classification of lands, the obligations are reduced to 10 per cent of the average for Type I and Type II lands and do not embrace lands in the department of Chocó.

Landowners failing to meet these obligations are subject to a tax of 2 per cent of the cadastral value of their property in 1958, 3 per cent in 1959, 4 per cent in 1960, 5 per cent in 1961, and 10 per cent in 1962 and subsequent years. The tax is reported and payable simultaneously with the basic income tax and complementary taxes.

The Livestock Tax

The livestock tax is closely related to the net wealth tax, for it is a special levy on one form of wealth. The tax is also integrated with the income tax, for it is reported, computed, and paid on the same form used for the basic income tax.

Taxpayers subject to the livestock tax include all livestock breeders and raisers, whether individuals, corporations, or other juridical entities whose livestock exceeds $15,000 in value at the close of any tax year from 1959 to 1970.[13]

[13] The term "livestock" includes cattle, horses, asses, sheep, goats, and hogs but not poultry, rabbits, or bees.

The rate for the livestock tax is 1 per cent of the net wealth value of stock owned at the close of the tax year. Instead of a cash payment, taxpayers may elect to subscribe and pay for shares of the Livestock Bank and Livestock Fund at par in an aggregate amount equal to the amount of the tax due. Since these shares are salable, even though at a substantial discount, the tax is normally paid by the purchase of shares. The livestock tax is deductible in full for Colombian income tax purposes from gross income of the year in which the livestock taxes are paid.

REVENUE PRODUCTIVITY

Before presenting information on assessments and collections for the income and complementary taxes, a few comments should be made on the availability and reliability of the data. Statistics on tax assessments and collections in Colombia may be obtained from a wide number of sources, the principal ones being the Central Bank, the Planning Department, the Budget Division, the Office of Economic Tax Analysis, the Division of National Taxes, the Comptroller General, and the National Department of Statistics.[14] It is also not unusual for there to be discrepancies in the data obtained from these various sources. This raises the important issue of which source of statistical information on taxation is the most reliable. Research on this issue provides the information that there are only two primary sources of information, and the other reporting units merely publish these data, sometimes with errors, and sometimes also providing estimates of assessments and collections without indicating the degree of reliability of the statistics.

The two primary sources of information on income tax statistics are the Comptroller

[14] Their designations in Spanish are respectively: Banco de la República, Departamento de Planeación y Servicios Técnicos, Dirección Nacional de Presupuesto, Oficina de Análisis Económico Tributario del Ministerio de Hacienda y Crédito Público, División de Impuestos Nacionales del Ministerio de Hacienda y Crédito Público, Contraloría General de la República, and Departamento Administrativo Nacional de Estadística.

General and the Division of National Taxes. Until December 31, 1960, the Comptroller General had the responsibility for the accounting and reporting of income tax statistics, but since January 1, 1961, this responsibility has been lodged with the Division of National Taxes. However, at the time that this transfer was affected, the Comptroller General was in certain cases four or five years delinquent in the reporting of income tax statistics. As of June, 1963, many of these omissions in statistical information still remain. For example, it is more difficult to obtain data on actual collections as compared to assessments and also more difficult to obtain statistics on earmarked taxes as compared to those that become budgetary revenues of the national government.

In the light of the foregoing, the approach taken in this study is to rely on the statistics of the Division of National Taxes, currently the only unit officially responsible for the provision of income tax statistics and, also, presently the single primary source of information. Second, the view is taken that a failure to obtain data is better than the presentation of unreliable statistics. Accordingly, only those data that can be verified as being reliable are used in this survey.

Table 2–8 presents a long-term historical series for the income and complementary taxes dating back to 1924. Because of accounting inadequacies, this series is available for the whole period only for assessments and not for collections, and the assessments include only those taxes that become budgetary revenues of the national government.

The series has two important implications. First, the data show very substantial increases in assessments, rising from the very modest amount of $652,974 in 1924 to $1,119 million in 1962. Even the increase from 1950 to 1962 has been very impressive in absolute amounts, rising by over 500 per cent. This long-term increase in assessments, of course, is attributable to several factors, not the least of which is inflation. Given long-term and chronic inflationary pressures, it is apparent from the evidence that reliance on income and wealth taxation is an important safeguard of government revenues.

Moreover, even if the assessments are deflated by a price index, as they are in the last column of Table 2–8, the increase is still substantial. When corrected for price level changes, income tax assessments rose from $360 million in 1950 to $851 million in 1961.

However, it is important to note that "real" assessments decreased from $896 million in 1960 to $851 million in 1961, and it is likely, in view of the degree of inflation in 1962, that "real" assessments continued to decrease. The second important implication in Table 2–8 is that there are very capricious movements in assessments from year to year.

TABLE 2–8
Assessments for the Income and Complementary Taxes, 1924 to 1962 [a]

Year	Assessments	Percentage Increase or Decrease Over Prior Year	Price Index [b] 1950 to 1961	Assessments Adjusted by Price Index 1950 to 1961
1924	$ 652,974	—		
1925	732,009	12.10		
1926	1,092,933	49.31		
1927	1,270,159	16.22		
1928	3,196,005	151.62		
1929	2,696,909	−15.61		
1930	3,323,553	23.24		
1931	2,278,771	−31.44		
1932	1,503,050	−34.04		
1933	1,709,561	13.74		
1934	2,026,926	18.56		
1935	4,340,444	114.14		
1936	12,907,192	197.37		
1937	15,279,063	18.38		
1938	18,115,379	18.56		
1939	19,607,463	8.24		
1940	21,564,170	9.98		
1941	22,890,418	6.15		
1942	28,127,831	22.88		
1943	45,287,032	61.00		
1944	53,281,600	17.65		
1945	60,438,448	13.43		
1946	72,971,752	20.74		
1947	96,153,660	31.77		
1948	118,547,687	23.29		
1949	144,387,722	21.80		
1950	192,608,704	33.40	53.5	$360,016,200
1951	250,000,701	29.80	59.0	423,730,000
1952	255,835,740	2.33	59.9	427,104,700
1953	263,375,903	2.95	62.8	419,388,300
1954	351,609,666	33.50	69.9	503,738,700
1955	407,624,921	15.93	69.8	583,989,800
1956	415,297,635	1.88	75.3	551,524,000
1957	537,096,063	29.32	88.2	608,952,400
1958	623,272,633	16.04	100.0	623,272,633
1959	875,273,884	40.43	106.1	824,951,820
1960	1,027,791,959	17.43	114.7	896,069,700
1961	1,058,915,681	3.03	124.4	851,218,300
1962	1,119,248,248	5.70	n.a.	—

a The amounts shown are "billings" or assessments and not actual collections. Also, the totals include only those taxes that become budgetary revenues of the national government and not those that are earmarked. Since 1960, the assessments shown include the basic income tax, the excess profits tax, the net wealth tax, the tax on absenteeism, the tax on underutilized agricultural land, two-thirds of the electric and steel development tax, and 34 per cent of the housing tax. Excluded as earmarked taxes are the livestock tax, one-third of the electric and steel development tax, and 66 per cent of the housing tax.

b Converted by means of a price index used in the national accounts. See *Cuentas Nacionales*, 1950–1961, Banco de la República, Departamento de Investigaciones Económicas, p. 19.

Source: Subdivisión de Recaudación, División de Impuestos Nacionales, Ministerio de Hacienda y Crédito Público.

In the thirty-nine years shown, there are only three years in which assessments declined over those of prior years, and assessments have risen consistently each year since 1933. Nevertheless, the percentage increases in assessments each year show wide variations. For example, assessments increased by 40.4 per cent in 1959 but only by 1.9 per cent in 1956. In particular, the percentage increases in assessments during 1961 (3.0 per cent) and 1962 (5.7 per cent) have been mild as compared to the increases experienced from 1957 to 1960. Thus, although the absolute level of assessments has continued to increase after 1960, there has been a very marked change in the rate of increase.

Reference has been made to the fact that Table 2-8 shows only those taxes that become budgetary revenues of the national government. In addition to these taxes, it has been traditional in Colombia to have a number of earmarked taxes for specific expenditure purposes. The distinction between budgetary and earmarked taxes is shown in Table 2-9. For most of the years from 1950 to 1962, earmarked taxes amounted to nearly 10 per cent of total assessments for the income and complementary taxes, although from 1961 to 1962 the proportion dropped from 11.50 to 8.13 per cent.

The number of earmarked income and wealth taxes in Colombia is undesirable on three counts. First, they complicate the tax system, both from the point of view of compliance and enforcement. Second, they constitute an undesirable way of financing particular government undertakings because there is seldom a close relationship between revenues derived from earmarked taxes and the expenditure needs that they are designed to satisfy. And finally, they prevent an orderly rationing of all government revenues among alternative expenditures by removing a source of revenue from budgetary discretion.

Perhaps the most relevant yardsticks for measuring the growth in income tax assessments and collections are two national accounting aggregates—the gross internal product and the national income. Table 2-9 also shows the relationship of total assessments for the income and complementary taxes to both of these measures for the period from 1950 to 1961. Once again, this comparison demonstrates developing strength in the income and complementary taxes for most of the period, with total assessments as a percentage of the gross internal product rising from 2.70 per cent in 1950 to 3.98 in 1961. For the national income, the comparable

TABLE 2-9

Total Assessments for the Income and Complementary Taxes, 1950 to 1962

Year	Assessments for Budgetary Revenues	Percentage of Total Assessments	Assessments for Earmarked Revenues	Percentage of Total Assessments	Total Assessments	Total Assessments as a Percentage of the Gross Internal Product	Total Assessments as a Percentage of the National Income
1950	$ 192,608,704	90.73	$19,673,314	9.27	$ 212,282,018	2.70	3.10
1951	250,000,701	90.70	25,645,364	9.30	275,646,065	3.08	3.60
1952	255,835,740	90.73	26,140,402	9.27	281,976,142	2.92	3.41
1953	263,375,903	95.52	12,357,883	4.48	275,733,786	2.57	2.99
1954	351,609,666	95.73	15,695,145	4.27	367,304,811	2.88	3.36
1955	407,624,921	92.74	31,901,962	7.26	439,526,883	3.32	3.91
1956	415,297,635	91.32	39,497,020	8.68	454,794,655	3.06	3.59
1957	537,096,063	90.61	55,638,354	9.39	592,734,417	3.33	4.01
1958	623,272,633	90.69	63,958,279	9.31	687,230,912	3.32	4.17
1959	875,273,884	90.74	89,362,496	9.26	964,636,380	4.11	5.05
1960	1,027,791,959	90.26	110,889,725	9.74	1,138,681,684	4.31	5.22
1961	1,058,915,681	88.50	137,609,400	11.50	1,196,525,081	3.98	4.76
1962	1,119,248,248	91.87	99,044,234	8.13	1,218,292,482	a	a

a Data not available for the gross internal product and the national income.

Source: Subdivisión de Recaudación, División de Impuestos Nacionales, Ministerio de Hacienda y Crédito Público.

increase was from 3.10 per cent in 1950 to 4.76 per cent in 1961. However, once more it should be noted that assessments weakened in 1961. Total assessments as a percentage of the gross national product decreased from 4.31 to 3.98 per cent from 1960 to 1961, while total assessments as a percentage of the national income fell from 5.22 to 4.76 per cent. Moreover, if it is assumed that the national income increased at the same rate in 1962 as it did in the previous year, total assessments as a percentage of the national income decreased again to 4.13 per cent. No better evidence could be offered that Colombia paid a heavy price in revenue foregone for the tax reforms of 1960.

Previous mention was made of the fact that statistical information on assessments is easier to obtain than on collections. In Colombia, reliable collection data for the income and complementary taxes are available only for the period from 1956 to 1962 and only for collections that become budgetary revenues of the national government.[15] Table 2–10 shows these collection figures and

[15] Many publications show an extended series designated as income and complementary tax "revenues," but for any period before 1956 these "revenues" are only estimates and not precise collection figures.

demonstrates that there is a tendency for collections to be some 5 to 7 per cent less than assessments in most years, although collections exceeded assessments in 1957 and 1958. For the seven-year period from 1956 to 1962, the percentage of total collections to assessments was 96.85 per cent.

The reason for a close, but not necessarily exact, relationship between collections and assessments in any year is that the assessment for the tax year is based on the income of the preceding year. Thus, the assessments for 1962 are based on incomes received during 1961. On the other hand, as Table 2–11 demonstrates, collections during any tax year are derived principally from assessments on incomes received during the previous year, but there are, in addition, receipts from delinquent taxes. For example, Table 1–11 shows that the total collection of $1,065,145,874 in 1962 for national government purposes is attributable in the most part to taxes on income earned in 1961, but that there were $126,691,406 attributable to income earned in 1960 and previous years.

When collections rather than assessments are related to the gross internal product and to the national income, as they are in Table 2–10, there is a noticeable reduction in the

TABLE 2–10
Assessments and Collections for the Income and Complementary Taxes, 1956 to 1962[a]

Year	Assessments	Collections	Percentage of Collections to Assessments	Collections as a Percentage of the Gross Internal Product	Collections as a Percentage of the National Income
1956	$ 415,297,635	$ 385,198,470	92.75	2.59	3.04
1957	537,096,063	573,201,964	106.72	3.22	3.87
1958	623,272,633	702,994,283	112.79	3.40	4.27
1959	875,273,884	809,788,378	92.52	3.45	4.24
1960	1,027,791,959	952,495,826	92.67	3.60	4.36
1961	1,058,915,681	989,970,013	93.49	3.29	3.94
1962	1,119,248,248	1,065,145,874	95.17	b	b
TOTALS	$5,656,896,103	$5,478,794,808	96.85		

[a] The totals include only budgetary revenues and not those taxes that are earmarked. Since 1960, budgetary revenues include the basic income tax, the excess profits tax, the net wealth tax, the tax on absenteeism, two-thirds of the electric and steel development tax, and 34 per cent of the housing tax. Excluded as earmarked are the livestock tax, one-third of the electric and steel development tax, and 66 per cent of the housing tax.

[b] Data not available for the gross internal product and the national income.

Source: Subdivisión de Recaudación, División de Impuestos Nacionales, Ministerio de Hacienda y Crédito Público.

TABLE 2–11

Tax Collections for the Income and Complementary Taxes Attributed to Years during
Which Income Was Earned [a]

Years during Which Income Was Earned	Years during Which Tax Was Collected		
	1960	1961	1962
1958 and previous years	$ 92,010,927		
1959 and previous years		$113,517,078	
1959	856,698,735		
1960 and previous years			$ 126,691,406
1960	3,786,164	873,207,154	
1961		3,245,781	931,083,394
1962			7,371,074
TOTALS	$952,495,826	$989,970,013	$1,065,145,874

[a] Collections include only those taxes that become budgetary revenues of the national government and not those that are earmarked.

Source: Subdivisión de Recaudación, División de Impuestos Nacionales, Ministerio de Hacienda y Crédito Público.

relationships. To illustrate, total assessments of the income and complementary taxes for budgetary purposes of the national government were 4.76 per cent of the national income in 1961, but total collections of the same taxes were only 3.94 per cent of the national income for the same year. Once again, total collections as percentages of the gross internal product and of the national income, as in the case of assessments, show steady increases from 1956 to 1960 and then a decrease in 1961 that was presumably followed by another decrease in 1962.

Among the fiscal systems of Latin America, Colombia is distinguished by the predominant role of income and related taxes. A comparative study made in 1960 shows that Colombia derived 51.7 per cent of its tax revenues from income taxes, the highest among nineteen Latin American countries.[16] Most of the other major countries trailed by some distance: Venezuela, 38.4 per cent; Chile, 32.3 per cent; Argentina, 29.3 per cent; and México, 36.8 per cent. Only Perú was close to Colombia with 47.1 per cent of its tax revenues being derived from income taxes.

[16] *Hearings,* Committee on Foreign Affairs, House of Representatives, 87th Congress, March 27–29, 1962, p. 477.

Table 2–12 shows that Colombia has continued to make progress with respect to the percentage of total tax revenues being derived from income and related taxes. From 1960 to 1962, the percentage increased from 51.9 to 56.5 per cent. At the same time, income

TABLE 2–12

Income and Complementary Taxes Related to Total Direct Taxes and Total Revenues of the National Government [a]

Year	Income and Complementary Taxes [b]	Percentage of Total Tax Revenues	Percentage of Total Revenues
1950	$ 192,608,704	47.1	40.5
1951	250,000,701	44.2	38.6
1952	255,835,740	45.8	39.0
1953	263,375,903	40.5	34.7
1954	351,609,666	41.9	36.1
1955	407,624,921	43.6	30.4
1956	385,198,470	43.2	39.7
1957	573,201,964	54.6	46.3
1958	702,994,283	49.9	43.5
1959	809,788,378	52.8	44.1
1960	952,495,826	51.9	46.8
1961	989,970,013	52.2	46.9
1962	1,065,145,874	56.5	51.5

[a] The data refer only to budgetary revenues of the national government.

[b] Assessments from 1950 to 1955 and collections from 1956 to 1962.

Source: Subdivisión de Recaudación, División de Impuestos Nacionales, Ministerio de Hacienda y Crédito Público.

and related taxes have increased from 46.8 per cent of total central government revenues in 1960 to 51.5 per cent in 1962.

Consideration may now be given to the several component parts of the system of income and related taxes, which numbered eight different levies in 1963. For convenience, these are presented in two tables. Those taxes that represent budgetary revenues of the national government appear in Table 2–13, while the taxes that represent earmarked revenues are shown in Table 2–14. As indicated in Table 2–13, the basic income tax is the dominant levy, representing 75.14 per cent of assessments for national government revenue purposes in 1961. Next in importance is the net wealth tax. It should be noted, however, that the net wealth tax was reduced appreciably in both relative and absolute importance when the tax was eliminated for corporations in 1960, assessments falling from 27.19 per cent of income and complementary tax assessments in 1960 to 20.48 per cent in 1961. The third tax in the trinity of complementary taxes—the excess profits tax—has always been relatively unimportant in terms of revenue productivity and, by the most recent statistics, apparently is becoming weaker. Table 2–13 indicates that the excess profits tax represented 4.19 per cent of income and complementary tax assessments for national government revenue purposes in 1961 as compared to 4.99 per cent in 1960.

Included in Table 2–13 are also a number of minor miscellaneous revenues: (1) Surtaxes were levied on the complementary taxes until they were eliminated in the income tax reform of 1960. (2) Penalties as a source of revenue are relatively unimportant and decreased from .63 per cent of total assessments for national government purposes in 1960 to only .19 per cent in 1961. (3) Included in the income tax assessments are five other levies: the tax on bachelors from 1950 until it was repealed in 1960; the tax on absenteeism from 1950 to 1962; 34 per cent of the housing tax during 1961 and 1962; the tax on underutilized agricultural land

from 1959 to 1962; and the electric and steel development tax in 1961 and 1962.

These miscellaneous taxes vary considerably in revenue importance. Assessments for the tax on absenteeism were only $310,305 in 1961 but were $1,475,790 in 1962. Since the tax on bachelors was eliminated in 1960, the last assessment year was 1961, when the tax reached an assessment level of $1,444,980. More important in terms of revenue were the housing tax with total assessments of $24,597,382 in 1962, and the steel and electrical development tax with total assessments of $34,480,807. The tax on underutilized agricultural land has been in effect since 1959, but there are no reportable assessments. Apparently, the tax is a dead letter.

Currently, there are three earmarked taxes, the assessments for which are shown in Table 2–14. These include one-third of the electric and steel development tax that is assigned to the *Paz del Río* steel plant, all of the livestock tax, and 66 per cent of the housing tax. As indicated previously, these taxes represented 8.13 per cent of total assessments for the income and complementary taxes in 1962.

In summary, it may be said that the Colombian system of income and complementary taxes shows developing strength in terms of revenue productivity from 1950 to 1960, but the tax reforms of 1960 reversed this trend. On the other hand, income and complementary tax assessments have continued to increase as percentages of central government total tax revenues and total revenues. Apart from the effect of the tax reforms of 1960, it can be said that this group of taxes has been instrumental in providing a relatively stable and increasing flow of revenue to the national government. The revenue productivity of the income and complementary taxes demonstrates one of the principal virtues of taxes on income and profits—that they are automatically self-adjusting to rising real incomes as well as inflationary conditions. As incomes and profits increase, whether in real or nominal terms, revenues from income and profits taxes under pro-

TABLE 2-13

Budgetary Assessments for the Income and Complementary Taxes, 1950 to 1962 [a]

Year	Income Tax [b]	Per Cent	Net Wealth Tax	Per Cent	Excess Profits Tax	Per Cent	Surtaxes	Per Cent	Penalties	Per Cent	Total
1950	$ 84,958,395	44.11	$ 37,145,863	19.28	$10,877,079	5.65	$ 58,850,652	30.55	$ 776,715	.40	$ 192,608,704
1951	112,344,386	44.93	45,706,313	18.28	11,087,697	4.43	79,835,904	31.93	1,026,401	.41	250,000,701
1952	110,778,453	43.30	52,833,028	20.65	10,915,535	4.27	79,993,277	31.27	1,315,447	.51	255,835,740
1953	169,627,680	64.40	68,467,941	26.00	13,190,320	5.01	10,183,104	3.87	1,906,858	.72	263,375,903
1954	240,850,174	68.49	93,271,208	26.53	12,314,763	3.50	2,125,254	.60	3,048,267	.87	351,609,666
1955	281,935,279	69.16	103,996,383	25.51	17,543,702	4.30	2,631,669	.64	1,517,888	.37	407,624,921
1956	279,627,161	67.38	110,876,254	26.69	14,262,390	3.43	7,713,828	1.86	2,818,002	.68	415,297,635
1957	343,172,682	63.89	150,788,976	28.07	16,562,344	3.08	23,751,261	4.42	2,820,800	.52	537,096,063
1958	412,480,030	66.17	156,946,825	25.18	26,853,067	4.31	24,151,095	3.87	2,841,616	.46	623,272,633
1959	545,869,719	62.36	233,944,164	26.72	42,154,757	4.82	46,775,590	5.34	6,529,654	.75	875,273,884
1960	652,015,569	63.44	279,435,244	27.19	51,299,535	4.99	38,597,964	3.75	6,443,647	.63	1,027,791,959
1961	794,775,871	75.14	216,635,450	20.48	44,288,868	4.19	c	—	2,045,380	.19	1,057,745,569 [d]
1962	1,060,170,059	—	n.a.	—	n.a	—	—	—	n.a.	—	1,119,248,247 [e]

[a] The assessments refer only to those taxes that become budgetary revenues of the national government and not to those that are earmarked.

[b] Income tax assessments include the surcharge for bachelors before the tax was repealed in 1960 and the surcharge for absenteeism. Income tax assessments also include 34 per cent of the housing tax, two-thirds of the electric and steel development tax for 1961, the net wealth tax, excess profits tax, the tax on underutilized agricultural land, and penalties for 1962.

c Surtaxes were repealed in 1960.

[d] This total disagrees with one reported previously due to accounting irregularities.

[e] Total includes assessments for 34 per cent of the housing tax amounting to $24,597,382 and assessments for two-thirds of the electric and steel development tax amounting to $34,480,807.

Source: Subdivisión de Recaudación, División de Impuestos Nacionales, Ministerio de Hacienda y Crédito Público.

TABLE 2–14

Earmarked Assessments for the Income and Complementary Taxes, 1950 to 1962[a]

Year	Instituto Crédito Territorial	Per Cent of Total	Paz del Río Steel Plant	Per Cent of Total	Livestock Tax	Per Cent of Total	Housing Tax	Per Cent of Total	Total Assessments
1950	$ 9,836,657	50.00	$ 9,836,657	50.00					$ 19,673,314
1951	12,822,682	50.00	12,822,682	50.00					25,645,364
1952	13,070,201	50.00	13,070,201	50.00					26,140,402
1953			12,357,883	100.00					12,357,883
1954			15,695,145	100.00					15,695,145
1955			31,901,962	100.00					31,901,962
1956			36,892,540	93.41	$ 2,604,480	6.59			39,497,020
1957			51,249,582	92.11	4,388,772	7.89			55,638,354
1958			58,864,347	92.04	5,093,932	7.96			63,958,279
1959			81,776,305	91.51	7,586,191	8.49			89,362,496
1960			93,272,155	84.11	17,617,570	15.89			110,889,725
1961			69,375,487	50.41	25,261,980	18.36	$42,971,933	31.23	137,609,400
1962			29,128,646	29.41	23,484,752	23.71	46,430,835	46.88	99,044,234

[a] The assessments refer only to those taxes that are earmarked. In 1962 these included one-third of the electric and steel development tax, all of the livestock tax, and 66 per cent of the housing tax.

Source: Subdivisión de Recaudación, División de Impuestos Nacionales, Ministerio de Hacienda y Crédito Público.

gressive schedules tend to rise more than proportionately to the increases in the taxable bases. Moreover, under progressive rates, the additional revenues are raised equitably from those taxpayers with the greatest capacity to pay. Of course, the converse is true when there are declines in business activity. Reliance on income and profits taxes under these circumstances may cause abrupt decreases in government revenues. Colombia's experience since 1950 indicates, however, that the advantages to be derived from upward adjustments to increasing capacity to pay far outweigh any disadvantages in revenue losses resulting from declines in economic activity. Undoubtedly, one reason for the relative revenue stability of the income and complementary taxes until 1960 is that the net wealth tax assured a degree of stability even when there were interruptions in the growth of income. On the other hand, the elimination of the net wealth tax from corporations in 1960 significantly reduced the importance of this tax. The excess profits tax also decreased in relative importance in 1961.

Finally, it should be noted that the system of income and complementary taxes is excessively complicated. The removal of several of the miscellaneous revenues would

facilitate compliance and enforcement. In particular, the three earmarked taxes should be eliminated because they detract from an orderly budgetary procedure.

CHARACTERISTICS OF TAXPAYERS

The number of taxpayers filing income tax returns in Colombia shows a vigorous growth similar to the increase in assessments. For natural persons, the number of taxpayers increased from 78,692 in 1950 to 486,113 in 1962 or by over six times. (See Table 2–15.) Reflecting this broadening of the tax base, the average assessment per taxpayer was actually lower in 1962 ($1,363) than in 1951 ($1,370). Although there has been an increase in the number of individual taxpayers in each year since 1950, the greatest percentage increase occurred in 1957, when withholding was introduced for six months before being rejected. Other contributing factors to the increase in the number of tax returns have been higher incomes, both because of inflation and rising real incomes, and an increase in the labor force.

Table 2–16 shows that the government has been even more successful in increasing

TABLE 2–15

Number of Taxpayers (Natural Persons) and Assessments for the
Income and Complementary Taxes, 1950 to 1962

Year	Number of Taxpayers	Index	Assessments [a]	Index	Average Assessment Per Taxpayer	Index
1950	78,692	100.0	$ 81,315,371	100.0	$1,033	100.0
1951	92,251	117.2	126,399,937	155.4	1,370	132.6
1952	106,126	134.9	107,661,219	132.4	1,015	98.2
1953	111,997	142.3	109,578,718	134.8	978	94.7
1954	110,953	141.0	181,613,306	223.3	1,637	158.5
1955	138,050	175.4	201,569,096	247.9	1,460	141.3
1956	150,725	191.5	226,710,600	278.8	1,504	145.6
1957	n.a.	—	n.a.	—	—	—
1958	293,271	372.7	n.a.	—	—	—
1959	342,713	435.5	n.a.	—	—	—
1960	414,317	526.5	n.a.	—	—	—
1961	477,039	606.2	n.a.	—	—	—
1962	486,113	617.7	662,385,489	814.6	1,363	131.9

[a] Assessments include only those taxes that become budgetary revenues of the national government and not those that are earmarked.

Source: Subdivisión de Recaudación, División de Impuestos Nacionales, Ministerio de Hacienda y Crédito Público.

TABLE 2–16

Number of Taxpayers (Juridical Persons) and Assessments for the
Income and Complementary Taxes, 1950 to 1962

Year	Number of Taxpayers	Index	Assessments [a]	Index	Average Assessment Per Taxpayer	Index
1950	1,067	100.0	$130,966,647	100.0	$122,743	100.0
1951	1,138	106.7	149,246,128	114.0	131,148	106.8
1952	1,268	118.8	174,314,923	133.1	137,472	112.0
1953	1,379	129.2	166,155,068	126.9	120,489	98.2
1954	8,465	793.3	185,691,505	141.8	21,936	17.9
1955	9,222	864.3	237,957,787	181.7	25,803	21.0
1956	9,690	908.1	228,084,055	174.2	23,538	19.2
1957	n.a.	—	n.a.	—	—	—
1958	12,033	1,127.7	n.a.	—	—	—
1959	13,432	1,258.8	n.a.	—	—	—
1960	14,755	1,382.8	n.a.	—	—	—
1961	14,578	1,366.3	n.a.	—	—	—
1962	15,481	1,450.9	555,906,993	424.5	35,909	29.2

[a] Assessments include only those taxes that become budgetary revenues of the national government and not those that are earmarked.

Source: Subdivisión de Recaudación, División de Impuestos Nacionales, Ministerio de Hacienda y Crédito Público.

the number of returns from juridical persons, with the number of these taxpayers increasing by over fourteen times from 1950 to 1962. Again, reflecting the broadening of the tax base by an increased number of taxpayers, the average assessment per taxpayer has decreased from $122,743 per taxpayer in 1950 to $35,909 in 1962.

The statistics in Tables 2–15 and 2–16 also show that the government has made progress since 1950 in shifting the burden

of taxation from juridical to natural persons. From 1950 to 1962, the proportion of total assessments attributable to natural persons increased from 38.31 to 54.37 per cent.

Despite this increase in the breadth of the tax base represented by a vigorous growth in the number of individual persons and societies filing taxable returns, there remains a marked tendency for the taxpayers to be concentrated geographically in a few districts. As shown in Table 2–17, the national tax office of Cundinamarca (the assessment district including Bogotá) collected 48.86 per cent of the total of income and complementary tax collections for budgetary purposes in 1962. Another 20.58 per cent was collected in Antioquia (principally from the city of Medellín), and 10.54 per cent from Valle (principally from the city of Cali). Thus, these three districts out of twenty-two, or more properly the three largest cities in Colombia, accounted for approximately 80 per cent of all budgetary income and complementary tax collections in 1962.

More serious in terms of tax policy is the concentration of income tax assessments among those taxpayers that are required to calculate their own tax (self-assessments) and those that merely file a declaration of relevant information and are given assessments by the government. Individuals having net

TABLE 2–17

Collections for the Income and Complementary Taxes by National Tax Offices, 1962[a]

National Tax Offices	Collections	Percentage of Total Collections
Antioquia (Medellín)	$ 219,175,632	−20.58
Atlántico	60,356,277	5.67
Bolívar	16,013,740	1.50
Boyacá	3,889,818	.36
Caldas	22,176,050	2.08
Armenia	9,022,768	.85
Pereira	17,037,691	1.60
Cauca	2,062,243	.19
Córdoba	5,218,371	.49
Cundinamarca (Bogotá)	516,056,627	48.86
Girardot	3,250,369	.30
Chocó	326,798	.03
Huila	4,537,604	.43
Magdalena	7,507,531	.70
Nariño	2,955,842	.28
N. Santander	9,599,194	.90
Santander	19,780,004	1.86
Tolima	8,016,526	.75
Valle (Cali)	112,257,836	10.54
Palmira	17,130,894	1.61
Tuluá	7,234,415	.68
Villavicencio	1,539,646	.14
TOTALS	$1,065,145,874 [b]	100.00 [b]

[a] The totals include only budgetary revenues and not those taxes that are earmarked.

[b] Totals do not add because of rounding.

Source: Subdivisión de Recaudación, División de Impuestos Nacionales, Ministerio de Hacienda y Crédito Público.

incomes of over $25,000 or net wealth of over $500,000 and all juridical persons must calculate their own tax liabilities. All other individuals are permitted, but are not required, to assess their own tax liabilities.

Table 2–18 shows that there were 501,594 taxpayers in 1962, but only 17.72 per cent of these were self-assessments, while the remainder, 82.28 per cent, were government assessments. On the other hand, the smaller proportion of self-assessed returns accounted for 84.18 per cent of total assessments. In other words, about one-sixth of the taxpayers accounted for about five-sixths of the assessments.

But the concentration of assessments among a relatively small number of taxpayers is even more extreme than the above evidence would indicate. Shown in Table 2–19 are the 88,901 taxpayers who filed self-assessments in 1962, classified by levels of assessment. According to this evidence, the largest single taxpayer in Colombia accounted for 3.69 per cent of total assessments for national government budgetary purposes; 92 taxpayers accounted for about one-third of all assessments; and 961 taxpayers out of 501,594, or only .19 per cent, accounted for over one-half of all assessments.

Statistics are not available for 1962 to identify these large taxpayers that bear the brunt of the burden of the income and complementary taxes, but the data for 1961 indicate that they are mostly juridical persons. In 1961, the one hundred taxpayers with the largest assessments accounted for 33.86 per cent of total assessments of the income and complementary taxes for national government revenue purposes. Out of these one hundred taxpayers, only five were natural persons, and these five accounted for only .65 per cent of assessments for the income and complementary taxes. Thus, the conclusion appears warranted that about one hundred juridical taxpayers account for approximately one-third of all assessments of the income and complementary taxes that are available for budgetary revenue of the national government.

TABLE 2–18

Assessments for the Income and Complementary Taxes Classified by
Self-Assessments and Government Assessments, 1962[a]

| | Taxpayers | | Assessments | |
Type of Assessment	Num-ber	Per Cent	Amount (Thousands)	Per Cent
Self-assessments	88,901	17.72	$ 942,189	84.18
Government assessments	412,693	82.28	177,059	15.82
TOTALS	501,594	100.00	$1,119,248	100.00

[a] The assessments refer only to those taxes that become budgetary revenues of the national government and not to those that are earmarked.

Source: Subdivisión de Recaudación, División de Impuestos Nacionales, Ministerio de Hacienda y Crédito Público.

TABLE 2–19

Percentages of Total Assessments Attributable to Taxpayers Filing Self-Assessments, 1962[a]

Levels of Assessment	Cumulative Number of Taxpayers	Cumulative Amount of Total Assessments	Cumulative Percentage of Total Assessments [b]
$41,000,000 to $42,000,000	1	$ 41,274,802	3.69
33,000,000 to 34,000,000	2	74,360,280	6.64
15,000,000 to 16,000,000	4	105,387,451	9.41
14,000,000 to 15,000,000	5	119,697,655	10.69
12,000,000 to 13,000,000	6	132,359,229	11.82
10,000,000 to 11,000,000	7	143,726,527	12.84
8,000,000 to 9,000,000	10	168,936,600	15.09
7,000,000 to 8,000,000	11	176,733,198	15.79
6,000,000 to 7,000,000	14	196,250,236	17.53
5,000,000 to 6,000,000	19	222,622,888	19.89
4,000,000 to 5,000,000	25	249,922,022	22.33
3,000,000 to 4,000,000	30	268,144,328	23.96
2,000,000 to ·3,000,000	43	298,667,742	26.68
1,000,000 to 2,000,000	92	367,148,156	32.80
500,000 to 1,000,000	159	417,089,477	37.26
100,000 to 500,000	961	574,633,831	51.34
1 to 100,000	88,901	942,188,789	84.18

[a] Assessments refer only to those taxes that become national government budgetary revenues and not to those that are earmarked.

[b] Total assessments include self-assessments and government assessments.

Source: Subdivisión de Recaudación, División de Impuestos Nacionales, Ministerio de Hacienda y Crédito Público.

CHAPTER 3

The Income and Complementary
Taxes—General Considerations

THE INCOME, EXCESS PROFITS, AND NET WEALTH TAXES

NO DEFENSE FOR taxation based on income needs to be offered, for this principle is firmly accepted in Colombia. Suffice it to say that the tax is the best available for purposes of placing the burden of taxation on those elements of the population with the greater ability to pay. It could be argued that the income and complementary taxes represent, in general, levies that are difficult to administer, but this argument has a rebuttal, for they are mutually reinforcing. Quite obviously, a net wealth tax, with the information that is required in the reporting of assets, should be of inestimable assistance in enforcing the income tax. And there is this same type of complementary relationship between the excess profits tax and the net wealth tax. Since the excess profits tax is based on certain percentage earnings as related to net wealth, the taxpayer has the incentive of declaring his assets at a fair value for purposes of the net wealth tax in order to reduce his excess profits tax liability.

The trinity of an income tax, excess profits tax, and net wealth tax represents a development that is essentially ingenious, progressive, and enlightened—both in terms of the goals of tax policy and administration. Although a great number of internal improvements to this system may be proposed, the general pattern should be retained.

But the other surtaxes and miscellaneous taxes on wealth and income are a different matter. With the exception of the tax on absenteeism, these contribute nothing but a complication of the system, both in terms of compliance and enforcement. They are essentially nuisance taxes that should be eliminated. For most of these taxes, their principle rationale for existence, apparently, is to provide earmarked revenues for particular government expenditures. But this, too, is indefensible from the point of view of desirable budgetary practices.

THE COMPARATIVE TAXATION OF NATURAL AND JURIDICAL PERSONS

A basic issue that should be raised in Colombia is the comparative income tax burden (as well as other related taxes) that should be borne by individual proprietorships as compared to the other forms of business organization. At the present time individuals are subject to income tax rates rising from .50 to 51.00 per cent; corporations have a three-rate schedule of 12, 24, and 36 per cent; partnerships have a two-rate schedule of 3 and 6 per cent; and limited liability companies have a progressive schedule of 4, 8, and 12 per cent.

There is also variation with respect to the income tax treatment at the individual level of the distributed profits of various forms of business organization. Profits from individual proprietorships, of course, are taxed only once under the income tax system, but the dividends of corporations are taxed in full, resulting in a double income tax burden on distributed corporate profits.[1] On the other hand, for both partnerships and limited liability companies, all income after payment of the income tax at the business level is construed to be distributed and is taxed again at the individual level.

As if this were not unneutral enough, there is no consistency in the application of the other related taxes. The excess profits tax applies to individuals and corporations but not to partnerships and limited liability companies; the net wealth tax applies to individuals but not to corporations, partnerships, and limited liability companies; the electric and steel development tax applies to individuals, corporations, and limited liability companies but not to partnerships; the hous-

ing tax is applicable to corporations, limited liability companies, and partnerships but not to individuals; the taxes on underutilized agricultural land and livestock are applicable to all taxpayers; and the tax on absenteeism applies only to individuals. To add to the confusion and unneutrality, in some instances different forms of business organization have different exemptions and exclusions from these taxes, so that their bases for the application of the tax rates are also different.

No attempt will be made to demonstrate the differential tax burdens that result from all of these variations, but an insight into the problem may be gained from the evidence in Table 3–1. This table shows four different forms of business organization: corporation, limited liability company, general partnership, and individual proprietorship. Each is assumed to have the same net wealth of $10,000,000 and the same net profits of $1,000,000. For purposes of simplifying the analysis, the table includes only the income tax and the other two taxes (housing and steel, and electrical development) that are surtaxes on income. Tax burdens have been calculated both at the business and individual levels.

[1] The only exception is that the first $5,000 of dividends is exempt if the shareholder's net income does not exceed $48,000.

TABLE 3–1

Illustrative Tax Calculations for Different Forms of Business Organization under Present Laws

	Corporation	Limited Liability Company	General Partnership	Individual Proprietorship
I. Business Level				
Net wealth	$10,000,000	$10,000,000	$10,000,000	$10,000,000
Net profits	1,000,000	1,000,000	1,000,000	1,000,000
Income tax	228,000	104,000	57,000	389,000
Effective rate	22.80	10.40	5.70	38.92
Housing tax	45,120	47,760	50,580	—
Effective rate	4.51	4.78	5.06	—
Steel and electric development tax	23,010	—	—	18,173
Effective rate	2.30	—	—	1.82
Total effective rate	29.61	15.18	10.76	40.72
II. Business and Individual Levels				
Total effective rate for Assumption I [a]	50.24	44.91	40.85	40.72
Total effective rate for Assumption II [b]	51.83	37.40	32.98	40.72

[a] Based on the assumptions that: (1) The corporation distributes 50 per cent of its after-tax earnings. (2) In the case of the corporation, limited liability company, and partnership, one principal owner receives 25 per cent of the after-tax earnings. (3) The income is taxed progressively at the individual level starting at the initial rate of .50 per cent.

[b] Based on the assumptions that: (1) The corporation distributes 50 per cent of its after-tax earnings. (2) In the case of the corporation, limited liability company, and partnership, one principal owner receives $100,000 of the after-tax earnings. (3) The income is taxed progressively at the individual level starting at the initial rate of .50 per cent.

At the business level, it may be seen that the effective rate of taxation for the corporation of 29.61 per cent is almost double that of the limited liability company (15.18 per cent) and almost three times the tax burden of the partnership (10.76 per cent). Bearing the heaviest burden is the individual proprietorship. Applying the individual progressive rates to a net profit of $1,000,000 for the individual proprietorship results in an effective rate of tax of 40.72 per cent.

But that is only part of the story, for corporations normally will distribute part of their earnings in dividends, and all of the earnings of the limited liability company and partnership (after deduction of the income tax at the business level) must be distributed for tax purposes. All of these distributed profits will be taxed again at the individual level. Table 3–1 shows the tax burdens that result under two sets of assumptions with respect to the ownership and distribution of profits for the corporation, limited liability company, and partnership.

Under the first set of assumptions, the corporation distributes 50 per cent of its after-tax earnings; one principal owner of the corporation, limited liability company, and partnership receives 25 per cent of the after-tax earnings of each entity; and the income received is taxed progressively at the individual level starting at the initial rate of .50 per cent. Under these assumptions, the total effective rate of tax on distributed income, counting both the burdens at the business and individual levels, is 50.24 per cent for the corporation as compared to 44.91 per cent for the limited liability company, 40.85 per cent for the partnership, and 40.74 per cent for the individual proprietorship. The burden of taxation on corporate earnings, of course, would be relatively higher or lower than this illustration depending on the assumed percentage of distributed earnings.

The second set of assumptions in Table 3–1 is probably more indicative of the unneutrality that exists. In this case, one assumption has been changed: that a principal owner of the corporation, limited liability company, and partnership receives $100,000 in after-tax earnings, and these earnings are taxed progressively at the individual level starting at the initial rate of .50 per cent. This results in an effective rate of tax on distributed income of 51.83 per cent for the corporation as compared to 37.40 per cent for the limited liability company, 32.98 per cent for the partnership, and 40.74 per cent for the individual proprietorship.

The objection may now be made that these assumptions show only the respective aggregative burdens on *distributed* earnings; they do not reflect the fact that the corporation retained one-half of its after-tax earnings and that these earnings were not taxed at the individual level. This factor may be taken into consideration by a further assumption—that all of the after-tax distributions of the corporation, limited liability company, and partnership are taxed at the same marginal rate of 20 per cent. These tax burdens may then be added to the tax liabilities at the business levels, and the totals expressed as a percentage of the net profit of $1,000,-000. When this is done, the effective rate of taxation for the corporation is 36.65 per cent as compared to 33.08 per cent for the limited liability company, 29.62 for the partnership, and 40.74 for the individual proprietorship. Once again, the tax burden on the corporation would be relatively higher if it had been assumed that more than 50 per cent of its after-tax profits had been distributed.

From the foregoing analysis, it is apparent that the income tax liabilities are relatively high on corporations and individual proprietorships as compared to limited liability companies and partnerships. Moreover, these disparities would be greater in the case of higher business incomes because of the relatively high marginal income tax rate of 36 per cent on corporations, and they would also be greater if the excess profits tax had been taken into consideration.

By comparison to the unneutralities that have been shown, the basic principle with respect to the income tax treatment of different forms of business organization is essentially that the tax burdens should be neutral in their impact. In other words, net income is net income, regardless of the vehicle through which it is earned, and it should be taxed neutrally. To do otherwise is to penalize certain forms of business organization and to encourage others, with no apparent purpose being served.

Anyone would agree that tax capacity in the case of a partnership rests with the individual shares rather than with the income of the firm before distribution. But what is true for a partnership is no less true for a corporation, for the latter, in effect, merely represents a larger number of owners associated together for business purposes. If corporations are taxed under an income tax, and there is no integration of the corporate and individual income taxes, low income shareholders of large and profitable corporations are likely to be overtaxed. On the other hand, the tax burden of a high income shareholder is not an enviable one either, for he is subject to both high corporate tax rates (in Colombia's case progressive up to 36 per cent) and to a progressive income tax on the dividends. As demonstrated in Table 3–1, he is being penalized for investing in the corporate form of business. Moreover, the cumulative tax burden on this shareholder's proportionate share of profits is unlikely to bear a rational relationship to his personal ability to pay. For example, two stockholders may receive the same amount of dividends from a corporation, but, even though they may have widely different total incomes subject to personal taxation, the tax burdens on their proportionate shares of profit at the corporate level will be the same.

Another irrational aspect of income taxation in Colombia is the taxing of corporations at progressive rates. When corporations are subject to progressive rates, large and profitable corporations are taxed at high effective rates even though the taxable income might represent an average or low rate of profit on invested capital. Subjecting corporations to progressive rates also results in maneuvers to circumvent the progressive impact of the

tax, such as the splitting of corporations or the utilization of other forms of business organization. These difficulties are all manifestations of a failure to realize that the concept of ability to pay, at least as measured by a progressive income tax, relates to individuals and cannot be applied rationally to corporations. They are manifestations, also, of the need to apply proportional rates to business organizations and to integrate income taxes at the business and individual levels of taxation. If this were done, all forms of business would be treated neutrally; there would be no encouragement to use certain forms of business for tax avoidance purposes; there would be no problem of corporate splitting to avoid taxes; and interpersonal equity on the part of owners of all forms of businesses would be achieved.

Thus, the principles involved in a rational and equitable system of income taxation are clear, as well as their means of achievement; but their implementation in Colombia is circumscribed by other considerations. There is, first, a very severe revenue problem, so that any adjustments that may be made to the present system should be productive of revenue. This means, in effect, that as far as the achievement of additional neutrality among various forms of business organization is concerned, the lower taxed forms of business organization must be scaled upward rather than the higher taxed scaled downward. Similarly, with respect to the progressivity of the corporate income tax, the rates should be adjusted so that the income tax burden is made heavier on medium and small firms, not made lighter on the larger firms.

There are also problems with respect to integrating the corporate and personal income tax burdens. One of the most severe social, political, and economic problems in Colombia is the concentration of income and wealth. It is also true that corporations in general are owned by upper income groups, much more so than in the case of more economically advanced countries of the world. On the other hand, any system of integrating the corporate and individual income taxes would provide tax relief for shareowners, and shareowners in general are low in the scale of priority for tax relief in terms of equity.

Furthermore, there is no convincing evidence that this relief is necessary for purposes of encouraging private savings and investment. Apparently, the returns from capital invested in corporations have adjusted to the double taxation of corporate earnings. This is not to say, of course, that tax relief would not be an inducement to further corporate investment. But again, there are other considerations. Would not a greater stability of the peso, made possible by the reduction of government deficits, also be an encouragement to corporate investment? In other words, would corporate investment be stimulated significantly if tax relief were provided but inflation continued unabated? Thus, one is left with the conclusion that an integration of the corporate and personal income taxes may be desirable in principle for purposes of tax relief for corporate investors and as an improvement in interpersonal equity, but there are other cogent reasons for not providing the relief.

This conflict in goals is not an uncommon dilemma in issues of tax policy. And, when one is confronted with such a dilemma, there is no alternative but to establish a priority for the several tax policy goals. In Colombia it would appear that the two most important considerations are the provision of additional financial resources for the government and the redistributive effects of the tax system. Accordingly, a policy of integrating corporate and personal income taxes does not appear to be warranted at this time. The present provision which exempts the first $5,000 of dividends if the shareholder's net income does not exceed $48,000 should be retained, however, for it is consistent with the objective of developing a strong progressive scale of personal income tax rates and the broadening of share ownership.

That is not to say, however, that no action whatsoever is warranted with respect to the unneutralities of taxation borne by the various forms of business organization. Upward adjustments may be made to the tax burdens of limited liability companies and partnerships to make them less favorably treated as compared to corporations. The progressivity of the corporate tax also may be reduced. These issues will be discussed more fully in later sections of this chapter.

THE TAX BURDEN OF INDIVIDUALS

In considering the tax burden of individuals under the income and complementary taxes, it is first desirable to repeat that the concept of ability to pay as measured by a progressive income tax relates more to individuals than to business entities as such. Thus, the long-term goal in Colombia should be to convert the income tax as much as possible to an *ad personam* levy and, at the same time, to de-emphasize the impact of the income tax on business entities. In principle, the income tax on business entities should be used principally as a collection device on owners, not as an end in itself.

Colombia has made some progress in strengthening the impact of the income tax on natural persons, but there remains much more that should be done. Previously, it has been shown that the proportion of total assessments attributable to natural as compared to judicial persons has increased from 38.31 per cent in 1950 to 54.37 per cent in 1962. This is all to the good. At the same time, however, it has been shown that ninety-two taxpayers in 1962 accounted for about one-third of all assessments, and most of these were juridical persons. This is undesirable and should be corrected.

The data in Table 3–2 show that direct taxes on individuals have increased from $78.4 million in 1950 to $600.0 million in 1960, an increase of over sevenfold. At the same time, the percentage of direct taxes on individuals to income received by individuals increased from 1.19 per cent in 1950 to 2.95 per cent in 1960. These are significant changes, but

TABLE 3–2

Relationship of Certain Components of the National Income to Direct Tax Burdens

	Income Received by Individuals [a] (Millions)	Index	Direct Taxes on Individuals [b] (Millions)	Index	Percentage of Direct Taxes to Income	Savings of Individual Persons (Millions)	Index	Percentage of Savings to Income
1950	$ 6,588.9	100	$ 78.4	100	1.19	$ 85.9	100	1.30
1951	7,341.2	111	107.2	137	1.46	86.4	101	1.18
1952	7,950.9	121	107.6	137	1.35	86.4	101	1.09
1953	8,854.1	134	109.5	140	1.24	109.7	128	1.24
1954	10,492.3	159	181.6	232	1.73	180.6	210	1.72
1955	10,750.0	163	201.5	257	1.87	171.2	199	1.59
1956	12,100.1	184	226.7	289	1.87	238.0	277	1.97
1957	14,090.4	214	315.3	402	2.24	326.6	380	2.32
1958	15,530.2	236	345.8	441	2.23	451.1	525	2.90
1959	17,851.6	271	530.0	676	2.97	614.0	715	3.44
1960	20,328.1	309	600.0	765	2.95	773.9	901	3.81

[a] Obtained from the sum of wages and salaries and income from property and from businesses not organized into societies of capital of family units.

[b] Obtained by subtracting direct taxes on juridical persons from total assessments for the income and complementary taxes.
Source: Departamento de Investigaciones Económicas, Banco de la República, *Cuentas Nacionales, 1950–1960*, p. 6.

one could never argue that a tax contribution on the part of individuals that represents, in the aggregate, 2.95 per cent of their income is oppressive. Moreover, Table 3–2 shows that the savings of individuals have increased from $85.9 million in 1950 to $773.9 million in 1960 or at a faster rate than the burden of direct taxes. From this evidence, it cannot be argued that the direct tax system has impeded the ability of individuals to save.

Can the trend toward obtaining relatively more income and related taxes from individuals be continued? Quite obviously it can, for all of the national income, all of the income that can be taxed under an income tax in the form of profit, rent, interest, and wages and salaries, is received in the final analysis by natural persons. Therefore, if the income tax on natural persons is relatively weak as a source of revenue, or if it is not as productive of revenue ·as it should be, the fault lies in low rates, a narrow base of taxation, or weak compliance and enforcement. Correctives must be sought, therefore, in raising rates, broadening the base, or strengthening compliance and enforcement.

Tax Rates

Tables 2–1 and 2–2 at the outset of Chapter 2 show the income tax rates on

individuals for the period from 1953 to 1959 and for the period from 1960 to 1963. Currently, the tax rate on individuals is in fifty-six brackets, from .50 per cent on taxable income up to $2,000 to 51.00 per cent on income over $2,000,000. By a comparison of the effective rates on taxable income in Tables 2–1 and 2–2 of Chapter 2, it may be seen that the revisions introduced in 1960 resulted in no changes in the tax burden up to $6,000 of taxable income, a saving in taxes on income from $6,000 to approximately $70,000, and higher burdens for taxable incomes over $70,000.

Table 3–3 provides a better understanding of the effect of the rate changes introduced in 1960. This table shows that substantial tax reductions were granted, from 13.39 per cent on $7,000 of taxable income to 27.49 per cent on $14,000, and then falling to a reduction of 13.88 per cent at $50,000. On the other hand, the increases in tax burdens beginning at about $70,000 were more modest. At a level of $100,000 in taxable income there was an increase in tax of 6.67 per cent, and at $400,000 there was an increase of 13.43 per cent. But after $400,000, the percentage increase in tax diminished until it was only 8.02 per cent on $1,000,000 of taxable income.

TABLE 3–3

Effect of the Tax Rate Change in 1960 on the Effective Tax Rates of Individuals

	Before Tax Rate Change			After Tax Rate Change		
Taxable Income	Amount of Tax	Effective Rate on Taxable Income (Per Cent)		Amount of Tax	Effective Rate on Taxable Income (Per Cent)	Percentage Increase or Decrease in Tax
$ 2,000	$ 10	.50		$ 10	.50	—
5,000	55	1.10		55	1.10	—
6,000	80	1.33		80	1.33	—
7,000	127	1.81		110	1.57	−13.39
8,000	177	2.21		145	1.81	−18.08
9,000	232	2.57		185	2.06	−20.26
10,000	290	2.90		230	2.30	−20.69
12,000	465	3.87		340	2.83	−26.88
14,000	662	4.72		480	3.43	−27.49
16,000	870	5.43		640	4.00	−26.44
18,000	1,092	6.07		820	4.56	−24.91
20,000	1,327	6.64		1,020	5.10	−23.13
30,000	2,980	9.93		2,320	7.73	−22.15
40,000	5,130	12.83		4,120	10.30	−19.69
50,000	7,455	14.91		6,420	12.84	−13.88
100,000	20,830	20.83		22,220	22.22	6.67
200,000	51,580	25.79		57,720	28.86	11.90
300,000	84,080	28.03		95,220	31.74	13.25
400,000	118,330	29.58		134,220	33.56	13.43
500,000	154,830	30.97		174,220	34.84	12.52
1,000,000	360,330	36.03		389,220	38.92	8.02
2,000,000	799,080	39.95		869,220	43.46	8.78

From the evidence presented in Table 3–3, it would appear that those responsible for drafting and enacting the tax changes in 1960 desired, in general, to keep the tax burdens the same on low income groups, to grant tax relief to the middle class, and to impose higher burdens on upper income groups. These goals are difficult to justify on equity grounds. If equity were the principal criterion motivating the changes, it would appear that taxpayers with a taxable income within the range of $2,000 to $6,000 were more deserving of tax reductions than persons with a taxable income within the range of $7,000 to $70,000. Tax reductions for those with taxable incomes of $50,000 to $70,000 appear particularly unwarranted, since these persons have enviable incomes by Colombian standards. The tax changes also appear to be difficult to justify on revenue grounds, since very substantial reductions were given in a taxable income range where the revenue productivity should be relatively strong as compared to more modest increases

where the productivity is probably weaker. Thus, the conclusion appears warranted that the tax changes in 1960 probably weakened the productivity of the tax on balance without contributing much, if anything, toward improving equity.

In considering possible reform measures, four general objections may be made to the Colombian income tax rate structure for individuals:

1) The beginning rate of .50 per cent is excessively low. Assume, for example, that a taxpayer has a gross income of $14,000 and that his exemptions and deductions amount to $13,000, leaving a taxable income of $1,000. The tax on this income amounts to $5, which at the current rate of exchange is approximately U.S. 50 cents. Because of the low beginning rate, there is probably a large number of returns in Colombia for which the amount of the tax does not justify the administrative cost of assessment and collection. Ideally, the beginning marginal rate would be about 10 per cent.

2) Fifty-six taxable income brackets and marginal rates is an excessive number. This type of refinement is unnecessary for purposes of achieving equity and only serves to complicate compliance and enforcement. In particular, this excessive number of marginal rates will be a burden if withholding is introduced. About one-half the present number of income brackets would be adequate for a progressive scale.

3) The highest marginal rate of 51 per cent on income over $2,000,000 appears to be desirable, at first glance, in the sense that no purpose is served in having marginal rates that are so high (70 or 80 per cent) that they encourage evasion and are essentially unenforceable. But this rate of 51 per cent is deceptive, since probably few individual taxpayers have an income high enough to be subject to the rate. Furthermore, it must be remembered that the marginal rate must be relatively high in order to have a substantial effective rate of taxation. It may be noted in Table 3–3, for example, that the marginal rate from $90,000 to $100,000 is 34 per cent, but the effective rate on $100,000 of taxable income is only 22.22 per cent.

4) The increases in the rates are capricious. For example, at the lower end of the taxable income scale, the percentage increases in the marginal rates on the first six successive income brackets of $2,000 are as follows: 200 per cent, 66.6 per cent, 40.0 per cent, 28.6 per cent, 33.3 per cent, and 16.7 per cent. While it is difficult to have a smooth progression and still have round numbers for the marginal rates for purposes of simplicity, some improvement is possible over the current rate progression.

It is easier to make these criticisms of the rate structure, however, than to offer proposals for reform. From a technical point of view the goal would be relatively easy if one could wipe the slate clean and start afresh. But this is not possible; instead, progress must be gradualistic for purposes of political and taxpayer acceptance. For example, although it would be desirable to have a beginning marginal rate of at least 10 per cent, merely to

increase the current rate of .50 per cent to 2.00 per cent would represent an increase in tax of 300 per cent. Or again, to attain symmetry in the rate structure, it would not be desirable to reduce some marginal rates abruptly and increase others precipitously. Moreover, it is necessary to bear in mind the broad tax policy goals of increasing the revenue productivity of the individual income tax and improving its equity by strengthening the progressivity of the rate structure. With all of these conditions and restraints, only limited progress can be made in reforming the rate structure in the short run.

Table 3–4 demonstrates the type of rate structure that would represent limited short-run progress. Several improvements over the current schedule may be noted:

1) The number of tax brackets has been reduced from fifty-six to nineteen.

2) The beginning marginal rate on the first $2,000 of taxable income has been increased from .50 to 2.00 per cent in order to increase the revenue productivity of those tax returns that are just above the exemption limit. This beginning rate actually should be increased to 5.00 or 10.00 per cent, but the lower rate of 2.00 per cent was selected in order to ease the transition problem.

3) The revenue productivity of the rate structure has been strengthened by increasing the effective rate of taxation at each level of taxable income. On the other hand, at no level of taxable income do the effective rates appear to be oppressive.

4) The progressivity of the rate structure has been increased. In this respect, special attention should be given to the last two columns of Table 3–4. At first glance it would appear that the proposed reform is prejudicial to low income groups, because the percentage increases in taxes are greater at the lower levels of taxable income. But percentage increases in taxes are misleading. When a tax payment is very low and it is increased, the increment of increase when expressed as a percentage is likely to be substantial. For example, if a taxpayer is subjected to a tax of one peso when he was

TABLE 3-4

Comparison of Proposed and Current Income Tax Schedules for Natural Persons

Taxable Income Brackets	Proposed Marginal Rates (Per Cent)	Taxable Income	Current Schedule Tax	Current Schedule Effective Rate (Per Cent)	Proposed Schedule Tax	Proposed Schedule Effective Rate (Per Cent)	Percentage Increase in Tax	Increase in Percentage Points of the Effective Rate
Up to $ 2,000	2.0	$ 2,000	$ 10	.50	$ 40	2.00	300.0	1.50
$ 2,000 to 5,000	3.0	5,000	55	1.10	130	2.60	136.4	1.50
5,000 to 10,000	5.0	10,000	230	2.30	440	4.40	91.3	2.10
10,000 to 20,000	10.0	20,000	1,020	5.10	1,440	7.20	41.2	2.10
20,000 to 30,000	15.0	30,000	2,320	7.73	2,940	9.80	26.7	2.07
30,000 to 40,000	20.0	40,000	4,120	10.30	4,940	12.35	19.9	2.05
40,000 to 60,000	28.0	60,000	9,220	15.36	10,540	17.57	14.3	2.21
60,000 to 80,000	36.0	80,000	15,520	19.40	17,740	22.18	14.3	2.78
80,000 to 100,000	42.0	100,000	22,220	22.22	26,140	26.14	17.6	3.92
100,000 to 150,000	44.0	150,000	39,720	26.48	48,140	32.09	21.2	5.61
150,000 to 200,000	46.0	200,000	57,720	28.86	71,140	35.57	23.3	6.71
200,000 to 300,000	48.0	300,000	95,220	31.74	119,140	39.71	25.1	7.97
300,000 to 400,000	50.0	400,000	134,220	33.55	169,140	42.29	26.0	8.74
400,000 to 500,000	52.0	500,000	174,220	34.84	221,140	44.23	26.9	9.39
500,000 to 750,000	54.0	750,000	278,720	37.16	356,140	47.49	27.8	10.33
750,000 to 1,000,000	56.0	1,000,000	389,220	38.92	496,140	49.61	27.5	10.69
1,000,000 to 1,500,000	58.0	1,500,000	623,220	41.55	786,140	52.41	26.1	10.86
1,500,000 to 2,000,000	60.0	2,000,000	869,220	43.46	1,086,140	54.31	25.0	10.85
Over $2,000,000	62.0	3,000,000	1,379,220	45.97	1,706,140	56.87	23.7	10.90

previously exempt, his percentage increase in tax is infinity, although the new tax in absolute terms is very light. For this reason, the last column in Table 3–4, showing the increase in the *percentage points* of the effective rates, is actually more indicative of the increase in the tax burdens at each level of taxable income. This column demonstrates that the tax burdens in general have been increased progressively.

Exemptions, Deductions, and Exclusions

To gain a general insight into the structural problems of the personal income tax, a sample of one hundred salary and wage returns was selected at random and analyzed intensively. This was a very illuminating experience, as it demonstrated one of the principal faults of the Colombian system of taxing individuals under the income tax: the base of the tax is very seriously eroded by an excessive number of exemptions, exclusions, and deductions. Therefore, what at first glance appears to be a rather formidable tax in terms of the rate structure applicable to taxable income is in reality a rather anemic tax in application. The tax is tough on paper but lenient in practice.

The first apparent problem caused by the erosion of the taxable base is the number of exempt returns. In Colombia there is a reporting requirement for income tax purposes if net income exceeds $2,500. Thus, despite the fact that all returns examined had an income in excess of this amount, only 45 returns were taxable. This information is consistent with the global figures, for 1,180,684 returns were filed in 1962, but only 501,594 returns or 42.5 per cent of the total were taxable.

Second, with respect to the 45 taxable returns, it was determined that the total gross income reported of $748,864 was reduced to a taxable income of only $271,503 or to 36.2 per cent of the total gross income. This total reduction also obscures the fact that several sizable individual gross incomes were reduced to very modest taxable incomes.

For example, one gross income of $34,810 was reduced to a taxable income of $309; another, from $42,287 to $3,066.

To ascertain the factors accounting for the erosion of the taxable base, the various deductions and exclusions for the 45 taxable returns were divided into four groups: requested deductions (*deducciones solicitadas*), personal exemptions (*personales y por personas a cargo*), exempt income (*rentas exentas*), and special personal exemptions (*exenciones personales especiales*). The analysis showed that 50.0 per cent of the total loss of taxable income was caused by personal exemptions, 23.5 per cent by exempt income, 14.0 per cent by requested deductions, and 12.4 per cent by special personal exemptions.

It should be observed also that the wide number of exemptions, deductions, and exclusions are a source of confusion to the taxpayers. Out of the 45 taxable returns, it is quite possible that not a single return was accurate in all respects, which means that the tax administration faces a difficult burden if the returns are to be policed adequately. And, although there are a number of outlandish claims, such as deductions for domestic servants and household food, in general there is an underutilization of available deductions. As a result, the erosion of the tax base would be even greater if taxpayers were better informed of the provisions of the income tax law.

Another insight into the problem of the erosion of the tax base may be gained by developing hypothetical examples of tax liability. Three illustrations are shown in Tables 3–5 to 3–7. The first table, showing the hypothetical tax liability of a well-paid secretary in the Ministry of Finance, shows that the various exemptions and exclusions reduce a gross income of $12,000 to a taxable income of $5,580. The tax on this income is $69, which at the current rate of exchange with the United States dollar represents an income tax payment of only U.S. $6.90. The effective rate of tax is only .58 per cent. In the case of a lawyer employed in the Ministry of Finance (Table 3–6), the gross in-

TABLE 3–5

Hypothetical Income Tax Liability for a Well-Paid
Secretary Employed in the Ministry of Finance

Gross salary		$12,000
Deductions		
Social security		
contributions	$ 360	
Interest	100	
	$ 460	
Exemptions		
Personal (single)	$2,500	
Transportation allowance	360	
Special personal		
exemptions:		
Medical and dental	500	
Educational	200	
Rent	2,400	
	$5,960	
Total deductions and exemptions	6,420	
Net taxable income	5,580	
Income tax	69	
Effective rate of taxation	.58 per cent	

TABLE 3–6

Hypothetical Income Tax Liability for a Lawyer
Employed in the Ministry of Finance

Gross salary		$24,000
Deductions		
Social security		
contributions	$ 720	
Interest	500	
	$ 1,220	
Exemptions		
Personal (married,		
four children)	9,000	
Special personal		
exemptions:		
Medical and dental	1,000	
Educational	1,000	
Professional	200	
Rent	3,600	
	$14,800	
Total deductions and exemptions	16,020	
Net taxable income	7,980	
Income tax	144	
Effective rate of taxation	.60 per cent	

come of $24,000 is reduced to a taxable
income of $7,980. The tax liability on this
income is only $144 (U.S. $14.40), and the
effective rate of taxation is only .60 per
cent.[2]

[2] The purpose of these illustrations is to demonstrate
the degree of tax base erosion. It should not be inferred
that one taxpayer or the other is relatively overtaxed or
undertaxed, for the two taxpayers obviously are not comparable.

Table 3–7, for a salaried business executive, is of more interest because it answers
the complaint that the upper middle income
groups are "penalized" by an undue burden
of taxation. On a gross salary of $100,000,
the taxable income through a normal use of
exemptions and deductions becomes $67,867,
the tax $11,659, and the effective rate of
taxation 11.65 per cent. This tax burden is
approximately the same as the federal income
tax of the United States. On a salary of
$10,000 in the United States, with six per-
sonal exemptions and using the standard
deduction, the tax is U.S. $1,108, and the
effective rate of taxation is 11.08 per cent.
In the United States, however, the taxpayer
bears much heavier tax burdens at the state
and local levels of government than is the
case in Colombia.

Personal Exemptions

Personal exemptions have remained at the
same level since 1953. They are $2,500 for
a single taxpayer, $5,000 for a married
couple, and $1,000 for each dependent. The
fact that these exemptions have not been
changed in the last ten years, despite inflationary pressure that has more than doubled

TABLE 3–7

Hypothetical Income Tax Liability for an Executive

Gross salary		$100,000
Deductions		
Social security		
contributions	$ 3,000	
Interest	8,000	
Real property tax	3,000	
	$14,000	
Exemptions		
Personal (married,		
four children)	9,000	
Special personal		
exemptions:		
Medical and dental	600	
Professional	200	
	$ 9,800	
Exempt income		
Service bonus	8,333	
Total deductions and exemptions	32,133	
Net taxable income	67,867	
Income tax	11,659	
Effective rate of taxation	11.66 per cent	

the price level, has let loose a storm of criticism. It is argued that exemptions should cover the indispensable living expenses of a taxpayer and his dependents, that taxpayers have a right to a basic subsistence that is not taxed by the state, that when inflation erodes away this basic minimum, exemptions should be increased.

All of these are specious arguments, at least in the way in which they are usually expressed. In 1963 the average per capita income in Colombia was about $1,600. This average obscures the fact that a maldistribution of income probably results in a significant part of the population having a per capita income of less than $1,000, and even not an insignificant part of the population having a per capita income of less than $500. And, in the face of this, it is argued that the exemption for a single taxpayer of $2,500 should be raised to provide him with a *subsistence* or an *indispensable living expense*. Quite to the contrary, the 486,113 natural persons that were income taxpayers in 1962 represent the income elite of the population of 16.5 million. It also is one of the compensations of secular inflation that a greater number of those that are relatively well off have been brought within the income tax system automatically as the exemption limits have been reduced in terms of real purchasing power.

What is the most desirable level for income tax exemptions? There is no absolute standard for this, any more than there is an absolute standard for the progressivity of the rates. If a standard is established in terms of an income that is a socially acceptable minimum, and, for the purpose of argument, this is considered to be the current exemption of $2,500 for a single person in Colombia, this means in effect that the income tax is being placed beyond the reach of the majority of the population. And the essential error of this is that the majority of the population is not being exempted from other taxes. In other words, the majority of the population is being spared the pain of an income tax in the name of protecting a socially acceptable

minimum income; but in the urgency of government demands for revenue, this majority is being subjected to regressive indirect taxes that are much more inequitable than an income tax. Thus, the argument for not taxing a socially acceptable minimum under the income tax only holds if taxpayers are in fact exempt from all taxes under this minimum. If they are not (and such is the case in Colombia), they would be better off with lower income tax exemptions accompanied by a reduction of indirect taxes.

Nevertheless, despite the fact that a case can be made for lower exemptions in Colombia, no positive government action is warranted. One reason for this is that the exemptions are reduced automatically as inflation continues. Another reason is that a lowering of exemptions would increase the number of tax returns, which would place a heavier burden on the income tax administration. At the present time, it is probably more important to use the available administrative resources for the improved enforcement of the current base rather than strain the resources further by an expansion of the base.

Special Personal Exemptions

The Colombian income tax law contains a number of "special personal exemptions" for medical, hospital, educational, and other expenses. Before considering each of these individually, there are four general reasons that may be advanced for either their elimination or drastic reduction:

1) The personal exemptions for the taxpayer, spouse, and dependents are sufficiently generous to provide protection from the vicissitudes that beset low income groups.

2) The exemptions erode the tax base and result in a loss of urgently needed revenue.

3) The exemptions are difficult to administer in order to control abuse.

4) There are more direct and efficient ways of subsidizing low income taxpayers than through the provision of income tax exemptions.

All of the exemptions have the common characteristic of being related to net income and the number of children supported. Taxpayers with a net income (before personal exemptions) of $36,000 or less, regardless of the number of children supported, are entitled to all of the exemptions; taxpayers with a net income exceeding $36,000, but supporting five or more children, are entitled to 50 per cent of the exemptions; and taxpayers with a net income exceeding $36,000, but supporting less than five children, are entitled to deduct only 20 per cent of all fees for professional expenses.

Medical and Hospital Expenses. These include (subject to the above restrictions with respect to the level of net income and number of dependent children) all payments to doctors and dentists and all payments to hospitals and clinics up to $500 for each case. Beyond the general criticisms of exemptions noted above, the principal objection that may be advanced to the medical and hospital exemptions is that they should provide relief only when expenses are unusually high and not for any ordinary family expense associated with sickness. Furthermore, if the principal of a deduction for unusual medical expenses is fair, it should be available to all taxpayers, for even the relatively well off can suffer a financial catastrophe through serious and prolonged sickness.

Recommended for consideration is the proposal that the exemption for medical and hospital expenses should be limited to expenses in excess of 5 per cent of net income, but the exemption should be available to all taxpayers regardless of the level of income or number of dependents.

Educational Expenses. The educational exemption includes all payments (subject to restrictions on net income and number of children) to educational institutions in Colombia of up to $500 for the taxpayer and for each of his dependents. To assess the desirability of this exemption, it is first necessary to realize that a child's attendance at either a free public school or a private school is based almost entirely on the income of the parent. In other words, a child invariably will be sent to a private school if the income of the parent will permit the necessary expenditure. In part, the explanation for this is the social status associated with private schools, but there is also a distinct difference between the two types of schools in terms of quality of education. Therefore, it is apparent that the net effect of the educational exemption is to subsidize and encourage the development of a private system of education. This is undesirable from a social point of view and is also quite unnecessary in view of the fact that private educational facilities are one of the principal booming industries of Colombia. Instead of granting this broad educational subsidy, that redounds to the benefit of middle and upper income groups, the government would be better advised to use the income for the provision of additional educational facilities for low income groups and for scholarships.

Payments to Professionals. This exemption includes 20 per cent of payments made to professionals other than doctors and dentists. Thus, the exemption includes payments made to lawyers, engineers, architects, optometrists, etc. The rationale for this exemption is uncertain. Perhaps the explanation lies in the strength of professional groups in the Congress. All professional expenses incurred in connection with the production of income should, of course, be deductible, but a clear case exists for the exclusion of all such expenditures that are in the nature of consumption items.

Rental Housing. This exemption includes payments up to $3,600 for rental housing that is inhabited by the taxpayer. For purposes of assessing the desirability of this exemption, the related issue should also be considered of taxing the imputed rent of owner-occupied residences. Under the present income tax law, every taxpayer has an exemption of the imputed income derived from the first $100,000 of value represented by an owner-occupied residence (and land) as this value is determined for cadastral purposes. Required to be included in gross income is an amount equal to 6 per cent of the cadastral value of land and buildings on that part of value between $100,000 and $300,000, 10 per cent on that part between $300,000 and $500,000, and 12 per cent on any value exceeding $500,000. In the event that there is no cadastral valuation of the property, the imputed income is based on acquisition price. The imputed income from summer or vacation houses, as well as normal residences, is included.

Since Colombia recognizes the justification of taxing the imputed income of owner-occupied residences, no elaborate defense of this principle is necessary. But since this principle is applied imperfectly, perhaps a brief reminder of the basic issue is in order. The purpose of taxing the imputed rent of owner-occupied houses is to place owners and renters on substantially equal terms with respect to the income tax. If a renter is not permitted a deduction for rent paid, and if an owner is not taxed on imputed rent, the latter in effect would be enjoying the same consumption standard as the renter but would be paying a smaller tax. Alternatively, it may be said that an owner should be taxed on his investment in housing to compensate for the fact that a renter is being taxed on whatever alternative investment he may have elected in lieu of investment in housing. This equality of tax treatment may be accomplished in one of two ways, by allowing renters to deduct part of their rents in computing their taxable incomes, or by taxing the imputed rents of owner-occupied residences.

In the light of this explanation, what is the rationale in Colombia for permitting a rental deduction as well as taxing imputed rent? The answer lies in the basic exemption enjoyed by taxpayers living in owner-occupied residences. In the original draft of Law 81 of 1960, an exemption of $60,000 was proposed. Thus, to compensate for this exemption, renters were given a deduction of 6 per cent of the amount of the exemption or $3,600. When the exemption was increased by Con-

gress to $100,000, the deduction for renters was not increased proportionately.

For purposes of simplicity, tax neutrality, and revenue productivity, it would be preferable to eliminate the deduction for renters and to subject taxpayers to the imputed rent of owner-occupied residences without any exemption. In addition, the amount to be included in gross income should be a flat rate of 10 per cent of cadastral value instead of the current progressive rates of 6 to 12 per cent. Justification for this higher rate is the relatively high return on capital in Colombia of at least 12 per cent. Because of the underassessment of real property, there is no need to allow deductions for such expenses as mortgage interest, property taxes, and repairs.

Requested Deductions

There is a section of the income tax law that provides for requested deductions (*deducciones solicitadas*). Most of these deductions are concerned with business expenses and are entirely legitimate, but there are three that are directly related to personal expenditures and should be eliminated.

Interest. The Colombian income tax law allows a deduction for interest on personal loans as well as interest incurred in business operations. The latter deduction, of course, is necessary to give a proper measure of net income, but there is little justification to allow a deduction for interest on personal loans. From an equity point of view, the saving in taxes from deducting interest is greater for upper income groups, for their marginal tax rates are higher. The interest deduction is also difficult to administer in the case of installment payments, for interest often is not distinguishable from other charges. The interest deduction for mortgages on owner-occupied houses is also unnecessary, as mentioned above.

Real Property Taxes. All real property tax payments are allowed as a deduction from income subject to the income tax. There is no persuasive argument to justify this deduction. It cannot be said that the deduction is necessary for purposes of tax relief, for the real property tax burden is not substantial. It cannot be argued that it is necessary for equity purposes, for low income groups probably, on balance, are renters rather than owners. Also, as in the case of all deductions, the saving in income tax is greater for upper income groups. Nor can it be argued that the deduction of real property taxes is necessary to prevent "a tax on a tax" unless all taxes are to be made deductible, including the income tax itself.

Contributions to Social Security and Pension Plans. All contributions to social security and other pension plans are deductible on the part of both the employee and the employer. Often, the deductibility of social security contributions made by employees is defended on the grounds that this is an expenditure of peculiar social importance, and for this reason should be encouraged. In Colombia this argument loses much of its appeal because social security covers only a select and privileged part of the labor force and, therefore, a part that is already subsidized by the mere fact of coverage. The tax treatment of contributions to social security and other pension plans also causes an unneutrality with those employees that provide for their own retirement income through annuities, for payments to an annuity fund are not deductible.

Exempt Income

Eroding the personal income tax base still further are several items of exempt income. These types of income must be reported, but they are fully deductible. Some are trivial in terms of their effect on narrowing the tax base, but others have a significant impact. Nevertheless, all of them should be eliminated because they represent income to the taxpayer, and they constitute an administrative burden in terms of verifying their accuracy:

1) By legal requirement, employees must be paid a service bonus of one-twelfth of their annual salary. All of this bonus is exempt from the income tax. Furthermore, if a collective agreement exists between employees and employers to grant a bonus in excess of one-twelfth of the annual salary, this additional amount is also tax-exempt. Another aspect of this unneutrality is that employees of the central government are not paid a service bonus, and thus they receive a larger percentage of taxable income than other workers. In addition, members of the police force and the armed services receive several cash subsidies as fringe benefits to their salaries, all of which are exempt.

2) If an employee elects to work rather than to have a vacation, his earnings during the vacation period represent exempt income. In a casual scrutiny of income tax returns, it appears that few workers in Colombia take a vacation.

3) There is a system of compulsory severance pay in Colombia *(cesantía)* whereby all workers, public and private, are provided with tax-exempt severance pay amounting to one month of earnings for each twelve months of employment. While the loss of employment may constitute a hardship, there is no guarantee that this will be the case, for many workers undoubtedly find other employment. It would seem that the personal exemptions available under the income tax would provide sufficient protection for hardship cases.

4) All social security and pension payments represent exempt income. These exclusions cannot be justified on equity grounds, for in Colombia the recipients of these payments, as indicated previously, are actually relatively well off as compared to the majority of workers that receive no such payments. Furthermore, the personal exemptions under the income tax provide sufficient protection for those taxpayers who would receive only social security or pension payments.

At this point, it is also appropriate to comment on the tax status of retirement income received in the form of an annuity. To illustrate the Colombian law in this regard, assume that a taxpayer retires at the age of sixty-five years, that by this time a total annuity fund of $100,000 has accumulated to his credit, and from this he will be paid $1,000 per month. According to the Colombian law, 6 per cent of the total capital of $100,000 will be construed as an interest return on capital. Thus, if the taxpayer receives $12,000 in annuity income during the first year, $6,000 will be taxable as interest, and $6,000 will be exempt as a return of capital. The $6,000 representing a return of capital will then be subtracted from the total capital of $100,000 in order to determine the taxable and exempt portions of the annuity payment in the second year, and so on.

This rule probably errs in understating the amount of net income that is involved in a series of annuity payments, principally because the interest return of 6 per cent is about one-half the interest return that is normal in Colombia. An improvement would result by adopting a rule with the following procedural steps: (1) Determine the total cost of the annuity at the time that the annuity payments are started. (2) Divide the cost of the annuity by the beneficiary's life expectancy and allow this amount as a tax-free return of capital in each benefit payment. (3) Tax the balance of each payment as taxable income.

5) All interest on governmental obligations is exempt from the income tax. Exempt interest also includes the obligations of an extensive list of autonomous and semi-autonomous institutions and interest earned on the first $5,000 of savings bank deposits. An objection may be made to the exemption of interest on government bonds on the grounds that it orients the capital market to the public rather than to the private sector, while the exemption of interest in general is undesirable because it is a greater advantage to upper income groups.

6) The 1960 income tax law provided for the exemption of emoluments earned by the religious of the Catholic Church. While most of the religious undoubtedly have modest incomes, this is not invariably the case. Therefore, it would seem that the personal exemptions would protect those with low incomes, while the others could be made to follow Christ's admonition to "render to Caesar the things that are Caesar's." Even if the exemption is retained, it should be broadened to include the religious of all faiths.

Income Splitting of Spouses

Under the 1960 law, if a husband and wife are living together, they are permitted to split up to $60,000 of their aggregate *earned* income on a fifty-fifty basis, whether such income is in fact earned by both spouses or not. This revision was an unfortunate mistake, for it represented a loss in revenue and decreased the progressivity of the income tax. Moreover, the better yardstick for determining ability to pay is family or aggregate income, not separate parts of the income.

Stock Dividends and Bearer Shares

Colombia taxes all dividends received in the form of shares at the market value of the shares and at the time of distribution. An objection to this may be made on the grounds that a stock dividend merely divides an existing equity interest into more shares with no fundamental change in the ownership. On the other hand, stock dividends are used frequently in Colombia as a means of capitalizing accumulated earnings and giving shareholders marketable securities that can be converted into cash. Thus, if stock dividends were not taxed, an avoidance device would be created. Why should any corporation pay taxable cash dividends if it could issue exempt stock dividends?

The principal justification for the existence of bearer shares is an anti-social one; i.e., they are popular because they make the enforcement of the income tax on dividends difficult by obscuring the identity of dividend receivers. Colombia attempts to overcome this enforcement problem with a withholding tax of 12 per cent on dividends payable on bearer shares. With individual income tax rates within a range of .50 to 51.00 per cent, quite obviously this withholding rate is not high enough to prevent evasion. Bearer shares should either be eliminated, or their use should be made more difficult by the adoption of a high stamp tax on their issuance and by raising the withholding tax rate to 20 per cent.

THE TAX BURDEN OF CORPORATIONS

Before examining the impact of the income and complementary taxes on corporations, certain general goals or principles of taxation may be postulated. Since some of these have been explained in a previous section, it is only necessary to restate them briefly: (1) The corporate form of business organization should not be penalized by an undue burden of taxation, for it is an important means of mobilizing national capital for economic development. (2) The application of progressive rates to corporations has a weak theoretical justification, for there is no reason to believe that the profitability of a corporation is directly or closely related (in an interpersonal sense) to the ability to pay of its owners. Moreover, applying progressive rates to corporations encourages them to split in order to avoid tax liabilities. (3) In general, it is desirable to strengthen the application of taxes on individuals and de-emphasize the burden of taxes on business enterprises, for decisions at the latter level with respect to investment are particularly sensitive to tax burdens. (4) Tax liabilities should be as neutral as possible with respect to the various forms of business organization.

With these guidelines in mind, consideration may now be given to the impact of the income and complementary tax system on corporations. Since 1960 corporations have been subject to six taxes: the income tax, the excess profits tax, the electric and steel development tax, the housing tax, the tax on underutilized agricultural land, and the livestock tax. Since the latter two taxes have a narrow and unique application, they may be ignored for purposes of considering the general impact of taxes on corporations.

Considering first the impact of the income tax on corporations, the 1960 tax reform, which substituted three tax rates (12, 24, and 36 per cent) for the previous forty-three rates, accomplished little but to allot heavier and lighter tax burdens in a rather haphazard fashion. As shown in Tables 2–3 and 2–4 in Chapter 2, the effective tax rates on taxable income were increased on incomes up to $50,000; reduced on incomes from $50,000 to $150,000; increased on incomes from $150,000 to $800,000; reduced at the level of $1,000,000; and were increased on all net taxable incomes in excess of $1,000,000. Quite obviously, if one of the purposes of the 1960 reform was to lighten the tax burden on corporations, at least as far as the income tax is concerned, the goal generally was not accomplished.

Nor was much done to reduce the progressivity of the tax. Referring again to Tables 2–3 and 2–4, it may be seen that the effective rates on taxable income before 1960 rose from 1.00 per cent on a taxable income of $2,000 to 28.8 per cent on a taxable income of $500,000. Since 1960 the progressivity through the same range of taxable income varies from 12.00 to 33.36 per cent.

Nor can it be argued that the new effective rates are unduly burdensome. At a level of taxable income of $50,000, the effective rate in 1960 was increased from 11.34 to 12.00 per cent; at $100,000, it was reduced from 16.16 to 12.00 per cent; at $500,000, it was increased from 20.83 to 21.60 per cent; at $1,000,000, it was reduced from 23.05 to 22.80 per cent; and on $5,000,000, it was increased from 28.18 to 33.36 per cent. These are all very minor changes. Therefore, if the tax burden on corporations is excessive, as has been charged repeatedly in Colombia, the reasons must be sought elsewhere than in the income tax.

Tables 3–8 and 3–9 have been prepared to illustrate the impact of the remaining direct taxes on corporations. Table 3–8 shows three groups of corporations that may be considered for illustrative purposes as large, medium, and small firms. Each of these groups, in turn, has three firms representing different levels of return on net wealth of 50, 25, and 10 per cent. From this illustration, it is apparent that the over-all tax burdens for all taxes and for any level of profit shown is moderate if the returns on net wealth are moderate. Even the largest corporation with a moderate return of 10 per cent of net wealth (Firm C) has an effective rate of taxation of only 37.79 per cent, while for the medium and small corporations with moderate rates of returns of 10 per cent (Firms F and I), the effective rates of taxation are only 29.61 and 17.22 per cent respectively.

When the corporations have excessive rates of return on net wealth, however, the tax burden is appreciably heavier. As shown in Table 3–8, the large corporation has an over-all effective rate of taxation of 51.51 per cent when the rate of return on net wealth is 50 per cent (Firm A), while the effective rate is 44.28 per cent when the rate of return is 25 per cent (Firm B). Moreover, the effective rates of taxation are also appreciably heavier when medium and small corporations realize excessive profits to the extent of a 50 per cent return on net wealth, as in the case of Firm D with an effective rate of taxation of 50.14 per cent, and Firm G with an effective rate of taxation of 42.12 per cent. In other words, there is a significantly higher tax burden attendant with the realization of excessive profits regardless of the size of the corporation. This may give rise to the objection that the application of the excess profits tax should be graduated in such a way that a greater burden is exacted from relatively large corporations; i.e., that if the effective tax burden on a medium-size corporation earning 50 per cent on net worth is 50.14 per cent, the effective rate should be more than 51.51 per cent on a large corporation earning the same rate of return.[3] But this argument defeats the purpose or rationale of the excess profits tax, which is to tax excessive profits. In effect it is an argument in favor of penalizing size itself rather than excess profits.

A more important argument with respect to the excess profits tax is that it is alleged to be unduly punitive. It has been charged, for example, that the application of the tax makes the group of direct taxes confiscatory. To substantiate this, it is customary for some experts to summate the several marginal tax rates borne by a large and very profitable corporation, and, indeed, in the manner in which this summation is done, the burden is confiscatory, namely:

Income tax	36 per cent
Excess profits tax	56 per cent
Housing tax	6 per cent
Electric and steel development tax	3 per cent
Total	101 per cent

Table 3–9 demonstrates, however, that there is no substitute for specific calculations in order to understand the impact of the several taxes borne by corporations. This table shows nine hypothetical corporations, each with the same net wealth but with varying returns on net wealth of from 12 to 75 per cent. In this table, both the effective and marginal rates of each tax have been calculated. It is apparent from these calculations that the application of all taxes on a corporation cannot be confiscatory at the margin, regardless of the rate of return, and cannot, in fact, exceed 92.72 per cent. Furthermore, this marginal rate of 92.72 per cent is not reached until a corporation realizes a rate of return of close to 75 per cent on net wealth. When the hypothetical corporation in Table 3–9 realizes a return of 25 per cent on net wealth (Firm D), the over-all marginal rate of the tax burden for all

---

[3] Small firms are already favored in the definition of profits that are construed to be excessive. For example, reference to Table 2–5 in Chapter 2 will show excess profits are those in excess of 42 per cent when the net wealth for excess profits tax purposes is from $100,000 to $120,000, but excess profits are those in excess of 12 per cent when the net wealth for excess profits tax purposes is over $200,000.

TABLE 3-8

Illustrative Tax Calculations for Corporations under Present Laws

	Firm A	Firm B	Firm C	Firm D	Firm E	Firm F	Firm G	Firm H	Firm I
Net wealth	$100,000,000	$100,000,000	$100,000,000	$10,000,000	$10,000,000	$10,000,000	$500,000	$500,000	$500,000
Net profits	50,000,000	25,000,000	10,000,000	5,000,000	2,500,000	1,000,000	250,000	125,000	50,000
Profits as a percentage of wealth	50.00	25.00	10.00	50.00	25.00	10.00	50.00	25.00	10.00
Income tax	17,868,000	8,868,000	3,468,000	1,668,000	768,000	228,000	48,000	18,000	6,000
Effective rate	35.74	35.47	34.68	33.36	30.72	22.80	19.20	14.40	12.00
Excess profits tax	5,490,160	826,400	—	594,160	106,400	—	44,480	10,420	—
Effective rate	10.98	3.30	—	11.88	4.26	—	17.79	8.34	—
Housing tax	1,597,310	917,136	206,880	163,070	99,036	45,120	8,251	4,595	1,440
Effective rate	3.19	3.67	2.07	3.26	3.96	4.51	3.30	3.68	2.88
Steel and electrical development tax	799,105	459,018	103,890	81,985	46,618	23,010	4,576	2,747	1,170
Effective rate	1.60	1.84	1.04	1.64	1.86	2.30	1.83	2.20	2.34
Total taxes	25,754,575	11,070,354	3,778,770	2,507,215	1,022,054	296,130	105,307	35,762	8,610
Effective rate	51.51	44.28	37.79	50.14	40.88	29.61	42.12	28.61	17.22

TABLE 3-9

Marginal Tax Rates on Corporations under Present Laws

	Firm A	Firm B	Firm C	Firm D	Firm E	Firm F	Firm G	Firm H	Firm I
Net wealth	$10,000,000	$10,000,000	$10,000,000	$10,000,000	$10,000,000	$10,000,000	$10,000,000	$10,000,000	$10,000,000
Net profits	1,200,000	1,500,000	2,000,000	2,500,000	3,000,000	4,000,000	5,000,000	6,000,000	7,500,000
Profits as a percentage of wealth	12.00	15.00	20.00	25.00	30.00	40.00	50.00	60.00	75.00
Income tax	300,000	408,000	588,000	768,000	948,000	1,308,000	1,668,000	2,028,000	2,568,000
Effective rate	25.00	27.20	29.40	30.72	31.60	32.70	33.36	33.80	34.24
Marginal rate	36.00	36.00	36.00	36.00	36.00	36.00	36.00	36.00	36.00
Excess profits tax	—	—	44,400	106,400	185,520	369,440	594,160	859,680	1,333,920
Effective rate	—	—	2.22	4.26	6.18	9.24	11.88	14.33	17.78
Marginal rate	—	—	20.00	20.00	26.00	32.00	38.00	44.00	56.00
Housing tax	52,800	64,320	80,856	96,336	110,789	138,154	163,070	185,539	214,685
Effective rate	4.40	4.29	4.04	3.85	3.69	3.45	3.26	3.09	2.86
Marginal rate	3.84	3.84	2.64	2.64	2.28	1.92	1.56	1.20	.48
Steel and electrical development tax	26,850	32,610	40,878	48,618	55,844	69,527	81,985	93,220	107,792
Effective rate	2.24	2.17	2.04	1.94	1.86	1.74	1.64	1.55	1.44
Marginal rate	1.92	1.92	1.32	1.32	1.14	.96	.78	.60	.24
Total taxes	379,650	504,930	754,134	1,019,354	1,300,153	1,885,121	2,507,215	3,166,439	4,224,397
Effective rate	31.64	33.66	37.71	40.77	43.34	47.13	50.14	52.77	56.33
Marginal rate	41.76	41.76	59.96	59.96	65.42	70.88	76.36	81.80	92.72

taxes is 59.96 per cent, which is considerably different from being confiscatory.

Table 3–9 demonstrates some other apparently little-known facts about the excess profits tax. It will be recalled from the descriptive section of Chapter 2 that net income for excess profits tax purposes is that in excess of a 12 per cent return on net wealth, when the latter exceeds $200,000. Some observers apparently believe that this actually means that all profits in excess of 12 per cent of net wealth are subject to the excess profits tax. But Table 3–9 demonstrates that such is not the case. Actually, for the corporations shown in this table, the excess profits tax has application when the profits on net wealth are between 16 and 17 per cent; that is, there is no excess profits tax if the return is 16 per cent, but there is an excess profits tax applicable if the return is 17 per cent. The reason for this is that the amount of the income tax paid is deductible from the excess profits tax base. Accordingly, it must always be borne in mind that excess profits are those that exceed 12 per cent of net wealth *after* income taxes have been paid on the profits.

This deductibility of the income tax from the excess profits tax base is a deceptive provision and results in two very irregular effects. Tables 3–8 and 3–9 show that the effective rate of the excess profits tax is actually regressive; that is, the effective rate of the tax on a 50 per cent return when the capital is $100,000,000 is less (10.98 per cent) than the effective rate when there is a 50 per cent return on a capital of $10,000,000 (11.88 per cent). The reason for this is the progressivity of the income tax, which makes its value as a deduction increase with the size of the income tax payment.

Second, because of the deduction of the income tax, the floor in terms of application of the excess profits tax rises as the amount of income tax paid increases. In this respect, it is easy to determine the point at which the excess profits tax is applicable in Table 3–9. For each firm, 12 per cent of profits is exempt from the excess profits tax as a basic exemption. If the amount of income tax paid is then converted into a percentage of net wealth, the remaining exemption is obtained. For example, in the case of Firm D, 12 per cent of net worth is exempt as a basic exemption plus 9.5 per cent as an income tax deduction. Thus, excess profits are those in excess of 21.5 per cent of net wealth when a return of 25 per cent is realized. Or again, in the case of Firm I, with a return of 50.00 per cent on net wealth, excess profits are those in excess of 12 per cent plus 16.7 per cent, or those in excess of 28.7 per cent of net wealth. Surely, this was not the intention of those who drafted and enacted the excess profits tax law!

Table 3–9 also illustrates a problem with respect to the application of the housing and steel and electrical development taxes. Besides complicating the tax system and being undesirable as earmarked taxes, both of these surtaxes are regressive in their application. For example, although the nominal rate of the housing tax is 6 per cent of net income, the marginal rate is 3.84 per cent on Firm A, with a net return of 12 per cent, and it decreases to only .48 per cent on Firm I, with a net return of 75 per cent. Therefore, once again the Colombian direct tax system on corporations has the anomalous contradiction of combining a progressive income tax with regressive taxes. And again, the reason for the regressivity of the housing and steel and electrical development taxes is that both the income and excess profits taxes are deductible from their bases. Thus, the greater the income and excess profits taxes paid, the smaller (relatively) the base for application of both the housing and steel and electrical development taxes.

Turning now to possible reform measures, the first and most apparent improvement is to eliminate both the housing and steel and electrical development taxes. Second, as a compensation for the loss of these two taxes, it would be possible to raise the rates of the income tax. However, with these adjustments, it would appear desirable to avoid much heavier impacts on relatively large corporations, where the tax burdens in the aggregate are already substantial. Third, the excess profits tax should be amended to eliminate the deduction of the income tax. And, finally, the net effect of all adjustments should be productive of revenue in view of the urgent demands for additional government revenue.

Table 3–10 has been prepared for the purpose of demonstrating the effect of these possible reforms. The table has been developed under three assumptions: (1) the elimination of the housing and steel and electrical development taxes; (2) an income tax with only two rates, 24 per cent up to $100,000 of net profits and 40 per cent on profits over $100,000; and (3) the retention of the excess profits tax, but without a deduction for the income tax, and with new schedules for both the determination of excess profits and for the excess profits tax rates.

The proposed new schedule for the determination of excess profits is:

Net Wealth for Excess Profits Tax	Excess Profits Are Those in Excess of:
$100,000 to $120,000	40 per cent
120,000 to 140,000	35 per cent
140,000 to 160,000	30 per cent
160,000 to 180,000	25 per cent
180,000 to 200,000	20 per cent

These excess profits would then be subject to the following proposed tax rates:

On That Part of Excess Profits:	Tax Rates (Per Cent)
Up to 5 per cent of net wealth	10
Between 5 and 10 per cent of net wealth	15
Between 10 and 15 per cent of net wealth	20
Between 15 and 20 per cent of net wealth	25
Over 20 per cent of net wealth	30

The suggested reforms shown in Table 3–10 may now be compared to the illustrative tax calculations in Table 3–8. Several improvements are apparent from this comparison: (1) The aggregate effective tax rates for each corporation have been increased so that the proposed reforms will be productive of revenue. On the other hand, the increases are moderate. (2) The aggregate effective rates have been made less progressive by raising the tax burdens proportionately more on small- and medium-size corporations. (3) The income tax has been made more proportional in its application with only two rates. (4) The fictitious nature of the excess profits tax has been eliminated by removing the deductibility of the income tax. Moreover, the proposed rates of 10 to 30 per cent on excess profits are more productive of revenue than the previous rates of 20 to 56 per cent. (5) The housing and steel and electrical development taxes have been eliminated. (6) The marginal rate of all taxes has been reduced to a maximum of 70 per cent—40 per cent for the income tax and 30 per cent for the excess profits tax. Currently, the marginal rate rises as high as 92.72 per cent, as shown in Table 3–9.

THE TAX BURDENS OF LIMITED LIABILITY COMPANIES AND PARTNERSHIPS

As it has been demonstrated previously, a problem of tax discrimination exists between corporations and limited liability companies. The elements of the problem are simple. With respect to the income tax, corporations are taxed under a three-rate schedule of 12, 24, and 36 per cent. Limited liability companies, however, are taxed under a three-rate schedule of 4, 8, and 12 per cent. Therefore, at the margin for equally large corporations and limited liability companies, there is a difference of 24 percentage points in the rate of the income tax.

On the other hand, corporate owners are more favorably treated with respect to the income taxation of their earnings at the individual level. While corporate earnings can

Table 3-10

Illustrative Tax Calculations for Corporations under Suggested Reforms[a]

	Firm A	Firm B	Firm C	Firm D	Firm E	Firm F	Firm G	Firm H	Firm I
Net wealth	$100,000,000	$100,000,000	$100,000,000	$10,000,000	$10,000,000	$10,000,000	$500,000	$500,000	$500,000
Net profits	50,000,000	25,000,000	10,000,000	5,000,000	2,500,000	1,000,000	250,000	125,000	50,000
Profits as a per cent of wealth	50.00	25.00	10.00	50.00	25.00	10.00	50.00	25.00	10.00
Income tax	19,984,000	9,984,000	3,984,000	1,984,000	984,000	384,000	84,000	34,000	12,000
Effective rate	39.97	39.94	39.84	39.68	39.36	38.40	33.60	27.20	24.00
Excess profits tax	8,000,000	1,250,000	—	800,000	125,000	—	40,000	6,250	—
Effective rate	16.00	5.00	—	16.00	5.00	—	16.00	5.00	—
Total taxes	27,984,000	11,234,000	3,984,000	2,784,000	1,109,000	384,000	124,000	40,250	12,000
Effective rate	55.97	44.94	39.84	55.68	44.36	38.40	49.60	32.20	24.00

[a] Assumed changes are: (1) the income tax has two rates, 24 per cent up to $100,000 of net profits, and 40 per cent on profits over $100,000; (2) the elimination of the housing tax and the steel and electrical development tax; and (3) the retention of the excess profits tax but with rates as shown in the text.

be retained to some degree in the firm without being taxed at the individual level, all of the earnings after payment of the income tax of a limited liability company are construed to be distributed for taxation at the individual level. This difference in the tax treatment of the earnings of corporations and limited liability companies at the individual level, however, does not serve to even the score. For example, for an equally large corporation and limited liability company, it would have to be assumed for equality of income tax treatment that the corporation pays no dividends and that the effective rate of taxation at the individual level on the earnings of the limited liability company approaches 20 per cent. These are very unreal assumptions. Unfortunately, the actual difference in the income tax burdens between corporations and limited liability companies at both the business and individual levels is impossible to calculate, because it depends on a host of considerations with respect to the ownership and the distribution of profits. There is no doubt, however, that the general bias in income taxation is in favor of limited liability companies, although the degree of the favorable treatment will vary from case to case.

But the income tax treatment is only part of the tax discrimination in favor of limited liability companies. As it has been demonstrated, the excess profits tax on corporations is quite substantial, and limited liability companies are exempt from this tax. It is true, of course, that the individual shareowners of the limited liability company are taxable under the excess profits tax, but it is unlikely that much excess profits tax liability would arise at this level after the profits have been divided among the shareholders. In any case, individual shareholders of a corporation are also subject to the excess profits tax on the relation between their net wealth and income. Finally, it should be noted that limited liability companies, unlike corporations, do not have to pay the steel and electrical development tax.

The position has been taken in Colombia by some experts that the structure of a limited liability company serves the purpose of a family enterprise or that of a small group of investors, and for this reason it is a desirable intermediate form of business organization between the individual proprietorship and the corporation. For this reason, also, these experts defend the policy of a relatively low tax burden on limited liability companies so that these businesses can grow and "graduate" into a corporation. But the evidence presented in the Appendix of this study proves just the contrary—that instead of a limited liability company developing into a corporation, the latter revert back to limited liability companies as a tax avoidance device. This is not only undesirable from a revenue point of view, but it also retards economic growth; for it is the corporation, rather than the limited liability company, that is a suitable vehicle for attracting a relatively large number of investors.

In the light of these arguments, the case seems clearly in favor of an upward adjustment of the tax burden on limited liability companies. This could be accomplished in one of two ways. One would be to tax limited liability companies as corporations, with the same income tax rates, as well as the imposition of the excess profits tax or any other taxes borne by corporations. This would be the preferred solution as it would insure neutrality of tax treatment between corporations and limited liability companies. If this were done, it would be necessary to make a distinction between distributed and undistributed profits of a limited liability company and tax only the former at the personal level of taxation.

Second, it would be possible to continue the policy of construing all the earnings of a limited liability company after payment of the income tax to be distributed for tax purposes at the individual level but to raise the present level of income tax rates on limited liability companies. To achieve neutrality with corporations, income tax rates on limited liability companies should be about two-thirds of those borne by corporations. In other words, if the recommendation is adopted to tax corporations at rates of 24 per cent on the first $100,000 of net profits and 40 per cent on the remainder, the respective tax rates on the profits of limited liability companies for the same brackets of income should be 16 and 27 per cent. But under this second alternative, as well as the first, limited liability companies also should be subject to the excess profits tax. This solution, at best, could only approximate neutrality of tax treatment between limited liability companies and corporations, but it would be an improvement over the present imbalance in rates between these two forms of business organization.

The problem is quite different for the tax treatment of partnerships. This form of business, apparently, is not competitive in Colom-bia with either corporations or limited liability companies, so there is not the same need to make a tax adjustment in order to reduce tax avoidance. Also, with the partnership there is a more legitimate and clear case that tax capacity rests with the individual shares rather than with the income of the firm before distribution. Therefore, the present system should be continued of construing all income after payment of the income tax at the business level as distributed for tax purposes at the individual level. However, if the tax burdens on limited liability companies are increased either by taxing them as corporations or by increasing their rates to 16 and 27 per cent, the tax burden on partnerships should also be increased at the business level. Suggested rates are 6 per cent on the first $100,000 of profits and 12 per cent on profits over $100,000.

CHAPTER 4

The Income and Complementary Taxes—Technical Issues, Administration, and Recommendations

THE TAXATION OF CAPITAL GAINS

THE BASIC CONCEPT of income in Colombia is defined in such a way that capital gains should be included, and there are very compelling economic and social reasons for taxing capital gains, yet the current income tax law represents merely a token gesture toward taxing capital gains as income. Before 1960 capital gains were not taxed, and since that date only gains from the sale of real property are taxable. And with respect to gains from real property, the treatment is so generous as to make their inclusion not much better than excluding them entirely. In the first instance, the application of the income tax to gains derived from real property was made exceedingly anemic by establishing that the beginning bases for measuring the gain are either the assessed value as of December 31, 1960, or, at the owner's option, on the basis of his sworn affidavit, the value during the period from January 1 to August 31, 1961. In other words, all gains derived before either of these two periods are ignored for taxation purposes.

But while there is no retroactivity in measuring gains, taxpayers unaccountably are allowed to reduce their gains by 10 per cent for each year that property has been held, provided that no sworn affidavit of value is made. In other words, retroactivity apparently is considered to be undesirable for purposes of measuring gains but quite acceptable for purposes of reducing gains. This procedure accomplishes little in terms of taxing capital gains, for it means that a taxpayer could own a piece of property from January 1, 1954, to January 1, 1963, but if it were sold on the latter date, the capital gain would be measured from January 1, 1961. On the other hand, this gain over a two-year period would be reduced by 90 per cent or by 10 per cent per annum for the nine years of ownership. Considering that the gains from real property are taxed in this way and gains from personal property remain excluded, it seems reasonable to conclude that the problem of taxing capital gains still needs to be resolved in Colombia despite the effort made in 1960.

Since Colombia recognizes, in principle, the theoretical justification of taxing capital gains, little needs to be said on this issue. Suffice it to say that there are at least two compelling reasons to extend and perfect the present system of taxing capital gains. The first is a matter of equity. Of all the structural weaknesses of the Colombian income tax, the failure to tax capital gains effectively is probably the most important in terms of tipping the scale in favor of middle and upper income groups. In other words, this is a major "loophole" and one that benefits directly the relatively wealthy.

The second reason that underscores the importance of taxing capital gains is equally important. When capital gains are not taxed effectively, investment in assets resulting in untaxed or lightly taxed gains are encouraged as compared to other forms of investment. This is another way of saying that an ineffective tax on capital gains encourages speculative activity, especially in the purchase of real property. In a society in which inflationary pressure has been chronic, there is already every incentive to use savings for the purpose of speculating on further increases in the price level. To deliberately encourage this activity through the tax system, then, is directly in conflict with other government policies devoted to the encouragement of investment opportunities that result in "real" investment and employment.

The principal problem with respect to taxing capital gains is the impossibility of taxing them on an accrual basis, as they should be, because of administrative difficulties. Thus, it is necessary to tax capital gains at the time of realization of the gains. But taxation on a realization basis, in turn, can be seriously discriminatory when an asset is held for a relatively long period and all the gain is taxed in one year at progressive rates. This problem can be resolved, however, in several different ways.

Another problem with respect to taxing capital gains is their illusory nature under inflationary conditions. The values of many assets, of course, increase more than the price level, and this is probably the general case. Moreover, if a person purchased a private residence ten years ago for $100,000 and sells it today for $200,000, there is no real gain in income if the price level during the intervening period increased by 100 per cent. Therefore, it could be argued that

capital gains, to be taxed equitably under an income tax, should be discounted by the increase in the price level.

Inflation has a variable impact on different groups. Its effect on the value of assets is relatively extreme and unique, but wage earners also suffer from inflation by a lag in their wage increases and by a reduction in the real exemption limits of the income tax. If no adjustment of the income tax is to be made for wage earners and others, should one be made for taxpayers realizing capital gains? And should an adjustment be made for the illusory character of capital gains when these gains in the most part redound to an economic class that uses investment in assets as a hedge against inflation? Would not such an adjustment only reward and encourage this activity all the more? These issues, it would seem, are sufficient to discourage the use of any adjustment factor for the illusory aspect of capital gains.

On the other hand, the justice of some device to alleviate the burden of taxation on capital gains because of their irregularity of receipt is indisputable. There are several ways of accomplishing this, some better than others. The discussion that follows will demonstrate that the Colombian method is relatively poor and could be improved upon by the use of an averaging device.

Colombia follows the procedure of allowing a reduction of 10 per cent of the gain for each year of ownership. This method has two serious faults: it is overly generous, and it is not related to the personal responsibility to pay taxes of the recipient of the gain. To demonstrate these problems, assume the case of a gain of $100,000 that arises over a ten-year period. If the gain had been taxed on an accrual basis, it would have been subject to an average marginal rate of 20 per cent, producing a total tax of $20,000. The problem, then, is not to eliminate this gain, simply because it accrued over ten years, but not to tax it excessively in one year, for example, at 40 or 50 per cent. How much of a reduction is necessary to tax this gain equitably in the year of realization? Assuming that the recipient of the gain has a marginal income tax rate of 20 per cent before the receipt of the capital gain and the goal is to tax the gain at an average rate of 20 per cent, it would be necessary under the current rate structure to reduce the gain from $100,000 to approximately $65,000. Quite obviously, therefore, it is excessive to reduce the gain to zero, as Colombia does, if the asset is held for ten years.

Second, the degree to which the gain is reduced should depend on the past and present level of taxpaying capacity of the recipient of the gain. For example, consider the case of a taxpayer who has never had a tax liability historically because of a relatively low income and several personal exemptions, and would not have had a tax liability on his asset even if the gain had been accrued annually for tax purposes. Under the Colombian system of taxing the gain, however, this factor is ignored—only the length of time that the asset is held is relevant for reducing the gain.

Appreciable improvement would result if Colombia shifted to a system of averaging the gains. The proposed solution is to divide the realized gain by the number of years the asset has been held, calculate the tax on this fraction, and then multiply the tax by the number of years the asset was held. For example, if the capital gain were $100,000 on an asset held for ten years, $10,000 would be added to the taxpayers income in the year that the gain was realized, and the tax on this $10,000 would then be multiplied by ten for the full tax liability on the gain. This procedure has the advantage of preventing an undue application of high marginal tax rates, but it also relates the tax on the gain to the level of income of the taxpayer. It has the further advantage of not requiring the burdensome recomputation of the tax for prior years, which is necessary in the use of other averaging devices.

This reform should also be combined with an abandonment of the principle that retroactivity in taxing capital gains is undesirable.

In Colombia the need for additional government revenues and the urgency to improve the equity of the revenue system are both so compelling that a philosophy of forgiving all prior gains before the enactment of a capital gains law is very imprudent.

Under the proposed recommendation, capital losses would be averaged in the same way as capital gains and would be allowed in full. However, in the event that there were both gains and losses in a single year, the gains would be reduced by the losses and only the net gains would be averaged. If the losses exceeded the gains, they would be deductible from other income, and if any unabsorbed losses remained, they would be carried forward to be offset against future income.

THE TAXATION OF FOREIGN INCOME

Under Law 81 of 1960, individuals that are residents of Colombia, whether citizens or aliens, are taxable on all income arising from sources outside Colombia. Only two exceptions to this general rule are made. First, the taxable amount of foreign income does not include foreign taxes paid. Second, resident aliens are taxed only on income derived in Colombia if the country of which they are nationals grants the same tax treatment to Colombians.

Some observers undoubtedly would object to these provisions on the grounds that they result in double taxation, as nearly all countries follow a principle of taxation on the basis of the source of income, and many, in addition, follow a world-wide basis. Thus, in the case of a Colombian investor in a United States corporation receiving a dividend payment of U.S. $1,000, this amount is first subject to a U.S. withholding tax of 30 per cent, and then the remaining amount of U.S. $700 is subject to the Colombian income tax. Certainly, this is to be decried in principle as inequitable and as an impediment to the free flow of capital between nations.

But what is the alternative? If Colombia

did not tax foreign income, it would encourage upper income groups to invest abroad in order to escape the impact of domestic progressive income tax rates. Thus, it would provide an income tax "loophole" for the rich. It would also encourage foreign, as compared to domestic, investment or be an added inducement to the flight of capital. Nor can a solution to this problem be found in offering a tax credit (rather than a tax deduction) for foreign taxes paid. A tax credit would not deter the movement of capital abroad, and it would result in little income to tax in Colombia since foreign taxes (in capital-exporting countries) are generally high as compared to those in Colombia.

The objection also may be made that foreign income should not be taxed because it is generally futile from an administrative point of view. The difficulties of taxing foreign income are real and should not be minimized, but the means are available through tax treaties that provide for administrative co-operation and exchange of information.

Under Colombian law, foreign residents are taxed only on income from Colombian source if their country of citizenship grants the same tax treatment to Colombian citizens. Since the United States does not accord this immunity to Colombians, United States residents in Colombia have a tax obligation to Colombia on all of their U.S. income, as well as retaining a U.S. income tax liability. However, much of the double tax burden is eliminated by the exclusion from U.S. tax of up to U.S. $20,000 in salary when foreign residence requirements are fulfilled. It also must be borne in mind that foreign personnel working in Colombia invariably receive salary increments and other perquisites that are usually more than adequate to compensate for their tax burdens.

In conclusion, the present rule of taxing residents on their income from all sources appears to be fully justified in order to discourage Colombian investment abroad and the flight of capital, and to achieve equity in the treatment of its residents by taxing all income regardless of source.

FOREIGN COMPANIES OPERATING IN COLOMBIA

Foreign companies doing business in Colombia are taxed as corporations regardless of their actual business form, but, unlike Colombian companies, they are taxed only on their income from Colombian sources. In addition, foreign companies paying dividends abroad are subject to a 12 per cent withholding tax on dividends. In the case of branches, the rate of this additional tax is 6 per cent of remittances.[1] The 6 per cent tax is levied only on that part of income not reinvested in Colombia or included in a dividend on which the tax of 12 per cent has been withheld.

Several of these provisions were enacted in 1960, each to correct a weakness in the income tax treatment of foreign companies. Before 1960 the tax on dividends paid abroad by a foreign company to its parent was only 5 per cent, and there was no tax on the remitted profits of a branch. As a result, this meant that favorable tax treatment was accorded either domestic subsidiaries or branches of foreign corporations, as compared to domestic corporations owned by Colombian shareholders, when taxes at the business level and the taxation of dividends at the individual level are both considered. A by-product of this favorable treatment of foreign corporations was a tendency for Colombian investors to form foreign companies in Panamá or Venezuela to do business in Colombia in order to evade taxes on their personal income. Also, the fact that foreign investors could select different forms of business organization (the branch, partnership, limited liability company, or corporation) for their activities resulted in strategems to avoid taxes and in difficulties for the tax adminis-

[1] This rate was raised to 12 per cent by Decree 3191 of December 26, 1963.

tration in identifying foreign entities for tax purposes.

All of the provisions adopted in 1960 were necessary and desirable. To tax as corporations all foreign companies doing business in Colombia is sound, because it eliminates tax considerations in the choice of a form of doing business. Imposing higher taxes on profit remittances abroad was also justified in terms of tax neutrality with domestic corporations owned by Colombian shareholders and, also, on the principal that it is proper to tax the individual shareholders of foreign corporations through a withholding tax on dividends. One may object that the individual shareholders of a foreign parent company are subject to tax on their dividends by their country of residence or citizenship, but there are tax credits available to the parent company (at least in the United States and in many European countries) to minimize the burden of the Colombian withholding tax. With the availability of tax credits, there is no reason to be overly concerned with the disincentive effects of the higher taxes on profit remittances. Furthermore, it is difficult to take the position that the Colombian withholding rate of 12 per cent on dividends is excessive when the U.S. withholding rate on non-resident aliens is 30 per cent.

Although Colombia made some progress in rationalizing taxes on foreign companies in 1960, two problems remain. One is the disallowance of deductions for personal services rendered abroad. Apparently, this is done in Colombia on the theory that the territorial concept of deductions is fair since Colombia asserts jurisdiction only over Colombian-source income. But this construction of allowable expenses is too narrow. Foreign businesses operating in Colombia incur several service expenses abroad that represent entirely legitimate deductions in determining their true Colombian income. Illustrations are home-office administrative expenses and technical services directly related to Colombian operations.

Colombia should adopt the rule that any expense is deductible if it is allocable by customary accounting practices to income earned in Colombia. Admittedly, such a rule would pose administrative problems, but the income tax laws should not turn primarily on the issue of administrative convenience. To ease the enforcement problem, it would be possible to require detailed proof that the claimed deductions are allocable to Colombian income.

The second problem that should be resolved concerns limitations placed on the deductibility of salaries. The salary paid to the president, director, or principal administrator of a business is deductible only up to $72,000 per annum, while the salary paid to lesser officers is limited to $48,000. Although these salary limitations apply to both domestic and foreign companies, on balance, they discriminate more against foreign companies, which, of necessity, usually employ a number of highly paid foreign personnel.

The salary limitations have their origin in an attempt to prevent a shifting of profit income into the salaries of managers, who are also stockholders. And in this case, some limitation of salaries is needed. But to extend the limitation to cover employees who are not shareholders, or only minor shareholders, is clearly undesirable, for it prevents an accurate determination of taxable income. For this reason, the specific limitations should be abandoned and the income tax administration should have the power and responsibility to determine dividends disguised as salary payments.

DEPRECIATION

Under current depreciation methods, depreciation may be calculated for tax purposes on a straight-line or declining balance basis or by any other recognized accounting method that is approved by the Division of National Taxes. The basis of depreciation is the original net purchase price plus subsequent additions to the assets, but depreciation accruals are allowed only on 90 per cent of cost, the remainder being considered salvage value. Computation of the salvage value is at the beginning of the term if straight-line depreciation is used and upon retirement in the case of the declining balance method.

There are no standard depreciation tables. The only guide available to taxpayers is the statement in the law that the useful life of an asset is assumed to be twenty years in the case of real property, five years for airplanes and motor vehicles, and ten years for other personal property. If taxpayers desire shorter write-off periods than these, they must offer justification.

An enigma exists with respect to the availability of the declining balance method. The principal justification of this method is that it provides for faster depreciation. Thus, with a factor of two for an asset that is depreciable over a ten-year period, the depreciation rate is 20 per cent applied to the full asset value in the first year and 20 per cent thereafter to the declining balance. Under this example, there are greater depreciation write-offs in the earlier years than if the straight-line method of 10 per cent per annum were used. But in Colombia, the authorized factor to be used with the declining balance method is one, and this provides a slower write-off period than the straight-line method. As a result, one cannot conceive of a taxpayer using the declining balance method. It can only be assumed that an error was made in drafting the article of the law legalizing this method.

In order to compensate for the higher costs of replacing depreciable assets due to inflation, the Income Tax Law of 1960 provided for an additional tax-free reserve for the replacement of machinery and industrial equipment acquired prior to June 1, 1957. Under this provision, corporations and limited share partnerships are permitted to credit annually to a special replacement reserve an amount up to 15 per cent of "net commercial profits." This amount is computed on the same basis as the amount that is accrued to the company's legal reserve in the preceding year. Annual accruals to the special reserve for depreciation cannot exceed 15 per cent of the historic cost or purchase price of the equipment, and the total accumulated reserve cannot exceed 100 per cent of the cost. Authorization to establish this special reserve must be obtained at the annual meeting of shareholders. Limited liability companies and general and ordinary limited partnerships are also entitled to establish these special reserves if the firms are under the supervision of the Superintendent of Corporations.

Taxpayers also are allowed a reasonable deduction for the amortization of investments in intangible capital assets. These include organization expenses, preliminary costs, development expenses, good will or other expenses incurred in the acquisition of a business, and the cost of trademarks, patent rights, and other intangibles. The minimum term for the amortization of these investments is five years.

It would appear that there are three interrelated issues that need to be discussed in Colombia before conclusions can be reached with respect to depreciation policy. The first is whether inflationary conditions warrant replacement cost depreciation. Second, is the desirability of the special reserve, introduced in 1960, for machinery and equipment. Third, is the question of whether the current depreciation methods, based on historical cost, are sufficiently liberal.

Replacement cost as a basis for depreciation is based on the argument that the net taxable income of a business cannot be ascertained fairly under inflationary conditions unless allowance is made for the increased cost of replacing investment in fixed assets. Although this argument has some validity, there are several objections that may be made to replacement cost depreciation. In the aggregate, these objections are important enough to establish the principle that replacement cost depreciation is not warranted unless inflation is particularly severe.

The first objection that may be made to replacement cost depreciation is on equity grounds. During an inflationary period all taxpayers have their incomes affected by price level changes. Therefore, if an adjustment is to be made for those who own fixed assets, should not similar adjustments be made for all taxpayers? In fact, it may be possible in terms of equity to develop a stronger case for an inflationary adjustment in the case of those who live on fixed incomes and wages and salaries than for those who own productive assets, for the latter are often able to adjust to inflation through higher prices for their products.

Second, there are technical difficulties involved with replacement cost depreciation. If an adjustment is to be based on price indices, which is the most direct and convenient method, there is the problem of selecting the most appropriate index. Should the index reflect the change in the domestic price level, or should it acknowledge the fact that many capital goods are imported by necessity, and therefore take into consideration changes in exchange rates? Quite obviously, whatever index is selected will result in an adjustment that essentially is only a rough approximation of the effect of inflation rather than an adjustment that is precisely correct for individual firms. Another technical problem is whether the revaluation of assets should be accompanied by a tax on the increase in the value of the assets. One could argue that a tax is warranted on the grounds that a revaluation of assets represents taxable income in the form of an increase in the value of the assets, but one can rebut this on the grounds that the income is illusory. And if a tax is to be levied, what is the appropriate rate?

Third, an objection can be made to replacement cost depreciation on the grounds of economic policy. If inflationary pressure is to be contained, certainly it is not desirable economic policy, in general, to remove its penalties through automatic adjustments. A more therapeutic method is to permit the painful effects of inflation to be manifested for whatever beneficial effects these will have as a restraint on inflationary pressures. This

is especially true of making an adjustment for a devaluation, for any adjustment, in effect, serves to defeat the basic purpose of the devaluation.

In the light of these arguments against replacement cost depreciation, the desirability of this method obviously depends on the degree of inflation. On this score, the proposition can be defended that Colombia's inflation has been relatively moderate, at least as compared to the inflationary pressures experienced in certain other Latin American countries. The consumer price index for Bogotá has increased from a base of 100 in 1954–55 to 137.6 in 1958, 155.3 in 1960, and 176.4 in 1962. The index for the price of machinery and transport materials has risen from a base of 100 in 1952 to 320.1 in 1962. The cost of construction materials has risen from 100 in 1951–53 to 215.9 in 1962. From an official rate of exchange of $2.51 for a U.S. dollar in the period from 1952 to 1956, the rate has fallen to $9.09 for a U.S. dollar in 1962. These evidences of inflationary pressure may appear significant, and they are certainly regrettable, but they are modest by comparison to the changes of one hundred times and more in the price level and exchange rates experienced by some countries.

Even if replacement cost depreciation is warranted in Colombia, and at best this seems dubious, the additional tax-free reserve introduced in 1960 was an undesirable way of making an adjustment for inflation for a number of reasons: (1) This reserve is available only for assets acquired prior to June 1, 1957, to compensate for a devaluation changing the rate of exchange to $6.03 to the U.S. dollar in 1957 as compared to $2.51 to the U.S. dollar in 1956. But this adjustment gives no recognition to the successive devaluations after 1957 and to the firms that acquired assets after 1957. (2) The provision, in effect, permits an accumulated tax-free reserve in addition to the normal depreciation of 100 per cent of the asset cost, but the availability of the reserve is based on the amount of commercial profits earned rather than being related to the amount of depreciable assets. Thus, the opportunity to take advantage of the reserve favors firms with relatively high profits and few eligible depreciable assets as compared to firms with more modest profits but with greater depreciable assets. (3) The provision is unnecessarily circumscribed by requiring stockholder approval for corporations and the supervisory control of the Superintendent of Corporations in the case of limited liability companies. (4) Without justification, the special reserve is denied to individual proprietors. (5) There is a provision that a company creating the reserve shall be taxed upon the amount exempted from tax if the reserve is distributed to shareholders as profits or if the reserve is capitalized within five years from the date of its creation. Quite obviously, however, this provision does not ensure that the amount of the special reserve will result in an equivalent reinvestment in capital assets. Nor does it ensure, in the absence of reinvestment, that the amount will be taxed, for it could be continued as a special reserve indefinitely.

Finally, there is the issue of whether the current depreciation rates based on historical cost are sufficiently liberal. In a country, such as Colombia, that is attempting to accelerate economic growth, depreciation allowances should be deliberately liberal. There is probably no better way of fostering new investment and increasing the productivity of labor through the tax system than to allow very substantial first-year allowances and generally short write-off periods. Provisions of this type encourage decisions to retire older pieces of equipment. In other words, faster depreciation encourages faster replacement. Also, faster depreciation facilitates the financing of new capital outlays, because debt may be retired sooner.

A final factor that weighs in favor of faster depreciation in Colombia is that this policy, in itself, is a compensation for higher replacement costs. Given the fact that inflation is not of the run-away type in Colombia, it would probably suffice to give whatever protection is necessary for higher replacement

costs through faster depreciation without such provisions as the special depreciation reserve.

To provide an improved system of depreciation allowances, Colombia first should develop tables for the various categories of depreciable assets, for the current classification of all assets into only three categories is wholly unsatisfactory. In developing these tables, the basic criterion generally should be realistic historical life in Colombia. For ease in compliance and enforcement, care should be taken not to develop an excessive number of categories. As a rough guide, perhaps twenty categories would be sufficient.

Second, to provide for faster depreciation, it is recommended that a factor of three be allowed under the declining balance method. With a machine that costs $100,000 and is depreciated over ten years, this would mean that 30 per cent of the cost could be depreciated in the first year and 65.7 per cent in the first three years. This faster depreciation should be allowed only for *new* industrial machinery and equipment.

As a further liberalizing gesture, the provision that reduces the value of the asset by 10 per cent for salvage value should be eliminated. Since the profit from any excessive depreciation is taxed as ordinary income in Colombia, there is no need for this provision.

DEPLETION

In the production of crude oil or natural petroleum gas, taxpayers may compute depletion either on a fixed percentage basis or on the unit cost of operation. Having made an election of either method, taxpayers may change the system only once and with the authorization of the Division of National Taxes.

Depletion on a fixed percentage basis is allowed at the rate of 10 per cent of the gross volume of crude oil or gas extracted but with the restriction that the deduction cannot exceed 35 per cent of the taxpayer's total net income prior to the deduction. The depletion allowance is permitted only for a period necessary to write off the cost of the investment, but during any subsequent operating period the taxpayer is permitted to exclude from his taxable income (as exempt income) an amount equal to 10 per cent of the gross value of his interest, again subject to the 35 per cent income limitation. Nor can the normal depletion deduction or exemption plus the amortization allowance for exploration costs exceed 45 per cent (50 per cent for the eastern zone)[2] of the taxpayer's net taxable income prior to depletion.

In addition to the normal 10 per cent depletion, the taxpayer may take a special depletion deduction of 15 per cent (18 per cent for the eastern zone) on petroleum operations started subsequent to January 1, 1955, subject to an aggregate depletion limitation of 45 per cent (50 per cent for the eastern zone) of the taxpayer's net income prior to depletion. After the total investment subject to the depletion deduction has been written off, a taxpayer entitled to the special 15 or 18 per cent depletion deduction is permitted to exclude from his taxable income (as exempt income) an amount equal to 15 per cent (18 per cent for the eastern zone) of his interest in the production. These combined normal plus special depletion exemptions once again are subject to the limitation of 45 per cent (50 per cent for the eastern region) of the taxpayer's net taxable income prior to depletion.

In order to qualify for the special 15 or 18 per cent depletion allowance after it becomes treated as an exemption, the taxpayer must reinvest in Colombia an amount equal to the allowance within three years of taking the allowance. This reinvestment must also be made in petroleum and related industries. In the event that a taxpayer fails to meet these requirements, he is taxed on the difference as taxable income during the period following the expiration of the three-year term, but he is given credit in future years for

any amounts invested in excess of the requirements.

Under the unit cost basis of depletion, the taxpayer must show the depletable cost of the properties being developed and submit to the Ministry of Mines a technical estimate of the amount of gas and oil reserves of the property. From this information is calculated the depletable cost per unit of reserve. The taxpayer's annual depletion deduction is then equal to the cost of the number of units produced. Taxpayers using the unit cost basis of depletion are not subject to the income limitations of 35, 45, and 50 per cent applicable to fixed percentage depletion.

In summary, the Colombian law permits either cost depletion, which represents a recovery of capital costs, or percentage depletion in excess of depletable cost. Percentage depletion initially is related to cost, but it has an open end whereby it is converted from an allowance to an exemption, and it can be increased to 25 per cent in the western region and to 28 per cent in the eastern region.

No one can object to cost depletion, for recovery of cost is essential in order to reflect true income. Percentage depletion, on the other hand, rests on more tenuous grounds, for the total depletion allowance (and exemption) is not related to cost. Rather, the total depletion allowed often results in many times the total capital cost of the property.

Percentage depletion can be defended in two ways. One is to argue that natural resources are distinctive in that their value may exceed their cost. But this is not a persuasive argument, for there are many other assets whose value in terms of future income exceed their cost, and the income tax law provides no allowance for this. Consider, for example, the output of a new machine in Colombia whose value in terms of future income will exceed its cost, although the value of the machine eventually will be exhausted. Should the machine qualify for percentage depletion in excess of actual cost?

The other argument in favor of percentage depletion is that it is necessary for incentive purposes. It is often maintained that the

---

[2] The relatively inaccessible eastern zone of Colombia, known as the "Llanos," is given higher depletion rates in order to encourage exploration in the area.

allowance is necessary because the oil industry is particularly risky. It is also said that the oil industry is uniquely subject to international competition, and if Colombia is to attract foreign investment to develop the industry, the incentives offered must be competitive. But placed in this light, the argument represents a justification for the subsidization of the oil industry—not for percentage depletion.

If, indeed, public policy dictates that the oil industry should be subsidized, percentage depletion, representing a several-fold recovery of a capital cost, is an undesirable method. It is undesirable, first, because it is a hidden and indirect subsidy. While it appears to the public that the oil industry is paying the normal income and complementary taxes, in fact, as much as 50 per cent of the income base is excluded. Second, the subsidy has no terminal date. Much to be preferred, therefore, is a system of subsidization that is open, measurable, and with a limit to its availability.

The depletion and amortization deductions permitted for mining operations and other extractive industries are much the same as those outlined above, and the same policy conclusions are applicable: if subsidies should be provided, there are better ways of providing them than through percentage depletion.

LOSS CARRY-OVER

Apart from a general operating loss carry-over of five years provided for farmers and a carry-over of five years applicable to casualty losses, Colombia has no provision for the carry-over of losses. This detracts from the equity of the income tax and discourages investment. It is inequitable, first, because the true measure of income is over a longer period of time than one year. A business firm with a net income for one year of $100,000 followed with a loss of the same amount really should not have a tax liability. It is evident, therefore, that in the absence of a loss carry-over, there is a discrimination against firms with fluctuating incomes. In

addition, the absence of a loss carry-over tends to encourage investment in secure rather than risky endeavors. Finally, it should be mentioned that the provision of a loss carry-over represents a further liberalization of depreciation in the sense that depreciation allowances, to the degree that they account for losses, may be carried forward to be offset against future income.

One issue that arises with respect to a carry-over of losses is whether there should be a carry-back as well as a carry-forward. The advantage of the carry-back of losses is that it provides funds immediately to a company when the assistance is needed the most —in the year of the loss. On the other hand, a carry-back is of no value to new firms, and it is also more difficult from an administrative point of view because past income tax returns must be reopened. Since any type of loss carry-over will constitute an additional administrative burden, it would appear more prudent for Colombia to adopt only a carry-forward provision. Also, in view of the fact that a carry-forward provision will represent a loss of revenue, three years rather than five would appear advisable.

Another issue concerning a carry-over provision is whether the loss to be carried forward should be determined on the basis of taxable income or total income. Under the taxable income concept, the loss to be carried forward is the amount determined for income tax purposes. Under the total income method, the loss is reduced by the amount of exempt income. Arguments appear to favor the total income method on the grounds that a failure to make an adjustment for exempt income compounds the advantages of exemptions, which is not the purpose of a carry-over provision. In addition, the total income method is less costly in terms of governmental revenues.

TAX INCENTIVES

There are two types of tax incentives offered in Colombia. One is general in scope for such purposes as encouraging the development of new industries, the use of Colombian raw materials, and the diversification of exports. The other type applies to specific business activities, such as agriculture and tourist hotels. A brief outline of the basic provisions for each of these two categories is presented first, before assessing Colombia's tax incentive policy. Consideration in this outline is confined to the income and complementary taxes, as the use of incentives with respect to other taxes is covered in other chapters of the study.

There are four exemptions that are general in scope:

1) *Economic Development Reserves*. The income tax law permits taxpayers to establish a special tax-free reserve of 5 per cent of their net commercial profits for a ten-year period, from 1961 to 1970. This reserve is exempt from the income tax if it is utilized to increase the production of raw materials and goods that would otherwise be imported. The National Council for Economic Policy and Planning is the arbiter for determining the desirability of producing particular types of goods for the purpose of obtaining the exemption.

2) *Basic Industries*. Established, as well as new, firms formed prior to December 31, 1965, may receive exemption from the income and net wealth taxes of up to 100 per cent for the period extending to 1969. For most industries the exemption is 100 per cent of income tax liabilities, but there are a few industries that have less than this percentage, some as low as 10 per cent. In the case of individual proprietorships, the exemption also includes the net wealth tax, and for new companies the exemption includes dividends and the net wealth tax on shares. To be eligible for the exemption, at least 60 per cent of the raw materials used must be of domestic origin, and for some industries this requirement is 100 per cent.

3) *Iron and Steel Fabricators*. Corporations and other companies engaged in the fabrication of articles made of iron, with over 50 per cent of their raw materials manufactured by the *Paz del Río* steel plant,

may receive an income tax exemption of 100 per cent until 1969.

4) *Exporters*. Income tax exemption is available to the exporters of all products other than unprocessed coffee, petroleum and derivatives, bananas, cowhides, and precious metals. For the purpose of computing the exemption, it is assumed that the net income derived from the export trade is 40 per cent of the gross sales value of the products exported, and the taxpayer may deduct the exempt income from income earned from all sources. There is the restriction, however, that this deduction cannot reduce the income from sources other than exporting by more than 50 per cent.

Tax incentives provided for specific business activities are generally more narrow in scope, but they cover a wide number of industries:

1) *Petroleum and Natural Gas*. Firms engaged in petroleum and natural gas operations, besides having special depletion and amortization allowances, have over-all limitations on their total taxes if their contracts were entered into before the Petroleum Code was revised in 1961. For eastern zone operations, the sum of taxes on income and wealth, including royalties and production taxes, cannot exceed 40 per cent of the taxpayer's net taxable income. In the case of operations other than in the eastern zone, the over-all limit of taxes is 50 per cent of net taxable income, but in this area there is also a minimal total tax of 40 per cent.

2) *Mining and Other Extractive Industries*. There are no income tax exemptions uniquely available to firms engaged in mining and extractive activities, but depletion and amortization allowances affect their net taxable income. In addition, since 1953 there has been an exemption from the net wealth tax (applicable to all enterprises) during the period of organization and installation, and investments in the mining of gold, silver, and platinum are exempt from the net wealth and excess profits taxes.

3) *Agriculture*. Several different types of tax incentives are offered to the agricultural

industry: (1) There are special income tax incentives offered to new plantings of rubber, cacao, olive trees, and other oil-producing trees and plants. For example, in the case of rubber trees, $20 may be deducted for each newly planted tree that is part of a planting of five thousand or more trees on holdings of one hundred hectares or over. This deduction must be taken over a three-year period, 50 per cent to be taken in the first year and 25 per cent in each of the following two years. (2) A special loss carry-over provision of five years is available for all agricultural operations except live-stock-raising. (3) Medium- and large-scale agricultural improvements undertaken after 1958 which amount to investments in excess of $100,000 exclusive of the value of the land entitle taxpayers to a reduction of their net taxable income of 50 per cent for the years from 1958 to 1968, as well as a reduction of 50 per cent in the net wealth tax and exemption from the excess profits tax for the same years. (4) These same exemptions are available without the $100,-000 investment requirement for taxpayers who convert inaccessible and unproductive land into prime agricultural land for sub-division purposes. (5) Taxpayers who sub-divide uncultivated or insufficiently cultivated land are granted an exemption of the first $5,000 in income from the activity. (6) Investments in agricultural machinery after January 1, 1958, are exempt from the net wealth tax, and investments in livestock for breeding and raising purposes are exempt from the same tax from 1959 to 1970, although they are subject to the livestock tax.

4) *Forestry*. The exploitation of timber-land is provided with the same depletion allowances as mining. In the case of investments in wood lots or permanent reforestation, there is a five-year exemption from the net wealth tax.

5) *Fishing*. Fishing companies and co-operatives were exempt from the income, net wealth, and excess profits taxes for the years from 1958 to 1962 inclusive.

6) *Real Estate*. Income from houses or apartments constructed after January 1, 1960, is exempt from the income, net wealth, and excess profits taxes if the initial assessed value per unit is not over $60,000 and the net income is not in excess of 20 per cent of cost. Houses built or acquired with loans from the Military Housing Bank or the Territorial Credit Institute are free of all taxes, including the income, net wealth, and excess profit taxes, as long as they are mortgaged by these institutions. Although this type of "mortgage" exemption is no longer available to non-residential housing, exemptions under prior laws (e.g., to the Hotel Tequendama) continue for the term of the mortgage.

7) *Colombian Airlines*. Colombian airlines are exempt from the income, net wealth, and excess profit taxes for ten years starting in 1960 if an amount equal to the tax exemption is invested in the maintenance, renewal, or expansion of their flight equipment, or if an amount equal to 50 per cent of the tax exemption is invested in Latin American international air transport enterprises.

8) *Investment Companies*. Investment companies are exempt from the income, net wealth, and excess profit taxes. The certificates issued by the companies are also exempt, but distributions of profits are taxable to the recipients. Mutual investment funds established by companies with a capital in excess of $500,000 and employing more than twenty persons are exempt from the income and net wealth tax, and these exemptions extend to the shareholder in the case of profit distributions and in the application of the net wealth tax to shares.

9) *Public Utilities*. Privately owned electric and other utility companies with rates approved by the Ministry of Development may pay their income tax by means of twenty-year notes carrying a maximum interest rate of 3 per cent if they invest a corresponding amount in the expansion of their facilities. They are also exempt from the net wealth tax. Government-owned public utilities are tax-exempt.

10) *Tourist Hotels*. Investments in tourist

hotels are exempt from the income and net wealth taxes for a period of ten years. In the case of existing hotels, the exemption period dates from October 29, 1957, while the exemption for new hotels is from the initiation of construction. Taxpayers must purchase shares in the Colombian Tourist Agency in an amount equal to one-half of the tax exemption. All hotels, restaurants, apartments, and industrial buildings in the territory of San Andrés and Providencia are exempt from the income, net wealth, and excess profit taxes for ten years dating from December 21, 1959.

11) *Automobile Assembly and Manufacturing*. The manufacture or assembly of motors, motor vehicles, or parts and accessories is exempt from the income, net wealth, and excess profit taxes for a ten-year period or until tax-free recovery of an amount equal to 150 per cent of paid-in capital.

12) *Publishing*. Taxpayers engaged in the publication of scientific or literary works or textbooks are exempt from the income and net wealth taxes from 1959 through 1968. Taxpayers engaged only partly in this business are entitled to a reduction in the tax in the proportion that net income from the publishing business bears to net income from all sources.

Operating Experience

For an adequate evaluation of Colombia's experience with the use of fiscal incentives for developmental purposes, the minimum requirements would be two items of information: (1) the number and characteristics (employment, investment, etc.) of the firms privileged with exemption; and (2) some conception, even if it is a rough approximation, of the total cost of tax incentives in terms of tax revenue foregone. Unfortunately, neither of these items of information is available. Nor could they be obtained without an expenditure of time and effort that was beyond the resources of this study.

Only fragmentary evidence of the extent of tax exemption is available. A great number of firms, of course, are eligible for the

special tax-free reserve of 5 per cent of their profits for a ten-year period, for the only requirement for this exemption is that the firms utilize domestic raw materials and produce substitutes for imports. Similarly, there are probably a significant number of firms that qualify for exemption because they use raw materials manufactured by the *Paz del Río* steel plant or because they are exporters of eligible products. In all probability, the use of special tax incentives in petroleum and natural gas, mining, agriculture, and real estate is also widespread. More narrow in application but probably important in the aggregate would be the number of firms privileged with tax exemption in forestry, fishing, air transportation, investment, public utilities, the hotel industry, automobile assembly, and publishing.

The only definitive information that could be obtained on the number of exempt firms of a particular category applies to basic industries, and this information is available only because the grants of exemption must be authorized formally, while most of the other exemptions are available simply on the basis of meeting the legal requirements. These contractual authorizations show a growth from four grants in 1960, to thirteen in 1961, and to seventeen in 1962.

When interviewed on the desirability of exempting these firms, the Minister of Development, who has been given the responsibility of authorizing these tax-exemption grants, acknowledged that there were at least three shortcomings in the present policy: (1) Exemptions are necessary for some industries, but the need for them has passed in others. (2) There is a problem in the loose definition of basic industries, with the result that several firms receiving tax exemption are not really basic. (3) There should be co-operation in the granting of exemptions between the Ministries of Finance and Development in order to guard against an undue loss of revenue.

In brief summary, then, very little evidence is available on the number of taxpayers that enjoy partial or complete exemption from the income and complementary taxes, although their number is undoubtedly large. From this it follows that no one in Colombia has even an approximate idea of the total cost of tax exemption as a subsidy. This is highly undesirable from the point of view of public policy, for, in effect, it means that the government is granting incentives in the vague hope that somehow the benefits to be derived will exceed an unknown cost.

Guidelines for a New Tax-Exemption Policy

If one were faced with the responsibility of recommending a new tax-exemption policy on the basis of a careful analysis of Colombia's experience, the assignment would be difficult, if not impossible, due to the paucity of available evidence. Fortunately, however, the use of tax concessions is not new. On the contrary, they are widely used throughout most countries of the world, and there is a consensus of informed opinion on both their effectiveness and their most expeditious use. This general experience may be used to offer some guidelines for the use of tax exemption in Colombia:

1) There are some doubts about the effectiveness of tax exemption on the grounds that investment responds to a multiplicity of factors, and in the total context of these motivations, exemption from taxes may be of only marginal importance.

2) It is probably more important in terms of economic development to provide permanent and positive fiscal incentives by the removal of major defects from the tax system than to offer temporary and essentially negative palliatives in the form of tax concessions. Reference is made to such improvements as eliminating the tax discrimination against corporations, providing a loss carry-over, and providing more generous depreciation allowances.

3) The extensive use of tax exemption results in a sizable loss in government revenue, and in Colombia's case, this is occurring during a period when there are urgent demands for higher revenues.

4) Tax exemption has a tendency to multiply throughout the whole of the tax system as each taxpaying group exerts pressure to receive the same privileges as exempt taxpayers. This process is facilitated because no direct appropriation is necessary by the government.

5) The granting of tax exemption is technically difficult. There are difficult problems with respect to differentiating between mature and growing firms, different types of firms within an industry, and high and low priority industries. There are also administrative problems involved in preventing abuses of the privileges.

6) Income tax exemptions, in particular, are an ineffective type of subsidy in the sense that they provide little assistance when it is needed the most, namely, during the initial operating period when losses or low profits occur.

In brief, these are some of the shortcomings in the use of tax exemption. These criticisms do not mean that tax exemption should not be used for developmental purposes, but they do establish a presumption in favor of caution and restraint. They suggest that the use of tax concessions should be confined to selective and short-run assistance.

Administration

While this survey of the income and complementary tax system primarily is concerned with functional and structural problems, the importance of tax administration warrants some consideration of the subject. One reason for this is that the best of laws can be defeated by slipshod administration. It is also true that in practice the design of a tax system and its administration are not separable and distinct issues; one should not be assessed without reference to the other.

A common debate among administrators and politicians is whether the improvement of a tax system or its administration should take priority. Often it is argued that emphasis should be given to strengthening enforcement on the grounds that it is inequitable to levy additional taxes on honest taxpayers when so much revenue is evaded with impunity by the dishonest. There is little merit in this argument, for a structurally imperfect tax system inhibits compliance and enforcement. Moreover, experience shows that the process of improving administration is a gradualistic one. No miracles can be worked. Therefore, to achieve a better revenue system, there is a need for improving both the structure and the administration of the system. Both are necessary, and both should be carried out simultaneously.

Evasion

Certainly, if one subscribed to the belief of the average Colombian, the conclusion would be that tax evasion is general and serious in degree. But apart from this intuitive insight into public morality, there is very little evidence. Nor is evidence on evasion easy to obtain. One cannot compare the totals of taxable income as reported in income tax returns with national income aggregates because of a lack of statistics. It is necessary, therefore, to rely on whatever insights may be gained by examining particular parts rather than the whole with the idea in mind that the evidence obtained may be meaningful for purposes of generalization.

One attempt along these lines undertaken for this study was a survey of professional workers. A sample of income tax returns was drawn in order to gain insight into the degree to which professional workers in Bogotá comply with the filing and reporting requirements of the income and complementary taxes. Names of professional workers were drawn at random from the business section of the Bogotá telephone directory, and the size of the sample should ensure some considerable degree of reliability for the results. In the case of medical doctors, each eleventh listed name was selected, for lawyers each seventh name, and for engineers and architects each fifth name. In this manner there was obtained a sample of 117 medical doctors, 112 lawyers, and 109 engineers and architects. For several reasons that will be explained later, this "gross" sample was

reduced to "net" figures for analytical purposes of 89 medical doctors, 81 lawyers, and 59 engineers and architects.

Table 4–1 summarizes the information obtained from the 1961 income tax returns filed by the professional workers in the "net" sample. This table shows, in general, average levels of reported income and tax liabilities that suggest serious degrees of income underreporting. In the case of medical doctors, for example, the average gross professional fees reported for 1961 was only $21,062, and the average net taxable income from all sources was only $15,466. Lawyers reported a higher average figure for gross professional fees of $25,783 but a lower average net taxable income of $13,401. On the other hand, the wealthiest (or most honest) group was engineers and architects, with average gross professional fees of $30,957 and average net taxable income from all sources of $24,426. From what is known about levels of income in Bogotá, this evidence suggests that the medical doctors and lawyers are under-reporting their income by at least 50 per cent. In other words, the average net taxable income from all sources for medical doctors should be at least $30,000 instead of $15,466.

The information in Table 4–1 with respect

TABLE 4–1

Survey of Income and Complementary Tax Returns for Professional Workers in Bogotá, 1961

	Medical Doctors	Lawyers	Engineers and Architects
Number in gross sample	117	112	109
Number in net sample	88	81	59
Average gross professional fees reported	$21,062	$25,783	$30,957
Average net taxable income, all sources	15,466	13,401	24,426
Average income tax liability	896	1,195	3,046
Average income and complementary tax liability	1,947	2,044	5,352

to tax liabilities is also very instructive. Average income tax liabilities in 1961 for the medical doctors was $896, for lawyers $1,195, and for engineers and architects it was $3,046. This evidence confirms the proposition advanced previously that middle income groups in Colombia are not over-burdened by the income tax. Relevant for tax policy purposes, also, is the relative importance of the complementary taxes in increasing the tax liabilities of these professional workers. In the case of the doctors, the average income tax liability of $896 is increased by over 100 per cent to $1,947 by virtue of the additional complementary taxes. This increase, undoubtedly due in the most part to the net wealth tax, gives added support to the contention that this tax is an essential component of the direct tax system.

Previous mention was made of the fact that it was necessary for several reasons to reduce the gross sample of professional workers to a smaller figure for analytical purposes. The reasons for this reduction are equally as instructive for an insight into compliance and enforcement in Colombia as the previous data on income-reporting and tax liabilities. Out of a gross number of 338 names selected, 109 returns were excluded or were not available for analysis. The reasons for this reduction are shown below:

	Number of Items
1. Technical errors (misspelling of names, etc.)	7
2. Filed returns outside of Bogotá	6
3. No professional income reported	37
4. Did not file income tax returns	36
5. Returns were filed, but they could not be located	10
6. Returns were filed, but no assessments were made	13
Total	109

The first three items in this tabulation are of no particular relevance for income tax compliance and enforcement, but the next three items are very important. Out of the total sample of 338 names selected, there were 36 instances in which income tax returns were not filed for 1961. Moreover, telephone calls confirmed that each of these "taxpayers" was currently resident in Bogotá and had been living in the city in 1961. In another 10 instances, there was evidence in the Ministry of Finance to show that the returns had been filed, but no assessment had been made because the returns could not be located. Finally, there were 13 instances in which the returns had been filed for 1961, but as of June, 1963, no assessments had been made. Thus, through various shortcomings of compliance and enforcement, there was a total of 59 instances (17 per cent of the gross sample) in which there was a failure to levy an income tax assessment.

The failure to file tax returns, of course, is not confined to professional workers. In a recent search for non-filers working in large industrial plants located in the city of Cali, it was found in one firm that 739 employees out of the total work force of 2,650 had a reporting liability and had not filed tax returns, although only 78 out of the 739 employees had a tax liability. In another industrial plant, 711 out of 1,500 employees were found to have a reporting liability and had not filed returns, but only nine out of the 711 had a tax liability. This evidence on compliance suggests two problems. There is, apparently, a marked tendency on the part of industrial workers not to file income tax returns unless enforcement action is taken. Second, even if this action is taken, the tax liability in terms of revenue is slight because of an erosion of the tax base through exemptions and deductions.

Admittedly, these two illustrations of evasion represent scanty information for the purpose of generalization. With more time and resources, additional and better evidence could be obtained. It should be borne in mind, however, that any social act like evasion, by the mere fact of its illegality, is difficult to measure. But this difficulty should not forestall public action. As long as a presumptive case can be established that evasion exists and is serious, this should be sufficient to justify corrective action.

Administrative Procedures

For reporting purposes, taxpayers are divided into two groups: those that are *required* to assess their own tax liabilities, and those that *may* do this. All juridical entities and individuals having net incomes of over $25,000 or net wealth of over $500,000 are required to assess their own tax liabilities; while all other taxpayers are permitted but are not required to file a self-assessment return. Accordingly, tax returns may be divided into two categories, self-assessments and government or official assessments. In 1962, 412,693 out of 501,594 assessments or 82.28 per cent of the total number of taxpayers were government assessments. On the other hand, the smaller number of 88,901 self-assessments represented 84.18 per cent of all assessments in terms of aggregate value.

In the case of self-assessments, the tax is paid in quarterly installments, but, if the total assessment in the previous year was more than $100,000, the tax may be paid in ten equal installments from February to November. For taxpayers that are given official assessments, there is a grace period of three months for effecting payment after the receipt of the assessment notice.

Payment of the income and complementary taxes may be made through either the 22 regional offices of the Division of National Taxes, the 786 collector's offices throughout the country, or through commercial banks. The use of commercial banks for collection purposes has proved a highly successful practice, with 60.08 per cent of total collections being made through this means in 1962 as compared to 35.50 per cent by major col-

lection offices and 4.42 per cent by minor collection offices.

Taxpayers' returns, whether accompanied by a self-assessment or not, are subject to the same procedure of analysis and official assessment of the tax. Assessments are normally made at the regional, rather than at the national level. The review of income tax returns is made, first, by an assessment section which sorts out the returns that are not liable to tax and then proceeds with an office audit for arithmetical errors and mistakes of law before making an official assessment. After the assessments are made, the investigation section undertakes audits on a selective basis. For the normal case, there is a two-year statute of limitations, but for persons who do not file returns or fail to pay their assessments, the limit on the recovery of tax liabilities is ten years.

Appeal procedures are extensive. After exhausting the appeal process at the administrative level, the taxpayer may appeal to one of the sixteen administrative courts, of which there is one in each department, and then to the Council of State, whose decision is final in all administrative claims. But a taxpayer also may petition the Supreme Court on any decree, resolution, or other act of the government as unenforceable on constitutional grounds.

Penalties and interest provisions on delinquent taxes are equally extensive. The principal ones are: (1) Interest is charged at the rate of 1.5 per cent per month for a delay in payment of the income and complementary taxes, but no interest is levied on the delay in paying the other related taxes. (2) A penalty is imposed for the late filing of returns varying from 10 per cent of the income and complementary taxes up to a maximum penalty of 100 per cent of the tax liability. (3) For any incorrect, incomplete, or falsified data that constitute misrepresentation, but excluding errors of judgement, the penalty is from five times the additional tax to a maximum of 100 per cent of the income and complementary tax liabilities. (4) Failure to file a return is penalized with a fine of 100 per cent of the income and complementary tax liabilities. (5) Failure to keep adequate accounting records is punishable with a fine of 1 per cent of the declared gross income in excess of $10,000 plus 1 per cent of the declared net wealth in excess of $100,000, but in no case is the fine less than $100 or more than $10,000. (6) There are criminal penalties subject to the Penal Code and Code of Penal Procedure, but there is no record in Colombia of criminal proceedings in a tax delinquency suit.

The enforcement of the income and complementary taxes in Colombia is facilitated by the fact that administrative decisions are enforceable immediately, without sanction of the courts. Collection officers have the authority to exercise powers of distraint, seizure, and attachment against property and to sell assets without the intervention of a court.

Administrative Performance

Table 4–2 summarizes some relevant information concerning assessments and collections of the income and complementary taxes during 1962. As of January 1, 1962, there was a total of $305 million of assessments for the income and complementary taxes made in 1959, 1960, and 1961 that had not been collected and an additional amount of $139 million of uncollected assessments made from 1935 to 1958. Adding accounting corrections of $2.5 million and new assessments made during 1962 of $1,119 million resulted in a total gross collectible amount during 1962 of $1,566 million. Actual collections made in 1962 were $1,100 million, leaving $465 million collectible. This amount, however, is reducible by a considerable number of items that were either not due in 1962 or would not be collected, with the result that the estimated net delinquency on December 31, 1962 (line 14 in Table 4–2) was $216 million.

A delinquency of $216 million out of total assessments of $1,119 million appears quite moderate, but the data in Table 4–2 provide an opportunity to identify several

TABLE 4–2

Statement of Assessments and Collections for the Income and Complementary Taxes, 1962

1. Balance not paid on January 1, 1962, on 1959, 1960, and 1961 assessments	$ 305,059,547
2. Balance not paid on January 1, 1962, on 1935 to 1958 assessments	138,866,159
3. Increase due to accounting corrections	2,528,675
4. Assessments made during 1962	1,119,248,248
5. Total collectible during 1962	1,565,702,629
6. Total collected during 1962	1,100,470,062
7. Balance to be collected, December 31, 1962	465,232,567
8. Less deposits (installment payments)	39,362,721
	425,869,846
9. Less assessments made but not due on December 31, 1962	33,908,189
	392,961,657
10. Less additional assessments not due on December 31, 1962	32,968,065
	359,993,592
11. Total gross delinquency, December 31, 1962	359,993,592
12. Less estimated reduction from appeals	100,000,000
	259,993,592
13. Less amnesty of 50 per cent of tax liabilities from 1935 to 1957	43,554,635
14. Estimated net delinquency, December 31, 1962	216,438,957

Source: Division of National Taxes.

problem areas. Starting first with assessments, there is a problem with respect to processing the assessments expeditiously. During 1962 most of the assessments are attributable to income earned during 1961, but an excessive amount of 12 per cent is attributable to income earned in 1960 and in prior years. The principal reason for this is that not all of the assessments that should have been made in 1961 on 1960 incomes were completed, and hence they were carried over to be completed in 1962. As a result, a considerable number of taxpayers are being assessed on their 1960 incomes during 1963. The number of these unduly late assessments can be stated explicitly for 1962. Out of 1,189,218 returns filed in 1962, 530,671 were given assessments during 1962, while most of the remainder were non-taxable. But, as of December 31, 1962, there remained 61,699 taxable returns filed in 1962 that had not been assessed. This number of taxpayers will be assessed in 1963 on income earned during 1961. Without any question, this is a serious administrative fault.

Considering next the collection efforts on delinquent accounts, it is apparent that there is this same undue delay. During 1962, 67,506 judicial proceedings were initiated to recover $101 million. But only 2.9 per cent of this amount was applicable to 1961 assessments, while 74.9 per cent applied to 1960 assessments, and 22.0 per cent was applicable to assessments made in 1959 and in prior years. It is not unusual, therefore, for a delinquency to be outstanding from three to five years before judicial proceedings are initiated.

As for the auditing performance, the little evidence that can be assembled reflects very badly on the administrative effort. It should be observed, first, that the net results attributable to office auditing are obscured by the fact that the assessment and office-auditing processes are combined for those taxpayers who do not calculate their own taxes. Thus, undoubtedly, the processing of official assessments itself represents a considerable auditing effort in the sense that items of income and deductions are reviewed and corrected as part of the assessment process. This auditing effort, however, is not measurable.

As it has been shown previously, 84 per cent of the value of all assessments in 1962 is attributable to self-assessments. Presumably, these are the returns that are field-audited or "investigated." The auditing effort with respect to these returns is far from impressive. For 1962, there is a record of 1,224 audits resulting in additional assessments of $19,600,000. At the same time, there were about 60,000 self-assessment returns. Accordingly, only about 2 per cent of self-assessment returns was audited.

It is reported by supervisory officials that the appeal process will reduce the total of additional assessments made in 1962 by approximately one-half or from $19,600,000 to about $10 million. This latter amount compares very unfavorably with the total of all assessments attributable to the income and complementary taxes of $1,119 million in 1962, being only about one-tenth of 1 per cent of total assessments.

Perhaps even more disturbing is the information that about 1,000 other audits were performed in 1962, but additional assessments were not processed because the two-year period of the statute of limitations had elapsed before the assessments could be made. In other words, there were actually about 2,224 audits performed in 1962, but, through procrastination and the mismanagement of staff resources, only 1,224 of these audits resulted in additional tax liabilities, and the remainder represented merely a wasted administrative effort.

Clearly, from this brief review of the enforcement effort, one must conclude that the administration of income and complementary taxes is critically weak. There quite obviously is an urgent need for new procedures, an increase in the work performance of personnel, and intelligent leadership.

Administrative Improvements

Without any doubt, the most important administrative reform that Colombia could introduce in the area of the income and complementary taxes is the withholding of the income tax on wages, salaries, dividends, and interest. There are two reasons for this. The first is a matter of equity, for there is little purpose in having a refined income tax law if thousands of persons are permitted to evade the tax with impunity. Second, and equally important, is the significant increase in revenues that would result from withholding.

Some appreciation of the beneficial effects that may be expected from withholding may be gained from the results experienced in 1957, when the device was used for six months before it was abandoned. Even this brief utilization of the procedure had dramatic results, increasing the number of individual taxpayers from 150,725 in 1956 to 293,271 in 1958.

Although the adoption of withholding would provide a permanently higher level of tax revenues, a particularly attractive feature of adopting the device at this time is that it also would result in a windfall gain during the period of introduction. If withholding were introduced on January 1, 1964, it would mean that the government would realize revenues during 1964 on 1963 incomes as well as revenues on 1964 incomes. To make this reform more palatable, 50 per cent of 1963 tax liabilities could be "forgiven." Even with this relief, telescoping two tax payments in one year would provide the government with a windfall gain of about $400 million.

It cannot be argued that Colombia does not have the administrative resources to conduct a system of withholding. Much smaller countries with less administrative expertise in Latin America, like the republics of Panamá and Honduras, have been administering effectively a system of withholding for a considerable period of time. Moreover, the implementation period, which is the most difficult, can be eased by limiting the procedure first to large businesses and governmental employees. It is also possible to obtain technical assistance for the introduction of the system.

If withholding is introduced on wages and salaries, it is important to extend the system to include interest and dividends, for experience demonstrates in other countries that evasion of the income tax with these two types of income is general and serious. At the present time, Colombia only withholds the tax on the dividends of bearer shares.

For income not subject to withholding, a system of current payment should be introduced. Taxpayers should be required to file estimates of anticipated tax liability for the year and pay taxes in quarterly installments. Current payment is important for revenue purposes, for it brings the government up-to-date in terms of receiving income as it is earned; but it is also important from an equity point of view if withholding on wages and salaries is introduced in order to treat all taxpayers neutrally and place all of them on a current basis.

A second major administrative improvement that is recommended is to place all taxpayers on a self-assessment basis, for one of the principles of effective income tax administration is to transfer as much of the routine burden of compliance as possible to the taxpayers. Under the present system, the administrative resources are being wasted in two ways. First, they are being consumed in the very onerous undertaking of calculating the tax liabilities for approximately 80 per cent of all tax returns. The taxpayers should assume this responsibility. Second, official notices of tax liability are being mailed to all taxpayers, even to those filing self-assessments. This procedure should be eliminated. If all taxpayers were required to calculate their own tax liabilities and to make payments on the basis of these calculations, then the administrative resources could be focused on the work that should be done, which is to review and audit the returns. In other words, taxpayers should be required to comply with the law, which should include the calculation of tax liabilities, while the enforcement staff should be used to ensure this compliance.

Another problem that is apparent is the length of the statute of limitations. This period should be long enough to convenience the income tax administration in its enforcement activities but short enough to be fair to taxpayers. In Colombia, however, the limit of two years is unduly restrictive for the income tax administration, and, in effect, serves to protect tax evaders. The period should be extended to at least four years for ordinary cases, and to ten years in those cases where auditing reveals deliberate misrepresentation.

Supervisory officials have supplied the information that at least 85 per cent of the audits resulting in additional assessments are accompanied by the application of penalties.

On the other hand, as compared to the total additional assessments made in 1962 of $19,600,000, the total assessment of penalties was only $2,045,320 in 1961. Therefore, penalties seem to be in the nature of a gentle slap on the wrist. Quite obviously, penalties of five times the additional tax are being levied very infrequently. On the other hand, the income tax administration would find that a fearless and vigorous application of penalties would be very therapeutic for purposes of improving compliance. And in this respect, the initiation in Colombia of the first criminal prosecution for income tax evasion is long overdue.

In the last analysis, the key to good tax administration, as it is the success of all group undertakings, is to have personnel with adequate technical ability, who are well motivated and have the benefit of capable leadership. There are serious failures in each of these requirements in Colombia, but perhaps the greatest failure of all is that the shortcomings are not fully realized, so that little is being done to overcome them.

SUMMARY OF RECOMMENDATIONS

1) The trinity of an income tax, excess profits tax, and net wealth tax should be retained and strengthened, but the miscellaneous surtaxes and earmarked taxes, with the exception of the tax on absenteeism, should be eliminated.

2) A deliberate attempt should be made to strengthen the revenue productivity and the progressivity of the income tax on natural persons. For this purpose, the rates should be increased from a range of .50 to 51.00 per cent to one of 2.00 to 62.00 per cent.

3) The base of the personal income tax should be broadened by a severe reduction or elimination of the following exemptions and deductions: (1) educational expenses; (2) payments to professionals; (3) rental housing; (4) interest on personal loans; (5) real property taxes; (6) contributions to social security and pension plans; (7) transportation allowances; (8) service bonuses; (9) pay-

ments in lieu of vacations; (10) severance pay; (11) interest on government obligations; and (12) emoluments earned by the religious of the Catholic Church.

4) The exemption applicable to the imputed rent of owner-occupied residences should be eliminated, and the amount to be included in gross income should be a flat rate of 10 per cent of the cadastral value. No deductions should be allowed for such expenses as mortgage interest, property taxes, and repairs.

5) Social security payments should be included as taxable income, and the following rule should be adopted for the taxation of annuities: (1) determine the total cost of the annuity at the time that the annuity payments are started; (2) divide the cost of the annuity by the beneficiary's life expectancy and allow this amount as a tax-free return of capital in each benefit payment; and (3) tax the balance of each payment as taxable income.

6) Eliminate the provision of the 1960 law that permits the splitting between spouses of earned income up to $60,000.

7) Bearer shares should either be eliminated or their use should be made more difficult by the adoption of a heavier stamp tax on their issuance and by raising the withholding tax rate on dividends to 20 per cent.

8) The system of taxing corporations should be rationalized by the elimination of the housing and steel and electrical development taxes; the adoption of an income tax with only two rates, 24 per cent up to $100,000 of net profits and 40 per cent on profits over $100,000; and the retention of the excess profits tax, but without a deduction for the income tax and with new schedules for both the determination of excess profits and for the excess profits tax rates.

9) Limited liability companies should be taxed as corporations, with the same income tax rates as well as the imposition of the excess profits tax or any other tax borne by corporations. If these reforms were introduced, it would be necessary to make a

distinction between the distributed and un-distributed profits of a limited liability company, and to tax only the former at the personal level of taxation. Alternatively, it would be possible to continue the policy of construing all of the earnings of a limited liability company after payment of the income tax to be distributed for tax purposes at the individual level but to raise the income tax rates on limited liability companies to 16 per cent on the first $100,000 of taxable income and 27 per cent on the remainder.

10) The present system of taxing partnerships should be continued, but the tax on partnerships should be increased to 6 per cent on the first $100,000 of taxable income and 12 per cent on the remainder.

11) The net wealth tax should be strengthened by including in the base all foreign assets, tangible as well as intangible. The provision for the depreciation of automobiles should be eliminated until such time as vehicles actually depreciate in value.

12) Capital gains from the sale of personal property should be included in the excess profits tax base.

13) All capital gains realized on real and personal property should be taxed under the income tax regardless of the length of ownership and with the application of an averaging device.

14) In the taxation of foreign companies operating in Colombia, the rule should be adopted that any expense is deductible if it is allocable by customary accounting practices to income earned in Colombia.

15) The limitations placed on the deductibility of salaries paid by business firms should be eliminated.

16) The special reserve, introduced in 1960, for machinery and equipment should be abandoned and replaced by a more generous depreciation policy that would include the availability of the declining balance method with a factor of three. Depreciation tables should be developed for various categories of depreciable assets based on realistic historical life in Colombia. The provision with respect to reducing the value of the asset by 10 per cent for salvage value should be eliminated.

17) Depletion should be based only on cost and not on a percentage basis. This applies to mining as well as to the oil and natural gas industry.

18) A loss carry-forward provision should be enacted covering a three-year period based on the total income rather than the taxable income method.

19) The availability of tax exemption needs to be curbed and rationalized.

20) The administration of the income and complementary taxes may be improved by the adoption of the following reforms: (1) the institution of withholding on wages, salaries, interest, and dividends; (2) the introduction of current payment for all other income; (3) the requirement that all taxpayers should calculate their own tax liabilities and pay their taxes on the basis of these calculations; (4) the elimination of all assessment notices except in the case of additional assessments; (5) the focusing of all personnel on the auditing of returns; (6) the extension of the statute of limitations to four years; and (7) the vigorous application of penalties.

CHAPTER 5

Death and Gift Taxes

GENERAL DESCRIPTION

Legislative Background

COLOMBIAN LEGISLATION ON death and gift taxation has had few changes during the last twenty-five years as compared to the revisions in other forms of direct taxation. Except for some minor modifications, Law 63 of 1936 is still the legal authority for these taxes. In fact, the only effective change in the intensity of death taxation has resulted from continuous inflation and its effect on the actual application of the progressive rate schedules.[1]

Structure, Jurisdiction, and Rates

Over-all Structure. Colombian death and gift taxation is a rather well-designed combination of the three standard levies on estates, bequests, and *inter-vivos* gifts. There is a progressive schedule of rates for the estate tax as well as separate schedules for the inheritance and gift tax levies. The latter are progressive but take account of the degree of affinity between the deceased or donor and the heir or donee. Except for some minor provisions as to deductions and exemptions, the rates for inheritance taxation are the same as those for *inter-vivos* gifts.

This means that there is no legal incentive for the distribution of wealth before death, at least in theory. However, the very low amount of taxes actually collected on gifts suggests the likelihood of concealed gifts, a practice that has been encouraged by the existence of loopholes in the definition of presumptive gifts.

The integration of estate, inheritance, and gift taxation is provided by a requirement that the valuation procedure of any estate, inheritance, or gift must accumulate the amount of previous gifts by the same donor to the same donee, taking account, of course, of tax credits corresponding to those previous gifts.

Jurisdiction. Death and gift taxes are administered by the Division of National Taxes. Proceeds of the taxes are received entirely by the national budget, with no participation by the departments or municipalities. All real and personal property located in Colombia must be included in the inventory of the estate, regardless of the nationality or residence of the deceased. In estate proceedings before a Colombian court, the inventory of the estate must also include all real and personal property belonging to the deceased, even though the property may be located abroad.

The same legal treatment applies to valuations of bequests and gifts. In these cases, however, property located abroad is subject to Colombian inheritance and gift taxation only if the transmission to the heir or donee

[1] After the research on this chapter was completed, the rates were raised 30 per cent by Law 21 of August 20, 1963. This action removed some of the urgency for reform, but does not in general invalidate the analyses and conclusions of the chapter.

can be affected by virtue of Colombian law or through the intervention of Colombian authorities.

Provisions for the Computation of Taxable Estates. The estate tax is imposed upon the aggregate value of all assets owned by the decedent at the time of his death, including the amount of all gifts made, obligations forgiven by the deceased during his life, as well as the total of all insurance, indemnities, and annuities payable on death for which no beneficiary has been designated. From the computed value of the gross estate, the following deductions are permitted: (1) expenses of the last illness, funeral, and burial; (2) expenses incurred in the estate proceedings, excluding the fees of executors, administrators, or representatives of the estate; and (3) certain debts of the decedent within statutory limitations. Exemptions permitted include that part of the gross estate that represents bequests and gifts to the government or public institutions, non-profit corporations, and foundations organized exclusively for public purposes, education, the advancement of the Roman Catholic religion, and for the encouragement of the arts and sciences.

Estate Tax Rates. It may be seen from Table 5–1 that the estate tax rates are rather moderate both in their level and degree of progression. Also, when more than five children inherit an estate, the amount of the estate tax payable is reduced 5 per cent for each child in excess of five up to a maximum of 25 per cent.

The moderation of estate tax rates is particularly apparent when a comparison is made with the income and net wealth taxes. While the estate taxes extend from 1 to 7 per cent, personal income tax rates range from .50 to 51.00 per cent, and net wealth taxes range from .1 to 1.5 per cent. This comparison suggests the need to modify the present estate tax structure for purposes of achieving greater progressivity and equity.

Computation of Taxable Legacies and Gifts. The inheritance and gift taxes are imposed upon heirs and donees and are applied to the net amount of any actual or presumptive inheritance or gift, excluding the proportional amount of the estate taxes paid. The taxable amount must include the value of all gifts previously made by the same donor or decedent to the same donee or heir, but a credit is given for previous inheritance and gift taxes paid. There are special provisions for the assessment of annuities, gifts or legacies with income, remainders, and gifts or legacies subject to a condition. Legally enforceable charges against gifts or legacies are deductible up to 75 per cent of the value of the bequest or gift.

All entities that are exempt for the purpose of the estate tax are also excluded from inheritance and gift taxation. The basic exemptions for the inheritance tax depend upon the category in which the beneficiary is

TABLE 5–1
Estate Tax Rates [a]

Taxable Estates	Marginal Rates (Per Cent)	Cumulative Tax	Average Rates (Per Cent)
Up to $ 3,000	—	—	—
$ 3,000 to 50,000	1.0	$ 470	.9
50,000 to 100,000	2.0	1,470	1.5
100,000 to 200,000	3.0	4,470	2.2
200,000 to 500,000	4.0	16,470	3.3
500,000 to 1,000,000	5.0	41,470	4.1
1,000,000 to 2,000,000	6.0	101,470	5.1
Over $2,000,000	7.0	—	—

[a] These rates were raised 30 per cent by Law 21 of August 20, 1963.

Source: Law 63 of 1936.

classified. Group A has an exemption of $500, while Groups B, C, and D have exemptions of $300, $200, and $150 respectively. Group E has no exemption. Definitions of these groups will be presented later. Life insurance payments are taxable for the purpose of the inheritance levy except for policies under $3,000.

Presumptive Gifts. Among those *inter-vivos* transfers that are subject to a rebuttable presumption that they are gifts for taxation purposes, the following are particularly worth noting: (1) transfers that distribute the property of a person among relatives within the fourth degree of consanguinity or second degree of affinity; (2) transfers to persons judicially declared bankrupt if made within the year following the declaration; (3) payments for the service of debts pursuant to agreements that are not evidenced by another document bearing a date certain or authenticated at least three months earlier; (4) transfers of property alleged to have been acquired by one person, using funds of another, when this fact is not set forth in the document by which the property was acquired; and (5) transfers of bare title with income and enjoyment (*usufructo*) retained.

Inheritance and Gift Tax Rates. Table 5–2 illustrates the different marginal tax rates for successive brackets of taxable amounts that are applicable both to bequests and *inter-vivos* gifts. In the case of bequests, exemptions are deductible before application of the rates.

On examination, Table 5–2 permits several observations: (1) In general, there is mild progressivity in the rate structure. (2) The progression is moderate in relative terms for the more distant degrees of affinity. (3) The marginal progressivity stops at the relatively low level of $100,000. (4) The number of groups is excessive and could be reduced without detracting from equity. (5) From a comparison of inheritance and estate tax rates, it is apparent that the Colombian legislation has placed greater emphasis on inheritance taxation. This latter observation will be confirmed later when information concerning assessments and collections of the two taxes are presented.

REVENUE PRODUCTIVITY

Assessment statistics for death and gift taxes are presented in Tables 5–3 and 5–4. Table 5–3 shows a breakdown of assessments by principal sources for the years 1950 to 1962, with a gap in the information for 1960 and 1961 due to the non-availability of data. The principal implications that may be inferred from Table 5–3 are the following:

1) The inheritance tax is the principal

TABLE 5–2
Inheritance and Gift Tax Rates [a]

Group	Degree of Affinity between Deceased or Donor and Heir or Donee	0–3	3–10	10–20	20–40	40–60	60–80	80–100	100 and Over
					Rates (Per Cent)				
A	Wife, children, and descendants	1	2	3	4	5	6	7	8
B	Ascendants, brothers, and sisters	3	4	5	6	7	8	10	12
C	Collaterals within the third degree of consanguinity: daughters-in-law and sons-in-law	6	7	8	10	12	14	16	18
D	All other relatives	10	12	14	16	18	20	22	24
E	All others and secret heirs and donees	12	14	16	18	20	22	24	26

(Header: Taxable Brackets (Thousands of Pesos))

[a] These rates were raised 30 per cent by Law 21 of August 20, 1963. The increase is immediately applicable in the case of inheritances but deferred to January 1, 1965, in the case of gifts.

TABLE 5–3

Assessment Statistics for Death and Gift Taxes

(Thousands of Pesos)

	Estate Taxes	Inheritance Taxes	Gift Taxes	Surtaxes for Inheritance and Gift Taxes[a]	Interest and Penalties	Assessments under the 1932 Law	Total
1950	$ 3,055	$ 5,516	$ 323	$1,137	$ 503	$42	$10,576
1951	4,216	8,296	794	1,837	1,018	92	16,253
1952	5,005	8,854	725	1,903	961	31	17,479
1953	4,695	10,576	4,090	2,719	1,227	—	23,307
1954	7,434	12,746	1,342	2,853	1,789	—	26,164
1955	8,888	19,514	2,297	4,268	3,354	—	38,321
1956	10,739	24,885	2,297	4,871	2,351	—	45,143
1957	7,277	15,350	2,353	3,622	3,254	—	31,856
1958	9,353	14,818	1,643	3,614	1,098	—	30,526
1959	11,595	24,025	2,292	5,063	6,783	—	49,758
1960	n.a.	n.a.	n.a.	n.a.	n.a.	—	n.a.
1961	n.a.	n.a.	n.a.	n.a.	n.a.	—	n.a.
1962	23,142	40,646	1,941	1,185	4,353	—	71,267

[a] According to the law, these surcharges should amount to 20 per cent of inheritance and gift tax assessments. The fact that they do not is apparently due to accounting discrepancies.

Source: Subdivisión de Recaudación, División de Impuestos Nacionales, Ministerio de Hacienda. Data for assessments are not available for 1960 and 1961.

TALBE 5–4

Death and Gift Taxes as Compared to Total Direct Taxes and the National Income

(Thousands of Pesos)

		Death and Gift Taxes as a Percentage of:	
	Death and Gift Taxes[a]	Total Direct Taxes	National Income
1950	10,576	5.1	.15
1951	16,253	5.9	.21
1952	17,479	6.3	.21
1953	23,307	8.0	.25
1954	26,164	6.8	.24
1955	38,321	8.5	.34
1956	45,143	10.3	.36
1957	31,856	5.2	.21
1958	30,526	4.1	.18
1959	49,758	5.7	.26
1960	53,430	5.3	.24
1961	55,707	5.3	.22
1962	67,901	6.0	n.a.

[a] Assessments from 1950 to 1959 and collections from 1960 to 1962.

Source: Subdivisión de Recaudación, División de Impuestos Nacionales, Ministerio de Hacienda.

source of revenue, accounting for nearly two times the amount of estate taxes in every year, even without counting the 20 per cent surcharge on the inheritance tax.

2) The yield of the gift tax is conspicu-ously low, accounting for less than 5 per cent of total death and gift tax assessments for most years. This low yield in large part is indicative of administrative defects and the relative ease of evasion. Moreover, unlike the estate and inheritance tax assessments, gift taxes show no tendency to increase in revenue productivity.

3) Inheritance and gift surtaxes should be 20 per cent of inheritance and gift tax assessments, except for 1962 when the surtax was eliminated. Table 5–3, however, shows significant discrepancies when the totals for the surtaxes are related to inheritance and gift tax assessments. Presumably, these differ-ences are due to accounting errors.

4) Interest and penalties are a relatively important component, accounting in many years for more revenue than the gift tax. Penalties are due to the delay in probate hearings and in collection.

Table 5–4 compares death and gift tax levies with total direct taxes and the national income. Except for 1957 and 1958, the death and gift tax levies show developing strength for the period from 1950 to 1962 in absolute terms of assessments and collections. But the trend is quite different when the data are related to total direct taxes and the national income. As compared to total direct taxes, death and gift taxes were not as productive of revenue in 1962 as they were a decade earlier in 1952. And when compared to the national income, death and gift taxes show a declining relationship from 1956 to 1958, and again from 1959 to 1961.

ADMINISTRATION

The administration of the estate, inheritance, and gift taxes is the responsibility of the Division of National Taxes, although many of the administrative procedures must be co-ordinated with probate proceedings under the jurisdiction of the judicial branch of the government. As it will be seen later, this joint responsibility accounts for certain advantages and disadvantages in the assessment and collection of the taxes.

The Division of National Taxes has a special unit charged with the responsibility of supervising the administration of death and gift taxes, while each regional office also has a special staff for assessment purposes. In other words, the same decentralized system of administering the income and complementary taxes is followed in the case of death and gift taxation; i.e., the actual assessments are made at the regional level, while activities at the national level are confined to supervision and review.

According to the law, the heirs must petition for an inventory and appraisal of the estate within six months of the decedent's death, and they are required to expedite the proceedings so that the tax will be paid within one year of the death. By legal requirement, the tax collector is empowered to file proceedings with the court and to take measures to prevent the loss, destruction, or consumption of the property if these deadlines are not met.

The inventory and appraisal of the estate are made by two experts, one appointed by the heirs and the other selected by the collector of taxes by lot from an official panel.

In the event that the two experts cannot agree, the court appoints a third, also from a panel. The tax may be computed once the court has notified the tax collector of the appraisal, and it must be paid before the probate proceedings may be continued, although the assessment may be revised subsequently. Reconsideration of the tax may be requested by the taxpayer within three days of the assessment notice. Appeals may be made to the regional administration or to higher levels. Before issuance of the final court decree settling the estate and ordering its distribution, the tax collector is afforded an opportunity to ascertain that no changes have occurred in the status of the property.

Estate and inheritance taxes are payable within ten days of the presentation of the tax bill, providing the presentation is made within one year of the decedent's death. After ten days, the taxpayer is liable to judicial process for collection. Unless mitigating circumstances can be alleged by the taxpayer, a surcharge of 1 per cent per month is imposed during the first year of delinquency, and 2 per cent per month thereafter.

The gift tax is due at the time of completion of the gift, the donee and donor being jointly liable. The Register of Public and Private Instruments will not inscribe any document evidencing a gift without proof of tax payment. The tax collector may investigate all transactions to determine whether or not an element of gift is involved.

The same procedures that are provided for estate valuation are available for the expert appraisal of gifts, but in most cases these procedures are by-passed and the tax collector uses more general principles established by the law. The taxpayer has the same appeal rights for gift taxes as for death taxes. Interest surcharges are also applied on delinquent accounts.

Administrative Problems

An investigation made by the research section of the Division of National Taxes shows that there were approximately 15,000 pending estate proceedings in June, 1963, in two-thirds of the regional offices of the country. A conservative estimate for the remaining one-third of the offices would raise this total to about 20,000. At the same time, the actual number of annual assessments is only about 7,000. Therefore, there is a backlog of pending estate proceedings of nearly three times the annual number of assessments. Most of these pending proceedings correspond to deaths that occurred more than a year ago and should, therefore, be already completed. Some of the cases have been pending completion for as long as forty years.

The conclusion that is warranted from this evidence is that the administration of death taxes is seriously frustrating the application of the law. Administrative improvements are equally, if not more, important than structural changes in the law.

A 1962 reform project proposed two administrative improvements. One of them is very elementary and merely authorizes the collector of taxes to appoint an expert for appraisal in the physical absence of the heirs or their representatives after a reasonable period has elapsed since an announcement was given to the heirs. Under present regulations, the appraisal can be indefinitely deferred by the heirs merely by their refusal to witness the selection of the government expert.

Another way that the heirs may defer assessment is by obstructing the inspection of the estate's assets. To overcome this problem, provisional assessment should be based on the latest income and net wealth tax returns of the deceased. This reform, the second recommended by the 1962 reform project, would help to reduce the large backlog of assessments.

How can heirs enjoy the use of property when the transfer of ownership is still pending and, as a result, be reluctant to have the estates settled? The answer is that many assets are transferable without the requirement of registration. Such is the case for livestock, farm products, inventories, furni-ture, etc. Furthermore, an heir can enjoy the income from his inheritance even if the title of ownership is not yet legalized. This enjoyment of income largely removes any incentive to transfer the ownership of assets.

Appraisal

In the opinion of the officials of the Division of National Taxes, the undervaluation of real estate assets seriously erodes the yield of death taxation. And in Colombia real property represents the principal type of taxable assets. A provision requiring an appraisal not lower than the cadastral valuation means little in practice, since in many parts of the country the cadastral valuations are only a small fraction of the market values.

A second factor that affects unfavorably the expert's appraisal is the practice of hiding assets like livestock and inventories. This problem could be resolved, as mentioned before, by provisional assessments based on the latest income and net wealth tax returns.

Assessment

The procedure of tax assessment varies considerably between single and married persons. For a married person, the assessment is more complicated in view of the provisions in the Colombian civil law for the acknowledgement of marriage contracts. It is, therefore, necessary on the part of the tax assessor to undertake a careful analysis of assets, debts, and expenses in order to make allocations between taxable and exempt portions of the estate. Assessments are made by specialists at the regional level, and their determinations are reviewed in the central office in Bogotá. The use of a standard form to systematize data processing, tax assessment, and review would facilitate the whole process of assessment and review.

Gift Taxation

As previously mentioned in this chapter, the relatively low total of gift tax assessments suggests that this levy is being evaded in Colombia to a serious degree. There are several reasons for this. First, the rebuttable presumption of gift in the case of transactions made by relatives within the fourth degree of consanguinity or third degree of affinity applies only when there are at least two transactions from the same seller to one or more buyers. Under these circumstances, a person can resort to fraudulent transactions that will result in no gift tax liability and a sizable saving of the death tax. Since the first registered transaction between relatives does not give origin to a presumption of gift, and since different transactions can be registered in different notarial offices, only a very careful co-ordination and supervision at the central office can prevent evasion. The Division of National Taxes is attempting to develop this co-ordination by means of periodical visits to different notaries in the country, but the problem is enhanced by the negligence of many officers in the judical branch. For example, one of the duties of a notary is to report to the tax authorities all transactions between persons with the same last name so that an investigation of consanguinity can be undertaken. This requirement is not complied with, since some reports of visits to a notary show instances of five or more transactions between sellers and buyers with the same last name without notification from the notary to the tax authorities.

Another difficulty with the administration of the gift tax is that a presumption of gift can be denied by the ruling of a court if proof is presented by the donor or donee. The essential problem here is that the responsibility to assess the evidence falls on officers of the judicial branch of the government and not on the tax authorities, and the latter are more competent to assess the evidence. In the opinion of officers of the Division of National Taxes, a great deal of evasion occurs in this way. Finally, it should be mentioned that when there is evasion of the gift tax, the mechanism of cumulating successive gifts for purposes of integrating gift and death taxes also breaks down.

CHAPTER 6

The Taxation of Agriculture

THE TAXATION OF THE agricultural industry in Colombia is of particular importance because Colombia is predominantly an agricultural country, despite the industrial advances that have been made. On the other hand, only a meager amount of public revenue is obtained from the agricultural sector. The problem of agricultural taxation, however, is more than an issue of raising additional revenue. In no other sector of the economy is it so apparent that the tax system should be used to accomplish such non-fiscal goals as a better tenure system and a more efficient use of the land. Because of this, consideration is given first in this chapter to the economic characteristics of the agricultural sector and to an analysis of the several problems that beset the industry. Once policy conclusions are reached concerning these problems, it is then possible to make suggestions for adapting the tax system to facilitate agricultural development in general.

ECONOMIC CHARACTERISTICS OF THE AGRICULTURAL INDUSTRY

Geographic Characteristics

The development of the land mass of Colombia, comprising an area of 1,140,000 square kilometers or 113.8 million hectares, has been affected by three features. The first is the division of the Andean Cordilleras into three mountain chains that separate the country into regions sharply isolated from one another, each having varied conditions of topography and climate. This physical partition has encouraged regionalism and, consequently, the development of several centers of economic activity. The second feature is the climate, which largely has determined the population distribution of Colombia. The bulk of the population lives in the western part of the country, the most mountainous area and, therefore, the most difficult with respect to communication and transportation. The climate has concentrated the inhabitants into two-fifths of the total area, leaving potentially rich, but climatically less attractive, regions unexploited. The third feature is Colombia's location in the continent. The country borders five other nations and is the only South American country with coasts on two oceans. This feature is a key element in regional and continental economic integration.

A wide variety of rainfall, temperature, and soil conditions is found in Colombia, which makes possible the growth of almost all crops of economic importance. Annual rainfall varies sharply among regions; for example, in the Guajira Peninsula, in the northeast, rainfall is negligible, while it may total as much as 500 inches along the Pacific Coast. With the exception of the Amazon region and the Pacific Coast, where rain occurs almost daily throughout the year, all parts of the country show a marked seasonal variation in precipitation.

Although information on Colombian soils

is scarce, some general observations may be made. Rich soils are found in some of the coffee-growing regions, in the upper Cauca Valley, and in the cotton area of Tolima. A recent study by aerial photography of 11.7 million hectares in the Atlantic Coast departments, the Guajira, and parts of the departments of Boyacá, Caldas, Antioquia, and Santander resulted in the following evaluation: [1]

400,000 hectares: well-drained alluvial soils suitable for agriculture, although some are deficient in rainfall.

2,000,000 hectares: poorly-drained alluvials.

1,300,000 hectares: subject to serious flooding.

1,500,000 hectares: natural grasslands of low fertility.

6,500,000 hectares: rough terrain, of which somewhat more than one million hectares are in varying stages of erosion.

Among the many problems of the agricultural industry in Colombia, soil erosion is undoubtedly among the more important. The problem is particularly acute in the departments of Norte de Santander, Boyacá, Cundinamarca, Huila, Nariño, and Cauca. Due to the vast area of land affected, however, erosion can be considered as a national problem. Among the factors that have contributed to increasing erosion are uncontrolled forest-cropping without reforestation and the practice of cultivating mountain slopes. The Coffee Grower's Federation has calculated that erosion results in a daily loss of soil equivalent to 583 hectares of arable land. In other words, the country loses annually through erosion 213,000 hectares of productive soil. [2]

Rural Population and Living Standards

Colombia's population in 1963 was approximately 16.5 million, and the annual rate of population growth is about 2.9 per cent. This relatively high rate of population increase prevails even though inadequate living standards for a sizable part of the population result in a relatively high death rate. The bulk of the population is concentrated in the higher regions. The highlands contain around 78 per cent of the population, the Caribbean plain 17 per cent, the Pacific Coast 3 per cent, and the Llanos the remaining 2 per cent. The rural population (those persons living in the country and in cities of less than 1,500 inhabitants) in 1961 was estimated to be 7.8 million or 51 per cent of the total population. By 1981 the rural population is expected to be only 35.0 per cent of the total population. [3]

The standard of living of the rural population, as indicated by income per capita, education, food consumption, housing, and health conditions is considerably lower than that of the urban population. The gross domestic product per capita for 1961 was about $1,550 (in 1958 prices). But for the 60 per cent of the active population that was employed in agriculture and the crafts in that year, the per capita output was less than one-half that of the workers employed in other sectors of the economy. Also, the wage level prevailing in agriculture was around one-half that in manufacturing.

Illiteracy and school absenteeism are much higher among the rural population than among the urban population. The 1951 census, although somewhat out of date, provides statistics on the magnitude of these problems. The census data show that 40 per cent of the male and 43 per cent of the female rural population had never attended school. Of those that had attended school, 58 per cent had completed only one year, and 16 per cent had completed five years. In 1959, 85 per cent of the rural schools offered only two grades of instruction. As a consequence, out of a total of 600,000 students that were enrolled in rural primary schools in 1959,

[1] Lauchlin Currie and Associates, *Programa del Desarrollo Económico del Valle del Magdalena y Norte de Colombia* (Bogotá, 1960).

[2] Rodríguez Guerrero, *Estudio de Erosión* (Departamento Técnico, Federación Nacional de Cafeteros, Chinchiná, 1956), p. 4.

[3] Departamento Administrativo Nacional de Planeación y Servicios Técnicos, *Colombia: Plan General de Desarrollo Económico y Social* (Bogotá, 1961), p. 60.

only 1,637 had completed the fifth grade. Obviously, the deficits in both classrooms and teachers in the rural areas are extremely acute.

The deficiencies in the nutrition of the population constitute one of the most conspicuous indications of economic underdevelopment in Colombia. Food consumption is above subsistence levels, but it is insufficient in both quantity and quality. Intake of calories per capita in Colombia during the period from 1956 to 1958 was 2,055 per day.[4] This amount is only 78 per cent of the level recommended by the National Nutrition Institute. The intake of proteins, vitamins, and calcium is equally low. For the rural population, malnutrition is due mostly to unbalanced diets, principally an underconsumption of protein. This problem is a consequence of the lack of education of the rural population and the technical inability of the small farmers to diversify their production.

Colombia also has very severe health and sanitary problems. Infectious diseases cause a high percentage of deaths in all age groups, but especially among the very young. The average life expectancy is less than forty years. Extremely poor housing conditions and inadequate sanitation and malnutrition contribute to the continuation of the vicious cycle of disease and poverty. Facilities for medical care are very inadequate in urban centers but are practically nonexistent in rural areas.

Considering the much higher percentage of illiteracy and absenteeism from school in the rural areas, the low health and nutrition standards, and the very low per capita output in some agricultural areas, it is apparent that a large proportion of the rural population is living on the fringe of the country's economic life. It is a part of the population that is, in effect, disenfranchised from active participation in the economy. This factor, in turn, is one of the most important drags on Colombia's economic development.

The fact that the bulk of the rural population lives under very precarious economic and social conditions has two other important consequences. The first is the creation of social tension, which is one of the principal causes of the persisting violence in the countryside. Second, is the surge to the cities, a common characteristic of population movements in many other Latin American countries. While the net increase in the rural population is 1 per cent per year, the urban population is increasing by more than 5 per cent, and in some large cities by more than 7 per cent. This situation is an essential factor in the development process, but it leads to other problems that must be resolved. The sharp increases in urban population make imperative the expansion of social services and an adequate development of the economy to provide work for the growing labor force.

Land Utilization and Tenure

Land Use. Although Colombia is large territorially relative to the size of the population, the topography and climate combine to restrict the area that is suitable for agricultural use. The total area of Colombia is 113.8 million hectares. Estimates of the area under agricultural exploitation vary widely, but the proportion is agreed to be somewhat less than one-third, that is, between 30 and 36 million hectares. Of this amount, the area in crop production is about 3.2 to 3.5 million hectares, while the remainder of the 30 to 36 million hectares is used as pasture. Table 6-1 summarizes the land use pattern.

Of the total land in crop production and pasture, about two-thirds, including practically all of the land in crop production, is located in the departments. Most of the remaining one-third of the agricultural land is in the Llanos, where it is used for cattle-raising. The agricultural areas in the departments are located principally in the mountain regions, the Cauca Valley, the Magdalena Valley, and on the northern coast. The area on the Pacific coast has little agricultural potential because of arid conditions. The

[4] *Colombia: Plan General de Desarrollo,* p. 70.

TABLE 6–1
Land Utilization in Colombia

	Hectares	Percentage
Agriculturally utilized	35,800,000	31.4
Crops	3,231,000	2.8
Fallow	2,569,000	2.3
Natural and artificial pasture	30,000,000	26.3
Area not economically used (jungles, productive but unused lands, unproductive lands, other non-agricultural uses)	69,435,000	61.0
Estimated area in cities and towns	3,240,500	2.9
Estimated area in rivers, lakes, and swamps	5,360,000	4.7
TOTAL	113,835,500	100.0

Source: S. J. Mejía, *Memoria al Congreso Nacional, 1957–1958*
(Ministerio de Agricultura, Imprenta Banco de la República,
Bogotá, July, 1958), p. 190.

Llanos, although large in size, is very sparsely populated.

A striking feature of Colombian agriculture is the disproportion between the area used for crops and for pasture. Of the country's total agricultural area, roughly 90 per cent is devoted to livestock production and only about 10 per cent to crop production. This ratio might suggest that Colombia's agricultural industry emphasizes livestock production. However, the output value of the two sectors indicates the exact opposite. For example, recent estimates for 1958 by the National Planning Board indicate that the output value of all crops represented 66 per cent of the total value of agricultural production, and livestock represented only 34 per cent. If coffee is excluded, the remaining output value of crops is about 36 per cent of the total value of agricultural output, still higher than that of livestock. This disproportion between the value of livestock output and the amount of land devoted to its production demonstrates the extensive, rather than intensive, use of land for raising livestock. In turn, this represents an important weakness of the agrarian structure, which will be more fully considered later as a problem of land tenure and distribution and its effect on land use and production.

The land used for growing crops in Colombia represents only about 3 per cent of the country's total area, and it is used primarily for the growing of coffee and cereals. Coffee alone accounted for 22 per cent of all land in crops in 1959, and corn accounted for another 24 per cent. Of the 3.5 million hectares under cultivation, only 715,000 hectares or 20.2 per cent, are cultivated by mechanical equipment. On the other hand, the total area that could be cultivated by mechanical equipment is about 10,000,000 hectares, not including the Llanos.

With respect to the future possibilities of land use, until land survey and land classification studies are completed, only estimates of the amount of undeveloped land suitable for agricultural use are possible. The World Bank's Mission to Colombia in 1956 estimated that the area of good undeveloped land that could be brought under cultivation at low cost is limited and probably does not exceed one million hectares. This estimate did not include the Llanos, the potential of which is yet to be explored. Present information suggests that this vast region is not likely to be much more than an extensive cattle-raising area, except for a few regions where certain permanent crops, such as African oil palm, appear to be economically feasible. As a result, the World Bank mission concluded that Colombia in the near future would have to obtain the bulk of increased agricultural output by a more intensive use of land already used for crops and pasture, unless the Llanos would prove to have a much greater agricultural potential.

Land Distribution and Tenure. Land distribution and tenure and, as a result, land resource use were molded largely by the character of the political and social institutions after the Spanish conquest of the sixteenth century. The influence of these institutions is still reflected, to some extent, in the pattern of the present agricultural economy.

The Spanish invasion laid the foundations of the large estates on the best lands through grants to the conquerors. These estates were largely self-sufficient in terms of food production, but the isolated nature of the country and the scarcity of labor relative to land resulted in an emphasis on livestock-raising rather than on the production of crops. The growth of population in the eighteenth and nineteenth centuries gradually altered the ratio of good land to population in the temperate climatic regions and started a migration into the mountainous regions. This led to the development of agriculture under adverse conditions on small farms and on unsuitable land. Thus, conquest and subsequent population increase produced two widely divergent systems of rural property distribution (size of holding) and tenure (the way in which land is held)—*latifundia* and *minifundia.*

Latifundia as a system of land holding represents generally the large-scale ownership of the best lands in Colombia and their utilization for cattle-raising under extensive and oftentimes wasteful methods. For many owners it represents a method of speculation in anticipation of increasing land values rather than the ownership of an economic asset from which income is earned through efficient use. In consequence, landowners have not acquired a knowledge of sound management of their land, nor, as a general rule, have they shown much interest in its improvement. A minimum of capital is invested in improvements, owner management is generally of the absentee variety, and little

attempt is made to acquire and train an efficient labor force.

Minifundia, on the other hand, is caused by the failure of the *latifundia* system to absorb population on the best agricultural land. It represents the overintensive use of land that is marginal for cultivation. As a result, the bulk of the rural population of Colombia is located on relatively poor land, particularly in the highland areas, which is cultivated under uneconomic conditions. The area of land per worker is small, while its topography is unsuitable for the use of mechanical equipment, even animal-drawn in most cases. In many instances, the soil and the size of the holding do not produce a surplus which permits an accumulation of capital to finance better production practices. Education facilities are at a low level, and the relative inability of workers to resist disease reduces their efficiency.

Another indictment of *minifundia* is that it keeps people idle and, consequently, in chronic poverty. For example, the average family occupying a two-hectare farm lives in a conflict between labor availability and labor requirements. Although this family of five can provide 400 work days per year, there is only work available for 146 days. This disguised unemployment not only retards agricultural development, but it also promotes social and political instability. On the other hand, the productivity of labor is also low on the *latifundia,* but it offers, at the other extreme, the evils of undersettlement and underutilization of land.

Scientific studies provide evidence of the discontent caused by the maldistribution of land in Colombia. Sociological studies of the municipalities of Tabio by Smith, of Saucio by Fals-Borda, and of Manta by Duque Gómez all show that diminutive landholdings are associated with low labor productivity.[5] In Tabio, 36 per cent of the farms are of five hectares or less, while in Manta 71 per cent are less than two hectares, and

[5] Robert Carlyle, "Land Distribution and Tenure in Colombia," *Journal of Inter-American Studies,* April, 1961, p. 281.

43 per cent under one hectare. Geographical studies by Crist reinforce these sociological and economic generalizations by showing both the lack of initiative on the part of the typical *latifundista* and the vivid discontent of the *campesino*.[6]

The widely divergent systems of rural property distribution just described—*latifundia* and *minifundia*—have thus given rise to a basically irrational and uneconomic use of land in Colombia and a maldistribution of population with respect to the land. Furthermore, the low level of general education and of technical knowledge in the rural areas, in addition to a shortage of capital, have combined to produce an inefficient and high cost system of agriculture.

Economic investigations of the past few years provide estimates of the distribution of land on a national scale that indicate the gravity of the problem inherent in the maldistribution of land. The distribution of farming units by size is presented in Table 6–2. Although these data are based on a sample taken from the 1951 census and cover only the sixteen departments, the statistics are adequate for a general indication of the problem.[7]

It may be seen from Table 6–2 that farming units of under five hectares—numerically equivalent to 56 per cent of the aggregate number of farms involved in the sample—occupy only slightly over 4 per cent of all the farm land, while farming units of five hundred hectares and over, representing 0.54 per cent of the total, occupy 31 per cent of the farm land. The farms of less than five hectares usually represent a form of tenure that is precarious and temporary, as for instance those worked under the share-cropping system. Farms of more than five hundred hectares are generally owner-operated, and some units have more area than that indicated in Table 6–2, the difference representing small or medium-sized holdings worked by sharecroppers or tenant farmers independently of the main undertaking. These large farms of over five hundred hectares include the *latifundia* already described. Although surveys have never been undertaken to determine the optimum size for different types of farm units in each area and at each climatic level, the ECLA survey of economic development of Colombia concluded *a priori* that farm units under two hectares and those over five hundred hectares are not economically desirable.[8]

[6] *Ibid.*

[7] More recent estimates based on data from the 1960 agricultural census show that the percentile distributions do not differ significantly except in the case of the percentage of the total number of farms falling within the first two groups of Table 6–2. In the more recent estimates, the percentage of farms under five hectares is 48

per cent, while that between six and twenty hectares is 41 per cent. The proportion of the total area accounted for by the combination of these two groups, however, remains the same, around 15 per cent.

[8] Economic Commission for Latin America, *Analyses and Projections of Economic Development, III: The Economic Development of Colombia, 1957*, p. 194.

TABLE 6–2
Distribution of Farming Units by Size

Size of Farms	Number of Farms	Percentage of Total	Area Occupied by Farms	
			Thousands of Hectares	Percentage of Total Area
Under 5 hectares	459,380	55.97	951	4.18
From 6 to 20 hectares	230,550	28.09	2,434	10.73
From 21 to 100 hectares	101,384	12.35	4,746	20.92
From 101 to 500 hectares	25,072	3.05	7,522	33.15
Over 500 hectares	4,456	0.54	7,036	31.02
TOTAL	820,842	100.00	22,689	100.00

Source: Economic Commission for Latin America, *Analysis and Projections of Economic Development—The Economic Development of Colombia, 1957*, p. 194.

Statistics presented in Table 6–2 should not obscure the fact that there exists a great variation in the size of farms according to different crops grown. For example, 64 per cent of the coffee farms have less than ten hectares.[9] According to the *Misión Económica y Humanismo* that made this finding, these coffee farms of less than ten hectares constitute the only acceptable *minifundia* in Colombia. It has also been determined that there is an extreme of *minifundia* in the case of tobacco, with 90 per cent of the farms having less than one hectare.[10]

Variations in farm size also exist among the various regions of the country. In northern Colombia and in the cattle regions of the Llanos, there are great differences in the size of cattle farms as compared to farms used for crop production. There are also considerable differences in farm size among regions, even though the crops grown may be the same.

Not only the size of holding, but also the way in which the land is held, contributes to the gravity of Colombia's agricultural problems. Data on the system of land tenure in Colombia indicate that a high proportion of the land is operated by landowners. From a sample including 26,108,000 hectares (a figure close to the total area under use of about 30 to 36 million), it was found that 87 per cent of the land was operated by owners, 3.3 per cent by tenants, 2.7 per cent by sharecroppers, 5.4 per cent by settlers, and 1.6 per cent by other forms of tenure. Table 6–3 provides statistics on the tenure system.

Table 6–3 provides information only on the distribution of the land area according to forms of tenure and does not indicate the distribution of farmers according to form of tenure. It should not be concluded, therefore, that the majority of the farmers operate their own land and that, consequently, there are few landless farmers. As it was shown earlier, a high proportion of the farm land is held by a few owners, and, conversely, a small proportion is held by the bulk of tenants, sharecroppers, and other non-owner operators. This means that a significant part of the agricultural output is produced by farmers who are not landowners—principally tenants renting land or squatters occupying private or public land. The circumstances under which these non-owners operate discourage them from making permanent improvements. Rental contracts are frequently oral and cover only one or two crop periods. The shortness of the rental period, associated with the constant possibility of eviction, is not conducive to permanent improvements. These factors encourage a wasteful use of soil as efforts are made to extract the maximum output during the uncertain short-run period.

Again, as in the case of the distribution

---

[9] Misión "Económica y Humanismo," *Estudio sobre las Condiciones del Desarrollo de Colombia* (Bogotá, October, 1958), p. 134.
[10] Ivan Pérez, "Sistema de Tenencia de la Tierra en Colombia," *Revista Facultad Nacional de Agronomía*, No. 56 (1962), p. 9.

TABLE 6–3
Land Distribution by Forms of Tenure

	Area in Hectares	Percentage	Less than 50 hectares	More than 50 hectares
Owners	22,710,000	87.0	6,123,000	16,587,000
Tenants	856,000	3.3	473,000	383,000
Sharecroppers	716,000	2.7	603,000	113,000
Settlers	1,419,000	5.4	381,000	1,038,000
Other	407,000	1.6	95,000	312,000
Total area studied	26,108,000	100.0	7,675,000	18,433,000

Source: Ivan Pérez, "Sistemas de Tenencia de la Tierra en Colombia," *Revista Facultad de Agronomía* (Medellín, 1962), p. 8.

of land by size, the distribution of farmers by forms of tenure varies greatly, depending on the crops produced. Cotton and tobacco farms, for example, are 44 and 25 per cent operator-owned respectively, while in the case of coffee farms, 77 per cent are operator-owned, 14 per cent sharecropped, 5 per cent rented, and 4 per cent held in other forms.

The foregoing analysis of the distribution of agricultural land has been concerned exclusively with privately owned lands, but the largest landholder in the country is the government. Approximately 76 per cent of the national territory is public domain. Most of the public land is *baldios,* sparsely inhabited and inaccessible. Some of the publicly owned land is slowly being developed by "spontaneous" squatters and by government-sponsored colonization projects. Public lands can become privately owned by squatters who occupy and exploit them.

Because of the limited funds and personnel of the Ministry of Agriculture and other agencies, the government has been unable to enforce adequately a systematic land use program for public lands. This neglect has in many instances led to the misuse of public lands and their resources, including widespread waste of valuable timber resources and severe damage to watersheds and streams. In turn, this has caused extensive soil erosion.

Colonization. In Colombia the term "colonization" may be defined as publicly assisted settlement of public lands. Colombia's first attempt at colonization began some forty years ago, when a Department of Colonization was established within the Ministry of National Economy. Four projects were undertaken in Caracolicito, Sumapaz, San Juan de Calima, and Bahía Solano. For a number of reasons, including political distractions, this effort did not succeed. A second attempt was made in 1948 when the Institute of Colonization and Parcelization was created. This agency was succeeded by the Institute of Colonization and Emigration in 1953, but this effort also failed due to poor administration, inadequate planning, and a lack of funds. Since 1956 the Agriculture Credit Bank (*Caja de Crédito Agrario*) has been given the responsibility for colonization. Efforts have been concentrated in five geographical areas, where over one thousand families have been settled. The number of "spontaneous" settlers is considerably higher, and these also have received assistance. Table 6–4 provides data on the colonization projects as of 1961.

One of the major obstacles to effective colonization has been the inaccessibility of the sites. One study reported in 1960 that the colonists had to transport their produce over 200 kilometers of trail passable only by mules or horses and across major streams by canoes.[11] A lengthy list of other problems faced by the colonist (the need for technical guidance, shortages of livestock and land clearing equipment, inadequate housing and schools, etc.) is discussed in a recent study based on interviews with twenty-four settlers in the Ariari project.[12] According to the author of this report, colonization efforts in practically all parts of the world have been accompanied by difficulties and have resulted sometimes in complete failures. The two principal reasons advanced are inadequate planning and insufficient resources. With respect to these deficiencies, Colombia does not appear to be an exception.

The interest in colonization still persists among some official and technical groups in Colombia, but others see limited possibilities for its success. It is argued that additional resources and more interagency co-operation would improve the results. Some defend the projects by calling attention to the thousands of marginal farmers who are working on steep and eroded lands and whose lot is being worsened by the competition of mechanized farms on the better lands. Others see colonization as the most practical way to

[11] Denny Byron, *et al., A Colonization and Land Utilization Program for Colombia* (Servicio Técnico Agrícola Colombiano Americano, 1960), p. 32.

[12] Jaime Pardo Sánchez, *Algunas Observaciones Sobre la Agricultura Actual y Las Condiciones de Vida en el Proyecto de Colonización del Ariari* (Servicio Técnico Agrícola Colombiano Americano, 1961), p. 8.

TABLE 6-4
Colonization Projects and Status of Accomplishments, 1961

Name of Project and Location	Lebrija in Santander	Sumapaz in Cundinamarca	Caquetá in Caquetá	Sarare[a]	Ariari in Meta
Year initiated	1960	1960	1959	1943	1959
Colonizable area in thousands of hectares	500	580	700	300	890
Area exploited	—	12	39	15	80
Distance from Bogotá (Kms.)	475	95	675	670	210
Number of families:					
Settled	—	—	450	175	450
Spontaneous	200	300	1,000	100	1,000
Planned	7,900	7,200	7,800	3,400	8,000
Probable cost through 1965 (Millions of pesos)	$195	$266	$295	$105	$205

[a] Located in Boyacá, Norte de Santander, Arauca.

Source: Reports of the Ministry of Agriculture and Caja Agraria.

settle low income farmers migrating because of the *violencia*. Still others see colonization as making an important contribution to national economic development. But in view of past experiences, the high cost of opening new lands, and other difficulties involved in transferring and settling displaced or landless peasants in new and isolated areas, enthusiasm over the results that can be expected from colonization does not appear to be warranted.

The parcelization program differs from colonization only in that it is based on the acquisition of idle private lands. As implemented by the Caja Agraria, available lands are being acquired through normal purchase procedures rather than expropriation or purchase at less than market value. The Caja Agraria and its predecessors in this effort have distributed about 21,000 hectares. The Tobacco Institute (Instituto Nacional de Fomento Tabacalero) also has a program of this type. By 1960 this agency had distributed 1,900 hectares (220 farms) in the departments of Bolívar and Santander as part of a program to eliminate sharecropping in tobacco. Under the current agrarian reform program, it is to be expected that official activities in the redistribution and parcelization of land will differ considerably in scope and procedure from those carried on in the past under the Caja Agraria.

Agricultural Production

Agricultural production is undertaken in Colombia by five relatively distinct systems of farming: (1) mixed subsistence-farming; (2) coffee-farming; (3) cattle-raising; (4) commercial-farming; and (5) farming by squatters.

Mixed subsistence farming has holdings ranging from one to ten hectares in size, with little capital invested except for the value of the land. Family labor is used almost exclusively and is applied intensively. Returns are low, due to the small-scale operations and the primitive techniques used. A great variety of crops are grown under this system (potatoes, wheat, barley, tobacco, hemp, yucca, beans, corn) depending on climatic conditions. In general, this system of farming is close to a subsistence level, with small surpluses being sold at the weekly market in the nearest town. Regional surpluses are marketed in the larger urban centers through middlemen, usually operating on a small scale.

The Colombian coffee *finca* is the foundation of the country's economy, as it provides the bulk of exports and hence is the principal source of foreign exchange. This type of farm is located at medium altitudes on the central and eastern Cordilleras, with the majority of the farms being located in the departments of Caldas, Valle, Antioquia,

Tolima, and Cundinamarca. Production is generally on a small scale with most of the labor supplied by the family. The coffee industry is thus a specialized segment of the *minifundia* system of land holding.

Cattle fincas comprise the bulk of the *latifundia*. They are generally located on the flat and rolling lands in the highland plateaus and valleys, the Cauca and Magdalena valleys, the North Coast lowlands, particularly the Sinu region, and the Llanos.

Commercial farming, as the name implies, is undertaken on a sizable scale and is found in many parts of Colombia. Normally, there is specialization of production. For example, banana production on a large scale for export is dominated by one company in the Santa Marta region. The larger proportion of this "banana zone," however, is cultivated by individual producers operating on a smaller scale. Large-scale sugar cane-growing for refineries is concentrated in the Cauca Valley, and small-scale growing for panela production is scattered throughout the country. A commercial-type of farming has developed recently in a few areas for the production of African oil palm.

Another recent development is large-scale mechanized farming of cereals and cotton on leased land. These operations are generally of a one-crop nature, designed to extract the maximum from the soil with little or no provision for restoring its fertility. These operations are undertaken frequently by urban residents who have adequate capital but little experience or personal interest in scientific farming methods. They are attracted by the speculative advantages of one-crop exploitation made possible by the relatively high price levels of certain products.

Squatters are farm workers and marginal farmers who establish themselves on land without obtaining legal titles or without even having the permission of the owners. Squatters occupy public as well as private lands, the latter often being abandoned or under-utilized *latifundia*. This use of the land is undesirable because it does not lead to permanent improvements or to the formation of a stable community. On private lands, squatter occupation frequently leads to friction, rural unrest, and even violence. Products sold by the squatters are mostly timber and miscellaneous cash crops.

Marketing and Price Stabilization Problems. The marketing system for agricultural products in Colombia presents striking contrasts. New methods and systems of distribution are appearing, but beside them exist antiquated systems that are primitive and incompatible with a developing economy. On the one hand, domestically processed foods and imported foodstuffs are being sold in retail outlets that resemble those in the United States. In contrast, the marketing of unprocessed food for domestic consumption shows little sign of change; it remains costly, unsanitary, primitive, and grossly inefficient.

Because a high proportion of agricultural commodities is grown on small holdings, where a large part of the crop is consumed, problems in marketing the surpluses have arisen. Each type of commodity has innumerable varieties that differ as to quality, size, shape, taste, color, appearance, and condition. Many of these products are perishable, but even the non-perishable are exposed to the risk of destruction or deterioration due to the lack of adequate storage facilities on the farms and inadequate means of transportation to the markets. Producers generally have no sales organizations, and in many parts of the country transactions are carried out in open-air markets, either directly between producers and consumers or between the farmers and the small middlemen supplying large urban centers. These middlemen are not organized nor have they the facilities for storing stocks and keeping them in good condition. Furthermore, the lack of uniformity among commodities of the same kind creates storage problems and prevents standardization for purposes of large-scale trade. Prices not only undergo enormous seasonal fluctuations, but they also differ from one locality to the other at the same date due to crop conditions, transport facilities, and the insufficient influence of organizations responsible for stabilizing the market. As a result, wastage is alarmingly high, and the appearance, state of preservation, and quality of the commodities that reach the consumer are very unsatisfactory.

The distribution of agricultural products is in need of producer organizations to stabilize the markets. Usually, distribution is handled by a few middlemen, who purchase products at relatively low prices from the small producers, taking advantage of their poor bargaining position, and transport the goods to the main consumption centers. An efficient system of co-operative markets would be a desirable solution to many of the existing structural deficiencies of the marketing system. In the past, however, the development of co-operatives, except in isolated cases, has not been successful enough to exert significant influence.

An extremely important need in the field of marketing is for price stabilization, particularly in the case of cereals. The basic problem involves seasonal price fluctuations, with the unduly low prices at the time of harvest resulting in a reduction of farm incomes and a discouragement to increased production. In this respect, there is a need to co-ordinate price and production policies so that guaranteed minimum prices will be established in such a way that they will encourage additional production.

The present price structure of agricultural goods in Colombia is characterized by its high level relative to world markets, rather wide fluctuations, and by variations in the prices of the same commodities in different areas of Colombia. These characteristics are due to a number of factors, among them government import policies, the influence of world coffee prices on domestic price levels, inefficiency in production and marketing, and inadequate internal transportation facilities.

In recent years, several agricultural products have been commanding prices on the domestic markets that are well above world prices. Quotas, tariffs, and exchange restrictions have prevented imports from equating world and domestic prices. Food prices are also high relative to wage income. The food bill of the lower income urban group accounts for an inordinately high proportion of its consumption expenditures. And during the first six months of 1963, the general increase in the consumer price index accentuated this problem.

The price received for coffee is determined principally by the world coffee market, which has been characterized by instability. Consequently, the income of the coffee sector, which represents the most important single determinant of consumer income, varies considerably both over short-run and long-run periods. In turn, this has an important influence on the general level of other commodity prices in the country.

The Colombian government has been active in the purchase and sale of farm products with the objective of regulating markets and stabilizing prices. These activities have been undertaken by the Instituto Nacional de Abastecimiento (INA), an autonomous agency with a broad range of responsibilities relating to the production, storage, and distribution of farm products. However, the typical scale of INA operations has been relatively small as compared to the magnitude of production. For example, INA purchased ten thousand tons of corn in 1960, or scarcely more than 1 per cent of total production. Except for wheat and sesame, the purchases of agricultural goods by INA represent very low percentages of production. It is generally recognized by both farmers and public officials that the stabilization efforts of INA have failed by a wide margin to stabilize prices to a desirable degree.

Water Resources, Irrigation, and Drainage. Poor water conditions exist throughout Colombia. Rainfall has an irregular distribution. While it is abundant in many parts of the country, in others it is too insufficient during part of the year to permit agricultural operations without a serious drought hazard. Drainage would assist in the development of many areas, as good flat land frequently is flooded. Water control, however, has been developing slowly, only a few dams having been built for flood control purposes. Of the total area under crops of about 3.2 to 3.5 million hectares, only around 260,000 hectares, or less than 10 per cent, are cultivated under irrigation. Studies made by different technical groups have concluded that considerable amounts of land could be brought into agricultural use by means of irrigation, drainage, and flood control.

The Four-Year Government Investment Plan has given consideration to twenty different projects (nine for irrigation, four for flood control, and seven for drainage and irrigation). These would benefit 1,032,000 hectares at a total cost of approximately $1.5 million.

Agricultural Credit. There are several sources of agricultural credit in Colombia, the principal one being the *Caja de Crédito Agrario.* Next in importance are the commercial banks, which are required to allot a certain percentage of their deposits to agricultural loans. Among the commercial banks, the two most important sources of agricultural credit are the *Banco Cafetero* and *Banco Ganadero.* In addition, there are other minor sources of credit such as cooperatives and producers' federations.

The volume of credit made available to agriculture has been expanding steadily in recent years, with a particularly sharp increase in 1959, when agricultural loans rose by 26.7 per cent, and in 1961, when loans increased by 24.4 per cent. Despite the increase in farm credit, however, the loans granted to agriculture reveal several structural defects. When comparing the distribution of credit within the agricultural sector, an imbalance is found. As shown earlier, livestock occupies a much greater proportion of arable land than crop production, but the latter contributes more to the gross internal product. On the other hand, the livestock industry absorbs a greater proportion of total farm credit than does crop production.[13] This is a clear example of the type of misallocation of resources that retards the agricultural development of the country. Moreover, the total amount of credit made available to all sectors of the Colombian economy increased by 80 per cent from 1955 to 1960, while the total credit granted to the agricultural industry during the same period increased by only 65 per cent.[14]

External credit to agriculture is also meager as compared to the credit extended to other sectors of the economy. The total amount of loans granted to Colombia by various international organizations during the period from January 1, 1958, to June 30, 1962, amounted to U.S. $592 million and Col. $312 million. Of this total only about U.S. $23 million and Col. $219 million were extended to agriculture.

Major Agricultural Products. Crops account for about two-thirds of the value of farm output as compared to one-third for livestock. Coffee, alone, accounts for somewhat more than one-fourth of the value of farm production. Rice, sugar cane, and in recent years cotton, are among the more important crops. Corn, potatoes, and plantain rank close behind.

Traditionally, Colombia has been an exporter of raw materials and an importer of manufactured products. These trade characteristics still persist. Currently, about 90 per cent of all imports are non-agricultural products. At the same time, the agricultural sector is the principal source of exports. Coffee, alone, represents 70 to 75 per cent of all exports and 90 per cent of agricultural exports. Given the economic characteristics of this commodity (inelastic demand, excess world production, and domestic surpluses), it is mandatory for the country to direct its development policy toward reducing marginal coffee-producing areas and promoting the diversification of crops. This policy should be executed jointly and integrated with the agrarian reform program.

As an export product, bananas have a

[13] See Asociación Nacional de Industriales, *Informe Industria Ganadera, 1961,* and Banco de la República, *Cuentas Nacionales, 1961.*

[14] Alfonso Fernández Cárdenas, *La Estructura de Crédito Agrícola en Colombia* (Servicio Técnico Agrícola Colombiano Americano, Bogotá, 1962), p. 25.

relatively favorable international market and an excellent internal organization with low production costs. Cotton has had an extraordinary export expansion since 1959. Other exports having favorable future outlooks are sugar, tobacco, soft fibers, oilseeds, cacao, and meat. In the case of meat, the difficulties are a relatively high price in relation to world prices and quality that must be improved. The need to increase exports and to find new exportable commodities in order to reduce Colombia's dependence on coffee as a source of foreign exchange is so obvious that it needs no elaboration.

Agrarian Reform

Public dissatisfaction with low rural incomes, the maldistribution of land, and the land tenure system led to the enactment of an agrarian reform law in December, 1961. The law created an autonomous executive agency for agrarian reform, the Instituto Colombiano de Reforma Agraria (INCORA), authorized a minimum annual budget of $100 million, and assigned broad powers to the new agency. The law has very ambitious objectives:

1) to reform the social agrarian structure by means of appropriate procedures, to eliminate and prevent the inequitable concentration of rural property or its uneconomic division, to reconstruct adequate farming units in the areas characterized by *minifundia,* and to distribute land to the landless;

2) to stimulate the economic use of uncultivated or undercultivated land in accordance with programs that have as their objective the orderly distribution and rational utilization of land;

3) to increase the over-all volume of agricultural and livestock production in harmony with the development of the other sectors of the economy;

4) to create conditions under which small renters and sharecroppers will have more security, and under which they, as well as salaried farmhands, will have better opportunities to become landowners; and

5) to assure the conservation, improvement, and adequate use of natural resources.

To attain these objectives, INCORA was vested with broad powers:

1) to administer the public domain;

2) to sponsor studies for the purpose of establishing programs of land use, tenure, and investment that will promote economic development;

3) to confirm land ownership dates and registrations;

4) to execute programs of land consolidation in areas of small-sized farms;

5) to distribute public and private lands;

6) to provide credit and technical assistance;

7) to grant title to public lands to private persons if they are able to demonstrate that two-thirds of the land for which title is requested is being exploited; and

8) to acquire privately held land by expropriation for such purposes as resettlement, reforestation, irrigation, drainage, erosion control, etc.

The projects undertaken by INCORA during 1962 will benefit around 118,000 hectares through irrigation and drainage, and 44,000 hectares were planned for redistribution. Also, the colonization projects in Nariño and Antioquia will result in the productive use of nearly 300 hectares of virgin forests. The number of families to be benefited by the land distribution projects will be around 10,400, while the colonization projects will permit the initial settlement of 3,000 families.

These specific accomplishments of INCORA during 1962 may be cited:

1) The law requires persons who owned land in excess of 2,000 hectares as of September, 1960, to show evidence of economic use. The purpose of this requirement was to obtain an inventory of large estates for possible expropriation proceedings. By the end of 1962, reports on 1,238 properties were filed by the owners. The properties covered a total of nearly 7.5 million hectares, of which 38 per cent was cultivated and 62 per cent was not being used. A total of 266

properties was visited by personnel of INCORA to initiate expropriation proceedings.

2) From July to December, 1962, INCORA initiated 510 resolutions declaring the acquisition of private properties to be in the public interest. The total area of these properties was about 136,000 hectares. As of December, 1962, 108 properties were visited to classify the lands, 30 properties were in the first stage of negotiation, 6 were in the second stage, and 3 properties, with a total area of 618 hectares, had been acquired.

3) The total number of land titles issued from land in the public domain was 1,627, amounting to 123,000 hectares.

These features and early results of the agrarian reform program suggest that a powerful instrument has been drafted. In general, both the government and public are giving support to the program. However, the agrarian reform program has not been free from criticism and opposition. For example, some public officials see the solution of Colombia's rural problems not as conceived in the agrarian reform program—through the redistribution of land and the settlement of landless farmers—but through urban absorption of the underemployed rural population into industry, with the concomitant establishment of large-scale commercial farming to supply the country's food needs.

Revenue Productivity of the Agricultural Sector

Agriculture in 1959 contributed $7.02 billion (1958 pesos) or 32.1 per cent of the total gross national product. The development plan estimates that agriculture will contribute $8.6 billion (1958 pesos) to the economy by 1965. But while agriculture is the highest single contributor to the gross internal product, it is also the lowest in terms of per capita output.

The amount contributed by agriculture to government revenues is not known with certainty. An estimate made by the Ministry of Finance indicates that only from 6 to 7

per cent of total government revenue is derived from the agricultural sector.[15] In Chapter 1 of this study, another estimate of 14.29 per cent of national government direct taxes in 1959 is presented. For the land tax, alone, that accrues to the municipalities, the amount collected in 1960 was about $115 million. More recent estimates and collection data are not available, but the statistics for 1962 probably were not much higher. Even on the basis of available data it is clear that the agricultural industry is very seriously undertaxed.

Public and Private Investment

Public investment in agriculture in 1959 was $16 million, which represents only 1 per cent of total public investment for that year. For the period from 1962 to 1965, the Ten-Year Development Plan has projected an average annual public investment of $149 million, or 6 per cent of total public investment. According to the recommendations made by the International Bank for Reconstruction and Development, however, agricultural investment should represent about 9 per cent of total public investment, an average of $262 million per year.

Colombia's economic development plan places major reliance on the private sector for achieving investment and output goals. This is also true of investment in agriculture. In 1959 private investment in agriculture was $47 million, or 17 per cent of total private investment. The Ten-Year Development Plan projects an annual average investment of $646 million for 1962 to 1965, or 16 per cent of total private investment.

The Ten-Year Development Plan

The development plan emphasizes agricultural development. One-fourth of the total increase in output is expected to originate in

[15] Comité Interamericano de Desarrollo Agrícola, *Inventario de Información Básica para la Programación del Desarrollo Agrícola en América Latina, Colombia* (Washington, 1962).

agriculture. Agricultural exports are scheduled to increase from U.S. $389 million in 1960 to U.S. $575 million in 1970, an increase of 48 per cent. Excluding coffee, the plan visualizes agricultural exports of $163 million in 1970, an increase of 256 per cent as compared to the 1960 total of $46 million. The comparable rate of increase projected for non-agricultural exports is only 110 per cent. The significance of possible overestimates in agricultural production is clear if it is realized that total exports are projected at U.S. $843 million in 1970. If agricultural exports other than coffee were to reach only one-half the amount planned, the total exchange earnings of the nation would fall short of the planned objective by 10 per cent.

A similar problem exists concerning import substitution. Imports of agricultural products were valued at U.S. $57 million in 1959. They are expected to decline to U.S. $42 million by 1970, a reduction of 27 per cent.

In addition to meeting these goals for export expansion and import substitution, agriculture faces a rapidly growing internal demand. This is inevitable, given the growth of population, the present level of food consumption per capita, and the effect of the expected increase in per capita income on the demand for foodstuffs.

PRESENT TAXATION OF THE AGRICULTURAL INDUSTRY

Taxes on Rural Property

The rural property tax (*impuesto predial*) represents the principal unique contribution of the agricultural industry to public revenues. It was established in 1908 by Law 20 as a municipal source of revenue, consisting of a tax of two mills on the assessed value of rural and urban property. Law 4 of 1949 gave the departmental assemblies regulatory responsibilities over the tax, but they were not permitted to exceed the tax rates established by national law or to allocate the

revenue to defray non-municipal expenditures.

The determination of cadastral assessments was delegated to municipal boards (*juntas municipales*), which usually assessed property every three or four years substantially below market values. This underassessment, together with the relatively low tax rate of two mills, made the land tax burden insignificant. In 1939, for example, the revenue collected represented an average of only $3.25 per holding (urban and rural), and resulted in only about 9 per cent of the aggregate income of the municipalities.[16]

Law 128 of 1941 assigned the responsibility of reassessing all property to the Instituto Geográfico Agustín Codazzi, and earmarked a cadastral surtax equivalent to 10 per cent for this purpose. Later, through Decree 2473 of 1948, the basic rate of the property tax was increased to four mills to finance the rural police force and to provide funds for municipal development.

In the Department of Valle, there is an additional rate of three mills levied on assessed properties. This surtax is allocated to the *Corporación Autónoma Regional del Valle del Cauca*. A similar surtax of two mills exists in the area comprising the *Corporación Autónoma Regional de la Sabana*.

The system of land assessments has undergone several changes since 1941. Decree 259 of 1954 transferred the responsibility for assessments from the Instituto Geográfico back to the municipalities. Self-assessment by the landowners was also tried but proved to be unsuccessful and was abolished in April, 1956. At this time, also, the assessment responsibility was transferred back to the Geographic Institute, where it has remained.

In 1957, the total assessed value of 1,762,812 rural properties and 873,377 urban properties was $23 billion, and the total land tax revenue was $83 million. The average tax collected per rural property was only

---

[16] Raleigh Barlowe, "Land Taxes and Rural Economic Development in Colombia," (Michigan State University, February, 1960), p. 13. Mimeographed.

$31.22. This average collection represented a considerable increase over the 1939 average of $3.25 due to inflation, higher assessments, and a tax rate of four mills instead of two. The total revenue collected from land taxes in 1960, the last year for which data are available, was $115 million. No precise distinction may be made between revenue collected from rural as compared to urban properties, but it is estimated by the Director of the Agrarian Reform Institute that $37.5 million were derived from rural properties in 1960.

The property tax also suffers from delinquency in collections. An indication of this problem is that only 51.8 per cent of the 1960 tax was collected in the thirty-four municipalities in the department of Cundinamarca. In some of these municipalities less than one-third of the land taxed was collected. Moreover, it is to be expected that the percentage of revenue collected by the municipalities in the rest of the country would be much lower because of the relatively efficient tax administration in the department of Cundinamarca. A rough estimate of the delinquency problem may be obtained from the total assessed value of rural properties in Colombia in 1960 of approximately $14.4 billion. With this total assessment, the land tax should produce a minimum revenue of $58 million with a rate of four mills as compared to estimated collections of about $37.5 million.

At the present time, the Instituto Geográfico Agustín Codazzi (Geographic Institute) is undertaking a program of land reassessment for tax purposes with foreign technical assistance. Unfortunately, however, this is a long-term undertaking, and it will be several years before Colombia has realistic land assessments. No one can estimate with precision how long this project will take to complete, but the most optimistic guess would be three to five years.

At first glance, the need for general reassessment is not apparent. Table 6–5 shows the year of last general reassessment for all

TABLE 6–5

Years of General Reassessment for Colombian Municipalities

Year of Last Reassessment	Number of Municipalities[a]
1951	1
1952	3
1953	1
1954	1
1955	17
1956	65
1957	171
1958	17
1959	49
1960	58
1961	69
1962	98
1963	27

[a] The Departments of Cauca and Nariño are not included.
Source: Instituto Georgráfico Augstín Codazzi, Departamento de Catastro.

the municipalities except for those in the departments of Cauca and Nariño. This table shows that practically all municipalities have been reassessed during the last ten years, and over 50 per cent of them during the last six years. This is a better record of reassessment than is accomplished by many local governments in the United States. But the data are deceptive for two reasons. First, even when properties are reassessed, they are valued at less than their market price. Second, the continuous inflationary pressure quickly invalidates the assessments. No one really knows the average ratio of assessed to real value in Colombia, but it is no higher than 50 per cent, and it is probably as low as 15 to 20 per cent in some areas.

The procedures used by the Geographic Institute in reassessment are extremely meticulous, but they are probably more refined than is warranted under the circumstances. A survey of a municipality is first made to determine the intrinsic value of the land through a careful analysis of soil fertility as well as topographic and climatic factors. Based on an internationally accepted classification table, the intrinsic value then is expressed in points according to the effect that each factor has on the productivity of the land.[17] Second, the Institute selects the lands most inaccessible and distant from the main urban center of the municipality, and through an investigation of market sales an average value for these lands is determined. These are assigned the minimum market value. Similarly, another selection is made of several properties in the main urban center of high market values due to location and low intrinsic value. Again, as in the preceding case, the sale transactions in the area are investigated to establish an average that constitutes the maximum market value. Based on these minimum and maximum values, the Institute then establishes the market values for intermediate locations.

Once this process is completed, the market values of particular properties are determined. Since a particular property is located in an area which already has an assigned value, the value per hectare may then be determined by considering the degree of exploitation. The value per hectare multiplied by the area of the property gives the assessed value of the land. To this figure is then added the value of the permanent improvements to arrive at the official assessmeht of the property.

In summary, rural property contributes a meager amount of revenue due to relatively low tax rates, underassessment, and tax delinquency. As a result, the tax has little effect on costs or prices, including the price of agricultural land. The Geographic Institute is undertaking a reassessment program, but only about 50 per cent of the project has been accomplished, and several years will be required for its completion.

----

[17] The point system used by the Institute is:

		Per Cent
1. Soil fertility	150 points	37.50
2. Topographic factors	125 points	31.25
3. Climatic factors	75 points	18.75
4. Degree of exploitation	50 points	12.50
	400	100.00

The degree of exploitation is considered in the second stage of assessment, that is, in the final assessment of each property.

Income and Related Taxes

In general, crop production and cattle raising both are subject to the same income and complementary taxes (net worth and excess profits taxes) as any other economic activity. There are, however, certain special provisions by which costs and income are to be computed. For crop production, gross income is the sum of all revenue in money or in kind that is realized by the taxpayer during the taxable year minus the cost of producing that revenue. For tax purposes, the annual income is differentiated between taxpayers who keep registered accounting books on an accrual basis and those who maintain their accounts on a cash basis. In livestock operations, gross income is determined by subtracting the cost of the livestock sold from the total income obtained during the year. Calves that are born and sold during the same fiscal year, however, do not result in taxable income. The cost of the livestock sold is the purchase price, if acquired during the tax year, or the inventory value of the livestock as of December 31 of the previous tax year.

Despite the fact that most capital gains in Colombia arise from the sale of land, this form of income remained exempt until Law 81 was passed in 1960. Action was taken to tax capital gains at this time because of the degree to which investment in land was undertaken for speculative reasons. Speculation was acute especially in the urban areas, where the buying and selling of real estate had become one of the most profitable activities in Colombia.

Present legislation on capital gains taxation stipulates that the basis for calculating the capital gains on real estate acquired before December 31, 1960, is the cadastral assessment as of this date or, at the owner's option, his self-assessed value. But gains may be reduced by 10 per cent for each year of ownership. This means that gains from the sale of real estate that has been owned for a period of ten years or more are not taxed. Losses resulting from the sale of real estate are treated in the same manner: a deduction of 10 per cent is allowed for each year of ownership. There is a presumption that these provisions have had little effect on the agricultural sector, due to both relatively weak compliance and enforcement of the income tax and the fact that rural land is usually held for relatively long periods and thus becomes exempt through the 10 per cent reduction in gains per year of ownership.

The great majority of farmers and cattlemen in Colombia, with the possible exception of the large-scale operators, do not maintain an adequate record of their income and expenditures. This shortcoming results in ignorance on the part of the farmers concerning the profitability of their operations and makes it impossible for them to compare results with prior years or with other business activities. This faulty record-keeping also makes tax enforcement difficult. In turn, the difficulty of enforcing the income tax within the agricultural sector causes the industry's contribution to the total national revenue to be sharply disproportionate to its importance. Also, the ease with which the income tax may be evaded has led some agricultural and livestock activities to be undertaken primarily for the purpose of obtaining fictitious losses that can be deducted from taxable income derived from non-agricultural activities.

The agricultural sector is specifically affected by Decree 290 of November, 1957, which imposed a tax on underutilized agricultural land. The purpose of this tax was to foster the more intensive use of arable land resources. The tax is in the nature of a penalty levied on the value of land if certain obligations are not fulfilled.

Under these obligations, owners and tenants of agricultural land of over 50 hectares are required to utilize their land in the following way: (1) 25 per cent of Type I land and 15 per cent of Type II land must be utilized annually; (2) Type III land must be cleared annually at the rate of 10 hectares per annum on properties of 50 to 200 hectares, and at the rate of 10 per cent of the area annually for larger properties; and (3)

Type IV land must be kept in pasture or timberland or be reforested. The government may also increase these obligations by as much as 50 per cent where government irrigation or drainage works have raised the productive capacity of the land and increased its value. Pending the classification of lands, however, the obligations are reduced to 10 per cent of the average for Type I and Type II lands, and do not embrace lands in the department of Chocó.

Landowners failing to meet these obligations are subject to a capital tax of 2 per cent of the cadastral value of their property in 1958, 3 per cent in 1959, 4 per cent in 1960, 5 per cent in 1961, and 10 per cent in 1962 and subsequent years. The tax is reported and is payable simultaneously with the income and complementary taxes.

This tax on underutilized agricultural land, however, is a good example that it is one thing to enact a tax but an altogether different problem to enforce it. As of July, 1963, there is no record of any collections despite the fact that the tax was enacted in 1957. Apparently, the land has not been classified into types, and, until this has been done, no assessments are possible.

Another special levy on the agricultural industry is the livestock tax, enacted in May, 1959. Taxpayers subject to the livestock tax include all livestock breeders and raisers, whether individuals, corporations, or other juridical entities, whose livestock exceeds $15,000 in value at the close of any tax year from 1959 to 1970. The rate for the livestock tax is 1 per cent of the net value of stock owned at the close of the tax year. Instead of a cash payment, taxpayers may elect to subscribe and pay for shares of the Livestock Bank and Livestock Fund at par in an aggregate amount equal to the amount of the tax due.

A large number of tax exemptions and special incentives also have been made available to the agricultural industry:

1) Article 18 of Decree 290 of 1957 provides that investment in agricultural machinery is exempt from the net wealth tax

from January 1, 1958. In addition, investments in fences, cattle corrals, silos, wells, windmills, dams, and electrical plants may be amortized over a five-year period.

2) Investments in housing for laborers are totally deductible within the tax year if they conform to certain standards.

3) Starting January 1, 1958, and until December 31, 1968, there are a 50 per cent reduction of the net wealth tax and the income tax and a 100 per cent exemption from the excess profits tax for agricultural and livestock operations undertaken on certain classified lands, providing that their investment exceeds $100,000 excluding the value of the land. Taxpayers purchasing Type III lands for the purpose of converting them into Type I have the right to this exemption regardless of the amount of their investment.

4) Taxpayers establishing new rubber, cacao, olive, and other permanent oil crops are entitled to the following deductions from gross income: (1) $20.00 for each rubber tree planted in new plantations of not less than 5,000 trees and with a minimum area of 100 hectares; (2) $10.00 for each cacao and olive tree planted in new plantations of not less than 4,000 trees and with a minimum area of 10 hectares; and (3) $10.00 for each permanent oil palm planted in new plantations of not less than 14,000 palms and with a minimum area of 100 hectares. Fifty per cent of these deductions are permitted in the first year and 25 per cent in each of the second and third years.

5) Investments in cattle for breeding or raising purposes, regardless of age, receive a 50 per cent reduction from the income and net wealth taxes and a 100 per cent exemption from the excess profits tax until December 31, 1968.

6) Lands dedicated to the planting of trees for timber or to the establishment of permanent forests are exempt from the net wealth tax and all departmental and municipal taxes. This exemption is granted for a period of five years with the approval of the Ministry of Agriculture.

7) Article 21 of Decree 290 of 1958

provided for a five-year carry-over of losses applicable to the agricultural industry in general.

THE DIRECTIVES OF THE ALLIANCE AND PREVIOUS AGRICULTURAL TAX PROPOSALS

The Act of Bogotá (1960) and the Charter of Punta del Este (1961) both made reference to the importance of efficient land use and the need for using tax reform as a means of accomplishing this goal. Specifically, the Act of Bogotá called for measures and systems of taxation and fiscal policy that would ensure the equity of the tax burden and, at the same time, promote the better utilization of land by bringing into use privately owned, productive lands that are held idle. Similarly, the Charter of Punta del Este recommended the efficient and rational utilization of financial resources by means of structural reforms of the taxation system that would include adequate and equitable taxes on high incomes and real property as well as measures to improve their enforcement.

Long before these directives were given, however, Colombia had the benefit of studies by several national and international groups in the field of agriculture, land use, and taxation that made specific recommendations concerning agricultural taxation. An early study by Lauchlin Currie for the World Bank in 1950 [18] maintained that the most effective method of achieving the maximum utilization of land is a system of taxation that would penalize the underutilization of good land. It recommended, as a first step, the reassessment of the best farm lands of Colombia to reflect the steady increase in land values. No change in the basic tax rate was considered necessary on the grounds that the increase in valuation would in itself provide a very substantial increase in taxes. But the study recommended that the basic rate should

[18] Lauchlin Currie and Associates, *The Basis of a Development Plan for Colombia* (Baltimore: Johns Hopkins University Press, 1950).

be increased progressively as the net income from the land fell below a certain percentage return on the current market value of the land as determined by the Instituto Geográfico. It was thought that this proposal would provide a direct stimulus to more intensive farming, and would also operate to reduce inflated land values, thus making land available to low income farmers. Moreover, the World Bank study stated that such a measure would tend to increase employment opportunities, since it had been the general experience that the conversion of land from cattle grazing to intensive cultivation, even with the use of machinery, created an increase in demand for agricultural labor.

A second World Bank Mission in 1956 [19] also maintained that the land tax system could achieve better land use, apart from the fact that it would also provide revenues for government activities of benefit to agriculture. Four specific recommendations were made: (1) The "technical" system of land assessment, abandoned in 1954 in favor of self-assessment by owners, should be re-established on the grounds that it was superior in principle, although admittedly difficult to administer. It was believed that the administrative problems could be overcome by the employment of an adequate staff of trained assessors and a more realistic attitude toward the true value of the land being assessed. (2) The assessed value of the land should be based on the optimum potential use that the quality and location of the land warrant, not on its current use. (3) Specific improvements, such as irrigation and drainage, should be encouraged by tax exemption or reduction for a limited period of time. (4) Speculative holdings of land and the withholding from cultivation of good quality land should be resisted by the levy of an income tax based on a presumptive return equal to 3 to 5 per cent of the value of land, livestock, and fixed farm capital.

In a second study by Lauchlin Currie,[20] it was maintained that the majority of the proposals advanced to promote a better use of land were either too difficult to establish or too easy to evade. The study recommended that efforts should be concentrated on achieving an adequate valuation of land for tax purposes. In the particular geographic region investigated in this study, it was found that tax evasion was characteristic and that underassessment of the land was notorious.

A study mission directed by Rev. Louis Joseph Lebret [21] maintained that in a country where land holdings were underexploited, especially the larger ones, relatively low land valuations and tax revenues from the land affected the smaller farmers adversely, and, therefore, the land tax was like a penalty that held back the productive efforts of small farmers. This study recommended a reduction of the land tax on properties that were adequately exploited and an increase of the burden for lands that were held idle or were not fully utilized.

Of more current interest, Colombia has had the benefit of two missions that assessed its development plan. The first of these, by the World Bank,[22] included land reassessment among the measures necessary to increase agricultural production. Through the effect of higher tax liabilities, it was felt that better land use and the adoption of modern production practices would be achieved over the long run. A heavier tax burden, it was thought, would improve the market for land by increasing its supply and decreasing demand. Also, it was believed that higher land appraisals would influence tax liabilities in three ways: (1) by creating higher land tax obligations; (2) by increasing collections from the net wealth tax; and (3) by raising income tax payments through a more intensive use of the land. To facilitate the re-

[19] International Bank for Reconstruction and Development, *The Agricultural Development of Colombia* (Washington, May, 1956).

[20] Lauchlin Currie and Associates, *Programa del Desarrollo Económico del Valle, del Magdalena y Norte de Colombia* (Bogotá, 1960).

[21] Misión Económica y Humanismo, *Estudio sobre las Condiciones del Desarrollo en Colombia*, (Bogotá, 1958).

[22] International Bank for Reconstruction and Development, *An Appraisal of the Development Program of Colombia* (Washington, August, 1962).

assessment of the land, the mission recommended that the Geographic Institute should be financed and staffed so as to enable completion of the undertaking by early 1964. If difficulty were encountered in obtaining staff and funds, it was proposed that resources should be diverted temporarily from the technical cadastral work now in progress. Based on detailed soil studies, this type of cadaster was considered to be a long-term effort, and it was felt that no great importance need be attached to a temporary interruption. In contrast, the fiscal cadaster, it was thought, was addressed to a more urgent problem.

The second assessment of Colombia's development plan, by the Panel of Nine of the Organization of American States,[23] also recommended new land assessments. This was viewed as the most efficient means of depressing the price of land to its real value.

The most recent study, prepared for the Comité Nacional Agrario,[24] advanced four recommendations for the reform of the land tax:

1) The valuation of lands should be an obligation of the owners, and the new valuations should be used by the government as the basis for levying both the land tax and the net wealth tax. The new assessments also should be used to determine the expropriation price of lands by the government.

2) The income tax liability on all agricultural enterprises should be terminated temporarily, and as a substitute there should be a 6 per cent presumptive income tax levied on the new valuations.

3) A five-year intensive cadastral survey should be initiated of all the municipalities for the purpose of determining the size of holdings, the exact boundaries and locations, and the market values of properties. Once these assessments are completed, they would be substituted for the valuations made by the owners.

4) Progressive rates should be used for the land tax, and when these rates are applied, the income tax based on presumptive income should be eliminated.

Some of the study missions concerned themselves with aspects of the revenue system other than reform of the land tax. The first World Bank study of 1950 recommended a capital gains tax with the level of rates indirectly related to the period over which the asset was held, thereby encouraging longer-term, as compared to speculative, investment. In addition, it was thought that the rates might be made to depend upon the extent to which the investment contributed to the country's economic development. Capital gains from unimproved land, for example, might be taxed at a relatively high rate, whereas gains from the sale of industrial plants could be taxed at a lower rate. All the studies mentioned above also considered the problem of tax evasion and concluded that it was one of the major obstacles preventing the development of an adequate agricultural tax system in Colombia.

PRINCIPAL CHARACTERISTICS AND PROBLEMS OF THE AGRICULTURAL INDUSTRY

From the foregoing material it is apparent that the agricultural industry is of strategic importance in Colombia but that it is beset by numerous and severe problems of production, marketing, and taxation. It is apparent, too, that tax reform is of vital importance for the rationalization and development of the agricultural sector in general. Before concluding with specific recommendations for tax reform, the principal characteristics and problems of the agricultural industry may be summarized briefly:

1) Colombia has a combination of factors favoring agricultural development. More than one-half of the population depends on agriculture for a livelihood, but the majority of farmers have a level of living close to subsistence.

[23] *Evaluation of the General Economic and Social Development Plan of Colombia* (Washington, July, 1962).
[24] Enrique Peñalosa, *Bases para una Reforma de la Tributación del Sector Agropecuario en Colombia* (Bogotá, May, 1963).

2) Despite Colombia's relatively large size, the additional area suitable for agricultural use is limited. It is estimated that the area of good land that could be brought into use at low cost is about one million hectares.

3) Of the 30 to 36 million hectares in agricultural use, only 3 to 3.5 million are in crops and the remainder is in artificial and natural pasture. Although about 90 per cent of the land is devoted to cattle-raising and only about 10 per cent to crops, the latter are more important to the economy in terms of their contribution to the gross internal product. This is demonstrative of a basic misallocation of resources.

4) Land distribution and tenure are characterized by the two divergent and undesirable systems of *latifundia* and *minifundia*. Land distribution data show that 3.6 per cent of the landowners occupy 64 per cent of the land, while 56 per cent of the landowners occupy 4.0 per cent of the land. The remainder of the land is occupied by tenants, sharecroppers, and squatters. As a result of this maldistribution of land, there is inefficiency and underutilization of the land held in very large units (*latifundia*) and subsistence farming on the many minuscule land holdings (*minifundia*).

5) The largest single landowner is the government, with 76 per cent of the national territory in the public domain. The government has undertaken colonization on public lands on several occasions, but without notable success.

6) Several pervasive production problems account for the relatively low agricultural productivity, such as the misuse of land, the low level of "know-how," high costs, single cropping, pests and diseases, and the inadequate use of fertilizers and improved seeds.

7) Agricultural marketing is inefficient, unsanitary, and costly. Prices undergo unduly high seasonal fluctuations, and small-scale farmers are victimized by middlemen.

8) Agricultural credit is generally insufficient, and inadequate amounts are available to small producers. The availability of credit to the agricultural industry is proportionally less than the industry's contribution to the gross internal product.

9) Crops account for about two-thirds of total farm output, and livestock for the remaining one-third. Coffee, alone, represents more than one-fourth of the value of farm production. Four agricultural products (coffee, bananas, cotton, and sugar) plus petroleum account for 90 to 95 per cent of Colombian exports. Coffee accounts for 70 to 75 per cent of exports. Agriculture is the single most important contributor to the gross internal product (about one-third), but this sector has the lowest per capita output.

10) The contribution of the agricultural industry to governmental revenues is greatly out of proportion to the industry's importance. One estimate is that only 6 to 7 per cent of total governmental revenue is derived from agriculture.

11) Several international and national study groups have reviewed agricultural taxation in Colombia. It is the general consensus that agriculture's contribution to government revenues is insufficient and that taxation has an important role to play in promoting a better tenure system and more efficient use of the land. A variety of methods have been proposed to achieve these goals, but none have been effective.

12) The present land tax system is characterized by relatively low rates, general underassessment, low revenue productivity, and undue collection delinquency. As a result, the land tax has a negligible impact on the price of agricultural land.

13) A technically well-oriented land reassessment program is being undertaken by the Geographic Institute, but only about 50 per cent of the country has been reassessed, and it will require several more years to complete the program with the resources presently available to the Institute.

14) The majority of farmers do not maintain adequate accounting records. This factor, accompanied by weak enforcement, results

in a high degree of income tax evasion. There is also a problem arising from the deduction of agricultural losses from other income. The effect of the capital gains provision enacted in 1960 is probably negligible in view of the reduction of gains by 10 per cent for each year that property is owned.

15) The tax on underutilized agricultural land enacted in 1957 has had no practical effect due to the failure to classify agricultural land into the necessary categories for application of the tax.

16) A large number of tax-exemption privileges has been made available to the agricultural industry. These incentives are undoubtedly in wide use, but data are not available to evaluate whether they have been successful in promoting significantly higher investments in agriculture.

RECOMMENDATIONS FOR TAX REFORM

An agricultural development program for Colombia should have as its principal objective the attainment of higher output levels. This is necessary to meet the increasing food requirements of an expanding population, to satisfy the needs of industry for raw materials, to contribute toward a resolution of the balance-of-payments problems by an expansion of exports, and to raise the level of living of the rural population. The objective of attaining greater output from the agriculture industry is possible only if measures are taken to bring new lands into productive use or if the present levels of productivity on already exploited lands are increased. In turn, this will require an agricultural development effort with broad ramifications, including the redistribution of land, the availability of credit, the provision of technical assistance, etc. Thus, tax reform measures have a dual role: (1) They should facilitate and encourage agrarian reform measures in general. (2) They should contribute toward the public revenues that are necessary to achieve agricultural development.

Taxation on the Basis of Presumptive Net Income

The application of a tax on the presumptive net income of rural land is recommended. Owners of rural land would be subject to the tax regardless of the type of agricultural production or degree of exploitation of the land. In the case of lands that have been leased, the tax would be levied on the tenant, and the owner would be taxed on rental receipts under the normal income tax rates.

The amount of the presumptive income should be determined by applying a rate of 10 per cent to the assessed value of the property. This amount would then be added to the taxpayer's net taxable income from other sources, if any, and the resulting total would be taxed according to the current income tax rate schedule. Normal personal exemptions would be allowed. Since the presumptive income would replace the current income tax liabilities on farm operations, income and costs would not have to be reported for tax purposes. Losses on non-farm operations would not be deductible from the presumptive income. The receipts from the tax would accrue to the national government.

Exemptions from the presumptive income tax should be provided under two circumstances: (1) for lands affected by natural catastrophies, such as earthquakes and floods; and (2) for lands affected by civil violence, provided that certification of this is made by the Division of National Taxes.

The reasons for proposing the presumptive income tax are based on considerations of revenue productivity, incentive effects, and administrative convenience. Reference already has been made to the scant contribution made by the agricultural sector to public revenues. In addition, a commonplace practice is to use losses in crop production and cattle-raising to reduce taxable income from other sources. Income tax evasion in crop production and especially cattle-raising is undoubtedly extremely high. This assertion, despite the absence of data to confirm it, is un-questionable, because it is known that the majority of farm operators do not maintain registered accounting books. And even if they did, in the case of agricultural and cattle operations, unlike in other businesses, it would be quite impossible for the tax admin-istration to control or verify items of income and expense. In view of these circumstances, it follows that the only feasible means of assuring an adequate contribution from all farm operators is a presumptive income tax that does not require the maintenance and verification of records.

It is recognized that there are certain shortcomings from an equity point of view in a presumptive income tax. However, it should also be obvious that any tax reform proposal, to be successful in the agricultural sector, must establish practicality as a high priority. This is evident from the many overly refined recommendations that have been proposed in the past that have either been discarded as impractical under Colom-bian conditions or have been adopted but have become inoperative. Moreover, the pre-sumptive tax has certain advantages in equity. The tax would exact a contribution from the many farmers who presently do not pay any income tax at all in spite of the receipt of taxable income. Also, the presumptive tax would eliminate the widespread practice of deducting fictitious agricultural losses to re-duce taxable income from other sources.

The presumptive tax would represent a fixed cost regardless of whether the land produces income. As such, it would act as an incentive to activate the land, for it would become expensive to keep useful land idle. At the same time, it would tend to reduce the inflated market value of land, and land speculation would become less attractive. Thus, the tax would serve as a means to improve the defective land tenure system and would help to achieve the goals of the agrarian reform program. While the presump-tive tax would penalize the underutilization of land, those willing and able to exploit land efficiently would be better off than under the present income tax system, as productivity above the presumptive rate of the tax would not be taxed. Consequently, farm produc-tivity and investment would be encouraged, thereby promoting the primary goal of agri-cultural development.

The presumptive income tax rate to be applied to the cadastral assessments of all rural lands to determine their presumptive net taxable income should be 10 per cent. This rate may appear high, but it should be remembered that actual assessments are no more than 50 per cent of true market value on the average, and possibly even less; so a presumptive rate of 10 per cent would be no more than 5 per cent of real value. As the Instituto Geográfico raises the ratio of assessed to market value of land, the presumptive rate could be decreased.

The revenue that may be expected from a 10 per cent presumptive income tax rate is shown in Table 6–6. The revenue calcula-tions in this table are based on the assump-tion that the personal exemptions available under the income tax would render tax-exempt all farmers with an average cadastral assessment below $21,900 (that is, all tax-payers with a presumptive income of less than $2,190). If the individual income tax rates are applied to income from properties with an average cadastral value of $21,900 or higher, the calculations in Table 6–6 show that total revenues of $26.6 million would result. If it is assumed, on the other hand, that the personal exemptions would exempt all taxpayers with an average cadastral value of below $63,800 (or with a presumptive income below $6,380), the total revenue would be $25.0 million. In addition, it may be assumed that a large proportion of the presumptive income from agriculture would be added to income from other sources and would be taxed at higher marginal tax rates than those used in Table 6–6. It is not pos-sible to calculate the effect of this influence, but if it is assumed that a multiplier of five is applicable, which seems to be a minimum considering the progressivity of the income tax schedule, the total amount of revenue

TABLE 6-6

Presumptive Income Tax Revenue Based on 10 Per Cent of Current Land Tax Assessments

(1) Size of Holdings (Hectares)	(2) Number of Properties	(3) Total Assessments (Thousands of Pesos)	(4) Average Assessment per Property	(5) Presumptive Income (Per Cent)	(6) Presumptive Taxable Income (Millions) (3) × (5)	(7) Presumptive Taxable Income per Property (4) × (5)	(8) Estimated Tax Rate[a]	(9) Average Tax per Property (7) × (8)	(10) Total Tax (Thousands of Pesos) (2) × (9)
Less than .5	292,679	$ 435,855	$ 1,500	10	$ 43.6	$ 150	—	—	—
.5 to 1	186,513	317,083	1,700	10	31.7	170	—	—	—
1 to 2	254,935	610,938	2,400	10	61.1	240	—	—	—
2 to 3	135,327	460,791	3,400	10	46.1	340	—	—	—
3 to 4	93,291	428,186	4,600	10	42.8	460	—	—	—
4 to 5	57,828	294,782	5,100	10	29.5	510	—	—	—
5 to 10	148,312	1,140,877	7,700	10	114.1	770	—	—	—
10 to 20	101,831	1,277,025	12,500	10	127.7	1,250	—	—	—
20 to 30	43,545	769,804	17,700	10	76.9	1,770	—	—	—
30 to 40	26,439	579,427	21,900	10	57.9	2,190	0.55	$ 12	$ 317
40 to 50	17,425	470,509	27,300	10	47.0	2,730	0.60	16	276
50 to 100	39,598	1,426,106	36,000	10	142.6	3,600	0.70	25	990
100 to 200	21,670	1,382,581	63,800	10	138.3	6,380	1.40	89	1,928
200 to 300	7,665	777,461	101,400	10	77.7	10,140	2.30	233	1,786
300 to 400	3,582	530,536	148,100	10	53.0	14,810	3.70	548	1,962
400 to 500	2,009	348,652	173,500	10	34.8	17,350	4.30	746	1,499
500 to 1,000	3,217	899,932	279,700	10	89.9	27,970	7.18	2,008	6,460
1,000 to 2,500	1,322	552,184	417,700	10	55.2	41,770	10.70	4,469	5,908
2,500 to 5,000	334	273,197	817,900	10	27.3	81,790	19.60	16,031	5,354
Over 5,000	68	15,891	233,700	10	1.6	23,370	6.00	1,402	95
					1,298.8				26,575

[a] Estimated from the individual income tax schedule.

Source: Computed from data presented by Enrique Peñalosa in *Bases de una Reforma Tributaria al Sector Agropecuario en Colombia* (Bogotá, May, 1963).

obtained would be about $125 million. This total also would be increased appreciably as the reassessment program raises the level of property assessments.

The Reassessment Program

It is hardly necessary to repeat that all rural properties should be adequately assessed if Colombia's agricultural sector is to contribute public revenues in proportion to its importance in the economy. Realistic land assessments are important for the property tax, but they become mandatory for a presumptive income tax. In addition, capital gains taxation and the net wealth tax depend on realistic assessments. Therefore, the Geographic Institute, which has the responsibility of assessing real property, should be given whatever resources that are necessary to complete the reassessment of all property in the shortest possible time.

The principal reason for the slow progress in assessing rural properties is insufficient financial resources. In its twenty years of existence, the total budget of the Geographic Institute has been about $40 million, but only a small fraction of this amount has been used for assessment purposes. Since 1959, the Institute has assessed about 50 per cent of the rural properties in the country.

Most of the international missions and study groups have recognized the importance of the Institute's cadastral responsibilities. Nevertheless, it has received little external financial assistance. The Institute appears, therefore, to be in a favorable position to apply for external funds to expedite the reassessment program. And certainly, such credit institutions as the Inter-American Development Bank, the Agency for International Development, and the World Bank should recognize the basic importance of realistic cadastral assessments in raising tax revenues and promoting agrarian reform and development.

The challenges involved in developing an adequate property tax system are great. Maps must be developed, valuations must be made,

property tax laws must be rewritten, administrative procedures must be developed, and a staff must be trained. In addition, the whole operation is politically sensitive, so that public support must be gained.

But the results would be worth the cost and effort. With a good property tax system, the need for national government subsidies to the municipalities would be eliminated. Property tax revenues could be as high as $1 billion instead of the paltry amount collected at the present time. In addition, revenues from the capital gains tax and collections from the net wealth tax would be enhanced. It would appear that expenditures made on property tax assessment would be returned a hundredfold.

The Tax Rate on Rural Land

It is clearly apparent that the current basic property tax rate of four mills, when associated with general underassessment, is inadequate. The revenue produced is meager, and the effect of the tax on the price of agricultural land is negligible. The tax does little to discourage *latifundia,* to encourage a better utilization of land, or to obtain an equitable contribution from the agricultural industry. Therefore, the tax should be made progressive, with the basic rate of four mills applying to that portion of assessments up to $10,000, a rate of six mills on that part of assessments from $10,001 to $100,-000, and a rate of eight mills on the part of assessments over $100,000.

A progressive rate structure for the real property tax would not be appropriate in an advanced industrial country, but it is entirely desirable in Colombia, where real property is the principal form of wealth, where it is concentrated in the hands of the few, and where it is used for speculative purposes. The progressive rates also should be applied to agricultural lands within the jurisdiction of regional development agencies on the grounds that the surtaxes on real property levied in these areas are in the nature of special assessments.

All of the revenues from the real property tax should be given to the municipalities. There is the temptation to earmark some of the revenue for the Geographic Institute to ensure that adequate funds will be available for reassessment purposes, but earmarking is undesirable in principle. Instead, the national government should realize that the work of the institute is of prime importance, and should provide the necessary revenue for its operations. It should be recognized that the work of the Institute not only will provide the foundation for an equitable and productive agricultural tax system, but that land-mapping and soil studies are also indispensable for agrarian reform and agricultural development.

Capital Gains Taxation

Fiscal reform in agriculture would be seriously inadequate without subjecting capital gains arising from the sale of land to income taxation. The chapters dealing with the income and complementary taxes point out that the present capital gains provisions are wholly inadequate both in terms of equity and the prevention of speculative investment.

SUMMARY OF RECOMMENDATIONS

1) A presumptive net income tax should be adopted for the agricultural industry, with presumptive income determined by applying a rate of 10 per cent to the assessed value of property. This amount would be added to the taxpayer's net taxable income from other sources, if any, and the resulting total would be taxed according to the current income tax rate schedule. Losses on non-farm operations should not be deductible from the presumptive income.

2) The reassessment project of the Geographic Institute should be completed in the shortest possible time. Additional funds should be obtained either through higher budgetary appropriations or from an external loan.

3) The tax rate on rural properties should be made progressive within the range of four to eight mills with all of the revenues being given to the municipalities.

4) The capital gains tax should be revised so that gains from the sale of real property are effectively taxed.

CHAPTER 7

Urban Real Property Taxation

GENERAL DESCRIPTION [1]

INCOME FROM REAL property has been subject to taxation under the income tax since the inception of the republic in 1821, but a unique tax on land and improvements was not enacted until 1859. At first the tax was a departmental source of revenue, and it was not until 1908 that it became principally a municipal tax (although still under the regulatory control of the departmental assemblies). Initially, the municipal tax rate was $2 per $1,000 of assessed valuation, but it was raised subsequently to $4 per $1,000. This is the current basic rate in all Colombian municipalities for general revenue purposes, but there are other rates that are earmarked for particular purposes, and special assessments are used in the larger cities. As will be shown in more detail later, the urban real property tax is principally a source of revenue for Colombian municipalities, but it represents a little less than 50 per cent of their tax revenues and only about 14 per cent of their over-all revenues.

Although the real property tax is principally a source of revenue for the municipalities, the departments of Boyacá and Cundinamarca still impose the tax for their own benefit to a minor degree. The national government also has authorized the depart-

ments to assess property for the purpose of highway construction. In addition, the national government levies assessments on real property for public improvements, and there is a surcharge levied for the support of the Agustín Codazzi Geographic Institute. Of particular importance from an assessment point of view is that the productivity of the national taxes on net wealth, estates, inheritances, and gifts, and capital gains under the income tax are dependent on the assessment level of the real property tax.

All levels of government are involved in the legislative and administrative processes. The national government establishes the basic rate structure, as well as limitations on rates, and within recent years has been instrumental in undertaking a program of general reassessment. The right to levy the tax is vested in the departments, but in most cases the departments merely determine the actual rate to be levied and assign the tax for assessment and collection to the municipalities. The departments, however, also retain a certain amount of regulatory control over the levy. The municipalities are not allowed to forgive delinquent taxes without departmental approval or to tax property subject to national or departmental taxes without authorization. An exception to these restrictions is the district of Bogotá, which is treated in the most part by the national government like a department, receiving its tax authority directly from Congress.

The real property tax is assessed on the

---

[1] The descriptive information on the urban real property tax is based on several sources but principally on a mimeographed study entitled "Taxation in Colombia," prepared by the Harvard Law School International Program in Taxation.

owner of record, but where property is of unknown ownership, it is assessed against the possessor. Unlike in the United States, the tax is not on the property itself, but is actually a personal rather than an *ad rem* tax. Thus, for assessment purposes it is necessary to determine ownership as well as boundaries and values, since the tax is not legally a charge on land and improvements but on the owners or possessors of the property. The determination of ownership, however, is facilitated by requirements for the registration of various types of contracts or acts that affect the ownership of land, such as gifts, sales, exchanges, and mortgages.

Exemptions

A number of exemptions from the real property tax have been authorized, and these result in a substantial loss of revenue. In 1960, the latest year for which information is available, there were 998,635 taxable and 97,769 exempt urban properties, or nearly 10 per cent of all parcels was exempt. The exemption problem is even more serious when related to the value of assessments. Exempt properties in 1960 were assessed at $3,578.4 million as compared to total urban property tax assessments of $21,171.9, or 16.9 per cent of total assessments was exempt.[2] Moreover, the average assessment per exempt property of $36,606 was nearly double the average assessment of $17,617 for taxable properties.

Exemptions may be classified into six categories:

1) *Government*. All properties owned by the national, departmental, and municipal governments are exempt from the real property tax. This exemption is also extended to most autonomous and semi-autonomous governmental agencies and to foreign embassies.

2) *Universities and Cultural Institutions.* Numerous educational and cultural institutions have been granted exemptions, such as

the Colegio de San Bartolomé Foundation and all public and private universities.

3) *Churches*. Exemption of church property is extended only to the Roman Catholic Church and is limited to property used for religious purposes. In practice, this means that the exemption applies to churches, seminaries, schools, and to the residences of the religious.

4) *Charitable Organizations*. Several charitable organizations are granted partial or total exemption from real property taxes. Examples are the International Red Cross, the Saint Vincent de Paul Society, and the Secretaría de Asistencia Social y Protección Infantil.

5) *Housing and Homesteads*. Several exemptions are provided to encourage low cost housing or to subsidize low income groups: (1) There is a ten-year exemption of the first $5,000 of the assessed value of houses or apartments constructed for workers or employees if the buildings are worth less than $10,000. If the buildings are assessed at less than $5,000, the exemption is extended to the municipal charges for street cleaning and lighting and to all other municipal taxes on real property. Since these provisions were enacted in 1936 and 1938, inflation has eroded away much of their effect. For example, the exemption of $5,000 is only equivalent to U.S. $500 in 1963. (2) Exemptions are granted to all housing financed by the Caja de Vivienda Militar and the Instituto de Crédito Territorial. (3) The municipalities may exempt houses up to $5,000 in value from real property taxes when they are inhabited by their owners and when they constitute the sole wealth of the owners. In the case of Bogotá, the limit for this exemption is $10,000.

6) *Industry*. Exemptions or limitations in the application of the real property tax are used as incentives in the following cases: (1) Mining activities that qualify for a five-year exemption from the net wealth tax may also petition for exemption from real property taxes. The taxation of mining properties is also limited by provisions that prevent the application of more than a single annual real

---

[2] Departamento Administrativo Nacional de Estadística, *Anuario General de Estadística, 1960* (Colombia, 1960), p. 623.

property tax; exempt the mine, subsoil, or precious metals; and exempt property devoted to a public use (schools, roads, etc.) or capital invested in prospecting and mining. Taxes on mining property are also given a 10 per cent annual deduction from the assessment for depletion purposes. (2) An exemption is granted for ten years dating from December 30, 1958, for real property used in the printing of literary, scientific, and educational works. (3) Exemptions are granted to enterprises engaged in maritime navigation and to firms engaged in the production of chemical or pharmaceutical products.

Tax Rates and Bases

The basic rate for the real property tax imposed by municipalities is $4 per $1,000 of assessed valuation. The proceeds from this tax may be used unconditionally. In addition, two surcharges are levied. One is 10 per cent, which is earmarked for the support of the Agustín Codazzi Geographic Institute. The other is also 10 per cent but is restricted to capitals of departments and municipalities with annual budgets in excess of $1,000,000. The rate of this second surcharge is left to the discretion of the municipalities, but the proceeds of the tax must be devoted to parks and the planting of trees. Municipalities are also authorized to impose taxes for street-lighting up to a maximum of $1 per $1,000 and for street-cleaning up to a maximum of $2 per $1,000. Finally, special assessments may be levied on particular properties assumed to be benefited by municipal improvements.

Certain municipalities have been authorized higher maximum rate ceilings. Bogotá and other municipalities with annual budgets of over $300,000 and cities that are departmental capitals may impose real property taxes up to $8 per $1,000 on vacant lots, while for Bogotá this limitation is $10 per $1,000. These ceilings include all the other real property tax rates except special assessments.

Special assessments are authorized in the district of Bogotá, the capitals of the departments, and other cities of over 25,000 population on properties that have benefited from a wide variety of public works, such as drainage, streets, markets, parks, plazas, sewers, and other public improvements. For municipalities with annual budgets of less than $2,000,000 special assessments must be approved by the governor of each department. Municipalities have considerable latitude in levying special assessments, for they do not have to be confined to a recovery of the cost of the improvement but may be levied on the basis of the degree to which the value of properties has been enhanced. In actual practice, the total assessed for particular improvements is the actual or budgeted cost plus 20 per cent.

For purposes of applying the special assessments, benefited properties are divided into zones based on distance from the public improvement, and each zone is assigned a coefficient of presumed economic enhancement. The municipal governments have full authority to apportion special assessments among property owners and to authorize the expenditure of funds, but the property owners may appoint an architect or engineer to represent them in both assessment and expenditure activities, the fee for which is paid from the assessment funds. Taxpayers with a net taxable income of less than $50,000 according to the latest income tax assessment are given from six to sixty months to pay the special assessments. The longer period is allowed if the assessment is more than 90 per cent of the taxpayer's net taxable income. Taxpayers with a net taxable income above $50,000 are given six to twenty months to pay the assessment, with the longer period permitted if the assessment exceeds 100 per cent of the taxpayer's income.

In addition to the 10 per cent national surcharge for the support of the Geographic Institute noted earlier, other levies are imposed for the benefit of various national agencies. One is for the National Irrigation and Drainage Fund, the purpose of the tax being to pay for public improvements extending beyond the boundaries of a single municipality. Also reaching beyond municipal limits is a provision for the financing of access roads constructed by private persons. If two-thirds of the owners representing one-half of the benefited properties approve of the construction of these roads, all landowners must contribute to their construction.

Only two departments levy real property taxes, and the amount collected from them is minor. The department of Cundinamarca, however, has been given special authorization to impose a tax on real property to cover the cost of highway construction, which is to be apportioned among property owners according to benefits received.

Of more importance than these national and departmental taxes are real property taxes established on a regional basis by the national government to support development agencies. There is a tax of $3 per $1,000 (on assessments over $100,000) to support the Cauca Valley Corporation (Corporación Autónoma Regional del Valle del Cauca or CVC). Depending on the location and value of the real property, the property owner receives CVC bonds in an amount varying from 25 to 100 per cent of the tax payment. The CVC also has administrative responsibility over assessments and exemptions of the property tax in the area, although collections are made by the municipalities in the region (together with their own property taxes) and part of the tax is given to the CVC.

Three other similar arrangements exist. There is a tax of $2 per $1,000 for the support of the Magdalena and Sinú Valleys Corporation (Corporación Autónoma Regional de los Valles del Magdalena y del Sinú) and for the support of the Bogotá Plains Corporation (Corporación Autónoma Regional de la Sabana de Bogotá y los Valles de Ubaté y Chiquinquirá). There is also a tax of $2 per $1,000 earmarked for the Cauca Electric Plants, Inc. (*Centrales Eléctricas del Cauca, S.A.*), the proceeds of which are turned over by the municipalities to the firm in exchange for common stock.

Of most recent origin, and still not implemented in any municipality, is a provision of the Income Tax Law of 1960 that authorizes the district of Bogotá, the capitals of the departments, and all municipalities with a population of over 100,000 to impose a property tax of up to 2 per cent on the assessed value of developed urban land and up to 4 per cent on undeveloped land. These tax rates are in the nature of ceilings and are inclusive of all other taxes. The new tax authorization applies only to the land and not to improvements, and it may be levied only on properties in excess of 1,000 square meters per taxpayer and on land used for residential purposes. Collections from this additional tax authorization are to be earmarked for the improvement of such services as electricity, telephone services, sewers, and other public works.

A principal purpose of this law was to promote the utilization of vacant or under-utilized properties, especially those that are held off the market for speculative reasons. It was thought that the tax would increase the supply of land, reduce land values, and encourage residential housing. In keeping with these objectives, the original proposal was for a graduated surcharge of from 30 to 200 per cent on that part of the net wealth tax imposed on real property appropriate for residential construction, but this proposal was changed to one authorizing a flat-rate levy on land with the actual taxing powers resting with the municipalities. A subsequent decree also authorized expropriation of lands vested with a public interest at their cadastral value. However, there have been no expropriations since the law was passed.

The normal exemptions are not applicable to this new tax authorization, but there are a number of other permitted exemptions. The tax does not apply: (1) if the landowner has requested permission to subdivide the property or to use it for residential construction; (2) to lands adjacent to industrial or certain other establishments; (3) to lands that are used for gardens or cultivation or are unsuitable for immediate urban development; and (4) to lands belonging to non-profit institutions or excluded from residential use by the national or departmental governments.

The Geographic Institute has been given certain responsibilities for implementing the new tax. Regional cadastral offices are required to reappraise all properties at current market values in zones designated for residential construction. Assessments are also required to be revised every two years.

Assessments, Appeals, and Collection

Formerly, municipal boards were responsible for assessments, but now most of the assessment responsibility for the urban real property tax is lodged with the Geographic Institute, an independent agency of the national government. Most of the departments have regional cadastral offices of the institute for the purpose of identifying ownership and assessing real property. The department of Antioquia and the district of Bogotá are exceptions, having their own cadastral offices that are not under the jurisdiction of the institute.

Assessments are to be made according to legislative mandate by classifying all land into zones, by determining averages for the lowest and highest valuations in each zone, and then by estimating the value of land per meter in each zone. For the assessment of buildings, a statutory formula is applied, which takes into consideration age, material, type of construction, quality, and the market value of fixtures, such as machinery and equipment. If this type of assessment is made, taking into account for each parcel its economic use or character, its fixtures and appurtenences, the valuation is designated a technical assessment. But there is also another type of assessment—a tax assessment—that is used only for tax purposes, and is intended only to approximate market value.

With respect to appeals, the taxpayer has one month, or fifteen days in Bogotá, from the date the appraisal is made public to request a reconsideration. After reconsidera-

tion, the decision may be appealed to the regional cadastral office within fifteen days, or within ten days in Bogotá. Appeals with respect to property valued at $100,000 or less are handled at the level of the regional cadastral office, while appeals involving valuations exceeding this amount are handled by a three-man committee composed of a representative from the Geographic Institute, the head of the regional cadastral office, and the president of the municipal cadastral board. When these appeal procedures are exhausted, taxpayers also have recourse to the administrative courts.

The municipal authorities have full responsibility for collection and enforcement of the real property tax. Payment of the tax is due within one month of the assessment notice. If the tax is not paid when due, the property may be attached and sold at public auction.

The District of Bogotá

Special mention should be made of the real property tax in the district of Bogotá, because the area is so important economically and, also, because Bogotá is a unique case, enjoying more autonomy than other municipalities. Bogotá may only levy taxes authorized by the national government, but unlike other municipalities, the city is not circumscribed by departmental restrictions.

Besides the exemptions listed previously, there are certain additional ones provided in Bogotá: (1) The Municipal Council may grant tax reductions in cases of poverty, property losses, or other hardship cases. (2) New or rebuilt apartment houses may be granted exemption from the payment of certain property taxes for a ten-year period following construction if they are for rental purposes and construction was completed between January 1, 1956, and December 31, 1961. (3) Cemeteries are exempt from the basic real property tax. (4) Real property assessed at less than $6,000 is exempt from the basic tax and the earmarked taxes for street cleaning and lighting. (5) New urban residences valued at less than $50,000 and constructed between September 1, 1955, and September 1, 1965, are taxed at $3.50 instead of $4.00 per $1,000. This reduced rate also extends to the land to the extent of an area twice as large as that upon which the building stands.

Table 7–1 shows that the rate structure in Bogotá consists of a basic rate of $2 per $1,000 and an additional tax of the same amount, that was originally earmarked for the police but is now used for general municipal purposes. Therefore, the basic rate is now really $4 per $1,000. Next in the table are two earmarked taxes, one for parks and trees and the other for the Geographic Institute. Two other taxes applying uniformly to all classes of property are for street cleaning and lighting ($3 per $1,000) and for the Bogotá Plains Corporation ($2 per $1,000).

For the remaining two taxes, a distinction is made for improved, unimproved, and non-urbanized property. Unimproved property is land without buildings or with buildings that are essentially uninhabitable. If this property is assessed at $1,500 or over, it bears a surcharge of $1, $2, or $3 per $1,000, depending on the zone in which it is located. This levy is in addition to all other taxes. Unimproved land within the district of Bogotá, but outside the urban limits, is exempt from the taxes for parks and trees, cadastral services, and street cleaning and

lighting for a period of ten years from September 1, 1955. The obvious purpose of this tax on unimproved property is to encourage owners to use the land more productively.

An additional tax burden is also levied on non-urbanized land, which is property within the city limits that has never been urbanized or subdivided. This type of land bears the same surcharge as unimproved property of $1, $2, or $3 per $1,000 but, in addition, bears a basic tax of $20 per $1,000 instead of $4 per $1,000 and also a levy of $5 per $1,000 for the Municipal Development Fund instead of $.50 per $1,000 as in the case of improved and unimproved property.

In summary, Table 7–1 indicates that the total tax burdens on the three classifications of property in the district of Bogotá are $10.40 per $1,000 for improved property, $11.40 to $13.40 for unimproved property, and $35.00 to $37.00 for non-urbanized property.

In addition to these tax rates on real property, there are special assessments. These are very substantial in Bogotá. In 1959 total collections from special assessments in the district of Bogotá were $39,184,985 as compared to total real property tax collections of $38,764,558.[3] When these two sources of

[3] Departamento Administrativo Nacional de Estadística, *Estadísticas Fiscales 1957–1958–1959* (Colombia, 1962), p. 304.

TABLE 7–1
Real Property Taxes Levied in the District of Bogotá

(Pesos Per Thousand)

	Improved Property	Unimproved Property	Non-urbanized Property
Basic property tax	$ 2.00	$ 2.00	$20.00
Surtax originally for police	2.00	2.00	
Parks and trees	.45	.45	2.00
National cadastral tax	.45	.45	2.00
Street cleaning and lighting	3.00	3.00	3.00
Municipal Development Fund	.50	.50	5.00
Bogotá Plains Corporation	2.00	2.00	2.00
Surcharge for unimproved property	—	1.00–3.00	1.00–3.00
TOTALS	$10.40	$11.40–$13.40	$35.00–$37.00

revenue are related to total cadastral valuations in Bogotá of $5,571,439,000 [4] in 1959, the result is a total tax burden of $13.99 per $1,000, the components of which are $7.03 per $1,000 for special assessments and $6.96 per $1,000 for real property taxes.

As indicated previously, the district of Bogotá is authorized under the 1960 income tax law to levy additional taxes for certain municipal improvements. As of August, 1963, this tax authority had not been utilized. These additional taxes established a ceiling of 4 per cent on non-urbanized properties within the urban limits of the municipality and 2 per cent on urbanized properties. These ceilings on the tax rates are exclusive of taxes for the Municipal Development Fund, the Bogotá Plains Corporation, and special assessments.

REVENUE PRODUCTIVITY

Total revenues received by the departmental and national governments from the real property tax are minor in amount. Collection statistics show that only two departments in 1960 received revenue from this source. The amounts were $3,444 in the department of Cundinamarca and $328,547 in the department of Boyacá. Although the national government levies a 10 per cent surtax of the basic property tax rate, this revenue is allocated entirely to the Geographic Insti-

[4] *Ibid.*, p. 309.

tute.[5] The amount of these revenues has increased from $3.1 million in 1950 to $12.2 million in 1962. As explained previously, there are a considerable number of regional, earmarked taxes, and other non-budgetary receipts that are allocated for special purposes, but collection data for these revenues are not available. Despite all of these ways in which the property tax is fragmented, however, the levy remains primarily a revenue source for the municipalities.

As a source of revenue for the municipalities, the tax on urban real property is surprisingly weak. Table 7–2 summarizes pertinent collection data for the years in which revenue statistics are available. From 1959 to 1961, total real property tax collections for all municipalities increased from $140.85 million to $157.62 million or by 11.9 per cent. During this period, also, property tax collections as a percentage of total municipal tax revenues increased from 42.8 to 49.2 per cent. Both of these indicators are signs of growing strength. However, there are also two indications of weakness. Table 7–2 shows that property tax collections as a percentage of total municipal revenues decreased from 18.6 per cent in 1959 to 14.0 per cent in 1961, and that property tax collections declined from .74 per cent of the national income in 1959 to .63 per cent in 1961.

[5] This technically is not an earmarked tax, as the receipts become budgetary revenues and are then transferred to the institute. In addition, the institute receives other sources of revenue.

TABLE 7–2
Municipal Income Tax Collections, 1959 to 1961[a]

| | Real Property Tax Collections (Millions) | Special Assessments (Millions) | Percentage of Property Tax Collections to: | | |
			Total Municipal Revenues	Total Municipal Tax Revenues	National Income
1959	140.85	75.71	18.6	42.8	.74
1960	139.27	58.66	16.3	44.7	.64
1961	157.62[b]	38.95[b]	14.0[b]	49.2	.63

[a] Comparable data for previous years and for 1962 are not available.
[b] Provisional.

Source: Departamento Administrativo Nacional de Estadística.

Two conclusions appear warranted from these data: (1) With a broad and lucrative base, the property tax should produce more than 14.0 per cent of municipal revenues. (2) Revenues should at least maintain a constant relationship with the national income.

Table 7–2 also provides data on special assessments. It is difficult to decide in Colombia whether these revenues should be construed to be a burden on real property in the same sense as the real property tax. Since they confer special benefits to particular property owners, special assessments are in the nature of charges made for particular public services. On the other hand, many of the special assessments levied in Colombia are very general in nature and cover expenditures that benefit most property owners. They are tantamount to being earmarked property taxes. Table 7–2 shows that revenues derived from special assessments decreased from $75.71 million in 1959 to $38.95 million in 1961. Thus, even if the special assessments are considered to be a burden on real property similar to a tax, since they have decreased sharply, the foregoing remarks with respect to the developing weakness of the property tax are even more valid.

Table 7–3 indicates, however, that care must be taken with respect to generalizations on the real property tax as a source of revenues for Colombian municipalities. Real property taxes represented as much as one-third of total municipal revenues in some departments in 1959, while in one department they accounted for only 8.9 per cent of municipal revenues, and in another 12.7 per cent. In Bogotá, the real property tax in 1959 represented 15.0 per cent of total municipal revenues. The variation in the use of special assessments is even more extreme, because they are used only in the larger cities. In most departments, special assessments are much less important than the property tax, but in Bogotá in 1959 they were approximately of equal importance.

Table 7–4 provides information on the growth in the number of parcels and the total value of assessments, with the relation-

TABLE 7–3
Taxes on Municipal Real Property
by Departments, 1959

	Percentage of Total Municipal Revenue Derived from:	
	Real Property Taxes	Special Assessments
Antioquia	12.7	11.4
Atlántico	26.9	8.9
Bolívar	16.6	.5
Boyacá	34.3	.7
Caldas	18.9	4.3
Cauca	24.1	.9
Córdoba	34.3	.6
Bogotá, D.E.	15.0	15.2
Cundinamarca	35.6	3.5
Chocó	9.9	—
Huila	19.4	.9
Magdalena	27.1	5.0
Nariño	n.a.	n.a.
Norte de Santander	17.7	6.4
Santander	30.7	9.1
Tolima	23.0	2.6
Valle del Cauca	24.5	7.3

Source: Departamento Administrativo Nacional de Estadística.

ship between taxable and exempt properties shown for each of these. Considering, first, the growth in the number of parcels, the table shows that there has been an increase from 970,682 in 1957 to 1,096,404 in 1960 or an average annual increase of about 4 per cent or about 40,000 parcels. To assess only these new properties is a demanding undertaking let alone the need for reassessment of older parcels.

Table 7–4 also shows that the total assessed value for urban real property has increased from $14,714.5 million in 1957 to $21,171.9 million in 1960. This is a substantial increase of 43.9 per cent, but it is not so impressive when it is related to the growth in the national income or when it is deflated by a price index. Expressed as a percentage of the national income, total assessments decreased from 99.4 per cent in 1957 to 97.0 per cent in 1960. When deflated by means of the price index used in the national accounts (1958=100), total assessments increased from $16,683.1 million in 1957 to $18,458.5 million in 1960, an increase of only 6.42 per cent. This increase

TABLE 7–4
Number of Parcels and Total Assessments for Urban Property, 1957 to 1959

	Taxable Property		Exempt Property		Total Property	
	Number of Parcels	Assessments (Millions)	Number of Parcels	Assessments (Millions)	Number of Parcels	Assessments (Millions)
1957	874,115	$11,776.8	96,567	$ 2,937.7	970,682	$14,714.5
Percentage of totals	(90.05)	(80.03)	(9.95)	(19.97)	(100.00)	(100.00)
1958	931,914	13,409.2	107,620	3,109.2	1,039,534	16,518.4
Percentage of totals	(89.65)	(81.18)	(10.35)	(18.82)	(100.00)	(100.00)
1959	956,649	15,197.0	102,762	3,454.9	1,059,411	18,651.9
Percentage of totals	(90.30)	(81.48)	(9.70)	(18.52)	(100.00)	(100.00)
1960	998,635	17,593.5	97,769	3,578.4	1,096,404	21,171.9
Percentage of totals	(91.08)	(83.10)	(8.92)	(16.90)	(100.00)	(100.00)

Source: Departamento Administrativo Nacional de Estadística.

over a three-year period probably is less than the real appreciation in property values.

Finally, Table 7–4 provides information on taxable and exempt property. Exempt parcels as a percentage of total parcels have declined from 9.95 per cent in 1957 to 8.92 per cent in 1960. There has also been a decline in the percentage of total assessments that is exempt, from 19.97 per cent in 1957 to 16.90 per cent in 1960. However, one can hardly view with unconcern the loss of 16.90 per cent of a total tax base.

THE IMPORTANCE OF URBAN REAL PROPERTY TAXATION

The tax on urban real property should be one of the most important sources of government revenue in Colombia, yet it is relegated to a rather minor role. Consider some of the relative magnitudes of particular tax revenues. In 1962 assessments for the income and complementary taxes were $1,065 million, and taxes on foreign commerce were $589 million, while the urban real property tax resulted in only $159 million in revenue for the municipalities in 1961. In fact, the urban real property tax does not produce much more revenue than the $125 million realized from national stamp taxes in 1962.

There are a multitude of reasons that may be advanced for strengthening the tax on urban real property:

1) At least insofar as the tax is borne by land, in general it is probably not shifted.[6] This resistance to shifting is of some value considering the likelihood that most other taxes that can be employed in a revenue system, especially at the local level, tend to be shifted to a greater degree.

2) Despite the large land mass of Colombia, urban land is relatively scarce and high in price. For example, it is not uncommon for a residential lot to cost one-half of the value of the building. There are several reasons for this, but one is that the property tax burden is so low that it does not depress prices through the process of capitalization. On the other hand, a higher tax burden would tend to decrease prices and make land more available for low income housing.

3) It is said in Bogotá that the best and easiest way to become rich is to invest in a large tract of land that will be valuable eventually for subdivision purposes. To the degree that this practice exists, it creates an artificial scarcity of land. And to the degree that the real property tax is increased, it would tend to discourage this practice.

4) Investment (or property speculation) in land is a principal hedge against inflation. This is an essentially unproductive use of

[6] The supply of urban land, of course, is not fixed in an absolute sense. Empirical research would be necessary to determine the degree to which the supply of urban land is sensitive to price increases, but casual observation in Bogotá and other Colombian cities suggests that the supply is relatively inelastic.

savings, and higher tax burdens on land would tend to channel savings to more productive uses.

5) There is no better tax for the use of local governments than the real property tax. It is easier to administer than other direct taxes, and it has (or should have) a broad productive base. The tax should be particularly productive in Colombia because real property is the principal form of wealth. Moreover, there is a direct and close relationship between tax payments and benefits received.

6) The tax comes close to being proportionate in its incidence, which is a virtue considering that most other taxes that could be used at the local governmental level are regressive.

7) A further exploitation of the urban real property tax would remove the necessity for transfer payments to the municipalities by both the national and departmental governments, which in turn would help to resolve the fiscal problems at the latter two levels of government.

8) The real property tax is important as a base for other tax assessments, especially the net wealth tax, capital gains under the income tax, and death and gift taxes.

ANALYSIS OF PROBLEMS

The lack of revenue productivity of the urban real property tax stems from several causes. It is a result of failures and weaknesses in exemption policy, assessment practices, the rate structure, collections, and the fractioning of the base among different levels of government.

Exemptions

Exemptions may be divided into two categories, conventional and special. By conventional is meant those exemptions that are granted to governments, churches, and charitable and non-profit institutions. Like most governments, Colombia has been too liberal in exempting non-profit institutions. The list

of these exempt institutions is so long, in fact, that it could not be repeated here for lack of space. What is wrong with exempting the Red Cross, or the Saint Vincent de Paul Society, or to take an extreme case, the Society of Morticians? One problem is that there is no logical stopping place in granting these exemptions. If labor unions are given exemptions, then the morticians demand equal treatment. If one extends exemptions to morticians, why not extend them to the boy scouts or to a country club? Second, an objection can be made to taxing charitable and non-profit institutions to support the government, but the payment of a property tax is a different matter. This is a payment, in general, for services, such as fire and police protection. If non-profit organizations are exempted from this payment, they are, in effect, being subsidized by local governments. On the other hand, if they are to be subsidized, it would be better in many cases if they were subsidized openly and directly by the national government. When the government entertains petitions for exemptions, it should bear in mind that 16.9 per cent of the property tax base was lost in this way in 1960.

Stronger objection may be taken to the special exemptions which are used in Colombia primarily for encouraging the development of housing and industry. Since property tax burdens are low relative to other tax burdens, it is unlikely that these exemptions influence investment decisions to any appreciable degree. Other factors are likely to be much more important and controlling in business decisions than a tax that represents probably less than one-half of 1 per cent of the real value of land and improvements. For this reason, tax incentives should be reserved to the income tax or customs duties, where the exemptions have a greater impact on business decisions.

Assessments

There is much that should be said about urban real property tax assessments in Colombia, but it is extremely difficult to obtain comprehensive and reliable evidence on assessment problems. It is taken for granted, although there is little evidence except casual observation, that there is general underassessment of real property in Colombia. The degree of underassessment also appears to vary widely. While the ratio of assessed to market value may be relatively high, for example, 50 to 75 per cent in the larger cities like Bogotá, Medellín, and Cali, in smaller municipalities the ratio may be only 10 to 20 per cent.

Underassessment is more than just a problem of revenue loss, for it also involves equity among taxpayers. When properties are underassessed, there is likely to be considerable dispersion around the average assessment ratio, which is another way of saying that assessments are likely to lack uniformity. In other words, if every property were assessed at 50 per cent of market value, there would be no cause for concern, but if property is assessed at 50 per cent, the underassessment tends to prevent this uniformity.

What has caused general underassessment in Colombia? Undoubtedly, part of the problem is attributable to a shortage of good assessment personnel. But this does not seem to be the principal problem. In Chapter 6 on The Taxation of Agriculture, it was shown that practically all municipalities have been reassessed during the last ten years, and over 50 per cent during the last six years. In Bogotá, the number of properties reassessed in 1961 was 21.6 per cent of the total number of parcels. This is a commendable record. It was also shown in Chapter 6 that the assessment procedures of the Geographic Institute were meticulous to the point of being too careful. Thus, it seems that the real villain may be inflation. What appears likely is that a typical municipality is completely reassessed only for the assessments to become invalidated by inflation within a few years.

The evidence in Bogotá corroborates this belief. The average tax payment per parcel increased from $139 in 1950 to $266 in 1960.

However, when the tax of $266 is corrected for the change in the purchasing power of the peso, the average tax payment per parcel in 1960 was only $128, less than it was in 1950.

In this case, what is needed in Colombia is to readjust the assessments every year for the effects of inflation. This could be done quite easily by determining the change in the prices of properties sold and by sampling the remaining properties. The Geographic Institute should have this responsibility of determining the degree to which property values in general have risen during the course of the year. If it were found, for example, that the value of real properties in Bogotá appreciated by 15 per cent in the course of a year, all assessments could be raised by 10 per cent, just to ensure that the process would not be too arbitrary.

This procedure would not eliminate the need for general reassessments, which should be undertaken every three to five years. In this respect, the recommendations in Chapter 6 are applicable equally to urban real property: the Geographic Institute should be given more resources so that it can expedite its reassessment program, and the institute should take a more pragmatic approach with respect to its procedures so that the work can be accelerated. It is fundamental that continued progress in property tax administration in Colombia depends on a continuation of assistance by the national government. More, and not less, centralization is desirable in property tax administration.

Rates

The present rate structure is so complicated, with earmarked taxes and variations in rates depending on population and the size of municipal budgets, that the first and most apparent need is for a simplification of the rate structure. For example, a particular part of the tax should not be earmarked for street cleaning or for the maintenance of parks. Rather, it should be the prerogative of the municipalities to allocate revenues according to their respective expenditure needs.

With respect to the level of rates, smaller municipalities are now permitted a rate ceiling of $7.40 per $1,000, while larger cities have a ceiling of $8.40 per $1,000. These are what might be called the "normal" ceilings. In addition, however, there is a considerable number of special surtaxes. In Bogotá there is a levy of $.50 per $1,000 ($5.00 per $1,000 on non-urbanized property) earmarked for the Municipal Development Fund. There are also regional surtaxes of $3 per $1,000 for the support of the Cauca Valley Corporation and $2.00 per $1,000 for the Magdalena and Sinú Valleys Corporation and the Bogotá Plains Corporation. Bogotá has been given the authority to levy special surtaxes of $1.00 to $3.00 per $1,000 on unimproved and non-urbanized land, and for the latter type of land, the basic tax rate is $20.00 per $1,000 instead of $4.00 per $1,000. Still not implemented in any municipality is the authority in the 1960 income tax law for larger municipalities to levy taxes on land up to a ceiling of 2 per cent on developed urban land and 4 per cent on undeveloped land. Finally, the larger municipalities can levy special assessments.

For all municipalities in Colombia, total urban collections from the real property tax were $139.27 million in 1960 from a total taxable base of $17,593.5 million. Therefore, the average effective rate of the tax was $7.9 per $1,000. However, if the average assessment ratio is 50 per cent, the average effective rate of tax is only about $4.00 per $1,000.

Although this average effective rate is too low, it cannot be concluded from the above information on the rate structure that the tax rates are excessively low in the larger cities or where there are regional development corporations. Rather, the fault seems to lie in a marked tendency to restrict increases in rates to the larger municipalities. Also, many of the municipalities are not taking full advantage of their taxing powers. When municipalities do not take advantage of their taxing authority, their grants from the national government should be reduced.

The special surtaxes on unimproved and non-urbanized properties applied in Bogotá are an excellent provision to discourage speculation and encourage the more effective use of land. This provision should be extended to other municipalities.

A conspicuous omission in the urban real property tax rate structure is that no attempt is made to penalize luxury residential housing. Since one of the principal forms of conspicuous consumption in Colombia by the wealthy is expensive housing, it is recommended that special surtaxes should apply to luxury residential housing with the following rates: on that part of assessments between $100,000 to $200,000, $5 per $1,000; on that part from $200,000 to $300,000, $10 per $1,000; and on that part over $300,000, $15 per $1,000. These surtaxes also should be applied to luxury-type apartments when the capitalized value of the rent per unit qualifies them for the surtax.

It must be admitted that there are good reasons for applying a proportionate rate to real property. In principle, progressivity should be applied to persons and not to property. When a progressive rate is applied to property, it ignores the fact that some of the holdings are encumbered by debt and that all persons do not own real property in proportion to their wealth or income. But there are even more valid reasons for applying a progressive rate to luxury residential property. In Colombia it has been shown previously that the over-all incidence of taxation is not sufficiently progressive. Since the income and complementary tax system does not have the impact that it should, the real property tax system and, in fact, every tax should assist in the development of a more progressive tax system. One may justify the tax also as a levy on a luxury consumption item. A progressive property tax will hardly prevent the wealthy from building ostentatious residences, but it would at least help to make the distribution of income more equal after taxes.

Collections

Nothing is more fundamental in taxation than the proposition that a tax should be collected after it has been assessed. To permit large numbers of taxpayers to become delinquent reduces government revenue, encourages other taxpayers to become delinquent, and creates inequities among taxpayers. In an inflationary environment, tax delinquency also means that the government is receiving less real revenue the longer that payments are delayed.

Despite this, the gleanings that may be obtained identify the collection of the urban real property tax as a serious problem. For example, real property tax collections in Bogotá in 1960 were $40.1 million. Relative to total taxable assessments of $7,525 million in that year, actual collections represented an average tax levy of $5.3 per $1,000. On the other hand, the minimum tax rate in Bogotá during 1960 was $8.4 per $1,000. The difference between these two rates is attributable to tax delinquency. On the average, only 71.3 per cent of the tax is collected when due in Bogotá. On December 31, 1961, the total property tax delinquency in Bogotá was $26.3 million, of which $13.6 million was attributable to 1961, $4.5 million to 1960, and $8.2 million to prior years. This means that there was a total delinquency at the end of 1961 of over 50 per cent of that year's collections. During the last eleven years, it is estimated that Bogotá has lost $54.3 million through tax delinquency, an amount equal to 23.8 per cent of actual collections. And since it may be assumed that Bogotá's administrative capabilities are relatively superior as compared to most of the other municipalities, the collection record is probably worse in the rest of Colombia.

What are the reasons for this delinquency? It results from a whole complex of problems, none easy to resolve. It stems from the employment of low-paid and badly trained employees, inefficient procedures, and probably more than anything else to a lack of militant enforcement action. At the same time, taxpayers can hardly be blamed for not paying their taxes when the penalties are relatively modest and the attachment of property infrequent. In Bogotá, the interest charge on delinquent taxes is only 9 per cent per annum. Only four properties have been sold at auction during the past four years, and in the same period there have only been 298 instances in which attachment proceedings have been initiated. Each of these collection problems should be resolved. There is an active organization and methods section in the national government, and this group could hardly find a better opportunity for their efforts than to improve the tax collections of the real property tax. Penalties for delinquency should be increased to at least 2 per cent of the delinquent taxes per month, since the interest earnings on a safe investment in Colombia are about 1 per cent per month. After taxes have been delinquent for six months, attachment proceedings should be initiated and the properties sold promptly.

Multigovernmental Use of the

Property Tax

At the present time, the real property tax is used to some degree by both the national and departmental governments. It is also used by regional development agencies and by certain national agencies for the financing of projects of benefit to more than one municipality. This fractioning of the tax base is undesirable, for it accounts, in part, for the reason that the tax is not a more important source of revenue for the municipalities. At the very least, the national government should abandon the 10 per cent surtax for the support of the Geographic Institute, and the two departments using the property tax should relinquish this field of taxation. The fact that so many other national taxes depend on a productive real property tax should be enough incentive for the national government to assume responsibility for its administrative improvement.

SUMMARY OF RECOMMENDATIONS

1) The national government and the departments should relinquish their use of the urban real property tax in favor of the municipalities.

2) The national government should increase its efforts with respect to improving property tax administration by making additional funds available to the Geographic Institute. But the institute, on the other hand, should lower its assessment standards in order to accelerate the reassessment program.

3) Property tax incentives to encourage housing and industry should be abandoned, and a restrictive attitude should be adopted in the granting of exemptions to educational, charitable, and non-profit institutions.

4) The following improvements should be introduced to the rate structure: (1) Rates should be simplified by consolidating the earmarked charges for parks, street lighting, and street cleaning into one rate and by removing the earmarking of revenues. (2) The smaller municipalities should be given more taxing authority. (3) The special surtaxes on improved and non-urbanized properties should be extended to all municipalities. (4) A special surtax with progressive rates should apply to luxury-type residential housing.

5) All assessments should be adjusted annually to compensate for changes in the value of real property due to inflation.

6) The collection problem should be resolved by: (1) the provision of technical assistance by the national government; (2) levying an interest charge of 2 per cent per month on delinquent accounts; and (3) selling properties promptly after taxes have been delinquent for six months.

CHAPTER 8

Revenues from Foreign Commerce

INTRODUCTION

REVENUES FROM FOREIGN commerce produce a large proportion of the receipts of the national government, amounting in 1961 to $695.2 million, or 31.61 per cent of the ordinary revenues of the national government.[1] In 1961 import duties accounted for 81.21 per cent of the total revenues from foreign commerce. The other receipts included consular fees and charges, navigation and shipping fees, profits on foreign exchange dealings with importers and exporters, stamp taxes, and export duties, although the latter have been abandoned since the beginning of 1962.

The tariff list is characterized by very high duties on so-called luxury items and high protective tariffs. In addition to tariffs, control over foreign trade is exercised by means of import and export prohibitions, quotas, advance licensing requirements, and various other foreign exchange and administrative regulations. These are motivated by the following explicit goals: to provide revenues, to protect and develop domestic industry, to conserve foreign exchange, and to promote domestic price stability. Conflict between these various goals necessarily results.

Due to high tariffs and import prohibitions,

there is an appreciable amount of smuggling. Estimates of the amount of contraband activity indicate that it is one of the country's more important "industries." Because of export quotas, mostly with respect to coffee, contraband exporting also occurs.

As a result of currency depreciation and prohibitions of certain heavily taxed imports from time to time, severe fluctuations in the relative importance of customs duties as a source of revenue have occurred over recent years. When revenues fall, drastic revisions in the tariff schedules are often enacted to restore the yield, but usually after a considerable time lag.

Protective tariffs, coupled with high domestic prices of some protected goods, create problems in distributing equitably the burden of development. The protective tariffs, while producing very little in the way of revenue, nevertheless impose a relatively high financial burden on consumers. The tariffs are so high, as a rule, that their incentive effect is dissipated. With foreign competition virtually eliminated, large profits can be made by restrictive practices and monopoly prices, which hardly can be considered a stimulus to production.

The prohibition of imports for the purpose of conserving foreign exchange (for example, in the case of automobiles) has provided windfalls for a few importers, including the diplomatic corps, without resolving the fundamental problem of balance-of-payments disequilibrium. Moreover, these prohibitions

[1] As of July, 1963, the official rate of exchange was Col.$9.00 to U.S.$1.00, while the free market rate was Col.$9.99 to U.S.$1.00. Unless otherwise indicated, all monetary values in this chapter refer to Colombian pesos. Although this research was undertaken in mid-1963, in several instances the most recent statistics available were for 1961.

make it even more difficult to achieve normalcy, since the developing shortages produce an overwhelming demand for the prohibited articles.

Total exemptions amounted to 21.96 per cent of total imports in 1961. The bulk of these exemptions was government or government-related imports. But in addition to the various government agencies, the autonomous government institutions, the departments and municipalities, and the diplomatic corps, an increasing number of exemptions is being granted as a development incentive to private enterprises.

Many agencies other than the Customs Division have responsibilities for administering various aspects of tariff policy. These include the Council on Tariff Policy (*Consejo de Política Aduanera*), the Import Control Agency (*Superintendencia Nacional de Importaciones*), the consulates abroad, and the Office of Exchange Registry (*Oficina de Registro de Cambios*). In addition, in the broader framework of foreign trade policy, there is the participation of the Central Bank, the Ministries of Agriculture and Development, and the Council on Economic Policy and Planning. The Colombian Ports Authority administers the taxes on navigation and shipping.

In brief summary, revenues from foreign commerce provide a significant part of the revenues of the national government. They have been subject to wide fluctuations over the years due to successive currency depreciations and other reasons. The administration of foreign trade policy, including customs, appears exceedingly complex. There are multiple duties on single items in the tariff list, and the import and export regulations include import licensing, import prohibitions, quotas, exemptions, and exchange regulations. There are many agencies, not counting legislative committees, which make and administer tariff and trade policies. There is a serious problem of contraband. And the economic effects of the tariff may not be what the legislature had intended. The protective tariffs appear to protect excessively, the administrative regulations produce results lacking in interpersonal equity, and the burden of tariff and international trade policies appears to be distributed regressively among the various income classes.

REVENUES FROM FOREIGN COMMERCE

The revenues from foreign commerce consist primarily of the duties on imports. However, some tariffs masquerade as consular fees and so-called development taxes. The taxes on imports proper produced the bulk of the revenues from foreign commerce in 1961. Of total receipts of $695.2 million, the listed tariffs, including cigarette duties, produced $564.6 million, or 81.21 per cent of total receipts. The consular fees, the development taxes, and the tonnage tax produced an additional 7.04 per cent. Import duties, however called, thus produced 88.25 per cent of the revenues from foreign commerce.

Export taxes, which have been abandoned since the beginning of 1962, accounted for only $3.49 million in 1961, or 0.50 per cent of total revenues from foreign commerce. The profits on foreign exchange reimbursements, however, an export tax in disguise, produced $68.7 million, or 9.89 per cent. Other receipts accounted for 1.36 per cent of total revenues from foreign commerce.

Table 8–1 shows the revenues from foreign commerce for the period from 1950 to 1961. The growth shown is largely deceptive because of inflation during the period and, also, because the 1950 data reflect the results of a very low effective rate. The latter problem is discussed below in the section on fluctuations in revenues from foreign commerce.

Table 8–2 shows the value of imports, taxes on imports, and total revenues from foreign commerce from 1950 to 1962, all expressed in 1958 prices. The implicit price ratios between national income reported in current and in 1958 prices were used to

FISCAL SURVEY OF COLOMBIA

TABLE 8–1

Revenues from Foreign Commerce, 1950 to 1961

(Thousands of Pesos)

	1950	1951	1952	1953	1954	1955
Import duties and surcharges	$ 97,557	$215,258	$195,750	$249,462	$335,084	$268,630
Tax on the importation of cigarettes	—	539	1,201	1,838	2,554	1,046
Tax to develop the production of basic materials	—	—	—	—	—	—
One per cent fee on consular invoices	—	—	—	—	—	—
Stamp tax on import registrations	—	—	—	—	—	123,278
Tonnage tax	2,435	2,803	2,821	4,081	4,959	4,583
Total taxes on imports	99,992	218,600	199,772	255,381	342,597	397,537
Tax on coffee exports	983	1,033	1,064	1,611	1,405	1,258
Tax to develop banana production	267	194	174	232	235	278
Other export taxes	27	277	13	2	1	42
Exports of hides	534	526	85	5	—	1
Total export taxes	1,811	2,030	1,336	1,850	1,641	1,579
Consular receipts	1,022	1,636	1,649	1,883	2,460	1,599
Foreign exchange reimbursements	—	—	—	—	—	—
Tax on certain foreign exchange transactions	—	—	—	—	—	—
Tax on drafts to foreign residents	1,367	747	1,292	1,362	616	619
Stamp tax on exchange transactions	36,560	5,116	27,402	40,135	42,592	13,883
Total miscellaneous taxes	38,949	7,499	30,343	43,380	45,668	16,101
Total taxes on foreign commerce	$140,752	$228,129	$231,451	$300,611	$389,906	$415,217

	1956	1957	1958	1959	1960	1961
Import duties and surcharges	$219,744	$184,132	$193,060	$361,390	$567,657	$562,833
Tax on the importation of cigarettes	1,597	—	2,050	1,434	1,533	1,782
Tax to develop the production of basic materials	—	—	—	—	17,160	22,109
One per cent fee on consular invoices	14,221	14,943	14,557	17,919	23,973	23,406
Stamp tax on import registrations	122,828	—	—	—	—	—
Tonnage tax	4,480	3,733	2,436	2,483	3,061	3,399
Total taxes on imports	362,870	202,808	212,103	383,226	613,384	613,529
Tax on coffee exports	1,028	1,049	1,678	2,550	1,872	2,159
Tax to develop banana production	263	—	—	—	—	1,327
Other export taxes	128	27	2	61	15	—
Exports of hides	—	—	—	—	—	—
Total export taxes	1,419	1,076	1,680	2,611	1,887	3,486
Consular receipts	1,374	1,553	1,243	4,594	3,358	3,341
Foreign exchange reimbursements	—	—	393,538	191,691	89,390	68,726
Tax on certain foreign exchange transactions	—	—	—	—	626	6,137
Tax on drafts to foreign residents	172	—	—	—	—	—
Stamp tax on exchange transactions	5,627	—	—	—	—	—
Total miscellaneous taxes	7,173	1,553	394,781	196,285	93,374	78,204
Total taxes on foreign commerce	$371,462	$205,437	$608,564	$582,122	$708,645	$695,219

Source: Subdivisión de Recaudación, División de Impuestos
Nacionales, Ministerio de Hacienda y Crédito Público.

TABLE 8–2

Value of Imports and Taxes on Foreign Commerce, 1950 to 1962

(Thousands)

	Imports in 1958 Prices[a]	Index (1951 = 100)	Imports in Current Prices (U.S. Dollars)	Index (1951 = 100)	Total Taxes on Imports[a] (Pesos)	Index (1951 = 100)	Total Revenues from Foreign Commerce[a] (Pesos)	Index (1951 = 100)
1950	$1,329,282	80.90	$364,673	87.03	$186,915	51.46	$263,108	69.41
1951	1,643,155	100.00	419,000	100.00	363,248	100.00	379,082	100.00
1952	1,699,249	103.41	415,363	99.13	326,907	90.00	378,746	99.91
1953	2,195,777	133.63	546,723	130.48	410,270	112.94	482,932	127.40
1954	2,515,981	153.12	671,779	160.33	513,245	141.29	584,118	154.09
1955	2,409,614	146.65	669,291	159.74	572,493	157.60	597,954	157.74
1956	2,171,858	132.18	657,193	156.85	479,678	132.05	491,036	129.53
1957	2,197,320	133.73	482,575	115.17	227,753	62.70	230,706	60.86
1958	2,543,543	154.80	399,932	95.45	212,103	58.39	608,564	160.54
1959	2,458,941	149.65	415,588	99.19	354,292	97.53	538,172	141.97
1960	2,872,980	174.85	518,585	123.77	515,243	141.84	595,262	157.03
1961	3,067,597	186.69	557,129	132.97	613,529	168.90	695,219	183.40
1962	2,928,857	178.20	536,866	128.13	n.a.	n.a.	n.a.	n.a.

[a] The implicit price index in reporting national income in current and 1958 prices was used as a deflator.

Sources: Anuario Comercio Exterior, 1961, and *Boletín Mensual de Estadística* (March, 1963).

adjust the data previously reported in Table 8–1. Indices were calculated utilizing 1951 as the base year.[2]

Revenues from foreign commerce increased 83.40 per cent from 1951 to 1961 in real terms, while imports increased 86.69 per cent. The actual dollar value of imports in current prices rose only 32.97 per cent. Since the prices of imported goods rose about 25 per cent during the period, it appears that the "physical volume" of imports remained about the same.[3]

Revenues from foreign commerce have failed to keep pace with the domestic purchasing power expended on imports. This means that the effective rate of the tax has declined. Table 8–3 shows that the rate has declined from 21.77 per cent in 1951 to 15.08 per cent in 1961.

Import Duties

The tariff list divides imports into three categories—a prohibited list, a list requiring

[2] Tariffs were adjusted markedly in 1951 and 1959. This accounts for the selection of 1951 as a base year.

[3] *New York Herald Tribune*, April 28, 1963, Section 5, page 3, quoting a United Nations source reporting that the price index for manufactured products rose about 25 per cent from 1950 to 1962.

an import license, and a so-called free or unrestricted list. The term "free" refers to the fact that the importation of the articles is unrestricted and does not require an import license, not that the item is free of duties.

On the prohibited list of imports may be found items from nearly every section of the tariff schedule. It includes most items produced in "adequate supply" in the country. It also includes so-called luxuries, which a previous law defined as "articles not used by a majority of the people and which can be restricted without detriment to the economy."[4] Some of the prohibited products are meat, milk products, most food products, smoking pipes, buttons, toys, animal raw materials (except those for medicinal or industrial use that are not produced within the country), soaps, hides, lumber, furniture, textiles, carpets, shoes, clothing, metal products (except machinery and spare parts), automobiles, and domestic appliances.

The unrestricted list includes such items as plants and seeds for medicinal purposes, raw materials for tanning and dyeing, vitamins and antibiotics, medical equipment, aviation

[4] Decree No. 331, February 16, 1955.

TABLE 8-3
Effective Rates of Import Duties

(Thousands of Pesos)

	Value of Imports	Duties Paid	Indicated Average Rate (Per Cent)	Duties Exempted	Duties Paid Plus Duties Exempted	Indicated Average Rate (Per Cent)	Indicated Rate on Non-exempt Imports
1948	$ 589,079	$ 57,868	9.82	$ 4,027	$ 61,895	10.51	n.a.
1949	515,921	39,981	7.75	3,108	43,089	8.35	n.a.
1950	711,112	97,156	13.66	10,754	107,910	15.17	n.a.
1951	988,840	215,258	21.77	28,160	243,418	24.62	n.a.
1952	1,038,407	195,749	18.85	36,669	232,418	22.38	22.65
1953	1,366,808	249,462	18.25	33,411	282,873	20.70	22.12
1954	1,679,448	335,084	19.95	39,668	374,752	22.31	23.12
1955	1,673,227	268,630	16.05	39,861	308,481	18.44	18.68
1956	1,642,982	219,744	13.37	65,051	284,795	17.33	16.22
1957	1,956,652	184,132	9.41	54,895	239,027	12.22	11.22
1958	2,543,543	192,713	7.58	86,707	279,420	10.99	9.22
1959	2,659,752	360,757	13.56	130,637	491,394	18.48	15.78
1960	3,420,214	567,657	16.60	234,018	801,675	23.44	19.95
1961	3,732,778	562,833	15.08	298,016	860,849	23.06	19.32
1962	3,658,327	n.a.	n.a.	n.a.	828,877[a]	22.66[a]	n.a.

a Provisional.

Sources: Anuario de Comercio Exterior, 1961, and Boletín Mensual de Estadística, December, 1962 and March, 1963.

fuel and parts, chemicals, photographic film, coloring materials, books, newsprint, safety glass, optical lenses, pipe for pipelines, sewing needles, automobile parts, and certain machinery.[5] Everything else requires an import license,[6] except the personal effects of travelers, or articles imported by persons or organizations privileged with exemptions.

There are, of course, exceptions even to the prohibited list.[7] Items on the prohibited list may be imported when scarcities occur in the domestic market, provided that they are important in the budget of low income families. This determination must be made by the Council on Economic Policy and Planning, and, following this determination, the board of the Import Control Agency directs their importation through official agencies. Donations to public agencies or foundations and charities are exempt from the prohibition. Bilateral trade agreements may provide for the importation of goods on the prohibited list "when domestic production is not sufficient to satisfy demand at fair prices."[8] Diplomatic missions, consular

officials, the Catholic Church, mining and petroleum companies operating in isolated areas, and other exempt persons and organizations may also import items on the prohibited list.

The tariff schedule includes both specific and *ad valorem* duties, and most items are subject to both types. As a rule, the specific duties are calculated on the basis of bulk weight, i.e., so much per gross kilogram. In a few instances, other liquid or dry measures are used, as in the case of beverages and cloth. The *ad valorem* duties are based on the c.i.f. value of merchandise, which is their f.o.b. value at the port of embarkation plus freight, insurance, and other transportation cost.

The average duty applicable to non-exempt imports amounted to 19.32 per cent in 1961. (See Table 8-3.) Since most items in the tariff list are subject to duties of 25 per cent or more, non-exempt imports are biased in favor of items subject to low duties. This cannot be attributed solely to exemptions or to the price effect of high duties, but rather more to the prohibitions and restrictions on certain imports. More will be said on this issue later. The exemptions also will be discussed sep-

5 Decree No. 3167, December 6, 1962.
6 Decree No. 3337, December 17, 1962.
7 Article 2, Law No. 1, January 16, 1959.
8 *Ibid.*, paragraph (d).

arately below. There are special tariffs applicable to countries in the Latin American Free Trade Area, but the volume of this trade has not achieved significant proportions. The special tariffs are also discussed separately below.

The Level of the Duties

There is a small list of free items in the general tariff schedule. Included among the items in this category are bulls for reproduction purposes, live plants and seeds for cultivation, crude oil, antibiotics, fertilizers, airplane tires, newsprint, books and periodicals, alloy steels, ships, art objects, and collector's items.

Duties of less than 25 per cent *ad valorem* are imposed on some animals, industrial raw materials not produced in the country and for which a protective policy has not been adopted, pharmaceuticals, rubber, safety glass, unfinished pearls and precious stones, cast iron, jeeps, buses, trucks, cocoa, most minerals, photographic film, hides, some sports equipment, and salt.

Duties of more than 25 per cent and of less than 50 per cent are imposed on intermediate goods and raw materials that require some processing in the country. Included among these are paperboard, raw silk, twisted silk (if not prepared for retail sale), sandpaper, plate glass, cylinder locks, machinery and electrical apparatus (except domestic appliances and machinery manufactured in the country), some office equipment, alarm clocks, records, and musical instruments.

Duties between 50 and 100 per cent are levied on many protected items and consumer goods, including meat and fish products, raw materials of animal or vegetable origin that may be substituted for those produced domestically, processed fibers and fabrics except cotton and wool, domestic appliances, radios and television receivers, buses for private use, bicycles, photographic instruments, golf equipment, and fountain pens.

Duties of 100 per cent or more are imposed on nearly all processed foods, alcoholic beverages, vinegar, tobacco products, cement, perfumes and cosmetics, soaps, leather goods, shoes, clothing, toys, furniture, and automobiles. This group includes either luxury goods or goods produced domestically.

The average duty assessed against imports in 1962 was 22.5 per cent, of which amount 6.8 per cent was assessed by specific duties and 15.7 by *ad valorem* duties. Exceptions in 1961 amounted to 34.6 per cent of total duties. If the same ratio applied in 1962, the average duty based on total imports would have been 14.7 per cent.

The highest average duties of the twenty-two sections in the tariff list, based upon actual imports, were 76.54 per cent applicable to oils and fats of vegetable or animal origin; 59.75 per cent applicable to food preparations including beverages; 62.03 per cent applicable to stone, clay, and glass products; 78.21 per cent applicable to arms and ammunition; and 44.49 and 41.89 per cent respectively applicable to merchandise and to products not included in any other category. The lowest duties applied to non-metallic minerals, including petroleum products, 14.17 per cent; chemicals and pharmaceuticals, 16.43 per cent; machinery and equipment including electrical apparatus, 15.98 per cent; and transport material and equipment, 15.45 per cent.[9]

Each of the above sections includes several chapters of the tariff schedule. Among the more important of the eighty-seven chapters, high rates are applied to beverages, including alcoholic beverages, 205.51 per cent; vegetable and fruit products, 114.43 per cent; tobacco, 59.75 per cent; lumber and wood products, 113.53 per cent; and stone products, 99.88 per cent. Low rates applied to fertilizer, free; cocoa, 6.65 per cent; petroleum products, 9.54 per cent; and machinery, 14.27 per cent.

Among specific products imported in sig-

[9] See Table 8–14 at the end of this chapter for additional detail.

nificant quantities, high rates may be noted for hydrogenated fats, 132.0 per cent; bottled wines, 190.4 per cent; electric irons, 68.5 per cent; domestic washers, 109.3 per cent; light bulbs, 69.8 per cent; electric wire, 64.8 per cent; private vehicles, 150 to 200 per cent; and motorcycles, 347.8 per cent. Low rates apply to agricultural tractors, equipment, and materials, free; automobile parts, 3.2 per cent; taxis, 4.4 per cent; jeeps, 5.6 per cent; airplanes and parts, free; large generators and transformers, 10 per cent; many kinds of industrial machinery, 10 per cent; basic metal shapes and sheet metal, 5 per cent; industrial chemicals, 20 per cent; medicines, either free, or if prepared for sale at retail, about 20 per cent; and newsprint, free.

Special Tariffs

The law provides that merchandise "originating from countries whose treaty with the Republic of Colombia is less favorable than for other states, or which endangers the vital interests of the nation, may be subjected to the maximum tariff, when it is so determined expressly and jointly by the Ministers of Foreign Relations and Finance." (*Arancel de Aduanas,* paragraph 7.) The maximum tariff is double that indicated in the tariff list with a minimum of 30 per cent *ad valorem.*

Ecuador has a special trade relationship with Colombia as a result of a 1945 treaty. Free trade between the two countries was established for a number of food products, vegetable and animal fibers, gas, and cement. Pharmaceuticals were added in 1959. Free trade is permitted in the border region between the two countries for all items destined for use and consumption in those areas. Through a 1938 treaty with Perú, a special tariff schedule also applies to the region bordering that country.

Colombia is a member of the Latin American Free Trade Association (*Asociación Latinoamericana de Libre Comercio*), formed by the Treaty of Montevideo of February 18,

1960. This agreement provided that the signatory countries would gradually eliminate the duties and restrictions on trade over a twelve-year period. Besides Colombia, the other members are Argentina, Brazil, Chile, Ecuador, México, Paraguay, Perú, and Uruguay.

By Decree No. 811 of March 30, 1962, and Decree No. 23 of January 8, 1963, duties were eliminated or reduced on a wide list of products originating within the Latin American Free Trade Association. These included livestock, fish, vegetables, chemical and pharmaceutical products, raw materials, minerals, and manufactured products. A longer list of free imports was extended to Paraguay. Advance licensing, however, remains a requirement for most of the products listed. Table 8–4 shows some of the products included with their former tariffs and the current tariffs applicable to the free trade zone.

In the first eleven months of 1962, imports from the free trade area in the special tariff list amounted to U.S. $8.55 million or 1.69 per cent of total imports during the same period of U.S. $507.41 million. Notable increases in imports have occurred from Argentina, Uruguay, and Ecuador. Imports on the special tariff list from Argentina during the first eleven months of 1962 amounted to U.S. $2.03 million compared with total imports from Argentina of only U.S. $0.25 million in 1960. Similarly, imports on the special list from Uruguay amounted to U.S. $2.01 million during the first eleven months of 1962 compared with total imports of only U.S. $0.14 million in 1960. Ecuador exported U.S. $3.07 million to Colombia of items on the special tariff list in the 1962 period compared to U.S. $2.37 million of total exports in 1960. Imports from all countries in the free trade area increased from U.S. $6.32 million in 1960 to U.S. $8.55 million in the first eleven months of 1962. (See Table 8–5.)

Authority was granted in 1959 to establish an Industrial and Commercial Free Zone in Barranquilla. All products may enter the

TABLE 8-4

Selected List of Products Showing Tariff Reductions to Countries in the Latin American
Free Trade Association, 1962

	Former Tariffs[a]	New Tariffs[a]
Horses (breeding)	20 per cent	Free
Heifers	20 per cent	Free
Queen bees	20 per cent	Free [c]
Fish (fresh water for breeding)	20 per cent	Free [c]
Fish (fresh water)	$3.00 + 50 per cent	$1.20 [c]
Fish (salt water)	$3.00 + 50 per cent	$1.00
Cheese	$3.00 +100 per cent	$3.00 + 50 per cent
Vegetables (except tomatoes and potatoes)	$2.00 + 50 per cent to $5.00 + 50 per cent	$3.50
Bananas	$2.00 + 50 per cent	$0.60
Brazil nuts	$3.00 + 50 per cent	$2.30 [c]
Raisins (not prepared for retail sale)	$3.00 + 50 per cent	$1.15 [c]
Tea	$10.00 + 50 per cent	$4.40 + 14 per cent
Wheat[b]	$0.10 + 20 per cent	$0.10 plus $0.10 development tax
Olive oil (liters)	$1.50 + 30 per cent	$1.20 + 10 per cent
Wines	$3.00 +100 per cent	$2.00 + 18 per cent
Iron ore	$0.05 + 5 per cent	5 per cent [c]
Other minerals	5 per cent	Free [c]
Morphine, codein, etc.	15 per cent	Free [c]
Synthetic rubber	10 per cent	Free [c]
Alpaca and llama hair	20 per cent	7 per cent [c]
Cotton (more than 29.4 mm.)	$0.35 + 20 per cent	13 per cent
Iron pipe and tubes	$0.40 + 25 per cent	$0.20 + 17 per cent
Radio and television tubes	25 per cent	16 per cent [c]
Binoculars	50 per cent	30 per cent
Taximeters	20 per cent	10 per cent [c]

[a] Specific duties are based on gross kilograms unless otherwise. indicated.
[b] May only be imported by the Instituto Nacional de Abastecimiento.

[c] Import license required.
Source: Decree No. 23, January 8, 1963.

TABLE 8-5

Imports from the Latin American Trade Area,
1959, 1960, and First Eleven Months of 1962
(Thousands of U.S. Dollars)

	Special Tariff List Items, First Eleven Months of 1962	All Items	
		1959	1960
México	$ 552	$1,467	$ 954
Argentina	2,034	274	252
Brazil	36	125	199
Chile	124	483	1,359
Ecuador	3,066	4,550	2,367
Perú	727	1,671	1,049
Uruguay	2,013	378	143
Total	$8,552	$8,948	$6,323

Sources: Auario de Comercio Exterior, 1960, and *Boletín Mensual de Estadística,* February 1963.

zone free of duties including consular fees. It is expected that the zone will be used for manufacturing as well as for transshipment. In the case of products manufactured in the zone consisting of both domestic and foreign materials and which are subsequently sold in Colombia, liabilities for duties will extend only to the extent that imported materials are incorporated in the products.

The islands of San Andrés and Providencia in the Caribbean are also free zones. Tourists returning from these islands are permitted to bring with them duty-free articles for personal or domestic use not exceeding $1,500 in value and 30 kilograms in weight.

Consular Fees

A consular invoice is required for each import into Colombia, and a 1 per cent consular fee is assessed based upon the f.o.b.

value of the merchandise.[10] While, in general, there can be no objection to a consular fee that more or less approximates the cost of the service rendered, a consular fee based upon the value of imports is simply an additional tariff. The fee bears no relation to the cost involved, for the expenses of operating the consulates are independent of the value of the merchandise being imported. Since consulates are designed to facilitate exports rather than imports, it would be more rational to assess consular fees on exports. Fees charged by consulates for visas, certifications of manifests, identifications of vessels bearing the Colombian flag, and similar services can be justified on the so-called benefit principle of taxation, which holds that those who receive the direct benefit of a government service ought to pay the costs of providing such service in the absence of any other overriding considerations.

The consular officials are not trained assessors, are not equipped for this work, and, in fact, do not value the merchandise that is subject to the fee. The assessment of the value of imported articles takes place when the merchandise is inspected at customs. This is the responsibility of the customs officials, and all *ad valorem* charges should be assessed by them. Since the fee charged for the consular invoice is simply an additional customs duty, it should be included in the *ad valorem* duties imposed by the tariff schedule. Doing so would avoid the duplication of tax collection officials and accounting. At present the consular fee is paid in advance of importation at the Central Bank.

The use of consular fees also distracts consular officials from their principal responsibility, which is to develop commercial opportunities for Colombian products. When the consular staff is engaged in bureaucratic "make-work," it is likely to neglect this very important objective. Maintaining bureaucrats abroad is also costly and wasteful of foreign exchange.

Finally, the need to validate import ship-

ments by referral to the consulates increases the cost of imports to Colombia and also increases the foreign exchange costs of the imports. Since the shipper is burdened with the additional expense of processing shipping bills through the consular offices, he must add this expense to the cost of the merchandise. On the other hand, the clerical work imposed on an importer in Colombia does not require any foreign exchange. Even if such costs are minor (and they are not minor relative to the value of small shipments), the fact that they involve foreign services is an additional reason for having the clerical work accomplished in Colombia. In summary, there appears to be no need to involve the consulates in the importation process, and there are several good reasons for removing them from the procedure.

Development Taxes

Several items in the tariff list are subject to special taxes that are earmarked for developing the domestic production of the items taxed. The products taxed are shown in Table 8–6. It will be noted that these so-called development taxes fall on products that are already protected by heavy tariffs. Many of the items are on the prohibited list, and nearly all the others require an import license.

The practice of funding taxes for particular purposes complicates the existing tax structure and also results in an arbitrary allocation of revenues to particular government expenditures. Expenditures necessarily are restricted to the revenues available, which may be more or less than their needs. Since these taxes are ultimately borne by the consumer, and there is no direct benefit to him from the expenditures, they also are financed arbitrarily. It would be an improvement from the standpoint of both equity and administration for these expenditures to be budgeted and financed out of general tax revenues. This would eliminate arbitrariness in the level of expenditures, simplify the tax structure, and distribute the tax burden more equitably.

---

[10] Decree No. 2,908 of 1960, paragraph 34.

TABLE 8–6
Imported Products Subject to Development Taxes

	Development Tax	Tariff[a]	Import Class[b]
Wheat	$0.10 per gross kilo	$0.10 + 20 per cent	P.
Oats	0.10 per gross kilo	0.30 + 40 per cent	I.L.R.
Wheat flour	0.10 per gross kilo	0.60 + 25 per cent	I.L.R.
Ground oats	0.10 per gross kilo	0.50 + 25 per cent	I.L.R.
Malt	0.05 per gross kilo	0.15 + 30 per cent	I.L.R.
Oil seeds	0.05 per gross kilo	0.10 + 20 per cent to 3.00 + 50 per cent	P. and I.L.R.
Cocoa	10 per cent	0.70 + 30 per cent	I.L.R.
Tobacco	5.00 per gross kilo	15.00 + 30 per cent	F.
Pipe tobacco	6.00 per gross kilo	15.00 + 50 per cent	P.
Cigars	10.00 per gross kilo	50.00 +100 per cent	P.
Cigarettes	.40 per package	20.00 + 50 per cent	I.L.R.
Other tobacco products	5.00 per gross kilo	20.00 +100 per cent	P.
Cotton	0.03 per gross kilo	0.35 + 20 per cent	F. and I.L.R.
Cotton thread	0.10 per gross kilo	6.00 + 40 per cent to 8.00 + 40 per cent	I.L.R.

[a] Specific taxes are based on gross kilograms.
Source: *Arancel de Aduanas, 1959*, pp. 296–97.

[b] P = prohibited; I.L.R. = import licenses required; and F = free of restrictions.

Other Import Taxes

In addition to the specific and *ad valorem* duties, consular fees, and the development taxes, each importation is subject to a U.S. $5.00 stamp tax on the consular invoice, a U.S. $5.00 stamp tax on the bill of lading, a one peso tax on each sheet of the import manifest, and a tonnage fee based on the gross weight of the shipment. Only so-called minor imports of U.S. $20.00 or less, the personal effects of travelers, and specifically exempted imports are free of these stamp taxes.

The stamp taxes are a nuisance. There is no reason for the offices to see the invoices, let alone tax them. All the import duties could and should be combined in a single levy and be collected by the Customs Division. These taxes only result in useless work, costly delays, and unnecessary handling of documents and complicate the collection of taxes. The bureaucracy required to administer and account for them is costly in terms of both domestic and foreign currency.

Foreign Exchange Transactions

A tax of 10 per cent payable in free market dollars is levied on exchange trans-actions made at the official rate.[11] Transactions made in the free money market are not subject to any tax or restrictions. This distinction is essentially quibbling, for the tax of 10 per cent on the remission of foreign exchange abroad applies only to transactions at the official rate, which is 10 per cent less than the free market rate.

The only transactions eligible for certificates of exchange, i.e., foreign exchange at the official rate, are payments for registered imports, repatriation of capital, interest, and profits under agreements approved after 1957, amortization and interest payments on private debts registered in 1957, payments of the government or its entities, expenses of students, payments on registered public debt, and 80 per cent of transportation and insurance costs of imported merchandise.[12] Registered imports, as well as remissions to students abroad, are exempt from the tax.[13] Remaining subject to the tax for all practical purposes are only the shipping costs of imports and private remittances abroad other than educational expenditures.

Reimbursable registered imports amounted to U.S. $444.55 million or 85.82 per cent

[11] Law 1 of January 16, 1959, Article 67.
[12] *Ibid.*, Article 39.
[13] *Ibid.*, Article 69.

of total imports in 1960.[14] At the current free market rate, these reimbursable imports are receiving a 10 per cent subsidy. Thus, during the first six months of 1963, the Central Bank was supporting the free market rate with one hand, while it encouraged the importation of goods with the other. Moreover, as long as the free rate exceeds the official rate, importers will be encouraged to maintain inventory levels as high as possible.

Advance Deposits

All imports, except as indicated below, require advance registration (*registro de importación*) in the Office of Exchange Registry and the payment of a so-called advance deposit (*depósito previo*) in the Central Bank. This deposit is not required in the case of: (1) foreign capital imported in the form of machinery and equipment to be used in the exploration, exploitation, or exportation of petroleum and minerals; (2) capital goods for which common stocks of Colombian corporations are delivered in payment or where the importer of capital goods delivers foreign exchange to the Central Bank and satisfies the latter that he did not recently convert pesos into U.S. dollars for that purpose; (3) personal effects of persons entering the country; and (4) imports from countries belonging to the Latin American Free Trade Association.

In May, 1963, after the 1962 devaluation, advance deposits reached the level of $1.03 billion. The amount of the deposit varies from 1 to 120 per cent, depending on the class of article to be imported. Books and materials for the fabrication of tires require a deposit of only 1 per cent; for motors, it is 5 per cent; for drugs, fertilizer, insecticides, and agricultural machinery, it is 20 per cent; and for other materials and articles, the deposit is 120 per cent. The exchange rate for this purpose is the so-called certified or official rate of $9.00 per U.S. dollar, while during mid-1963 the free market rate was

approximately $10.00 per U.S. dollar. The term of the deposit is ninety days counted from the date of importation, but the deposit may be returned in sixty days if it is used to pay for the merchandise abroad. No foreign exchange is disbursed against the deposits if there is no necessity to pay for the merchandise by a foreign exchange draft, or if it is a capital import. Foreign exchange is issued only on the basis of the f.o.b. value of the merchandise and for 80 per cent of the shipping expenses. The remaining shipping expenses must be paid at the free rate.

When the requirement of an advance deposit was first imposed in 1951, the Minister of Finance justified the action as follows: "This deposit, which may be done away with in the future, is made necessary as security that the imports will be made and to avoid false registrations that would completely distort the import statistics." [15] Rather than being eliminated, the initial rate of the advance deposit of 10 per cent has been increased to as high as 120 per cent. Moreover, the reasons offered by the Minister for the deposits, if they were the only ones, would not justify the basic effect of the advance deposits, which is to make imports more costly.

As far as the reference to import statistics is concerned, no one appears to be concerned with *ex ante* information on imports. Nearly all countries of the world predict future foreign exchange requirements by other methods. But even if the advance registration of imports is desirable to provide these data, the advance deposit itself certainly is not required for statistical purposes.

Moreover, the advance deposit is not a tax. It must be returned to the importer at the expiration of the waiting period. Therefore, it produces no revenue for the government.

The advance deposit means that importers are required to set aside capital for sixty or ninety days. At the expiration of this period, the deposit may be utilized to pay

[14] *Revista del Banco de la República, 1963,* p. 69.

[15] *Memoria de Hacienda, 1951,* p. 36.

import duties, to pay for the imported merchandise, or it may be refunded. If a businessman imports goods more or less continuously, his deposits are maintained more or less permanently with the Central Bank. Thus, the deposits absorb working capital in an economy where capital is relatively scarce and should be economized. The deposits are financed directly by importers or exporters or indirectly by banks. Thus, imports bear a direct or indirect interest expense, raising their costs. Even if importers use their own capital instead of borrowing, or if the exporter finances the deposit, an implicit interest expense is involved, and the costs of imported merchandise are increased. What could be paid to the government in increased import taxes is thus channelled into the banks or to exporters abroad who may finance the deposits. In the latter case, the deposits increase foreign exchange expenditures.

In addition, the small manufacturer, producer, or merchant is discriminated against by the advance deposits. Access to capital, to loans, or to credit from the exporter is limited for small businessmen. On the other hand, the larger businesses or the foreign enterprises are much less likely to be restricted. The advance deposit therefore works particular hardships on the smaller firms and favors the larger domestic and foreign enterprises.

A more sophisticated argument in favor of the advance deposits is that they are counter-inflationary, because capital on deposit is not available for spending. To the extent that bank reserves are decreased by the amount of the advance deposits, the effect on bank loans for this purpose (nominally prohibited) is to produce a secondary restriction on bank lending.

The amount of bank lending is subject to the control of the Central Bank through a variety of devices. Aside from establishing the required level of bank reserves, open-market operations and selective controls are available. Of the various controls, those that restrict the capital of enterprises are probably the least desirable. How is it possible to

defend restrictions on capital when durable consumer goods may be purchased with no down payment, when merchants may borrow to finance inventories of consumer goods, when the Central Bank finances the deficits of the government, and when the Central Bank supports the coffee market by a monetary issue? The latter two policies are the most inflationary monetary devices conceivable.

Export Duties

Although most taxes on exports have been abolished, some exports, particularly coffee, continue to be subject to charges that are in the nature of an export tax. Exporters are required to sell to the Central Bank the foreign exchange obtained from the exported goods. The rate of exchange for the sale is specified by the Board of the Central Bank after consultation with the Council on Economic Policy and Planning and with the approval of the Minister of Finance. Exporters of coffee and precious metals (except platinum) are reimbursed at the rate of $7.10 per U.S. dollar,[16] which is considerably less than the official rate of $9.00 per U.S. dollar. Coffee exporters are required, in addition, to deliver to the account of the National Coffee Stabilization Fund without compensation a quantity of unhulled, prime coffee equivalent to 5 per cent of their export volume plus a quantity of second-grade coffee equal to 6 per cent of export volume.

Exporters of all other goods are reimbursed at the free market rate. An exception is made in the case of manufactured articles employing imported raw materials or intermediate goods valued at more than 50 per cent of the f.o.b. export price of the articles. If such goods were imported using certificates of exchange, i.e., at the official rate, then the reimbursement of foreign exchange is at the official rate. A certificate from the Minister of Development is required showing that imported goods do not exceed 50 per cent

16 On January 10, 1964, the rate was increased to $7.30 per U.S. dollar.

of the export price in order for the exporter to be eligible for reimbursement at the free rate. For coffee, bananas, and platinum, the f.o.b. value is specified. For example, coffee exports are valued at U.S. $59.00 per sack of 70 kilograms regardless of the actual price at which the coffee might be sold.

Exporters of so-called minor exports are required to register with the Minister of Development, produce a certificate showing payment of income and complementary taxes (*Paz y Salvo*), and execute a guarantee in favor of the Central Bank ranging from 5 to 30 per cent of the value of the exports at the official rate of exchange. A tax of 2 per cent, later reduced to 0.125 per cent, was levied until recently on all minor exports.[17] The tax was collected by the Central Bank and was credited to the account of the exporter for the promotion of exports. All exports also must be registered with the Office of Exchange Registry, except those with a value of less than $1,000 accompanying tourists.

Many exported articles are subject to quotas or other restrictions established by the Ministers of Development, Agriculture, and Mines and Petroleum. In establishing these restrictions, the ministries are required to consider the need for foreign exchange, national consumption requirements, and the obligation to maintain "a level of prices in the domestic market that is equitable to the producer and the consumer."[18] Among the products whose export is prohibited by the Minister of Agriculture are rice, cocoa, beans, milk and its derivatives, beef, pork, live animals, poultry, sheep, vegetables, vegetable oils, sugar, cotton, and barley.[19] The Minister of Development has prohibited the export of hides.[20] Quotas have been established for cattle, which are administered by the

Colombian Federation of Cattlemen.[21] There are also quotas on sugar and cotton seed.[22]

As an export stimulus, income originating from exports is exempt from the income tax. The law presumes that the income originating from exports is equal to 40 per cent of the value of the exported merchandise. The effect of this provision is to exempt the firm from part of the income tax on its domestic production as well as on its exported products. A better and more equitable rule would be to exempt that proportion of income that foreign sales bear to total sales.

Revenue Fluctuations

The Colombian peso in 1950 was valued officially at $1.95 per U.S. dollar. From April, 1951, until June, 1957, the official rate was $2.50 per U.S. dollar. In July, 1957, a system of gradually changing rates was introduced, with the official rate rising to $6.70 to the U.S. dollar by May, 1960. In December, 1962, a further depreciation to $9.00 to the U.S. dollar occurred. These currency depreciations affected very seriously the revenues from tariffs.

Currency depreciation affects tariff revenues in two ways. First, by changing the relative prices of foreign goods, that is, by making them more expensive, it tends to reduce imports and to encourage the consumption of domestically produced goods. Second, where the duties are specific, a fixed amount per physical unit, they become a smaller percentage of the value of imports. On the other hand, *ad valorem* rates are not changed by currency depreciation, and the revenues are affected adversely only to the extent that the imports are reduced.

Prior to 1951, the tariff list consisted principally of specific duties. The Minister of Finance, in his report for that year, observed that a defect of the existing tariff list was that it provided for:

---

[17] Article 53 of Law 1 of 1959 authorized the 2 per cent tax, which was reduced by resolution of the Board of the Institute of Industrial Development on March 7, 1961, to 0.125 per cent, and then was subsequently eliminated.

[18] Law 1 of 1959, Article 30.

[19] Ministry of Agriculture, Resolution No. 0118, January 29, 1959.

[20] Ministry of Development, Resolution No. 214, May 21, 1959.

[21] Ministries of Agriculture and Development, Resolution No. 606, November 14, 1960.

[22] Ministries of Agriculture and Development, Resolution Nos. 1,194 and 1,195.

. . . a system of specific tariffs that did not accommodate themselves to the international oscillations in prices, nor to the fluctuations in the purchasing power of the nation's money. Within this system and in liquidating the duties by weight of the articles, the defensive power of the tariff remained fixed and could become affected in case of a rise in prices or a rise in the rate of exchange. Thus, for example, a burden of $0.10 per kilo, established in 1931, when the price of the respective article was $1.00 per kilo, bore a tax of ten per cent. Today, when the price of such an article, due to the phenomenon of the devaluation of our money or of its rise in foreign markets is $3.00 per kilo, it bears a tax of only three per cent.[23]

Unfortunately, the minister was more concerned with the protectionist aspects of a decline in effective rates of the tariff, which he noted fell from 22.03 per cent in 1936 to 10.3 [sic] per cent in 1947. (See Table 8–7.) The minister then concluded with respect to the nature of the reform adopted in 1951:

> There was imposed, therefore, in this field, a radical modification of our system, adopting, at least partially, the *ad valorem* tariff, and therefore in the new statute it is combined with the specific, a formula which I consider the most suitable, both for the ascending phase of the economic cycle like the present as well as for a period of depression, for which the specific duty can preserve a greater protectionist power.[24]

The argument that specific tariffs exert a greater protectionist effect over the business cycle is a rather specious one. It is true that the effective rates of the specific duties rise as foreign prices fall, and, conversely, the effective rates fall when foreign prices rise. But the argument assumes that the forces accounting for changes in foreign prices over the business cycle will not apply in Colombia. In a dynamic world, prices are always changing. Some of the forces are temporary, and others are more permanent. If prices fall in

[23] *Memoria de Hacienda, 1951,* p. 53.
[24] *Ibid.,* p. 54.

TABLE 8–7

Effective Rates of Duties on Imports, 1944 to 1960
(Thousands of Pesos)

	Total Imports c.i.f. Value[a]	Import Duties[b]	Indicated Effective Rates (Per Cent)
1944	$ 174,666	$ 25,881	14.82
1945	281,182	41,047	14.60
1946	403,043	48,691	12.08
1947	638,625	65,082	10.19
1948	589,079	57,868	9.82
1949	515,921	39,981	7.75
1950	711,112	97,156	13.66
1951	988,840	215,258	21.77
1952	1,038,407	195,749	18.85
1953	1,366,808	249,462	18.25
1954	1,679,448	335,084	19.95
1955	1,673,227	268,630	16.05
1956	1,642,982	219,744	13.37
1957	1,956,652	184,132	9.41
1958	2,543,543	192,713	7.58
1959	2,659,752	360,757	13.56
1960	3,420,214	567,657	16.60
1961	3,732,778	562,833	15.08
1962	3,658,327	n.a.	n.a.

Sources:
 a *Anuario de Comerico Exterior,* various years.
 b *Boletín Mensual de Estadística,* December 1962, p. 30.

Colombia, the level of protection increases when it is less necessary.

Thus, in addition to the business cycle as a cause of changes in foreign prices, increases in efficiency and changes in foreign exchange rates may likewise affect the relative prices of foreign and domestic goods. With respect to the former, the domestic industry also must become more efficient, and if it is not able to do so, it suggests that the protection is misplaced. Costs of production in Colombia of protected goods should fall more rapidly than the costs of comparable foreign goods, since productivity increases are greater during an industry's infancy. Presumably, foreign production has already achieved a high level of efficiency or there would be no reason for protection. The specific tariffs are not likely, by themselves, to be very important in the event of a serious deflation in the developed economies of the United States and Europe. Besides, the argument appears irrelevant with respect to the period since World War II, when not falling, but rising, prices have been the rule in the developed countries, and depreciation of the peso and inflation have been the chronic problems in Colombia. In the actual postwar situation, the specific tariffs not only caused a loss in revenue, but they contributed to the balance-of-payments problem and provided less protection for Colombian production. The successive devaluations also have been followed by off-setting rises in domestic prices. In such a situation, specific tariffs tend to lose their protectionist effect compared with *ad valorem* tariffs.

This contention can be demonstrated by an example. Assume that the c.i.f. cost of an imported article is $1.00, and that it is subject to a specific duty of $1.00. Assume, further, that the domestic cost of production is $1.50, and that there is a currency depreciation of 50 per cent. The c.i.f. cost of the imported article would then rise to $2.00, and if the duty remained at $1.00 the devaluation would increase the amount of protection. But if the domestic price level rises to nullify the depreciation, and if the domestic cost of producing the good rises to $3.00, the imported product is now competitive. But if the duty is *ad valorem,* say 100 per cent, and if the assumed conditions before depreciation are identical, greater protection would be afforded the domestic industry. After depreciation the imported article would cost $4.00, the $2.00 c.i.f. value plus the 100 per cent duty. Even if the domestic cost of the product rose by 100 per cent to $3.00, it would still be protected. Thus, not only do specific tariffs produce less revenue than *ad valorem* tariffs as a result of depreciation, but they also afford less protection.

The purpose of a currency devaluation is to discourage imports and increase exports. But specific tariffs, as shown in the above example, are less of a discouragement to imports than are *ad valorem* tariffs. Moreover, the effect is opposite to that intended by devaluation. Although specific tariffs may provide more protection against falling foreign prices, there is obviously no reason to

apply them to non-protected items in the tariff list. For non-protected items, they simply produce less revenue without any gain to the domestic economy.

Finally, there is little need to provide protection automatically. What is really "automatic" are the cries of domestic producers for more protection when they are being hurt by foreign competition. There are ample powers for adjusting *ad valorem* tariffs when a good case can be made for protection. More often than not, the cries for protection will be unjustified. If anything should be automatic, it should be the gradual elimination of the protective tariff. If the industry never can withstand foreign competition, it ought not to have been protected in the first place.

Lack of Neutrality and
Regressivity of Specific Tariffs

The principal advantage of specific tariffs is the simplicity of the calculation, obviating the need to be concerned over whether the declared value is in fact the true value. But this advantage does not exist when both specific and *ad valorem* duties are assessed, as is the usual case in Colombia. The necessity of determining the true value for tariff purposes exists with respect to the *ad valorem* duties, and the specific duties, therefore, require additional calculations.

In addition to the adverse revenue effects noted above, there are other objections to specific duties. They tend to discriminate against the less expensive goods in the class of merchandise to which they apply, and therefore to distort the consumption pattern of the community. Specific duties are not harmful in their effects as long as the object of the tax is a homogeneous commodity and the tax is based on the net weight or other physical characteristics of the product. When the goods are not homogeneous, or when they are based on gross weight, specific duties result in changes in relative prices that distort the allocation of resources and are regressive in their effect.

As an illustration, assume that a tax of $10.00 is imposed on imported liquors. If the c.i.f values of two brands are $7.50 and $15.00, or in the ratio of one to two before tax, as a result of the tax they become $17.50 and $25.00 respectively, or in the ratio of seven to ten. Thus, their relative prices have narrowed as a result of the specific duty. On the other hand, if an *ad valorem* tax of 100 per cent had been levied, the price after tax of the first would become $15.00, and of the second $30.00, retaining the same price relationship as before.

Specific duties in the Colombian tariff list are usually levied on gross weight, which includes the packaging. Therefore, the tax tends to favor products with packaging materials of lighter weight. Since these are usually the more expensive products, the specific tax penalizes the heavier and usually less expensive products. Because neutrality is a desirable characteristic of any tax system, the specific duties should be based on net weight to avoid discrimination due to packaging.

As a final argument against specific tariffs, there is the fact that the amount of protection is concealed. Legislators are often victims of lobbies which prey upon the illusion created by small specific duties that they afford only minor protection. But what may appear to be a small specific tax may result in a rate of 100 per cent or more. In the case of *ad valorem* duties, however, the rate of protection is obvious, and grossly excessive inefficiency and monopolistic pricing practices can be more easily detected.

In summary, the imposition of both specific and *ad valorem* duties does not provide even the advantage of simplicity, since both duties must be calculated. Specific duties produce excessive fluctuations in the effective rates of the duties as a result of currency depreciation, defeat the intended effects of a devaluation, and have unneutral effects on relative prices.

Import Controls as a Cause of
Fluctuations in Customs Revenues

Another cause of the wide fluctuations in customs revenues is government policies that periodically restrict or prohibit certain imports. These actions usually are taken to conserve foreign exchange. While they certainly do so, at the same time they reduce government revenues. This forces the government into deficit financing when it is trying to achieve price stability. On the other hand, a release of the restrictions and prohibitions produces a windfall in tax revenues.

In 1954 the list of prohibited imports was eliminated.[25] As a result, imports rose from $1,366.8 million in 1953 to $1,679.4 million in 1954, or by 22.9 per cent, and import duties rose from $249.5 million in 1953 to $335.1 million in 1954, or by 34.3 per cent. (See Table 8–8.) Falling coffee prices led to the reimposition of the prohibited list later in 1954. Although total imports showed little decline, revenues from duties fell to $219.7 million in 1956, a decline from 1954 of 34.4 per cent. Translated into U.S. dollars, the revenues rose from U.S. $99.8 million in 1953 to U.S. $134.0 million in 1954 but then fell to U.S. $87.9 million in 1956. This result cannot be attributed to devaluation, since there was no devaluation during the period.

By reducing import demand from U.S. $671.8 million in 1954 to U.S. $399.9 million in 1958, there was a saving of foreign exchange of U.S. $271.9 million. At the same time, however, there was a decline in government revenue from U.S. $134.0 million in 1954 to U.S. $30.3 million in 1958, or a decrease of U.S. $103.7 million. In addition, one must add the social costs of regulatory bodies, the increased complexity and its attendant private costs, windfall gains that result from shortages, and the fact that the exchange difficulties continued.

[25] *Memoria de Hacienda, 1954,* p. 139.

TABLE 8–8
Imports and Import Duties, 1948 to 1961

(Thousands)

| | c.i.f. Value of Imports | | Indicated Rate of Exchange[a] | Import Duties | |
	(U.S. Dollars)	(Pesos)	(Per Cent)	(Pesos)	(U.S. Dollars)[b]
1948	$323,670	$ 589,079	54.95	$ 57,868	$ 31,798
1949	264,575	515,921	51.28	39,981	20,502
1950	364,673	711,112	51.28	97,156	49,822
1951	419,000	988,840	42.37	215,258	91,205
1952	415,363	1,038,407	40.00	195,749	78,300
1953	546,723	1,366,808	40.00	249,462	99,785
1954	671,779	1,679,448	40.00	335,084	134,034
1955	669,291	1,673,227	40.00	268,630	107,452
1956	657,193	1,642,982	40.00	219,744	87,898
1957	482,575	1,956,652	24.66	184,132	45,407
1958	399,932	2,543,543	15.72	192,713	30,294
1959	415,588	2,659,752	15.16	360,757	56,386
1960	518,585	3,420,214	15.16	567,657	86,057
1961	557,129	3,732,778	14.93	562,833	84,031
1962	536,866	3,658,327	14.68	n.a.	n.a.

[a] Column 1 divided by column 2.
[b] Column 3 multiplied by column 4.

Sources: For c.i.f. value of imports, *Anuario de Comercio Exterior, 1960,* p. 3; and for import duties, Division de Impuestos Nacionales, Subdivisión de Recaudación, and *Boletín Mensual de Estadística,* December, 1962, p. 30.

Exemptions

In addition to the conventional exemptions granted to governmental units and non-profit institutions, exemptions are granted to certain private firms as a development incentive.[26] These include companies engaged in the exploration and development of petroleum and mineral resources, the fishing industry, and government-sponsored industrial enterprises such as the *Paz del Río* steel plant (*Acerías Paz del Río*) and the Colombian Petroleum Company (*Ecopetrol*). Firms that employ raw materials produced by the steel mill to the extent of not less than 80 per cent of total materials also used have a customs exemption on their imports. Firms that export all or part of their production may enter into a contract with the Minister of Development and receive an exemption for imported materials and parts. Chassis for buses imported by urban transport enterprises are exempt.[27] In the case of petroleum and mining companies a lengthy list of personal consumption items may be imported for use

[26] Decree No. 3,387, Article 3, December 31, 1959.
[27] Decree No. 578, Article 1, March 11, 1960.

at the exploration sites.[28] These imports may not enter into commercial outlets nor consist of items produced in Colombia "in equal conditions of quality and availability." [29]

Many public utilities—telephone, electricity, water, and transport companies—are owned by the national and local governments. The exemptions for these firms are limited to those imports' that are "essential for fulfillment of their proper functions."

From 1952 to 1961, exemptions increased from 16.75 per cent of the value of total imports to 21.96 per cent. (See Table 8–9.) Moreover, the duties exempted increased as a percentage of total duties (receipts plus exemptions) from 15.78 per cent in 1952 to 34.62 per cent in 1961. The estimated average rate of the duties on exempted imports rose from 21.06 per cent in 1952 to 36.76 per cent in 1961, while the estimated average rate on taxable imports fell from 22.65 per cent to 19.32 per cent during the same period. (See Table 8–10.)

By far the largest importer of exempt

[28] Central Bank, Resolution No. 21, Articles 1 and 8, October 1, 1958.
[29] *Ibid.,* Article 2.

TABLE 8–9
Exemptions Related to Total Imports and Assessed Duties, 1952 to 1961

(Thousands)

	Imports (U.S. Dollars)	Exemptions (U.S. Dollars)	Exemptions as a Percentage of Imports	Assessed Total Duties (Pesos)	Duties Exempted (Pesos)	Percentage of Duties Exempted to Total Duties
1952	$415,363	$ 69,557	16.75	$232,418	$ 36,669	15.78
1953	546,723	95,551	17.48	282,873	33,411	11.81
1954	671,779	92,007	13.70	374,751	39,668	10.59
1955	669,291	94,040	14.05	308,491	39,861	12.92
1956	657,193	115,196	17.53	284,795	65,051	22.84
1957	482,575	77,882	16.14	239,027	54,895	22.97
1958	399,932	71,142	17.79	279,420	86,707	31.03
1959	415,588	58,468	14.07	491,395	130,637	26.58
1960	518,585	87,199	16.81	801,675	234,018	29.19
1961	557,129	122,336	21.96	860,850	298,016	34.62

Source: *Boletín Mensual de Estadística*, December, 1962, p. 30.

TABLE 8–10
Effective Rates on Exempted and Non-Exempted Imports, 1952 to 1961

(Thousands of Pesos)

	Imports	Per Cent of Imports Not Exempted	Non-Exempted Imports	Duties Collected	Indicated Rate	Exempted Imports	Duties Exempted	Indicated Rate
1952	$1,038,407	83.23	$ 864,267	$195,749	22.65	$174,140	$ 36,669	21.06
1953	1,366,808	82.52	1,127,890	249,462	22.12	238,918	33,411	13.98
1954	1,679,448	86.30	1,449,364	335,084	23.12	230,084	39,668	17.24
1955	1,673,227	85.94	1,437,971	268,630	18.68	235,256	39,861	16.94
1956	1,642,982	82.47	1,354,967	219,744	16.22	288,015	65,051	22.59
1957	1,956,652	83.86	1,640,848	184,132	11.22	315,804	54,895	17.38
1958	2,543,543	82.21	2,091,047	192,713	9.22	452,496	86,707	19.16
1959	2,659,752	85.93	2,285,525	360,757	15.78	374,227	130,637	34.91
1960	3,420,214	83.19	2,845,276	567,657	19.95	574,938	234,018	40.70
1961	3,732,778	78.04	2,913,059	562,833	19.32	810,719	298,016	36.76

Sources: *Anuario de Comercio Exterior*, 1961, and *Boletín Mensual de Estadística*, December, 1962, p. 30.

goods is the government. In 1961 the national government and its decentralized institutions and enterprises imported 46.99 per cent of the total exempted imports, while departments and municipal governments imported an additional 15.22 per cent for a total of 62.43 per cent. (See Table 8–11.) Private enterprises imported 37.11 per cent of the total, while embassies and consular officials imported 0.47 per cent.

Significantly, exemptions granted to private enterprises have been rising sharply. As shown in Table 8–12, the amount of duties exempted was only $1.51 million in 1956

and $6.24 million in 1959, but the total rose to $22.47 million in 1960. Not included in these data are agricultural machinery, equipment, fertilizers, and insecticides, which are free of duties.

The imports of the government sector were dominated in recent years by those of the Institute for National Supplies (*Instituto Nacional de Abastecimientos*, or INA), which imported $189.87 million of foodstuffs in 1961 to maintain adequate supplies in the domestic market.[30] This total represented

[30] *Informe del Instituto Nacional de Abastecimientos, 1962*, p. 10.

TABLE 8-11

Summary of Exemptions by Entities

(Thousands of Pesos)

	Calendar Year 1960					Calendar Year 1961				
	Exempted Imports	Percentage of Total Exempted	Duties Exempted	Percentage of Imports	Percentage of Total Duties Exempted	Exempted Imports	Percentage of Total Exempted	Duties Exempted	Percentage of Imports	Percentage of Total Duties Exempted
Departments and municipalities	$ 90,476	16.24	$ 23,312	25.77	9.89	$126,525	15.44	$ 30,959	24.47	10.31
National government	328,661	58.98	140,586	42.78	59.63	385,131	46.99	149,607	38.85	49.84
Private enterprises	135,901	24.39	68,268	50.23	28.96	304,132	37.11	114,613	37.69	38.18
Foreign governments	2,164	.39	3,594	166.08	1.52	3,863	0.47	5,012	129.74	1.67
TOTALS	$557,202	100.00	$235,760	42.31	100.01	$819,651	100.01	$300,191	36.62	100.00

Source: Boletín Mensual de Estadística, December, 1962, p. 31.

TABLE 8–12

Exemptions of Duties Granted to a Select List of Entities, 1956 to 1961

(Thousands of Pesos)

	1956	1957	1958	1959	1960	1961
Government	$34,406	$34,145	$54,477	$ 84,286	$118,260	$129,408
Institute of National Supplies	17,938	24,739	42,974	73,584	91,563	90,590
Antioquia	153	1	33	11	316	1,397
Medellín	361	157	75	875	3,353	8,755
Institute of Industrial Development	245	358	440	1,288	697	2,295
Ministry of Communications	271	495	1,626	1,238	1,034	1,314
Ministry of Education	—	171	311	772	758	2,147
Ministry of War	8,537	4,389	1,880	2,890	8,080	7,032
Ministry of Health	795	359	1,298	692	2,935	1,970
Ministry of Public Works	6,019	3,472	5,227	2,293	7,437	8,577
Institute of Municipal Development	87	4	611	614	1,720	2,712
National Training Service	—	—	2	29	367	2,619
Utilities and Government Enterprises	2,250	3,262	3,801	9,148	21,552	34,342
Central Hydroelectric de Río Anchicayá	114	182	28	377	495	3,839
Empresa Paz del Río	774	540	723	1,917	2,710	2,918
National Railways	411	1,166	100	663	4,609	4,470
Institute of Water Supply	12	5	20	383	3,705	10,242
Empresa Colombiana de Petróleos	939	1,369	2,930	5,469	9,092	4,528
National Airports	—	—	—	339	941	1,206
Bogotá Electric	—	—	—	—	—	7,139
Private	1,513	2,694	3,175	6,243	22,474	53,077
Unites States Government	177	303	14,075	17,816	39,051	57,741
Gifts	63	91	13,323	15,697	37,412	55,639
Embassy	114	212	752	2,119	1,639	2,102
Total exemption of duties	$38,346	$40,404	$75,528	$117,493	$201,337	$274,568
Total expenditures	$65,051	$54,895	$86,707	$130,637	$234,018	$298,016

Source: *Boletín Mensual de Estadística*, December, 1962, pp. 30–31.

49.30 per cent of national government imports. The duties exempted on INA's imports were $90.59 million, indicating an average effective rate of 47.71 per cent. Notwithstanding the large increase in INA's imports from 1956 to 1961, when its exempt duties increased from 2.76 to 30.40 per cent of total exemptions, the exempt duties on government imports actually declined from 52.89 per cent of total duties exempted in 1956 to 43.42 per cent in 1961. (Table 8–12.)

The impact of the development program also is revealed by the statistics on exemptions. Public utilities and government enterprises imported 19.02 per cent of exempted merchandise in 1959 but 29.35 per cent in 1960. (See Table 8–13.) The enterprises in this category listed in Table 8–11 accounted for 3.46 per cent of exempted duties in 1956 but 10.03 per cent in 1961.

Utilities and government enterprises imported goods that were subject, on the average, to the lowest tariffs. As shown in Table 8–13, the average rate applicable to the merchandise imported was only 10.33 per cent in 1959 and 20.19 per cent in 1960.[31] Private enterprises were next, with tariffs averaging 10.41 per cent in 1959 and 14.42

[31] Tables 8–12 and 8–14 were prepared from different sources and the totals do not equal. Public utilities and government enterprises are shown as a separate group in Table 8–14, while in Table 8–12 they are grouped according to ownership by different levels of government.

TABLE 8–13

Exemptions Granted by Entities, 1959 and 1960

	Calendar Year 1959					Calendar Year 1960				
	Value of Imports Exempted	Percentage of Total Imports Exempted	Duties Exempted	Duties Exempted as a Percentage of Imports	Percentage of Total Duties Exempted	Value of Imports Exempted	Percentage of Total Imports Exempted	Duties Exempted	Duties Exempted as a Percentage of Imports	Percentage of Total Duties Exempted
Government	$268,358	60.14	$ 80,060	29.83	67.68	$226,571	40.09	$119,236	52.63	48.81
Utilities and government enterprises	84,873	19.02	8,768	10.33	7.41	165,889	29.35	33,486	20.19	13.71
International and charities	19,818	4.44	17,148	86.53	14.50	31,640	5.60	56,347	178.09	23.06
Private	73,161	16.40	12,313	16.83	10.41	141,071	24.96	35,237	24.98	14.42
TOTALS	$446,210	100.00	$118,289	26.51	100.00	$565,171	100.00	$244,306	42.23	100.00

Source: Memoria de Hacienda, 1960 and 1961.

per cent in 1960. Government imports were subject to average duties of 29.83 per cent in 1959 and 52.63 per cent in 1960. The highest average rate applied to the imports of embassies and consulates, economic aid missions, and educational and charitable organizations. Taken as a group, these rates were 86.52 per cent in 1959 and 178.09 per cent in 1960. The relatively high average tariffs applicable to government imports may be explained by the fact that many government imports are subject to high protective tariffs for the purpose of stabilizing domestic prices.

The Central Bank reported that U.S. $368.75 million in foreign exchange was spent in 1960 and U.S. $435.53 million in 1961 for the importation of merchandise (f.o.b. plus transportation costs). This represented an increase of U.S. $66.78 million or of $477.43 million at the official rate of exchange existing in 1961.[32] The total increase in imports from 1960 to 1961 was $312.56 million, of which the increase in exempted imports represented $262.45 million or 83.97 per cent. Thus a large part of the increase in foreign exchange expenditures must necessarily be attributed to the increase in exempted imports.

The increase in exempted imports not only resulted in a drain on foreign exchange but also contributed to a decrease in government receipts from import duties. The latter declined from $567.66 million in 1960 to $562.83 million in 1961.

While the granting of exemptions on imports to enterprises engaged in exporting may be justified on the grounds that this policy helps the firms to become competitive in international markets and creates no foreign exchange problem, the same arguments do not apply to firms that sell their products in the Colombian market. Firms selling their products domestically should be exempted on their imports only to the extent that their products should be subsidized. The notion that all goods produced in Colombia should

not be taxed, regardless of the social utility or in utility of the products, is untenable, and it is especially unwarranted when scarce foreign exchange is involved.

A more desirable policy would be to exempt imports only when they will be incorporated into exported goods or when no claim on foreign exchange is involved, as in the case of diplomats and technical assistance missions. The development of industries that produce only for the domestic market, but which will require large amounts of imported capital goods, intermediate goods, and raw materials, or which will require remittances of profits and repatriation of capital, requires a more cautious policy with respect to exemptions.

The rate at which exemptions accorded private firms is increasing suggests that the exemption policy may be stimulating imports at the expense of a loss of revenue. Of the increase in exempt duties of $64.43 million between 1960 and 1961, private firms accounted for $46.35 million or 71.93 per cent. Similarly, of the increase in exempted imports from 1960 to 1961 of $262.45 million, private firms imported $168.23 million or 64.10 per cent. (See Table 8–11.)

No breakdown of the exempted imports for 1961 and 1962 is available in sufficient detail to enable an assessment of the relative importance of petroleum and mining companies, exporters, and others. In 1959 petroleum and mining companies accounted for 78.4 per cent of the imports of private firms according to a study made by the Customs Division.[33] In 1960 these firms accounted for 45.7 per cent of total imports, and it may be assumed that this percentage continued to decline in 1961.

The data on exports does not appear to show significant increases in the export of manufactured goods from 1959 to 1961. Petroleum exports continued to be important, and there were increases in tanned hides, textiles, sugar, and pharmaceuticals. Manufacturers continued to be noteworthy by their

[32] *Revista del Banco de la República,* January, 1963, p. 69.

[33] *Memoria de Hacienda, 1960,* pp. 343–44 and 1961, pp. 300–1.

insignificance. To the degree that it is possible to draw conclusions from such evidence, it may be deduced that a large proportion of the increased exemptions granted to private firms were not for export industries or for mining and petroleum but were largely for producers supplying the domestic market. If so, the exemptions accorded firms producing for the domestic market probably involved an unnecessary cost in revenues foregone. These producers can be encouraged by protective tariffs for a short period of time without the added cost of exemptions. Moreover, the firms should be encouraged to find domestic substitutes for their imported materials, but exemptions encourage reliance on foreign sources of supply. A continuation of exemptions to private firms in view of the government's chronic budget deficits and Columbia's balance-of-payments difficulties appears to be unwarranted.

High duties, combined with prohibitions and restrictions on certain imports, have resulted in tremendous differentials between foreign and domestic prices of certain luxury goods, such as automobiles. This has had not only the effect of stimulating contraband activity but has conferred windfall gains on those privileged to import these goods. Those who are able to import these goods free of duties have enjoyed even greater benefits.

Since the number of diplomatic and technical assistance missions is quite large, regulations have been introduced regarding the resale of automobiles. The chief of a diplomatic mission may import two automobiles every two-year period, and other members of diplomatic missions may import one vehicle every two years. These vehicles may be resold free of duties. There seems to be no reason other than diplomatic niceties that justifies the sale of these vehicles free of duty. Because of the effect on market prices of restrictions on the importation of automobiles, a clear profit of several thousands of U.S. dollars may be realized on such sales. Clearly, Colombian residents purchasing vehicles from members of the diplomatic or consular corps should be considered as importers and should be required to pay the import duty.

A member of a technical assistance mission not accorded diplomatic privileges may similarly import one automobile free of duty, but he must pay the duty on the automobile when it is sold. There seems no reason why this same rule should not be applied to diplomatic and consular officials. Whenever an automobile is resold by a person who has imported it free of duty, the duty should be paid.

Diplomatic and technical assistance personnel imported 206 automobiles in 1961 and 300 in 1962.[34] The duty on smaller vehicles is 150 per cent, and on larger, 200 per cent. At the end of a two-year period, these vehicles will be worth three to four times their import c.i.f. value, judging by experience in the past. If the average c.i.f. value is assumed to be U.S. $3,000, and if only one-half the vehicles are free of duties, the loss of revenues would be U.S. $600,000 in 1963 and U.S. $900,000 in 1964.

[34] Information supplied by the Customs Division.

TABLE 8–14

Imports and Duties Assessed by Section and Chapter of the Tariff Schedule, before Exemptions, 1962

(Thousands of Pesos)

Chapter or Section	Description	Value of Imports, c.i.f.	Specific Duty	Per Cent	Ad Valorem Duty	Per Cent	Total Duties	Per Cent
Section I:	Animals and their products	$ 10,096.45	$ 132.98	1.32	$ 1,693.87	16.78	$ 1,826.85	18.09
1.	Live animals	8,648.37	—	—	1,294.29	14.97	1,294.29	14.97
2.	Meat, fresh	34.45	.23	.67	.03	.09	.26	.75
3.	Fish	14.13	—	—	.08	.57	.08	.57
4.	Milk products, eggs, honey	672.81	131.56	19.56	250.90	37.29	382.46	56.85
5.	Raw materials of animal origin	726.69	1.19	.16	148.57	20.44	149.76	20.61
Section II:	Vegetable products	163,538.67	24,742.41	15.13	34,948.21	21.37	59,690.62	36.50
6.	Live plants and flowers	234.03	—	—	11.28	4.82	11.28	4.82
7.	Vegetables	571.50	176.39	30.86	93.14	16.30	269.53	47.16
8.	Edible fruits	1,081.53	230.49	21.31	145.91	13.49	376.40	34.80
9.	Coffee, tea, and spices	2,807.22	844.99	30.10	582.55	20.75	1,427.54	50.85
10.	Cereals	97,789.96	15,811.89	16.17	19,987.49	20.44	35,799.38	36.61
11.	Flour, malt, and starches	751.74	100.72	13.40	148.56	19.76	249.28	33.16
12.	Oleaginous seeds and fruits	51,528.90	6,904.98	13.40	12,626.08	24.50	19,531.06	37.90
13.	Raw materials for tanning	8,479.12	651.82	7.69	1,275.89	15.05	1,927.71	22.74
14.	Wicker, cane, and bamboo	294.67	21.13	7.17	77.31	26.24	98.44	33.41
Section III: 15.	Oils and fats of animal or vegetable origin	73,761.35	30,601.23	41.49	25,855.92	35.05	56,457.15	76.54
Section IV:	Food preparations	54,741.50	18,896.59	34.52	13,788.12	25.19	32,684.71	59.71
16.	Meat and fish preparations	650.90	82.34	12.65	245.27	37.68	327.61	50.33
17.	Sugar and sweets	1,555.24	165.60	10.65	426.20	27.40	591.80	38.05
18.	Cocoa	31,482.18	917.48	2.91	1,175.16	3.73	2,092.64	6.65
19.	Preparations from grains	144.07	39.32	27.29	35.30	24.50	74.62	51.79
20.	Vegetable and fruit products	729.35	665.97	91.31	168.60	23.12	834.57	114.43
21.	Miscellaneous food products	1,714.28	120.18	7.01	454.66	26.52	574.84	33.53
22.	Beverages	9,691.58	11,677.92	120.50	8,156.65	84.16	19,834.57	204.66
23.	Food scraps	1,459.87	175.06	11.99	96.62	6.62	271.68	18.61
24.	Tobacco	7,314.03	5,052.72	69.08	3,029.66	41.42	8,082.38	110.51
Section V:	Mineral products, non-metal	147,659.59	8,084.71	5.48	12,841.71	8.70	20,926.42	14.17
25.	Salt, sulphur, cement, etc.	31,075.54	5,368.93	17.28	4,612.91	14.84	9,981.84	32.12
26.	Mineral, other	4,002.07	7.02	.18	200.18	5.00	207.20	5.18
27.	Combustible mineral products	112,581.98	2,708.76	2.41	8,028.63	7.13	10,737.39	9.54
Section VI:	Chemical products	592,604.69	18,760.91	3.17	78,593.45	13.26	97,354.36	16.43
28.	Chemicals and pharmaceuticals	376,387.86	12,971.84	3.45	55,934.41	14.86	68,906.25	18.31
29.	Chemical preparation, film, etc.	17,635.42	1,730.68	9.81	2,752.35	15.61	4,483.03	25.42
30.	Dyes and paints	59,154.52	3,063.74	5.18	9,307.49	15.73	12,371.23	20.91
31.	Essences and perfumes	14,544.83	129.02	.89	5,537.55	38.07	5,666.57	38.96
32.	Soaps, candles, etc.	16,001.23	154.98	.97	2,705.59	16.91	2,860.57	17.88
33.	Caseins, glues	3,035.28	695.35	22.91	864.38	28.48	1,559.73	51.39
34.	Explosives, matches, fireworks	13,342.04	14.29	.11	1,484.86	11.13	1,499.15	11.24
35.	Fertilizers	92,503.51	1.01	—	6.82	.01	7.83	0.01

TABLE 8–14 (Continued)

Imports and Duties Assessed by Section and Chapter of the Tariff Schedule, before Exemptions, 1962

(Thousands of Pesos)

Chapter or Section	Description	Value of Imports, c.i.f.	Specific Duty	Per Cent	*Ad Valorem* Duty	Per Cent	Total Duties	Per Cent
Section VII: Skins and hides		1,891.00	150.08	7.94	341.86	18.08	491.94	26.01
36.	Skins and hides	313.86	—	—	62.77	20.00	62.77	20.00
37.	Products of skins and hides	1,519.60	145.88	9.60	275.05	18.10	420.93	27.70
38.	Fur products	57.54	4.20	7.30	4.04	7.02	8.24	14.32
Section VIII: Rubber and rubber								
39.	products	84,010.90	4,335.44	5.16	13,148.80	15.65	17,484.24	20.81
Section IX: Wood and cork products		7,080.41	1,586.44	22.41	1,243.70	17.57	2,830.14	39.97
40.	Lumber and wood products	1,805.13	1,360.34	75.36	689.08	38.17	2,049.42	113.53
41.	Cork	5,188.91	213.72	4.12	549.17	10.58	762.89	14.70
42.	Straw articles, etc.	86.37	12.38	14.33	5.45	6.31	17.83	20.64
Section X: Paper and paper products		179,379.31	12,358.57	6.89	22,962.01	12.80	35,320.58	19.69
43.	Materials used to make paper	43,070.18	4,420.46	10.26	6,430.51	14.93	10,850.97	25.19
44.	Paper and cardboard	127,819.25	7,870.79	6.16	15,594.73	12.20	23,465.52	18.36
45.	Books, graphic arts	8,489.88	67.32	.79	936.77	11.03	1,004.09	11.83
Section XI: Textile materials		137,780.44	6,176.89	4.48	30,040.05	21.80	36,216.94	26.29
46.	Silk and synthetic fibers	11,014.32	1,907.53	17.32	2,811.30	25.52	4,718.83	42.84
47.	Wool and hair	68,991.94	2,091.55	3.03	14,638.69	21.22	16,730.24	24.25
48.	Cotton	4,101.30	140.28	3.42	690.19	16.83	830.47	20.25
49.	Linen, vegetable fibers	981.88	222.15	22.62	263.34	26.82	485.49	49.44
50.	Felts, cords, rope	32,872.33	1,389.79	4.23	11,363.88	34.57	12,753.67	38.80
51.	Clothing accessories	779.61	138.46	17.76	112.48	14.43	250.94	32.19
52.	Clothing	19,036.34	280.13	1.47	157.45	.83	437.58	2.30
53.	Rags and scrap	2.72	7.00	257.35	2.72	100.00	9.72	357.35
Section XII: Shoes, hats, etc.		2,542.95	371.83	14.62	426.83	16.78	798.66	31.41
54.	Shoes	1,151.60	91.05	7.91	117.12	10.17	208.17	18.08
55.	Hats	529.11	36.27	6.85	200.64	37.92	136.91	44.77
56.	Umbrellas and canes	694.72	244.39	35.18	109.05	15.70	353.44	50.88
57.	Feathers, flowers, wigs	167.52	.12	.07	.02	—	.14	.01
Section XIII: Stone, ceramic, glass		55,959.06	18,355.58	32.80	16,362.72	29.24	34,718.30	62.03
58.	Stone and mineral products	26,524.57	15,821.53	59.65	10,671.38	40.23	26,492.91	99.88
59.	Ceramics	5,755.09	435.08	7.56	1,168.62	20.31	1,603.70	27.87
60.	Glass	23,679.40	2,098.97	8.86	4,522.72	19.10	6,621.69	27.96
Section XIV: Pearls, precious stones		1,101.86	4.11	.37	199.50	18.11	203.61	18.48
61.	Pearls, precious stones	1,101.86	4.11	.37	199.50	18.11	203.61	18.48
62.	Coins	—	—	—	—	—	—	—

TABLE 8–14 (Continued)
Imports and Duties Assessed by Section and Chapter of the Tariff Schedule, before Exemptions, 1962

(Thousands of Pesos)

Chapter or Section Description	Value of Imports, c.i.f.	Specific Duty	Per Cent	*Ad Valorem* Duty	Per Cent	Total Duties	Per Cent
Section XV: Common metals	428,760.87	55,647.16	12.98	64,315.67	15.00	119,962.83	27.98
63. Iron and steel	321,367.04	44,277.91	13.78	46,216.08	14.38	90,493.99	28.16
64. Copper	36,020.91	3,417.20	9.49	7,392.14	20.52	10,809.34	30.01
65. Nickel	2,537.94	152.54	6.01	389.34	15.34	541.88	21.35
66. Aluminum	41,442.63	2,983.06	7.20	5,341.47	12.89	8,324.53	20.09
67. Lead	769.16	74.27	9.66	85.95	11.17	160.22	20.83
68. Zinc	5,521.87	1,384.93	25.08	1,163.72	21.07	2,548.65	46.15
69. Tin	3,133.35	79.91	2.55	345.78	11.04	425.69	13.59
70. Other	1,607.49	7.24	.45	225.11	14.00	232.35	14.45
71. Miscellaneous	16,360.48	3,270.10	19.99	3,156.08	19.29	6,246.18	39.28
Section XVI: Machinery and equipment	1,154,764.41	19,808.20	1.72	164,688.93	14.26	184,497.13	15.98
72. Boilers, machinery	842,542.70	8,408.10	1.00	111,805.89	13.27	120,213.99	14.27
73. Electrical machinery	312,221.71	11,400.10	3.65	52,883.04	16.94	64,283.14	20.59
Section XVII: Transport equipment	417,461.27	561.24	.13	63,940.86	15.32	64,502.10	15.45
74. Railroad equipment	14,238.80	2.94	.02	2,290.82	16.09	2,293.76	16.11
75. Automotive vehicles	360,159.51	551.50	.15	61,297.98	17.02	61,849.48	17.17
76. Aviation	43,062.96	6.80	.02	352.06	.82	358.86	.83
Section XVIII: Precision Instruments	67,287.14	1,352.53	2.01	13,515.51	20.09	14,868.04	22.10
77. Scientific instruments	52,981.30	196.64	.37	8,757.35	16.53	8,953.99	16.90
78. Watches and clocks	6,245.36	381.51	6.11	2,137.95	34.23	2,519.46	40.34
79. Musical instruments	8,060.48	774.38	9.61	2,620.21	32.51	3,394.59	42.11
Section XIX: Arms	12,335.72	4,339.81	35.18	5,348.12	43.35	9,687.93	78.54
80. Arms	7,725.62	2,623.34	33.96	3,194.02	40.83	5,817.36	75.30
81. Ammunition	4,610.10	1,716.47	37.23	2,154.10	46.73	3,870.57	83.96
Section XX: Merchandise	11,635.91	1,888.09	16.23	3,288.85	28.26	5,176.94	44.49
82. Plastic products	6,563.32	1,280.42	19.51	2,016.11	30.72	3,296.53	50.23
83. Brushes and sieves	383.81	20.69	5.39	115.80	30.17	136.49	35.56
84. Games, sports equipment	2,547.20	382.15	15.00	718.49	28.21	1,100.64	43.21
85. Fountain pens, pipes, etc.	2,141.58	204.83	9.56	438.45	20.47	643.28	30.04
Section XXI: Art and collector's objects							
86. Art and collector's objects	88.23	—	—	—	—	—	—
Section XXII:							
87. Other products not specified elsewhere	79,188.52	22,024.62	27.81	11,151.26	14.08	33,175.88	41.89
TOTALS	$3,683,670.25[a]	$250,179.42	6.79	$578,695.95	15.71	$828,875.37	22.50

[a] Subsequently revised to $3,658,327. See *Boletín Mensual de Estadística*, March, 1963.

Source: Departamento Administrativo Nacional de Estadística.

CHAPTER 9

Tariffs and Development

GOVERNMENT POLICY

THE GOVERNMENT'S POLICY with respect to imports as stated in the tariff reform law of 1958 is to keep the level of imports down ". . . to the limited amount of foreign exchange available during the coming years and to prevent disequilibrium in the balance of payments"; to ". . . stimulate a rapid substitute of imports in raw materials, consumer goods, and intermediate and capital goods, which can be produced economically in the country, in order to encourage a fuller utilization of the natural resources of the country"; and ". . . to seek the optimum utilization of the existing industrial capacity and stimulate investment preferentially in basic industries for the economic development of the country." In addition, the reforms were designed " . . . to bring up to date the tariffs that have lost their effect as a result of the monetary devaluations of recent years." To accomplish these objectives, protective tariffs, import licensing, and exemptions were to be utilized, and an organization was to be created to implement and advise with respect to tariff policies.[1]

The problem of maintaining the effective rates of the tariffs was considered in the previous chapter. The other objectives of tariff policy as stated above may be summarized as follows: (1) to conserve foreign exchange; (2) to encourage the substitution of domestic production for imports by employing both import restrictions and protective tariffs; (3) to encourage industrial development by means of low tariffs on capital imports, raw materials, and intermediate goods not produced domestically; and (4) to offer exemptions to oil and mining enterprises, to firms using *Paz del Río* steel, and to enterprises engaging in the export trade. All of the foregoing enterprises currently are protected from foreign competition by protective tariffs designed to promote import substitution. In addition, whether or not it is stated specifically as a government policy, the tariffs and controls ought to be designed to raise revenues and to distribute equally the burden of the tariffs and of development.

High protective tariffs and import prohibitions tend to serve the first three objectives, but they also reduce revenues, at least from the tariffs, and probably have a regressive effect, the burden being borne by consumers who are forced to pay higher prices. By reducing the amount of imports, they clearly tend to conserve foreign exchange, and by prohibiting or making imports expensive, they encourage the development of domestic production of the protected goods. But the advantageous effects may be offset by negative effects for the community, not only in lower revenues or in higher prices but in excessive protection, which invites monopolistic practices. Moreover, the protected industry may save little foreign exchange if

[1] Law 100, December 31, 1958.

174

it is dependent on imported raw materials and intermediate goods.

Low tariffs on imports of capital goods or exemptions from duties of these imports encourage the development of domestic industry, but they do not conserve foreign exchange, at least initially, and they reduce tariff revenues. Moreover, whether they conserve foreign exchange eventually depends on whether the industry continues to be dependent on foreign raw materials and intermediate goods, and whether or not, and how much, it exports.

High tariffs on luxury imports serve the objective of raising revenues equitably, and they may encourage the domestic production of these articles. In the past decade the higher priority of conserving foreign exchange by import prohibition has seriously affected government revenues from this source.

EFFECTIVENESS OF THE POLICIES

The early part of the decade from 1953 to 1962 was a period of relaxed controls as a result of relatively high coffee prices. Total imports rose from U.S. $546.7 million in 1953 to U.S. $671.8 million in 1954. Because of falling coffee prices, however, strict controls were effected, and imports reached a low of U.S. $399.9 million in 1958. Although controls remained, an easing of import restrictions occurred in 1960 and 1961, with imports rising to U.S. $557.2 million in the latter year. The decade ended with the imports in 1962 of U.S. $540.4 million, amounting to slightly less than the imports of 1953. From the standpoint of conserving foreign exchange, the import policy during the decade must be considered to have been moderately successful, especially in view of the fact that with a rising national income, averaging about 4 per cent per annum, the demand for imports must have increased considerably.

There is no room for complacency, however, since sizable deficits in trade have occurred in the last three years, imports

exceeding exports by U.S. $54.0 million in 1960, U.S. $122.6 million in 1961, and U.S. $81.5 million in 1962. The difficulties with respect to maintaining a balance of trade are amply indicated by devaluations in 1957 and 1962.

The substitution of domestically produced, durable consumer goods for imported, finished durable goods, which entails heavy and prolonged expenditures on imported raw materials and intermediate goods, is simply a disguised way of increasing the imports of consumer goods. The policy may require the employment of some domestic resources, and, thus, it may be more economical of foreign exchange for the new level of consumer goods consumption, but it also uses more foreign exchange resources than did the former level of imports.

Table 9–1 indicates the changes in the character of imports from 1958 to 1962. It shows an increase in total imports from the austerity level of 1958 of U.S. $140 million, or an increase of 35.1 per cent. Because of the relatively large amount of imports unallocated in 1958, the absolute increases shown in Table 9–1 are somewhat misleading. Table 9–2 shows the imports of the various years with the unallocated imports apportioned on the basis of percentages shown in each category for the given year. The table shows that the imports of finished consumer goods increased by $7.2 million, or by 23 per cent; intermediate goods by $51.9 million, or by about 21 per cent; and capital goods by U.S. $81.3 million, or by 68 per cent.

Finished consumer goods decreased as a proportion of total allocated imports from 7.8 per cent in 1958 to 7.1 per cent in 1962. Intermediate goods likewise decreased from 62.4 per cent in 1958 to 55.8 per cent in 1962. Capital goods during the same period increased as a proportion of the total from 29.8 per cent to 37.1 per cent. For the unallocated imports, no attempt was made to determine if a bias existed in favor of one category or another. However, in an analysis based upon registered imports shown

TABLE 9–1

Imports of Important Articles, 1958 to 1962[a]

(Millions of U.S. Dollars)

	(1) 1958	(2) 1959	(3) 1959	(4) 1960	(5) 1960	(6) 1961	(7) 1961	(8) 1962
Finished consumer goods	$13.8 (5.0)	$13.7 (4.8)	$16.3 (4.7)	$17.7 (4.0)	$17.2 (3.9)	$19.2 (4.0)	$19.2 (3.9)	$14.2 (3.3)
Durable consumer goods	7.8 (2.8)	7.9 (2.8)	10.9 (3.1)	19.3 (4.3)	20.6 (4.7)	40.2 (8.3)	40.2 (8.2)	16.6 (3.8)
Total consumer goods	21.6 (7.8)	21.5 (7.6)	27.2 (7.8)	37.8 (8.3)	37.0 (8.6)	59.4 (12.3)	59.4 (12.1)	30.8 (7.1)
Primary products	41.3 (14.9)	33.2 (11.7)	34.8 (10.0)	31.6 (7.1)	31.5 (7.1)	44.3 (9.1)	44.3 (9.0)	35.7 (8.2)
Intermediate goods	131.7 (47.5)	130.5 (45.9)	172.2 (49.3)	208.8 (47.0)	202.1 (45.8)	218.1 (44.9)	218.2 (44.3)	207.1 (47.6)
Total intermediate goods	173.1 (62.4)	163.7 (57.6)	207.0 (59.3)	240.4 (54.1)	233.6 (52.9)	262.4 (54.0)	262.5 (53.3)	242.8 (55.8)
Capital goods	82.8 (29.8)	98.9 (34.8)	114.9 (32.9)	166.9 (37.6)	169.9 (38.5)	163.9 (33.7)	170.1 (34.6)	161.6 (37.1)
Total important goods	277.5 (100.0)	284.1 (100.0)	349.1 (100.0)	444.3 (100.0)	441.4 (100.0)	485.7 (100.0)	492.1 (100.0)	435.2 (100.0)
Total important goods	277.5 (69.4)	284.1 (68.4)	349.1 (84.0)	444.3 (85.7)	441.4 (85.1)	485.7 (87.2)	492.1 (88.3)	435.2 (80.5)
Not allocated	122.5 (30.6)	131.5 (31.6)	66.5 (16.0)	74.3 (14.3)	77.2 (14.9)	71.4 (12.8)	65.1 (11.7)	105.1 (19.5)
Total imports	399.9 (100.0)	415.6 (100.0)	415.6 (100.0)	518.6 (100.0)	518.6 (100.0)	557.1 (100.0)	557.1 (100.0)	540.3 (100.0)

Sources: Anuario de Comercio Exterior, 1959, 1960, 1961, and Boletin Mensual de Estadística, May, 1963.

Totals do not add because of rounding.

[a] Columns (1) and (2), (3) and (4), (5) and (6), and (7) and (8) are based on the same list of goods. Therefore, columns (1), (3), (5), and (7), or (2), (4), (6), and (8) are not strictly comparable because the list of goods varies.

TABLE 9-2

Estimated Imports of Consumer, Intermediate, and Capital Goods, 1958 to 1962[a]

(Millions of U.S. Dollars)

	(1) 1958	(2) 1959	(3) 1959	(4) 1960	(5) 1960	(6) 1961	(7) 1961	(8) 1962
Finished consumer goods	$19.9	$20.0	$19.4	$20.7	$20.2	$22.1	$21.7	$17.7
Durable consumer goods	11.2	11.6	13.0	22.5	24.2	46.1	45.5	20.6
Total consumer goods	31.1	31.6	32.4	43.2	44.4	68.2	67.2	38.3
Primary products	59.6	48.6	41.4	36.9	37.0	50.8	50.2	44.3
Other intermediate goods	189.9	190.9	205.0	243.7	237.5	250.2	247.0	257.1
Total intermediate goods	249.5	239.5	246.4	280.6	274.5	301.0	297.2	301.4
Capital goods	119.3	144.5	136.8	194.8	199.6	188.0	192.6	200.6
Total	399.9	415.6	415.6	518.6	518.5	557.2	557.0	540.3
Actual Total	399.9	415.6	415.6	518.6	518.6	557.1	557.1	540.3

[a] Columns (1) and (2), (3) and (4), (5) and (6), and (7) and (8) are based on the same list of goods. Therefore, columns (1), (3), (5), and (7), or (2), (4), (6), and (8) are not strictly comparable because the list of goods varies.

Source: Table 9-7.

TABLE 9-3

Registered Imports According to Class of Goods, 1958 to 1961

(Millions of U.S. Dollars)

	1958	1959	1960	1961[a]
Transport equipment	$ 45.1 (16.3)	$ 83.5 (22.1)	$100.0 (22.5)	$100.7 (21.8)
Other capital goods	63.6 (23.0)	98.8 (26.2)	130.0 (29.2)	129.4 (28.0)
Sub-Total	108.7 (39.3)	182.3 (48.3)	230.0 (51.7)	230.1 (49.8)
Consumer goods	141.5 (51.2)	168.0 (44.6)	176.4 (39.7)	187.7 (40.6)
Drugs, books, and others	26.3 (9.5)	26.8 (7.1)	38.1 (8.6)	44.7 (9.7)
TOTALS	276.5 (100.0)	377.1 (100.0)	444.5 (100.0)	462.5 (100.0)

[a] Provisional.

Source: Informe Anual del Banco de la República, July, 1960, to December 31, 1961, p. 64.

in Table 9-3, the Central Bank showed that capital goods imports increased relatively, as well as absolutely, from 1958 to 1961, while consumer goods imports increased absolutely but declined relative to total registered imports. These results are consistent with the data in Tables 9-1 and 9-2, although the composition of the categories obviously is different. In avoiding the intermediate goods category in Table 9-3 and allocating all goods to the capital or consumer goods categories, it is interesting to note that consumer goods result in about 50 per cent of total imports. Although there is cause for

some satisfaction in that the proportion of consumer goods has been declining, the substantial increases in their absolute amount obviously has contributed to the balance-of-payments difficulties.

ECONOMIC DEVELOPMENT

As noted earlier, agricultural equipment and materials are practically free of duties, and very low duties apply to machinery and materials not produced in the country. Both agricultural production and factory output increased substantially during the decade of 1950 to 1960. Gross domestic product rose from $14,581 million to $22,784 million, both expressed in 1958 prices, or by about 56 per cent. Factory output (gross product) rose from $1,608 million to $3,138 million, or by 95 per cent.[2] Manufactures of smaller producers (employing less than five persons) increased from $572 million to $787 million, or by 37.6 per cent. Agricultural production, including forestry and fishing, rose from $5,631 million to $7,901 million, or by 34.7 per cent.[3]

During the same period (1950 to 1960) factory employment grew from 170,000 to 252,000, or by 48 per cent, and artisan employment from 379,000 to 496,000, or by nearly 31 per cent.[4] Employment in the primary sector increased from 2,113,000 in 1951 to 2,334,000 in 1961, or by 10 per cent.[5] Referring to the production data in the previous paragraph, real output per worker obviously grew in both the manufacturing and primary sectors. Gross output per worker increased over 31 per cent in the factories, by about 5 per cent among the artisans, and by about 27 per cent in agriculture.

One may conclude that genuine progress is demonstrated in general. Nevertheless, the picture is uneven among various industries, and given the serious problems of unemployment and underemployment, the question must be asked whether government efforts and resources, including revenues foregone, were allocated efficiently.

THE CHANGING PATTERN OF IMPORTS[6]

It was noted earlier that total imports in 1953 and in 1962 were nearly at the same level, U.S. $546.7 million and U.S. $540.4 million respectively. In both years, mechani-

[2] *Plan General de Desarrollo Económico y Social*, Part II, p. 7.
[3] Departamento Administrativo de Planeacíon.
[4] *Plan General de Desarrollo*, Part II, p. 19.
[5] Departamento Administrativo de Planeación.
[6] For additional detail on the changing pattern of imports, see Appendix Tables 9–8 and 9–9 of this chapter.

cal and electrical machinery and appliances were the most important classes of imports, accounting for 26.1 per cent of total imports in 1953 and 31.4 per cent in 1962. Common metals and their products and transport material accounted for 15.3 and 14.9 per cent respectively in 1953 but dropped in relative position behind chemicals and pharmaceuticals by 1962, their proportions declining to 11.6 and 11.3 per cent respectively. Chemicals and pharmaceuticals showed the greatest absolute and relative change, increasing by U.S. $34.3 million, from 9.7 per cent of the total imports in 1953 to 16.2 per cent in 1962.

The increased imports of machinery and equipment, which includes industrial and agricultural machinery and electrical products, were undoubtedly affected by the government's policy of encouraging industrial development. Similarly, the increase in the chemicals category reflects this policy. There are no duties on agricultural machinery and equipment, and the average duty on the whole section of machinery and equipment was 15.98 per cent in 1962. Similarly, the average duty on chemicals and pharmaceuticals was 16.43 per cent in 1962. Other increases related to industrial development were in rubber and rubber products, from U.S. $8.6 million to U.S. $12.3 million, an increase of 43.9 per cent, and in paper and paper products, from U.S. $17.8 million to U.S. $26.3 million, an increase of 47.5 per cent. Both of these groups represent, in the most part, raw materials and intermediate goods.

Two other increases are worth noting, mainly because they illustrate programs of import substitution which have not been successful. Imports of agricultural products increased 15 per cent between 1953 and 1962. Nearly all of the increase was in the importation of cereals under Public Law 480 from the United States. The other is the importation of oils and fats of animal and vegetable origin, which increased by 12.8 per cent from U.S. $9.7 million to U.S. $10.9 million. Substantial increases in the production of wheat, soy beans, and cotton seed are projected under the development plan and could be successfully accomplished given the land resources of Colombia.[7]

Successful programs of import substitution may be noted in the import reduction of processed agricultural products, a decrease of 43.6 per cent, or U.S. $6.2 million; non-metallic minerals, principally petroleum products, which decreased 33.9 per cent from U.S. $33.0 million to U.S. $21.8 million; textile and textile product imports, which decreased 54.8 per cent from U.S. $44.8 million to U.S. $20.2 million; and imports of common metals and their products, which decreased 25.1 per cent from U.S. $83.8 million to U.S. $62.6 million. In textile products, the reduction was mostly in cotton imports, which decreased from imports of more than U.S. $21 million in 1953 to a negligible quantity in 1962. Other reductions, especially in transport material and equipment, instruments, and merchandise mainly reflect import restrictions of consumer goods.

From 1953 to 1962, the imports of capital equipment, raw material, and intermediate goods increased enough to offset the combined savings in foreign exchange from the import substitution programs in raw materials and soft goods and the import prohibitions of luxury consumer goods. If the imbalance between exports and imports did not exist, there could be no criticism made of the increased imports of raw materials and intermediate goods. But given the sustained trade imbalance over the past three years, it appears likely that it would have been better to concentrate on developing exports than on industrialization, at least at this stage of Colombia's development.

IMPORTS OF PARTICULAR INDUSTRIES

In 1959 manufacturing payrolls amounted to 31.5 per cent of value added in manufacturing. (See Table 9–4.) The range was from

[7] *Plan General de Desarrollo*, Part I, p. 143.

9.7 per cent of value added in the tobacco products industry to 71.0 per cent in the manufacture of transport materials and equipment. On the other hand, total imported materials (excluding capital equipment) amounted to $1.49 billion compared to payrolls of $1.22 billion. In other words, it required $1.21 of imports to provide $1.00 of payroll. Imports were 293.4 per cent of payrolls in the paper and paper products industry, 281.9 per cent in electrical products, 225.4 per cent in the rubber products industry, and 231.7 per cent in chemicals and pharmaceuticals. Other industries with high ratios of imports to wages included food processing, publishing, basic metals, metal products, and diverse manufactures. Imports were a relatively low percentage of payrolls in wood furniture, 10.9 per cent; shoes and clothing, 18.4 per cent; wood and cork products, 24.6 per cent; non-metallic mineral products, 39.5 per cent; and petroleum, 44.6 per cent.

Manufacturing industries as a whole imported 23.3 per cent of their total purchases. Imports were only 4.7 per cent of total purchases in the manufacture of shoes and clothing, 7.6 per cent in wood and cork products, 7.0 per cent in wood furniture, 3.7 per cent in petroleum, 8.5 per cent in basic metals, 11.7 per cent in food processing, and 14.4 per cent in leather and leather products.

On the negative side, imports were as high as 74.7 per cent in the rubber products industry, 72.8 per cent in electrical products, 70.6 per cent in transport materials and equipment, 57.5 per cent in metal products, 57.3 per cent in machinery, 56.6 per cent in diverse manufactures, 59.2 per cent in chemicals, and 53.9 per cent in the paper and paper products industry.

If these industries are ranked with respect to the percentage that imports bear to payrolls (the lowest receiving "1" and the highest "20") and with respect to imports as a percentage of total purchases (the lowest similarly receiving "1" and the highest "20"), and the two scores are summed, the lowest and, therefore, the best rankings are made by shoes and clothing, wood furniture, petro-

TABLE 9–4

Value Added, Wages, and Imports in Manufacturing, 1959[a]

Industry	Value Added	Total Remuneration	Per Cent	Imported Materials Excluding Capital Equipment	Imports as a Percentage of Remuneration	Total Purchases of Materials	Imports as a Percentage of Total Purchases
Food processing	$ 562,214	$ 148,166	26.4	$ 275,101	185.7	$2,344,006	11.7
Beverages	557,883	101,829	18.3	89,858	88.2	364,231	24.7
Tobacco	242,920	23,464	9.7	17,544	74.8	79,042	22.2
Textiles	614,015	231,168	37.6	222,139	96.1	992,623	22.4
Shoes and clothing	213,010	94,176	44.2	17,303	18.4	368,214	4.7
Wood and cork	39,938	18,968	47.5	4,675	24.6	61,039	7.6
Wood furniture	33,667	20,204	60.0	2,200	10.9	31,581	7.0
Paper	64,327	20,544	31.9	60,266	293.4	111,774	53.9
Publishing	104,911	52,867	50.4	84,213	159.3	97,975	86.0
Leather (except shoes)	58,707	22,707	38.7	17,706	78.0	123,286	14.4
Rubber	92,953	37,100	39.9	83,638	225.4	111,906	74.7
Chemical	371,149	98,202	26.5	227,489	231.7	384,337	59.2
Petroleum	166,324	33,327	20.0	14,853	44.6	398,257	3.7
Non-metallic minerals	237,065	93,575	39.5	36,975	39.5	143,088	25.8
Basic metals	101,043	20,165	20.0	23,245	115.3	272,319	8.5
Metal products	127,680	56,077	43.9	98,613	175.9	171,412	57.5
Machinery	32,500	16,276	50.1	18,241	112.1	31,846	57.3
Electrical products	81,283	28,702	35.3	80,909	281.9	111,106	72.8
Transport materials and equipment	98,008	69,550	71.0	66,801	96.0	94,582	70.6
Diverse	75,408	32,041	42.5	46,583	145.2	82,285	56.6
TOTALS	$3,875,005	$1,219,108	31.5	$1,488,352	122.1	$6,374,909	23.3

[a] Includes establishments with five or more employees or with more than $24,000 in output.

Source: Anuario General de Estadistica, 1960.

leum, wood and cork, leather, tobacco, non-metallic mineral products, basic metals, textiles, and beverages. On the other hand, the highest and worst scores are made by electrical products, rubber products, publishing, chemicals and pharmaceuticals, paper, metal products, diverse manufactures, transport materials and equipment, machinery, and food processing.

PRICING POLICIES

The average gross margin on sales in manufacturing, which covers profits, depreciation, and taxes, was 26.4 per cent in 1960. (See Table 9–5.) Among the industries with lower-than-average margins were food processing, 15.0 per cent; wood and cork products, 18.3 per cent; transport materials and equipment, 15.5 per cent; petroleum and coal

products, 19.5 per cent; and shoes and clothing, 20.9 per cent. Leather, wood furniture, textiles, basic metals, and metal products were also below the average.

The highest margins were recorded in tobacco products, 67.0 per cent; beverages, 50.3 per cent; chemicals, 38.0 per cent; and non-metallic mineral products, 30.7 per cent. Other industries with above average margins included diverse manufactures, machinery, electrical products, rubber products, paper, and publishing.

In general, the industries which performed well with respect to imports, payrolls, and domestic purchases also showed the lowest gross margins on sales with the exception of beverages and tobacco products. On the other hand, showing an unexpectedly low gross margin were transport materials and equipment.

While some of the difference in gross

TABLE 9–5
Value Added and Wages in Manufacturing, 1960

Industry	Gross Product (1)	Value Added (2)	Salaries, Wages, and Fringe Benefits (3)	Percentage of Value Added (4)	Col. (2) Minus Col. (3) (5)	Gross Margin for Profits, Depreciation, and Taxes Col. (5) Divided by Col. (1) (6)
Food	$ 3,219,033	$ 657,819	$ 176,278	26.8	$ 481,541	15.0
Beverages	1,118,685	688,134	125,414	18.2	562,720	50.3
Tobacco	347,390	259,396	26,563	10.2	232,833	67.0
Textiles	1,817,082	727,785	280,848	38.6	446,937	24.6
Shoes and clothing	631,490	233,746	101,828	43.6	131,918	20.9
Wood and cork	117,566	44,253	22,681	51.3	21,572	18.3
Wood furniture	74,363	38,553	21,816	56.6	16,737	22.5
Paper	227,509	84,959	25,336	29.8	59,623	26.2
Publishing	254,022	132,572	64,659	48.8	67,913	26.7
Leather	183,502	67,369	23,492	34.9	43,877	23.9
Rubber	234,980	104,350	40,037	38.4	64,313	27.4
Chemicals	911,524	471,845	125,305	26.6	346,540	38.0
Petroleum and coal	636,329	163,035	39,246	24.1	123,789	19.5
Non-metallic minerals	494,314	269,524	117,604	43.6	151,920	30.7
Basic metals	554,060	157,290	25,422	16.2	131,868	23.8
Metal products	378,240	165,350	75,229	45.5	90,121	23.8
Machinery	80,370	40,791	17,890	43.9	22,901	28.5
Electrical products	267,610	111,337	39,029	35.1	72,308	27.0
Transport, materials and equipment	226,127	117,520	82,364	70.1	35,156	15.5
Diverse manufactures	204,021	94,685	33,671	35.6	61,014	29.9
TOTALS	$11,978,217	$4,630,313	$1,464,712	31.6	$3,165,601	26.4

Source: Boletín Mensual de Estadística, No. 141, December, 1962.

margins represent varying amounts of capital invested per dollar of product, there is also the possibility that the degree of monopoly in the industry is a major factor. It is not surprising to find such traditionally competitive industries as food-processing, wood products, shoes and clothing, textiles, and leather products among those with low margins. Tobacco and chemicals are traditionally monopolistic and therefore cause no surprise with their high margins. Petroleum firms must compete with a government-owned firm, which presumably does not price monopolistically.

While the data are inconclusive with respect to the cause of the variations, one should expect competitive industries to behave well in the face of protective tariffs and controls. On the other hand, monopolists will find it relatively easy to abuse their privileges. Of necessity, the number of firms producing sophisticated industrial products will be few. In such cases, protective tariffs should certainly be low, for this is the only effective means of preventing abuses.

The narrow gross margin on sales in transport materials and equipment suggests that this is due to the fact that the products produced—trucks and spare parts—are subject to foreign competition. The duties on trucks and automobile parts are very low. The domestic industry, in the absence of import licensing, would face strong competition. The margin, therefore, probably reflects the competitive pricing practices in the industry. The effect of low tariffs can be seen here—good industry performance and reasonable margins.

It is interesting to note that protection by means of import licenses rather than by high tariffs prevents the usual practice of charging what the market will bear. There is a conspicuous tendency to price domestic products at just below the sum of import c.i.f. prices plus duties; in other words, domestic products tend to be priced at a level just sufficient to prevent their importation given the existing tariffs. If the latter are high, the domestic prices tend to be high; if low, the domestic prices tend to be low.

The pricing policies for alcoholic beverages and cigarettes are of particular interest from the point of view of government revenue. Since the firms in these industries must compete with foreign producers, if the differential in market prices is too small, the contraband problem is aggravated. In the case of liquors, there is the additional problem that the domestic industry has failed to develop a whiskey, either bourbon or scotch-type. As a result, local products must compete with foreign products that are quite different, and, therefore, price differences have a lesser impact. Domestic liquor prices, if they included heavy taxes as part of their present prices, would not be too high. But if their present prices reflect monopolistic pricing, they provide neither government revenues nor adequate competition. Furthermore, high profits on gins and rums are not an inducement to compete against contraband whiskeys and cognac.

A similar criticism may be made of cigarette-pricing. Cigarettes are very lightly taxed, yet the range in prices per package is $.70 to $1.50, a spread of $0.80. The range in the United States for comparable cigarettes is only three U.S. cents. One may reasonably suspect that most of the Colombian differential reflects monopoly pricing. If the price of $1.50 included a tax of Col. $0.75, the price would appear to be justified. As it is, the price of $1.50 merely encourages the consumption of contraband imported cigarettes without appreciably increasing government revenues.

INTERMEDIATE GOODS AND VERTICAL INTEGRATION

The preceding analysis reveals that many Colombian industries, particularly those producing durable goods, chemicals, paper, and rubber products, require large amounts of imported raw materials and intermediate goods. The consequent drain on Colombia's foreign exchange resources appears excessive. For some industries, there even may be a question as to whether any foreign exchange is, in fact, economized. The basket of imports assembled in Colombia may cost nearly as much in foreign exchange, perhaps more per unit if repatriated profits are taken into account, as finished imports. In that event, the employment of Colombians in the industry is paid for entirely by the consumer in the form of higher prices. There is no real saving in foreign exchange, and there is no economic advantage to the country.

What is at issue is not the desirability of industrialization but the best strategy to attain this end. Clearly, a greater degree of integration of production in Colombia would be desirable. In general, the development of raw materials and the production of some intermediate goods should precede, or at least accompany, the development of industry. If it preceded industrialization, the export of raw materials would provide the foreign exchange necessary for the subsequent development of industry.

This is particularly true of such industries as rubber products and paper and, probably, also of chemical products and fertilizers. The quantity and quality of domestic rubber production leaves much to be desired. Since it is a product for which an international market exists, resources applied to its development would earn foreign exchange through exports as well as save a substantial part of the U.S. $12.3 million in rubber imported in 1962. Similarly, cocoa imports of U.S. $4.6 million, oils and fats of U.S. $10.9 million, fertilizers of U.S. $13.8 million, wool of U.S. $10.2 million, oleaginous seeds of

U.S. $7.2 million, and cereals of U.S. $14.5 million offer better possibilities of development and import substitution than do complicated, industrial durable goods.

The organization of production in the durable goods industries, especially of those products which offer possibilities of mass production, also leaves much to be desired. Many of the consumer goods industries have a relatively small domestic market. The Colombian market for autos, refrigerators, and electric appliances can be satisfied, in view of the present limited market, only if production is concentrated in a single firm or, at the most, two or three firms. Parcelling the limited market among several firms not only prevents the realization of economies of large-scale production but, in fact, deters the rapid substitution of domestic production for imported intermediate goods.

Unless the scale of production of the firm is large enough, it will not pay to produce the necessary parts in Colombia, or, if the firm is forced to do so, it will cost more to produce them in Colombia in foreign exchange because of small-scale operations than the cost of the imported parts. The recent negotiations by the Minister of Development with several automobile firms for assembly plants in Colombia is a case in point. If there were several automobile plants in Colombia, they would not produce engines and many other parts, because each firm would find it more advantageous to import parts than to produce them. On the other hand, the market probably would justify a single, integrated firm.

By and large, import substitution has been more beneficial in industries in which Colombia has, or can be expected to have, a comparative advantage because of its natural resources. Cotton, textiles, leather, shoes, clothing, beverages, food-processing, and petroleum products have proven highly successful in terms of import substitution. It is no accident that these industries also afford the greatest promise of foreign exchange earnings. It is possible, in fact very likely, that the

development of consumer durable goods industries will eventually prove to Colombia's advantage. But in the meantime, this development is likely to cause a serious drain on Colombia's limited foreign exchange resources for many years if considerations of the economies of large-scale production and the integration it makes possible are neglected.

FOREIGN OPERATIONS

Many of the firms producing chemical products and durable goods are subsidiaries of large foreign corporations that have integrated operations abroad. As a result, many of them import intermediate goods (parts, materials, etc.) from either their parent companies or from other subsidiaries of their parent companies. A conflict-of-interest problem thus arises. While on the one hand the interest of Colombia is to have as much integration of industrial operations within Colombia as possible, the parent company may be reluctant to invest in additional facilities that duplicate operations it already possesses abroad.

There is also the problem of conflict of interest with regard to export operations and the pricing of imports purchased from affiliated companies. International companies are naturally reluctant to have their various subsidiaries undercut one another or invade markets profitably being exploited by other affiliates. Whereas the Colombian interest is not only to substitute for imports but to earn foreign exchange, the primary interest of the foreign company may be to exploit the Colombian market.

The parent company of a Colombian subsidiary is interested in maximizing its profits from its total operations. It will try to earn profits where it is most advantageous to do so. If some operations are located in tax havens, it will try to maximize its profits in those locations. It will tend to under-invoice its shipments to subsidiaries or affiliates in those locations, and overinvoice its shipments from those locations.

FOREIGN REMITTANCES OF INTEREST AND PROFITS

As a possible further complication, it may be noted that the attempt to develop from the top down, instead of the bottom up, requires skills and talents not available in Colombia. Except in agriculture and mining, where the government traditionally has played a major role, these skills must be provided by private firms. As a result, many of the firms that dominate the durable goods market are foreign firms. They expect, sooner or later, to repatriate their capital and profits. In this respect, they may not differ very much from domestic firms whose owners send their capital abroad for "safe-keeping." But the likelihood of their doing so is greater. Therefore, to the cost of imported raw materials and intermediate goods, one must add the likely loss of foreign exchange in the future through the repatriation of capital and profit.

In the decade from 1950 to 1959 inclusive, factor payments to the exterior averaged about U.S. $40 million annually. In the three years of 1957 to 1959, the average annual remittances of profits were U.S. $38.1 million and of interest, an additional U.S. $16.8 million.[8] This is not a serious problem when the foreign firm engages in export trade and earns its own foreign exchange requirements. It can be a serious matter, though, when no foreign exchange is earned by the firm.

This problem is not peculiar to foreign companies. It is notorious that rich Colombians send large amounts of capital abroad. If they have not earned foreign exchange sufficient to cover their remittances abroad, they place a serious burden on the economy.

There are, at present, no restrictions on foreign remittances. Foreign companies that possess guarantees with respect to the repatriation of capital may do so at the official rate,

but any company or individual may convert pesos into foreign exchange at the free rate, which during 1963 was 10 per cent higher than the official rate.

While investment, whatever the source, is likely to aid the development of Colombia, it is clear that some forms of investment are better than others. Foreign investment in industries that will earn foreign exchange, or in those that will require relatively small amounts of imported raw materials and intermediate goods, are preferable to those which will neither earn foreign exchange nor save much foreign exchange on import substitution. As a case in point, the foreign oil companies, while they may be subject to certain conflicts of interest mentioned above, are expected to meet their foreign exchange requirements out of exports. At least, that is the rationale of the Petroleum Law, which permits them to keep whatever foreign exchange earnings they realize on exports. But all that this means, in effect, is that they may repatriate capital and profits at the official rate.

While many Colombians are forced by import restrictions, tariffs, and protective policies to tighten their belts, it does not seem equitable to allow foreign remittances to be entirely free of taxation. If foreign exchange is not to be rationed, then those who remit abroad should be subject to special taxes whenever they cannot show that their economic activities have actually earned foreign exchange for the economy.

FOREIGN TRAVEL

No restrictions on foreign travel are imposed by the Colombian government. In 1960 some 27,000 Colombians made trips abroad as tourists, about two-thirds going to Europe, the United States, and Canada, and about one-third to Latin American countries.[9] These numbers do not include those who may have traveled to neighboring countries not having

---

[8] *Plan General de Desarrollo*, Part I, pp. 298 and 302.

[9] *Anuario General de Estadística, 1960*, pp. 130–33.

visa requirements. The balance-of-payments accounts for 1960 show foreign exchange expenditures for travel purposes of U.S. $28.3 million.

High import duties on luxuries result in a reallocation of the consumer's income in favor of untaxed purchases. The expenditure on travel is thus encouraged by the relative changes in prices of imported goods and protected goods as compared to untaxed travel expenditures. If only to have a neutral effect on expenditures, a tax on travel abroad based on assumed foreign daily expenditures would be justified. In addition, since travel expenditures are almost entirely restricted to upper income groups, the tax would have desirable effects on the distribution of the tax burden. Finally, the levy would penalize the expenditure of scarce foreign exchange.

It might not be amiss, in addition to the foregoing tax, to restrict the granting of credit for travel abroad. In the face of balance-of-payments difficulties, it is an anachronism to permit the encouragement of travel abroad on credit. Colombia's limited credit resources obviously could be allocated more usefully.

IMPORT SUBSTITUTION IN THE PRIMARY SECTOR

Agricultural production has grown significantly during the past decade, but agricultural products, with few exceptions other than the perennial exports like coffee and bananas, have not contributed directly to foreign exchange earnings. One exception has been cotton, which has been successful both with respect to import substitution and exports. In 1953 the textile industry was forced to import U.S. $21.26 million of cotton, but by 1962 cotton exports amounted to U.S. $15.64 million. The few other exceptions include lumber, with exports rising from U.S. $203,000 in 1951 to U.S. $2.23 million in 1962, and seafood, with exports rising from a negligible amount in 1959 to U.S. $1.53 million in 1962.

Excluding cotton and processed foods, other agricultural imports rose slightly from 1953 to 1962. Appendix Table 9A–1 shows that imports in the first three sections of the tariff list rose from U.S. $32.49 million to U.S. $36.18 million, or by more than 10 per cent. As noted earlier, cereals, oils and fats, and oleaginous seeds and fruits showed increases and accounted for 90 per cent of the total imports of the first three sections of the tariff list in 1962. On the other hand, the agricultural industry made significant progress in meeting the increasing food requirements of the population. During the decade from 1950 to 1960, the value of agricultural output measured in 1958 prices, including forestry and fishing, rose from $5,630.9 million to $7,901.4 million, or by over 40 per cent.

It is possible to be very optimistic about the future of the agricultural industry. As shown in Chapter 6 on agricultural taxation, 3.2 million hectares are in crops, 2.6 million in fallow, over 30.0 million in pasture, and 69.4 million are unexploited. An appreciable part of the land now farmed extensively could be utilized in crops.[10] Some of the unutilized land needs only adequate transportation facilities to make it accessible, and much of it requires public investment for the development of water resources. The development plan anticipates that total agricultural exports, excluding forestry and fishing, can be increased by 48 per cent by 1970. Excluding coffee, the plan anticipates an increase in exports for the decade from U.S. $31.5 million to U.S. $155.2 million.[11]

Public investment in the agricultural sector should have a high priority in the short run, and perhaps in the long run as well. Higher agricultural output would make possible the successful industrialization of Colombia by providing a better market for industrial goods, raw materials for industry, and foreign exchange earnings for the importation of capital goods. The variety of climatic conditions makes it possible to grow almost anything in

[10] *Plan General de Desarrollo*, Part I, p. 26.
[11] *Ibid.*, Part I, p. 350.

Colombia and to produce many crops during seasons when production is not possible in the temperate zones. Development of the agricultural sector also would make possible higher living standards for the masses of the people, something which the industrialization program in the durable goods sector offers only in the very long run because of its dependence on imports.

PROSPECTS FOR HIGHER TARIFF REVENUES

Revenues from tariffs are dependent on the level and composition of the rates, the level of imports, the composition of imports, and exemptions. The level of the rates established by the tax reform of 1959 was considerably higher than the level that existed from 1956 to 1958.[12] Nevertheless, the rates effective on actual imports were somewhat less from 1960 to 1962 than from 1952 to 1954. In 1961 imports were slightly higher than in 1953, U.S. $557.1 million compared to U.S. $546.7 million, but duties collected in 1961 were U.S. $92.9 million compared with U.S. $102.2 million in 1953, or about 9.1 per cent less. The difference must be attributable to the composition of imports and exemptions. The increasing proportion of capital goods imports noticeable in recent years, which are subject to low rates or are exempt, and the decreasing proportion of consumer goods, which are generally subject to the highest rates, tend to reduce revenues from the tariffs. The increasing amount of exemptions likewise tends to reduce the yield of the tariffs. Emphasis on industrial development should tend to reduce further the effective rates of the tariffs.

Most of the goods exempted to private enterprises are capital goods, judging by the low average rate of the exempted duties in this category. It is easy to exaggerate the importance of exemptions as a development incentive. The saving is primarily in the

12 *Ibid.*, Part II, p. 55.

interest cost on the taxes saved. But since the domestic industry is protected in practically every case by high tariffs, the firms would have no problem in passing the increased interest cost on to consumers.

It may be objected that the exemption reduces the amount of capital that the firm needs to raise. This is true, but this criticism suggests not that the duties should be exempted but only that they should be postponed. The government could permit the duties to be amortized (plus interest) in cases where this would be desirable.

On the other hand, exemptions probably should be given to firms that engage in the export trade, but only to the extent that their exported products bear to the total sales of the firms. In such cases, the exemptions may be defended as a means of giving firms a better competitive position with foreign competitors. But the same argument does not apply to protected sales in the domestic market.

Unless it is the desire of the government to subsidize the consumers of products to be manufactured with exempt capital equipment, there is little justification for the exemption. But even when subsidization is warranted, it cannot be assumed that the consumer will benefit when the industry is protected by high tariffs. Duties exempted to private firms totalled $53.1 million in 1961, or U.S. $7.9 million. Many of these exemptions could and should be terminated.

A second aspect of tariff policy is that raw materials and intermediate goods that are manufactured into luxury goods in Colombia are subject to relatively low duties. If a refrigerator is subject to high duties on the grounds that it is a luxury good, its components should not be subject to low duties simply because they are assembled or produced in Colombia. The policy of import substitution through protective tariffs should not be permitted to reduce an important revenue source that is progressive in its impact. The prices of these luxury-type goods produced domestically tend to be extremely high, reflecting the lack of competition as well as the small scale of production. What is to be avoided is a shift of taxes that would have been collected on the imported, finished products into the pockets of the domestic producers with no gain and, in fact, a serious loss to the consumer.

As noted earlier, the industries producing durable consumer goods tend to import a high proportion of their raw materials and intermediate goods. As a result, little is saved in foreign exchange by their development, while the loss of revenue is considerable. To prevent this loss of revenue and to increase customs revenues, intermediate goods incorporated into consumer durable goods should be taxed more heavily, or a substantial internal excise tax should be levied on the finished products. It is estimated that the effective rate of the duties on intermediate goods, some of which are subject to protective tariffs, is 28.2 per cent.[13] If this *average* were raised to 40 per cent, revenues would be increased by $35.6 million, or U.S. $5.3 million, based on total estimated imports of intermediate goods in 1962.

In Colombia's concern to use tariff policy for development purposes and to conserve foreign exchange, the revenue aspects of the tariffs generally have been neglected. Earlier in this chapter, there was also occasion to comment on the wide fluctuations in tariff revenues and the declining yield of the tariffs due to import restrictions. High duties on luxury imports are one way of distributing the tax burden according to ability to pay and, at the same time, reducing the demand for imports. Nearly always, when it becomes necessary to conserve foreign exchange, the action taken is to restrict luxury imports. For much of the past decade, import licenses were denied for luxury goods such as automobiles. But with automobiles subject to duties of 200 per cent, the government may forego $2.00 of revenue in order to save $1.00 of foreign exchange. At the same time, the government has never taken serious action to restrict foreign travel and foreign remit-

[13] *Ibid.*, Part II, p. 53.

tances. A restriction of $1.00 in foreign travel or in a foreign remittance would enable the government to realize $2.00 in revenue on a highly taxed import. It would seem desirable to abandon emergency and stop gap measures like import restrictions and to adopt a long-range policy with respect to luxury imports that would be less costly to the government in terms of revenue foregone.

The prejudice against luxury imports in the face of balance-of-payments difficulties is justified at first glance. On reflection, however, in the light of the possibility of collecting taxes as high as 200 per cent on such imports, it appears to be a case of cutting off one's nose to spite one's face. A government which can realize 200 per cent on a foreign exchange expenditure would be justified in borrowing foreign exchange for such a purpose. If these revenues are wisely invested, government investment should yield foreign exchange greatly in excess of the interest on the borrowed foreign exchange. There are many projects, for example in agriculture, which require expenditures in domestic resources, but which would yield foreign exchange through increased exports. Another aspect of this, and equally important, perhaps, is that at a cost of $1.00 in foreign exchange, the government has induced $2.00 in savings. The expenditure on an imported vehicle may well result in the foregoing of a trip abroad; the saving thus may even be a saving in foreign exchange. In any case, it is a saving, and it would help to fulfill the needs for public investment.

From 1950 to 1962, nearly 90,000 automobiles, including jeeps and taxis, were imported, or an average of about 6,800 per year. Imports ranged from a low of 630 vehicles in 1958 to a high of 16,729 in 1954. In 1961 imports reached 16,393, but they decreased to only 4,225 in 1962.

These troughs and peaks should be evened out by planning for vehicle imports over the next decade. In view of present balance-of-payments difficulties, imports of automobiles could be projected at a level of only 5,000 per year, but with the limiting factor being the tariff. If the demand for imported vehicles at a duty of 200 per cent exceeded the number of planned imports, the duties could be raised higher. Assuming that the applicable tariff would be 200 per cent for vehicles, and that the average c.i.f. value per vehicle is U.S. $2,000, revenues from this source should result in U.S. $20 million per year with a foreign exchange expenditure of U.S. $10 million.

Previously in this chapter, there was occasion to note the privileged treatment accorded diplomats and certain personnel of technical assistance missions, who are able to sell their automobiles free of duty after two years, or after six months if they are transferred to another post. Diplomatic conventions merely require that these personnel be permitted to use their automobiles free of duty, but they do not require exemption upon resale. Duties that are foregone, at present, from this source are estimated at nearly U.S. $1 million per annum.

Automobile parts are subject to duties ranging from 3 to less than 10 per cent if they are not produced in Colombia. Agricultural machinery and tractors are subject to no duties at all. In both cases, also, the importation of these goods is subsidized inasmuch as they can be imported at the official rate of $9.00 to the U.S. dollar in 1963 instead of at the free rate of $9.99 to the dollar in 1963. In view of the importance of agricultural development, it is probably desirable to continue the policy of exempting agricultural machinery and equipment. In the case of automobile parts, however, the low duties in effect are a subsidy for the most privileged income groups in Colombia.

Duties on automobile parts resulted in $121.8 million in 1962. If the rates on these imports were increased by 10 per cent, the revenues would increase by $12.18 million. If taxis were taxed at 100 per cent instead of 4.4 per cent, additional revenues would be $14.6 million. If jeeps were taxed at 100 per cent instead of 5.6 per cent, an additional $26.0 million would be realized.

Automobiles are subject to two levels of duties, depending on whether they weigh more or less than 1,650 kilos. Those weighing less than that amount are subject to duties of 150 per cent, the others to duties of 200 per cent. The use of weight as the basis for a distinction in rates results in an expensive sports car being subject to a rate of 150 per cent, while a standard sedan is subject to a rate of 200 per cent. It would be more equitable to draw a distinction on the basis of c.i.f. value according to the following schedule: less than $15,000, 150 per cent; $15,000 to $25,000, 200 per cent; $25,000 to $35,000, 250 per cent; and over $35,000, 300 per cent.

Taxis are subject to the extremely low rate of 4.4 per cent. Since they are used in public service, it is considered undesirable to tax them as heavily as private vehicles. Although this argument appears reasonable, it ignores the following considerations:

1) The subsidy is small in terms of the amount of travel per mile. Suppose that a 100 per cent duty applies to a taxi with a c.i.f. value of $15,000. The tax would be $15,000, or an additional $13,400 in duties, compared with the 4.4 per cent duty currently levied. Assuming that the taxi will be used for 150,000 passenger miles during its useful life, the difference in duty amounts to only 8.93 centavos per mile, or less than one U.S. cent per mile.

2) Since taxi owners are small businessmen, in the most part, and are universally noted for their evasion of income taxes, the subsidy appears to redound to a group not deserving of the benefit.

3) Not all taxis are in the public service. Because of the import prohibition of private vehicles, there has been a leak of taxis into private service.

4) Taxis must be employed in the public service for five years, but they may be sold to other operators after one year of ownership. Due to the scarcity of private automobiles and the high import duties to which they are subject, taxis customarily appreciate in value. As a result, a taxi owner who imports a new vehicle may realize a profit of

60 to 90 per cent after one year of owner-ship.

5) Taxi owners benefit from the government's policy of restricting importation of private automobiles, for this creates a stronger demand for taxi services. Higher import duties could be justified as a payment for this special benefit.

6) It is argued, in justification of the low duty on taxis, that the owners could not afford higher tariffs on their vehicles. If this were true, the government could authorize the payment of the duty in installments over a period of years or permit the operators to arrange with foreign exporters for credit. The argument does not justify the low duty.

Jeeps are taxed at rates of only 10 per cent. This low rate has been justified because of their use in agriculture. On the other hand, there can be no doubt that a large proportion of jeeps is used for non-business purposes, for they are excellent substitutes for passenger vehicles. Their "bargain" price is an encouragement to their importation, and their resale value is relatively high. In fact, it is so high that the successful jeep importer is in a position to enjoy its use at practically no cost. As long as the shortage of passenger vehicles continues, a substantial import duty on jeeps would appear to be justified.

EFFECT OF TARIFF POLICIES ON PRICES

All tariffs, whether they are revenue-producing or protective, tend to raise prices. The rise in prices is an intended effect of the revenue tariffs, while, in the case of the protective tariffs, it is expected to be merely a temporary effect until the industry can achieve efficiency and economies of scale. By raising the prices of foreign goods relative to domestic, tariffs will cause a shift in demand in favor of domestic products and untaxed products and services. The more perfect the domestic product is as a substitute for the imported product, the greater the elasticity of demand and the more the shift to the domestic product.

But there are other effects, which policy-makers often ignore, and which should be taken into consideration. The protective tariffs, if they are so high as to prohibit imports, or if they are accompanied by import prohibitions, may encourage monopolistic pricing by domestic producers. Such pricing is the more likely the fewer the number of producers. Monopolistic pricing in turn tends to reduce sales, and by permitting high profits on low volume, provides little stimulation to efficiency and to the expansion of output and employment.

Another effect which should not be ignored is that by making the internal market profitable, there is a tendency to reduce resources devoted to the export market. Import duties thus tend to reduce exports as well as imports. This effect will depend on the elasticity of substitution of resources between the two sectors, the domestic and the export.

Among the reallocations of consumer expenditures resulting from the tariffs, the most important appears to be a shift to untaxed foreign travel, which was considered earlier in this chapter. Since imported products have only imperfect domestic substitutes, the shift among other consumer expenditures tends to be somewhat subtle and immeasurable, but expenditures on services, housing, and domestic products are probably increased by making imported products more expensive.

There can be no doubt that there are abuses under the protective umbrella of high protective tariffs and import prohibitions. Prices in the United States and Colombia are compared for a small list of consumer goods in Table 9–6. Fresh foods, including fruits and vegetables not shown in the table, tend to be priced comparatively low in Colombia. In the clothing industry, where there is considerable competition even under tariff protection, prices are generally low, although there are exceptions. Products made by artisans and by several firms, such as shoes and men's suits, are relatively low, while those made by only a few firms are relatively high, e.g., men's shirts and undershirts. Processed foods, as distinguished from fresh foods,

TABLE 9–6

Prices in Bogotá, Colombia and Washington, D.C. of a Selected List of Retail Goods, Summer, 1963

(U.S. Dollars)

	Colombia	United States	Percentage of Colombian to U.S. Price
Processed Foods			
Fresh milk, qt.	$ 0.15	$ 0.28	53
Butter, lb.	0.88	0.68	130
Sweet peas, 14 oz. can	0.65	0.18	361
Baked beans, 22 oz.	0.49	0.22	223
Tomato catsup, 14 oz.	0.39	0.22	177
Soda crackers, lb.	0.65	0.37	176
Swiss cheese, lb.	0.80	0.59	136
Frankfurters, lb.	0.65	0.49	133
Salt, iodized, kg.	0.05	0.14	36
Sugar, lb.	0.10	0.18	56
Grape jam, lb.	0.50	0.37	135
Condensed milk, 14 oz.	0.34	0.17	200
Coffee, roasted, lb.	0.34	0.65	52
Vegetable soup, 10½ oz.	0.29	0.18	161
Fresh Foods			
Chicken, whole, lb.	0.45	0.35	129
Rice, kg.	0.27	0.41	66
Beef, chuck, lb.	0.30	0.57	53
T-bone steak, lb.	0.34	0.99	34
Hamburger, lb.	0.30	0.44	68
Rib roast, lb.	0.34	0.89	38
Manufactures			
Toothpaste, 130 gm.	0.65	0.53	123
Talcum powder, 9 oz.	0.68	0.59	115
Toilet soap, med.	0.14	0.09	156
Detergent powder, 100 gm.	0.69	0.53	130
Electric bulbs, 75 watt	0.28	0.21	133
Automobile tires, 6.50 x 15	13.00	17.50	74
Automobile battery, 6 volt	20.00	13.95	143
Electric iron	10.65	6.25	170
Typewriter, portable	115.00	62.50	184
Vacuum cleaner, cannister type	129.00	34.95	369
Pressure cooker, 4 qt.	10.81	8.95	121
Refrigerator, standard, 9.5 cu. ft.	349.50	189.95	184
Coffee percolator, aluminum, 6 cups	2.20	1.70	129
Washing machine, wringer type, 6 lb. capacity	219.50	120.00[a]	183
Gas range, 20 inches, standard	134.50	90.00	149
Luggage, 24 in. Pullman, plastic and cloth	18.30	11.95	153
Brief case, leather	13.50	21.95	62
Clock radio	29.50	20.00	148
Nylon stockings	0.97	1.03	94
Men's all-wool suits	38.00	52.69	72
Men's drill pants	4.10	4.29	96
Men's overalls	2.95	2.50	118
Men's blue jeans	3.50	2.19	160
Men's undershirts	1.25	0.84	149
Men's dress shirts	2.55	1.97	129
Men's shoes	6.70	11.95	56

[a] 9 lb. capacity.   *Source:* Survey of retail stores in Bogotá and *The Washington Post.*

likewise are relatively expensive compared to those in the United States. Again, the exceptions are noteworthy. Those products that require a minimum of processing, and salt that is produced by a virtual government monopoly, are the lowest in price.

It is in manufactures, except where there is artisan competition, that the highest prices appear. Refrigerators, typewriters, electrical appliances, gas ranges, and radios are all priced very high relative to the United States. Less elaborate products, like pressure cookers and percolators, are less expensive relatively. The differences in prices between Colombia and the United States cannot be explained entirely by the tariffs on raw materials and intermediate goods, for these duties tend to be low. Thus, in the case of typewriters, they probably amount to less than $15.00 per typewriter; in the case of refrigerators, probably less than $40.00, and so on.

To prevent monopolistic abuses, the appropriate policy would be to provide protection at a level of 25 per cent or less. To remove all foreign competition is to invite abuses. In interviews with manufacturers, it was pointed out repeatedly that the parts purchased in Colombia are nearly always priced at just under the imported c.i.f. cost of a similar part plus the duties. In some cases, however, the price is higher when the import control agency prohibits imports because the product is made in Colombia.

It is widely believed that protective tariffs should be high, and, generally, they are the highest in the tariff list. Actually, they should be the lowest, since their purpose is not to raise revenue but to stimulate domestic production. If very high tariffs are imposed at first, they should be reduced gradually over time in order to maintain some competitive pressure on domestic firms. If, in the long-run, the industry cannot survive without high protective tariffs, it was undoubtedly uneconomic to produce the product in Colombia in the first place.

Tariffs, especially for protective purposes, tend to encourage resources to be devoted to domestic production. The more profitable the domestic market, the less resources will be utilized in production for export. Given the large amount of unemployment and underemployment, it is probable that labor is not taken away from production for export. The allocation of insufficient investment to exports probably is the greatest cause of suffering in the export market.

Colombia's principal export is coffee, which accounted for 72.9 per cent of Colombia's registered exports in 1962. Petroleum and fuel oil resulted in 14.9 per cent; bananas, 2.3 per cent; cotton, 3.4 per cent; tobacco, 1.2 per cent; and textile products, 1.0 per cent. The latter two exports achieved significant amounts only in the past three years. (See Table 9–7.)

Exports of manufactured goods other than textile products were negligible. Yet, except for petroleum and textiles, nearly all foreign investment and nearly all industrial investment were designed to produce import substitutes. Given Colombia's foreign exchange needs, the priorities ought to be reversed: production for export should precede import substitution as a priority, especially the import substitution of complicated industrial products that will demand large amounts of imported intermediate goods for many years. Past experience suggests that investment directed to agricultural production should receive a higher priority, because it is in this area that Colombia appears to have a decided comparative advantage.

ADMINISTRATION OF TARIFF POLICY

Numerous government agencies administer various aspects of tariff policy. They include the Council on Tariff Policy, the National Import Control Agency, the Central Bank, the Office of Exchange Registry, the Ministries of Agriculture, Mines and Petroleum, and Development, the National Planning Council, and the Ministry of Finance.

The Council on Tariff Policy was established in 1959 in connection with the tariff reform

TABLE 9–7

Changes in the Composition of Exports, 1951 to 1962

(Thousands of U.S. Dollars, F.O.B. Value)

Articles	1951	1955	1959	1960	1961	1962	Percentage of 1962 Exports
Coffee	359,782	487,386	361,246	332,249	307,826	332,021	72.9
Petroleum	73,542	61,484	73,292	79,998	68,189	60,584	13.3
Bananas	8,778	16,849	13,876	13,687	14,055	10,644	2.3
Fuel oil	—	2,334	8,715	7,466	4,765	7,131	1.6
Tobacco	2,031	2,132	1,995	2,376	4,044	5,690	1.2
Cement	194	572	2,310	2,000	2,406	1,997	0.4
Shellfish	—	—	1,298	1,691	1,420	1,527	0.3
Platinum	1,433	1,838	379	302	1,478	1,030	0.2
Tanned hides	547	805	573	83	301	1,038	0.2
Lumber	203	717	1,349	2,079	2,242	2,230	0.5
Carboxylic acids and naphtha	—	—	553	710	572	138	—
Pharmaceuticals	46	158	231	444	639	899	0.2
Domestic appliances	—	123	453	728	647	586	0.1
Medicinal balms	748	105	129	122	172	199	—
Ipecacuana	776	638	378	309	—	—	—
Cotton	—	—	6	12,709	10,128	15,638	3.4
Textile products	—	—	—	—	1,413	4,494	1.0
Other	15,217	8,755	6,221	7,221	7,307	9,587	2.1
TOTALS	463,297	583,896	473,004	464,174	427,604	455,433	100.0

Sources: *Anuario de Comercio Exterior, 1961,* and *Boletín Mensual de Estadística,* March, 1963.

of that year. The functions of the council are: (1) to modify the tariffs within authorized limits, which are 10 per cent of the c.i.f. value, except where the changes are designed to stimulate Latin American trade or involve automotive vehicles; (2) to establish prices as the bases of the *ad valorem* duties, taking into consideration the need to prevent dumping; (3) to modify the development quotas in accordance with development needs; (4) to revise the exemptions; and (5) to advise the government on all matters concerning foreign commercial policies.

The members of the council include the Minister of Finance, two members of Congress, the Director of the Department of Planning, the Minister of Development, the Minister of Agriculture, and the Director General of Customs. The council's decisions on tariffs, prices of imports, and quotas require the approval of the National Council of Economic Policy and Planning and the Board of the National Import Control Agency.

The National Import Control Agency is attached to the Ministry of Development for administrative purposes, but otherwise it is autonomous. The board consists of the same ministers and representatives who constitute the Council on Tariff Policy. In addition, it includes the Director of the Central Bank and the Chief of the Office of Exchange Registry. The board's principal functions are to administer the granting of import licenses, to approve exceptions to the prohibited list of imports, to prescribe the necessary rules and regulations for imports, and to advise with respect to desirable modifications.

As noted earlier, the Central Bank is the custodian of the advance deposits and operates the Office of Exchange Registry. The Minister of Agriculture is charged with the responsibility of administering export quotas for agricultural products, and the Ministers of Development, and Mines and Petroleum for quotas of products within their purview.

The number of agencies dealing with tariff policy and the number that have power to control or restrict imports should be reduced.

The Central Bank should be divorced from administrative responsibilities concerning imports and exports, except to be represented on the Council on Tariff Policy so that tariff policy can be co-ordinated with monetary policy. The advance deposits have as their primary purpose to restrict the money supply. The Central Bank ought to accomplish this by other means. It is difficult to understand the functions of the Office of Exchange Registry. The statistics collected by this unit should be assembled by the Customs Division from its manifests. If all transactions were made at the free rate, it would remove the necessity for a tremendous amount of unnecessary paper work.

Similarly, the controls exercised by the various ministries would be largely unnecessary if there were less arbitrating among vested interests and if domestic prices were not artificially controlled below the world level. These controls are confusing, largely self-defeating, and encourage contraband and speculation. They create more problems that need more controls, that create more problems, *ad infinitum*. It would be better if the ministries were occupied less with such political problems and concerned themselves more with promoting agricultural and industrial development.

Moreover, the powers invested in the various ministries and the Import Control Agency enable them to reward favorites, and this invites bribery and corruption. A government that cannot eliminate the open sale of contraband on its streets, and that governs in an environment in which it is popularly believed that anything can be purchased at a price, invites little confidence in its ability to administer controls with neutrality and effectiveness. It should avoid giving officials tremendous power to reward and punish.

In general, imports should be restricted by sufficiently high tariffs, and domestic prices should be allowed to find their equilibrium level with world prices. The establishment of price controls and quotas is a herculean task, since prices affect the consumption and production of the items. The most highly trained and qualified economists would hesitate to set prices and quotas. How much more difficult it must be to achieve the "correct" price when the regulatory agencies are staffed more by lawyers and politicians than by highly qualified economists.

It may be difficult to effect the transition to equilibrium prices, but it will be more difficult to maintain artificial prices. Let the market determine the appropriate relationships between domestic and foreign prices, with the tariffs intervening to provide the necessary protection and discouragement of imports. In such a way, favoritism will be avoided, and the government will be permitted to concentrate on the real task of development. The considerable amount of resources that would be released by ending excessive regulation would contribute a great deal to the country's development.

CONTRABAND

High tariffs and import prohibitions have created a large differential in the prices of luxury goods between Colombia and the outside world, which makes contrabanding attractive. Long coast lines and equally long boundaries with neighboring countries create a difficult problem in preventing the introduction of contraband. Also, the relatively low wages paid customs personnel encourage bribery and create an environment in which contraband can thrive.

Contraband cigarettes and other articles are sold openly on Bogotá's main thoroughfare by dozens of hawkers. It is not unusual to be accosted on the street with proposals for the sale of contraband. In some neighborhoods, vendors will offer to obtain practically anything in short supply, from watches and fountain pens to silverware and tableware.

It is estimated that non-registered imports, principally luxury consumer goods, amount to about U.S. $20 million per year.[14] Customs enforcement officials reported that they had

[14] *Ibid.*, Part II, p. 11.

seized $26.2 million (U.S. $3.9 million) in contraband merchandise in 1962. The increase in the enforcement effort is indicated by the growth of such seizures from only $7.4 million in 1960[15] Nearly $20.0 million of contraband was seized in the first five and one-half months of 1963. The principal items confiscated were liquors, cigarettes, vehicles, radios, watches, and fountain pens.

It is unfortunate that import prohibitions on liquor and cigarettes are nullified by contraband activity. The same amount of foreign exchange is involved, almost the same prices are charged, but what the government could collect in revenue disappears into private pockets. For taxpayer morale, if for no other reason, the open sale of contraband should be terminated.

But there does not appear to be a will to end the contraband activity. One excuse offered is that the activity is giving employment to those who would otherwise be unemployed. Perhaps the government really is not giving up any more to achieve employment in this way than with other exemptions. But in that case, the government should permit the imports and receive revenue. Another excuse is that those who do the vending are relatively unimportant and are not the real culprits. This is probably true, but the government's attitude of disinterest makes it easy for the real criminals to vend their merchandise. Besides, it would not involve undue effort or intelligence to identify the ones who are responsible for the illegal activity.

The contraband, except what is sneaked in through customs, comes from offshore or from neighboring countries. No doubt, Colombia's neighbors are also injured by contraband from Colombia. The easiest way to curb this wholesale smuggling is to stop it at the source. An agreement between Colombia and neighboring countries, perhaps including all members of the Organization of American States, would do much to terminate large-scale smuggling activities. In the mean-

time, each country probably looks the other way when its nationals engage in smuggling goods into other countries.

Oddly enough, there is also considerable smuggling of exports. Unregistered exports of coffee and cattle were estimated to be U.S. $28.4 million in 1959 and U.S. $20.2 million in 1960.[16] Exports of these products are subject to quotas, and in the case of coffee, the exporters are reimbursed at less than the free market rate. This results in an incentive to smuggle the goods out of the country.

Currently, there are similar problems with respect to sugar, the export of which is prohibited in order to maintain adequate domestic supplies. Leather exports are also prohibited. Once again, these are illustrative of the type of controls that are not fully comprehended in terms of all of their consequences. The reason for the controls is the low internal fixed price of these products, while the reason for the contraband is the higher prices that can be obtained abroad. If prices were allowed to adjust to their equilibrium levels, there would be no need for quotas on exports. In the face of continuing foreign exchange difficulties, one could make out a good case for severely rationing sugar internally to make exports possible. As it is, producers are reluctant to sell at the artificially low domestic prices, and shortages plague the economy. It would be better to permit the domestic price to seek its market level and for the government to assure that those who profit thereby pay their income taxes. It would appear that the government, after introducing a devaluation, then attempts to neutralize all of its effects, including the windfall gains it gives to exporters. In following this policy, the government is preventing the adjustments necessary for a solution of the balance-of-payments problem.

The responsibility of the price control agencies and the Ministers of Agriculture and Development to protect domestic sup-

---

[15] División de Aduanas.

[16] *Plan General de Desarrollo*, Part II, p. 11.

plies should not be construed in terms of keeping domestic prices below their equilibrium levels. Obviously, if all prices were maintained low enough, all goods would be in short supply. Prices serve a rationing function, and higher prices serve to limit the consumption of scarce and expensive goods. They also serve to call forth more production. The present controls neglect foreign exchange requirements. Also, by maintaining low domestic prices, they result in artificially high domestic consumption and reduced exports.

SUMMARY OF RECOMMENDATIONS

1) Since the fee charged for the consular invoice is simply an additional customs duty, it should be included in the *ad valorem* duties imposed by the tariff schedule. This would remove the need for involving the consulates in the importation process.

2) The so-called development taxes should be eliminated in order to remove arbitrariness in the level of earmarked expenditures, simplify the tax structure, and distribute the tax burden more equitably.

3) The stamp taxes on consular invoices, bills of lading, and import manifests and the tonnage fee should be eliminated, for they are nuisance taxes that result in useless work, costly delays, and the unnecessary handling of documents.

4) The present exemption of imports and 80 per cent of transportation costs from the 10 per cent tax on foreign exchange should be eliminated.

5) The advance deposit (*depósito previo*) should be abandoned. These deposits produce no revenue, absorb working capital, are the worst possible type of anti-inflationary device, and discriminate against small business firms.

6) With respect to the income tax exemption on exports, the rule presuming that the income originating from exports is equal to 40 per cent of the value of the exported merchandise should be changed to an exemption of that proportion of income that foreign sales bear to total sales.

7) *Ad valorem* instead of specific duties should be used on the grounds that the latter produce excessive fluctuations in the effective rates of the duties as a result of currency depreciation, defeat the intended effects of a devaluation, and have unneutral effects on relative prices.

8) Import exemptions need to be curbed. With respect to private firms, exemptions should be given only when goods will be incorporated into exports or when no claims on foreign exchange are involved, as in the case of diplomats and technical assistance missions.

9) Vehicles and household furnishings, when they are purchased from members of diplomatic and technical assistance missions, should be subjected to import duties.

10) The development of industries that require and will continue to require large amounts of imports of raw materials and intermediate goods should be discouraged, and encouragement should be given only to those which use or can reasonably be expected to use large proportions of domestic materials.

11) Excessive levels of protective tariffs encourage monopolistic pricing practices. Reliance should be placed on modest protective tariffs, and import restrictions either should not be used or should be used very infrequently for purposes of protecting domestic industry.

12) An excessive number of firms are being encouraged in mass-production industries, like automobiles and electrical appliances, which prevents a realization of economies of scale and results in low productivity and high prices and discourages the import substitution of intermediate goods.

13) Operations of foreign firms must be carefully scrutinized to avoid conflicts of interest between the parent companies and Colombia's national interest. This might be of special importance when the parent is reluctant to permit its Colombian subsidiary to compete in markets abroad.

14) Foreign remittances should be taxed, except where the taxpayer can show earnings

of foreign exchange in excess of the remittances.

15) A tax on foreign travel should be levied based on assumed daily expenditures abroad or the cost of the fare, and credit for foreign travel should be severely restricted.

16) Increased public resources should be devoted to import substitution and export development in the agricultural sector, where Colombia appears to have a decided comparative advantage.

17) Exemptions from import duties given to private firms should be limited to those firms that export part of their output and should be allowed in the proportion that the exports bear to total output.

18) Duties should be increased on raw materials and intermediate goods incorporated

in consumer durable goods, on taxis and jeeps, and on automobile parts.

19) Automobiles are currently subject to varying rates of tariffs depending upon their weight. It would be more equitable to distinguish the classes of automobiles on the basis of their c.i.f. value.

20) Restrictions of exports to maintain domestic supplies of commodities at artificial prices should be avoided. Domestic prices should be allowed to seek their equilibrium levels as soon as possible.

21) The number of agencies dealing with tariff administration should be reduced. The intervention of foreign consulates and the Central Bank in the import process appears unnecessary.

22) Luxury imports should not be prohibited, but their quantity should be re-

TABLE 9–8

Changes in Imports by Section of the Tariff Schedule, 1953 to 1962

(Thousands of U.S. Dollars)

Section	Description	1953 Imports	Percentage of Total Imports	1962 Imports	Percentage of Total Imports	Percentage Change 1953 to 1962	Absolute Change 1953 to 1962
I	Live animals and animal products	$ 2,146	0.39	$ 1,490	0.28	−30.6	$ −656
II	Agricultural products, n.s.e.[a]	20,676	3.78	23,788	4.40	+15.1	+3,112
III	Oils and fats	9,669	1.77	10,906	2.02	+12.8	+1,237
IV	Processed agricultural products	14,110	2.58	7,964	1.47	−43.6	−6,146
V	Non-metal mineral products	33,038	6.04	21,848	4.04	−33.9	−11,190
VI	Chemicals and pharmaceuticals	53,118	9.72	87,425	16.18	+64.6	+34,307
VII	Skins, hides, leather products	995	0.18	277	0.05	−72.2	−718
VIII	Rubber and rubber products	8,563	1.57	12,323	2.28	+43.9	+3,760
IX	Wood, cork, and products	2,284	0.42	1,048	0.19	−54.1	−1,236
X	Paper and products	17,832	3.26	26,311	4.87	+47.5	+8,479
XI	Textiles and products	44,782	8.19	20,221	3.74	−54.8	−24,561
XII	Shoes and hats	1,233	0.22	366	0.07	−70.3	−867
XIII	Stone, mineral, glass	10,830	1.98	8,259	1.53	−23.7	−2,571
XIV	Precious stones, metals	284	0.05	163	0.03	−42.6	−121
XV	Common metals and products	83,776	15.32	62,644	11.59	−25.2	−21,132
XVI	Machinery, electrical apparatus	142,563	26.08	169,402	31.35	+18.8	+26,839
XVII	Transport materials	81,600	14.93	61,134	11.31	−25.1	−20,466
XVIII	Scientific, musical, and other instruments, watches	11,493	2.10	9,863	1.83	−14.2	−1,630
XIX	Arms and munitions	3,163	0.58	1,793	0.33	−43.3	−1,370
XX	Merchandise and miscellaneous, n.s.e.[a]	4,282	0.78	1,693	0.31	−60.5	−2,589
XXI	Objects of art	236	0.04	13	0.00	−94.5	−223
XXII	Products, n.s.e.[a]	50	0.01	11,420	2.11	2,274.0	+11,370
	TOTAL IMPORTS	$546,723	100.00	$540,351	100.00	−1.2	$−6,372

[a] n.s.e. = not specified elsewhere.

Source: Anuario de Comercio Exterior, various years.

stricted through the price mechanism in the form of high tariffs to reduce the fluctuations in the revenues from year to year and to make additional tax resources available to the government for development. In the case of luxury imports such as cigarettes and liquor, import prohibitions encourage smuggling.

23) The open sale of contraband should be discouraged by firm action against the vendors and their suppliers.

24) The government should attempt to reduce large-scale contraband activity by means of agreements with neighboring governments designed to stop this activity at its source.

TABLE 9–9

Value of Imports, C.I.F., by Section and Chapter of the Tariff Schedule, 1953 to 1962

(Thousands of U.S. Dollars)

Chapter	Description [a]	1953	1955	1957	1959	1960	1961	1962 [a]
1.	Live animals (excl. fish)	$ 1,708	$ 8,470	$ 223	$ 331	$ 1,982	$ 807	$ 1,277
2.	Meat	17	55	3	6	4	12	5
3.	Fish, shellfish	11	8	2	—	2	1	2
4.	Milk products, eggs, honey	378	4,198	1,090	143	157	27	100
5.	Raw materials of animal origin	33	49	45	69	97	82	106
	Total Sec. I: animal products	2,146	12,779	1,363	550	2,243	929	1,490
6.	Live plants and flowers	34	48	4	1	5	22	35
7.	Vegetables	401	496	30	8	13	1,551	84
8.	Edible fruits	611	785	84	76	68	264	159
9.	Coffee, tea, and spices	416	423	449	351	200	446	417
10.	Cereals	3,322	6,027	11,839	9,358	8,351	21,765	14,480
11.	Milled grains, malt, and starches	8,699	7,283	7,503	8,176	4,549	3,418	110
12.	Oleaginous seeds and fruits, other seeds and plants	6,474	16,211	15,248	9,492	10,799	8,711	7,199
13.	Raw materials for tanning and dyeing, gums and resins	640	560	747	486	663	697	1,262
14.	Wicker, cane, bamboo	79	76	80	31	30	39	43
	Total Sec. II: vegetable products	20,676	31,909	35,984	27,979	24,677	36,913	23,788
15.	Oils and fats, animal or vegetable origin, Sec. III	9,669	8,029	6,291	8,721	9,842	4,961	10,906
16.	Meat and fish preparations	1,528	2,782	26	41	37	23	96
17.	Sugar and sweets	1,350	471	3,314	949	229	177	231
18.	Cocoa	6,180	8,556	7,789	5,636	2,461	3,713	4,583
19.	Preparations from grains and starches	193	652	258	29	13	18	20
20.	Vegetable and fruit products	171	339	154	189	152	125	105
21.	Miscellaneous food products	297	943	653	152	114	113	251
22.	Beverages, soft, alcoholic, and vinegar	2,901	2,416	1,376	898	1,653	1,079	1,384
23.	Food scraps	159	1,182	322	29	57	53	216
24.	Tobacco	1,331	879	660	1,305	1,379	1,629	1,080
	Total Sec. IV: processed foods	14,110	18,220	14,552	9,228	6,695	6,930	7,964
25.	Salt, sulphur, cement, lime, etc.	3,184	3,974	3,696	3,433	3,544	4,094	4,591
26.	Minerals	52	71	119	271	281	296	556
27.	Combustible minerals and products	29,802	29,197	25,997	11,947	13,670	16,372	16,701
	Total Sec. V: non-metallic minerals	33,038	33,242	29,812	15,651	17,495	20,762	21,848

TABLE 9–9 (*Continued*)
Value of Imports, C.I.F., by Section and Chapter of the Tariff Schedule, 1953 to 1962

(Thousands of U.S. Dollars)

Chapter	Description	1953	1955	1957	1959	1960	1961	1962[a]
28.	Chemicals and pharmaceuticals	33,364	49,700	50,222	46,671	53,480	57,929	55,438
29.	Chemical preparations, films	2,272	2,580	2,037	2,167	2,166	2,545	2,601
30.	Dyes, paints, etc.	8,716	11,346	9,004	6,637	8,319	8,408	8,737
31.	Essences and perfumes	1,986	2,188	1,543	1,716	1,742	1,834	2,127
32.	Soaps, candles, etc.	1,120	3,377	1,353	1,602	1,591	2,110	2,371
33.	Caseins, glues, etc.	548	1,055	808	498	445	530	452
34.	Explosives, matches, fireworks	1,002	1,874	2,366	1,407	1,666	1,152	1,948
35.	Fertilizers	4,110	9,720	11,981	7,139	9,235	13,286	13,751
	Total Sec. VI: chemicals	53,118	81,840	79,314	67,838	78,645	87,794	87,425
36.	Skins and hides	570	1,666	210	291	116	118	47
37.	Products of skins and hides	364	683	254	219	263	170	222
38.	Furs and fur products	61	7	—	5	12	6	8
	Total Sec. VII: hides, skins, and fur products	995	2,356	464	515	391	294	277
39.	Rubber and rubber products, Sec VIII	8,563	12,432	8,892	8,387	13,256	9,890	12,323
40.	Wood and wood products	1,554	1,435	688	254	459	293	267
41.	Cork and cork products	701	1,260	1,701	1,744	1,289	1,450	769
42.	Articles made of straw, etc.	29	52	1	36	20	13	12
	Total Sec. IX: wood and cork products	2,284	2,747	2,390	2,034	1,768	1,756	1,048
43.	Materials used to make paper	1,356	4,012	4,724	4,867	4,847	5,922	6,301
44.	Paper and cardboard and their products	14,618	19,630	19,226	16,604	20,372	20,392	18,758
45.	Books and graphic art products	1,858	2,938	701	561	957	1,238	1,252
	Total Sec. X: paper products	17,832	26,580	24,651	22,032	26,176	27,552	26,311
46.	Natural silk and synthetic fibers	5,452	8,122	3,009	4,036	3,725	2,383	1,622
47.	Wool, hair	12,539	16,797	13,364	9,552	10,559	13,188	10,191
48.	Cotton	21,260	6,332	12,893	4,266	802	392	609
49.	Linen and other vegetable fibers	859	332	160	210	201	121	144
50.	Felts, cords, and ropes	4,195	4,394	3,956	3,053	4,172	2,984	4,808
51.	Clothing accessories	30	144	57	547	417	127	113
52.	Clothing	429	1,970	920	1,740	3,368	2,414	2,733
53.	Rags and scrap	18	19	9	7	1	—	—
	Total Sec. XI: textile products	44,782	38,110	34,368	23,412	23,244	21,609	20,221
54.	Shoes	167	65	7	141	185	106	161
55.	Hats	970	939	123	51	54	47	78
56.	Umbrellas and canes	95	122	82	91	129	62	102
57.	Feathers, flowers, wigs	1	3	—	61	28	17	24
	Total Sec. XII: shoes, hats, and accessories	1,233	1,129	212	344	396	232	366
58.	Stone and mineral products	1,158	1,600	1,550	1,305	1,461	1,915	3,923
59.	Ceramics	3,560	4,330	1,991	815	1,065	683	849
60.	Glass	6,112	6,667	5,789	4,691	5,172	5,274	3,486
	Total Sec. XIII: stone, ceramic, and glass	10,830	12,597	9,330	6,811	7,698	7,872	8,259
61.	Pearls, precious stones	284	1,178	310	31	161	445	163
62.	Coins	—	—	—	4	—	—	—
	Total Sec. XIV: pearls, precious stones, coins	284	1,178	310	35	161	445	163

TABLE 9-9 (*Continued*)

Value of Imports, C.I.F., by Section and Chapter of the Tariff Schedule, 1953 to 1962

(Thousands of U.S. Dollars)

Chapter	Description	1953	1955	1957	1959	1960	1962	1962[a]
63.	Iron and steel	73,112	74,987	65,599	40,832	54,999	49,644	46,974
64.	Copper	3,149	3,460	4,425	3,867	4,632	5,750	5,315
65.	Nickel	201	280	350	723	529	523	377
66.	Aluminum	2,662	4,450	5,058	3,318	4,096	4,859	5,956
67.	Lead	199	369	557	384	466	387	112
68.	Zinc	160	586	439	703	1,013	660	800
69.	Tin	276	407	441	597	323	488	467
70.	Other	119	330	230	195	175	241	237
71.	Miscellaneous products	3,898	4,570	1,987	2,541	2,005	2,068	2,406
	Total Sec. XV: common metals	83,776	89,439	79,086	53,160	68,238	64,620	62,644
72.	Boilers, machinery, and mechanical apparatus	107,604	118,086	80,261	73,422	109,681	113,398	123,677
73.	Electrical machinery and apparatus	34,959	52,317	36,635	29,887	36,676	45,302	45,725
	Total Sec. XVI: machinery and equipment	142,563	170,403	116,896	103,309	146,357	158,700	169,402
74.	Railroad vehicles and materials	2,009	4,499	1,123	1,682	3,232	7,642	2,116
75.	Automotive vehicles, motorcycles and bicycles	74,453	90,423	19,720	45,963	68,983	68,638	52,915
76.	Aviation and navigation equipment	5,138	7,000	4,372	7,127	5,111	13,384	6,103
	Total Sec. XVII: transport	81,600	101,922	25,215	54,772	77,326	89,664	61,134
77.	Scientific instruments	5,748	6,266	5,191	4,648	5,911	6,196	7,756
78.	Watches and clocks	2,724	1,605	638	634	1,047	1,136	923
79.	Musical instruments	3,021	2,162	270	898	781	1,225	1,184
	Total Sec. XVIII: precision and musical instruments	11,493	10,033	6,099	6,180	7,739	8,557	9,863
80.	Arms	2,037	1,982	2,179	317	572	455	1,117
81.	Munitions	1,126	7,646	2,961	561	339	702	676
	Total Sec. XIX: arms	3,163	9,628	5,140	878	911	1,157	1,793
82.	Products and materials for cutting or molding	1,912	2,398	1,345	689	958	840	959
83.	Brushes and sieves	194	227	44	68	73	83	56
84.	Games and articles for sports	728	704	219	297	418	413	371
85.	Buttons, fountain pens, pipes for smoking	1,448	1,186	364	214	198	252	307
	Total Sec. XX: merchandise, n.s.e.[b]	4,282	4,515	1,972	1,269	1,646	1,594	1,693
86.	Art and collector's objects	236	187	57	40	14	19	13
	Total Sec. XXI	236	187	57	40	14	19	13
87.	Products, n.s.e.[b]	50	15	87	2,444	3,665	4,880	11,420
	Total Sec. XXII	50	15	87	2,444	3,665	—	—
	GRAND TOTAL	$551,723	$669,290	$482,575	$415,588	$518,585	$557,129	$540,351

[a] Provisional.
[b] n.s.e. = not specified elsewhere.

Totals may not equal because of rounding.
Source: Anuario de Comercio Exterior, various years.

CHAPTER 10

Internal Indirect Taxes

IT IS NOT POSSIBLE, in general, to be very enthusiastic about the internal indirect taxes used in Colombia. Most of them are not based on ability to pay, while others are a nuisance and obstruct business, are difficult to administer, and are capricious with respect to their burden. Some of the indirect taxes are so undesirable, in fact, that they constitute the rubbish heap of public finance. Regardless of this, however, probably all the indirect taxes are popular with politicians, mostly because they are concealed in prices and their cumulative burden goes unnoticed by the taxpayers.

That is not to say, however, that all indirect taxes are without a rationale. Some of these taxes may be justified by the cost-of-service principle—that the taxpayer consuming certain taxed goods or services receives a benefit from the government roughly equivalent to the charge. Other indirect taxes may be defended on the grounds that they are easier to administer (or less easy to evade) than direct taxes. In Colombia, there are two other important reasons for the use of indirect taxes. First, is the urgent need for additional government revenues. Second, is the increasing internal production of luxury and semi-luxury goods and the need to substitute internal excises on these goods for the former customs duties imposed on their importation. This would serve not only to raise revenues but also to discourage expenditures on these goods and to shift resources from import substitution to exports.

In terms of revenue productivity, internal indirect taxes are relatively unimportant in Colombia. In fact, they are probably less important in this country than in any other nation of Latin America. The indirect taxes traditionally have been a principal source of revenue for the departments, but they are also levied by the national government and the municipalities, and there actually is a bewildering array of taxes at each level despite their general revenue weakness.

In developing this chapter, the indirect taxes are first described and commented upon briefly at each level of government. Following this, information is provided on the revenue importance of these taxes. Finally, the indirect taxes are analyzed, and recommendations are proposed for their improvement.

NATIONAL INDIRECT TAXES

Stamp Taxes

National stamp taxes are used to collect a great variety of fees and taxes. The establishment of stamp taxes dates from the origin of the republic in 1821, and since that time there have been innumerable changes in the taxed items and rates. All of the scattered laws and regulations were codified by Decrees 3,908 of 1960 and 900 of 1961. For purposes of description, the stamp taxes may be grouped into seventeen categories. These are listed below in detail, with deliberate intention, for there is probably no better way to convince a reader that many of these stamp taxes obstruct business, are irrational, and are a nuisance pure and simple. By reading through this list, the unavoidable conclusion is that many of them should be eliminated.

1) *Official Activities*: (1) naturalization papers for farmers, skilled mechanics, and artisans, $100; (2) other naturalization papers, $1,000; (3) passports, $100, and renewals, $20; (4) passports issued abroad, $30, and renewals, $5; (5) group passports for ten or more persons, $10 per person; (6) passports for students, $10, and renewals, $1; (7) travel documents issued in favor of foreigners, $100, and renewals, $20; (8) ordinary resident visas, $10; (9) temporary visas, $5; (10) group visas, $1 per person; (11) certification of signatures, $.50; (12) certification of signatures by Colombian consuls, $5; (13) certificates issued abroad by Colombian diplomatic or consular officials, $5; (14) official proceedings presented to private persons, $1; (15) sanitation or health certificates, $2; (16) certificates issued by government officials, $1, certificates of freedom from debt, $.50; (17) official translations, $.50 per page; (18) authentication of official publications, $2; (19) copies of official documents, $.10 per page; (20) copies of marriage certificates, $.20; (21) licenses to introduce goods requiring official certification, $100; (22) books registered at the chambers of commerce, $.20 per sheet; and (23) petitions seeking exemptions or reductions of taxes, $5.

2) *Mining Activities*: (1) claims, $50; (2) terminations, $50; (3) possession, $100; and (4) titles—for vein mines, $50, placer, $1,000, and sediment mines and precious stones, $500.

3) *Concessions and Permits*: (1) petroleum, $2,000; (2) radioactive minerals, $1,000; (3) forests covering over 500 hectares, $500; (4) other mining concessions, $200; (5) forests and deposits of sand, gravel, and stones, $50; (6) emerald mines, $1,000; (7) idle public lands, $.50 per hectare; (8) occupancy of streets and plazas,

$500; (9) hydraulic water rights, $500; (10) water concessions, $1 per liter per second; (11) to carry firearms, $10; and (12) sale of firearms, $100.

4) *Industrial Property*: (1) applications for patents, trademarks, models, and industrial designs, $50; and (2) grants of patents, trademarks, models, and industrial designs, $100.

5) *Transportation*: (1) licenses for ships, $1 per ton; and (2) registration of aircraft, $5 per each kilogram of operating gross weight.

6) *Appointments*: of government officials and officers of private companies, 2 per cent of monthly salary if not over $1,000, or 4 per cent if over that amount; if remuneration is contingent, $5; if partly fixed and partly contingent, $5 plus 2 per cent or 4 per cent on the fixed portion.

7) *Payrolls and Accounts Presented by Government Employees for Payment at Government Offices*: $.20 per $100 or fraction of gross monthly wages if over $1,000, or on total of accounts presented; and half-rate on wages of $1,000 or less.

8) *Income Tax Returns*: for late filing, $10.

9) *External Trade*: (1) consular invoices, 1 per cent of the net f.o.b. value of the goods; (2) presentation of commercial invoices to customs authorities, 2 per cent of the net f.o.b. value of the goods; (3) excess of foreign goods brought into the country by travelers, 2 per cent of the value of the excess; (4) original of each bill of lading or airway bill, $5; (5) each additional copy of consular invoices, bills of lading, or airway bills, $2; (6) navigation permits, $5; (7) ship's manifests, $45 up to 1,000 net tons, $60 from 1,001 to 2,000 tons, $75 from 2,001 to 3,000 tons, $90 from 3,001 to 4,000 tons, $105 from 4,001 to 5,000 tons, $120 from 5,001 to 7,000 tons, $135 from 7,001 to 10,000 tons, and $150 for over 10,000 tons; (8) certificates of air worthiness, $10; and (9) manifests for importing goods, $2 per page.

10) *Notarized Documents*: (1) original

copy of public deeds, $2; and (2) notarial copies, $.20 per page.

11) *Appraisals of Property*: (1) for civil trials or administrative actions concerning estate inventories, $.40 for each $100 or fraction; and (2) in other civil proceedings, $.20 for each $100 or fraction.

12) *Documentary Evidence*: (1) decisions, invoices, i.o.u.'s, collection accounts, receipts, copies of denial or admission in litigation, acknowledgements or confessions, all of which when used as evidence in civil suits or administrative proceedings, $.20 per $100 or fraction of the value of the indebtedness, but where the value is indeterminate, $10; (2) documents not requiring notarization, $.20 for each $100 of value, and for undetermined value, $10; and (3) documents on agreements, promises, or options, $10.

13) *Transfers of Money*: (1) the remittance or transfer of cash or currency within the country, $.20 for each $100 or fraction, and (2) assignments of contracts, debts, or rights, $.20 for each $100 or fraction of the amount.

14) *Professional and Technical Licenses*: (1) recording of professional qualifications, $2; (2) registration of merchants or tradesmen in the Public Trade Registry, $2; (3) professional licenses, $10; and (4) certificates and diplomas upon completion of secondary, university, or technical studies, $10.

15) *Financial Activities*: (1) issuance of bonds, 1 per cent of nominal value; (2) issuance of bearer bonds, 2 per cent of nominal value; (3) capitalization of savings certificates, $.20 for each $1,000 of nominal value; (4) issuance of corporate shares, $4 per $1,000 of the nominal value of the certificates; (5) endorsement, assignment, or transfer of nominal shares traded on the stock exchange, $2 per $1,000 of the average stock value in the month preceding the transaction; and (6) the endorsement, assignment, or transfer of nominal shares not registered with the stock exchange, $3 per $1,000 of the value determined by the Division of National Taxes.

16) *Air Transportation*: air and sea transportation tickets from Colombia to foreign ports, 5 per cent of the value of the tickets.

17) *Cargo and Parcel Transportation*: (1) bills of lading, transportation bills, letters of safe conduct, or any other document covering the transportation of cargo, $.05 for each $100 of value; and (2) parcel post packages, $.20 for each.

Administrative Procedure. The national stamp taxes are administered through the sale of stamps, by the use of stamping machines, by the receipt of cash payment, or by the withholding of the fees by business firms. For noncompliance, there is a penalty of three times the value of the fee.

Official Stamped Paper

Official stamped paper (*papel sellado*) must be used in the following instances: (1) documents addressed to law-making bodies; (2) written proceedings before government agencies; (3) summary enforcement proceedings; (4) notarial acts, copies, certificates, and other documents; (5) public and private documents evidencing the creation, amendment, or termination of contractual rights; (6) copies and certificates relating to civil status (birth, citizenship, marriage, etc.) issued by civil or ecclesiastical authorities; and (7) proceedings before chambers of commerce and arbitration tribunals.

Comments on National Stamp Taxes and Stamped Paper

Some of these taxes are actually fees, for which the service rendered by the government is directly related to the charge; some are partly taxes and partly fees, where there is only an element of service related to the charge; and others are taxes where no service is received. Generally speaking, wherever there is a direct benefit to the taxpayer, the charge made by the government should be based on the cost of providing the service. Quite obviously, however, this is not the case in Colombia in many instances, for there can be no relation between the number of pages of a document and the benefits received. In instances such as the filing, certification, and recording of documents, the government should make an attempt to determine the cost of providing the service and charge accordingly. There are some documents, however, that should be free of any charge. These involve petitions or grievances presented to the government. In a democracy, these should be viewed as a right and should not be discouraged by a fee.

Many of the stamp duties are in the nature of taxes, for the government accords little service relative to the tax paid. This is true of licenses, appointments of government officials and officers of private companies, consular invoices, the transfer of cash holdings, professional certificates, etc. With many of these taxes, the principal rationale is that they are considered to be desirable for the purpose of raising revenue. But, on this score, they have several shortcomings: (1) They are a nuisance and obstruct business. One gets the impression, in fact, that it is hardly possible to do anything in Colombia without an official stamp or the use of stamped paper. (2) They are not very productive of revenue. (3) They fall arbitrarily on the consumers of particular products. (4) They are usually regressive.

In the case of those stamp duties that are actually in the nature of taxes, the only ones that appear to have some merit are those levied on mining concessions, licenses for ships and aircraft, the issuance of corporate bonds and shares, and the tax on air transportation. The latter, in particular, is fully justified on the ability-to-pay principle. On the other hand, taxes on credit instruments increase the cost of doing business and are a nuisance to businessmen and consumers alike. These should be eliminated.

*National Consumption
and Production Taxes*

The remaining national indirect taxes comprise a group of twenty miscellaneous consumption and production taxes, varying from taxes on liquor and lotteries to levies on cotton and insurance premiums:

1) *Distilled Liquor.* This tax was originally levied in 1955 at the rate of $1.00 per bottle (720 grams or fraction thereof), and was earmarked for the National Public Services Corporation (Corporación Nacional de Servicios Públicos). Later, 50 per cent of the tax was allocated to the Municipal Development Institute (Instituto de Fomento Municipal) and 50 per cent to the Electrical Institute (Electroaguas). Finally, Decree 1,361 of 1961 provided that 10 per cent of the tax should be allocated to the Central Bank for educational purposes, 45 per cent to the departmental unit of the Municipal Development Institute, and 45 per cent to the Electrical Institute.

2) *Public Shows.* This tax, enacted in 1932, has a distinction in tax rates between cultural and non-cultural entertainment. Entertainment of a cultural nature has the following rate schedule: 5 per cent on tickets up to $.20; 6 per cent on tickets of $.21 to $.30; 7 per cent on tickets of $.31 to $.40; 8 per cent on tickets of $.41 to $.60; and 10 per cent on tickets of more than $.60. Due to inflation, only the 10 per cent rate is currently applicable. The tax rate on non-cultural entertainment, such as bullfights, moving pictures, and horse races, is a flat 10 per cent. For application of the tax on public shows, departmental and municipal entertainment taxes are deductible from the value of the tickets to determine the national tax base.

3) *"Five-and-Six" Tax.* The "five-and-six" is a betting arrangement in horse-racing in which the individual wins if he selects five or six winners. The tax on this form of gambling, created in 1958, has rates of 20 per cent on the amount wagered, $1.00 on each of the forms, and 20 per cent on gambling gains. Collections from the tax on the amount wagered are earmarked for the Ministry of Health to maintain hospitals, while the other revenues are earmarked for welfare and public assistance agencies at the local levels of government.

4) *Football "Totogol."* "Totogol" is another gambling activity in which a person attempts to select winning soccer teams. This tax was established in 1963 and consists of the same tax rates and earmarking of revenues as described above for the "five-and-six" tax.

5) *Hotel Occupancy.* This tax was enacted in 1954 for the purpose of subsidizing the activities of the Colombia Tourist Agency (Empresa Colombiana de Turismo). The rate of the tax is 5 per cent on hotel rooms for which $10 or more is charged for food and lodging. Revenues are earmarked for the Colombia Tourist Agency.

6) *Classification of Motion Picture Films.* Enacted in 1960, the purpose of this tax is to provide funds for the Ministry of Education for the classification of motion picture films. The rate of the tax is $50 per film.

7) *Consumption of Cotton and Cotton Yarns.* This tax was originally established in 1948 for the purpose of developing the production of cotton. The tax was abolished in 1957 and was replaced with a development tax of $.03 for each kilogram of cotton consumed by textile factories and $.10 for each kilogram of imported cotton. Collections are earmarked for the support of the Cotton Development Institute (Instituto de Fomento Algodonero).

8) *Sales under the "Club System."* A "club" is formed by retail stores, the members of which are the customers buying on credit. The members contribute weekly to a fund, and the proceeds are raffled off each week. A tax was levied on this activity in 1946 with a rate of 2 per cent on the value of the goods given by the retail stores as prizes.

9) *Fund for the Blind (Fondo de Ciegos).* Originally, this tax was a departmental source of revenue used for the maintenance of institutions for the blind, deaf, and dumb, but since 1942 the tax has been a national government source of revenue. The tax is levied on theatres, circuses, racetracks, and similar establishments and is based on capacity according to the following schedule: up to 500 persons, $5.00 per month; from 501 to 1,000 persons, $10.00 per month; and for more than 1,000 persons, $20.00 per month.

10) *Matches.* This tax dates from 1917, when the rate was one-half cent for each box of fifty matches and another one-half cent for any amount in excess. In 1932 the tax rate was increased to one cent per box of thirty matches, plus an additional cent for any excess. Finally, the rate was increased in 1960 to two cents for each box of sixty matches and one cent for each additional thirty matches. The tax is collected by means of a stamp tax.

11) *Playing Cards.* Levied since 1960, the rate of this tax is $.02 per card, which is also collected by means of a stamp tax.

12) *Oils and Greases.* This tax has been in effect since 1931 and has a rate of $.20 per gallon of lubricating oil and $.06 for each kilogram of grease consumed domestically.

13) *Insurance Premiums.* Premiums are taxed according to the following schedule: individual life insurance premiums, $3.00 per $100 or fraction; group life insurance, $2.50 for each $100 or fraction; general or commerical insurance, $4.00 per $100 or fraction; other insurance, $4.00 per $100 or fraction; and reinsurance premiums paid by foreign companies, $2.00 per $100 or fraction.

14) *Lotteries.* There are two national taxes on lottery tickets and prizes. One of these is collected by the departments for the benefit of municipal welfare agencies. This tax has a rate of 5 per cent on tickets and 10 per cent on prizes. The other tax has a rate of 2 per cent applicable to all lottery prizes, the revenue from which is received by the national government.

15) *Raffles.* Levied since 1946, the tax has a rate of 10 per cent of the value of raffle tickets and 15 per cent on prizes exceeding $1,000.

16) *Forest Exploitation.* This tax is in the nature of a royalty on the exploitation of public property. The rates are 5 per cent

of the value of products when a government concession or license has been granted, and 7 per cent in the absence of a concession or license.

17) *Tobacco Products*. National government excises are levied on the manufacturer of tobacco products according to the following rates: on each package of eleven to twenty cigarettes, $.12; on each package containing ten or fewer cigarettes, $.06; on each box, package, or container of cigars, pipe tobacco, or chewing tobacco, $.50. For cartons or packages containing more than twenty cigarettes, the tax is imposed on multiples of twenty, but the other taxes on tobacco products remain the same regardless of quantity or weight.

18. *Oil Production*.

1) Producers of government-owned petroleum are required to pay a tax of one-third of a cent U.S. currency per barrel of petroleum produced, which is used to provide scholarships abroad for Colombian students.

2) There is a pipeline tax for operations in the eastern zone of the country of 2 per cent of the transportation charges computed at the per barrel rates fixed for each pipeline. For pipelines from fields in other parts of the country, the rate is 6 per cent.

3) There is a surface tax in the eastern zone of U.S. $.10 per hectare during the first and second years of a concession, U.S. $.20 during the third year, U.S. $.30 during the fourth year, U.S. $.50 during the fifth year, and U.S. $1.00 during the sixth, seventh, and eighth years. In the remainder of Colombia, the tax is U.S. $.20 for the first year, U.S. $.60 for the second year, U.S. $1.00 for the third year, U.S. $2.00 for the fourth year, and U.S. $3.00 for the fifth and sixth years. A part of the surface tax is allocated to the departments and municipalities where the fields are located.

4) Concessionaires engaged in the exploration, exploitation, and extraction of government-owned petroleum are required to pay the government a royalty at the rate of 11.5 per cent of the gross output in the eastern

zone and 14.5 per cent in the remainder of the country. For concessions in the eastern zone that enter into commercial production prior to December 31, 1970, the rate is reduced to 7 per cent for the first ten years of the operating period. On natural gasoline in either zone, the royalty is one-thirtieth of gross output.

5) Operators extracting privately owned petroleum, who commenced operations after March 16, 1961, must pay a production tax on both gas and oil production at the rate of 6.5 per cent of gross output in the eastern zone and 8.5 per cent in the remainder of the country. On natural gasoline, the production tax is one-sixtieth of gross output.

19) *Gold Production*. The extraction of gold is subject to the payment of royalties ranging from 2 per cent on deposits of up to 150 milligrams of gold per cubic meter to 20 per cent on deposits of over 800 milligrams per cubic meter. In addition, there is a production tax of $2.50 per troy ounce of fine gold that is collected for the benefit of the municipalities within whose boundaries the gold is produced. The municiplities also receive 50 per cent of the royalties collected.

20) *Registry and Recording Taxes*. A tax is imposed on the registry and recording of documents, contracts, and acts that are required to be registered, certified, or cancelled at official registry offices. The tax varies from $.50 for documents of minor importance to $30 for contracts with a value of $500,000 or over. There is a charge of $.50 for each sheet of paper over five, and a surcharge for certifying documents over twenty years of age, computed at $.10 per year for each year in excess of twenty. The fee for registry, certification, or cancellation of share-cropping contracts or other crop division contracts is $2.00 per contract. These fees are in addition to charges for stamps or stamped paper. Of the revenue collected from registry and recording taxes, 80 per cent is allocated to the departments to cover departmentally operated registry offices, except in those cases where the national government maintains the

offices. The remaining 20 per cent is to be used principally by the Ministry of Justice in preparation for the eventual transfer of all public registry offices to the national government.

Comments on National Consumption and Production Taxes

Several criticisms may be made of this group of taxes:

1) There is an exaggerated use made of earmarking. For a wide number of these taxes, the government either allocates the revenues to particular agencies or activities of the national government or to the departmental and municipal governments. In either case, this is an undesirable practice. When revenues are allocated to particular agencies or activities, there is only a slight chance that the revenue received is appropriate— it probably is either more or less than should be spent. In other words, this type of practice prevents an orderly and efficient budgetary procedure. When revenues from particular national government indirect taxes are allocated for the support of other government units, the tax source itself should be relinquished by the national government. Obviously, no purpose is served by the national government administering a tax from which it receives no revenue. This practice could only be condoned on the basis of administrative necessity, but this factor does not appear to be controlling in Colombia.

2) As a group, the national consumption and production taxes do not emphasize the taxation of semi-luxuries or luxuries. Several, in fact, are decidedly regressive, such as the taxes on liquor and tobacco products, public shows, gambling, cotton and cotton yarns, matches, playing cards, and lotteries. An improvement in equity would result if many of these taxes were de-emphasized and if luxury-type articles were taxed.

3) The consumption and production taxes do not represent a *system* of taxation but merely a conglomerate group of items that have been singled out haphazardly for taxa-

tion. As a result, the taxation of consumption and production at the national level distorts the price system, results in a misallocation of resources, and lacks consumer interpersonal equity.

4) Many of the taxes are specific instead of *ad valorem,* which means that inflation erodes away their bases. Specific taxes are also regressive as between low- and high-priced articles.

5) As in the case of stamps and stamped paper, the registry and recording taxes should be levied on the basis of a fee (cost equated to service) rather than a tax, for they represent a service provided by government.

6) The various royalties and production taxes levied on the oil industry are unduly complicated and should be combined into a single levy.

DEPARTMENTAL INDIRECT TAXES

The departmental assemblies may establish only those taxes that the national Congress authorizes. This authorization may be given in such a way that minimum and maximum limits are established for the rates, with the departments being free to select particular rates within these limits. In other cases, all details of the tax are enacted by the Congress, and the levy is then turned over to the departments for administration. Because of these two methods, there is considerable variation among departments in the use of particular taxes, while other departmental indirect taxes are uniform throughout the country. Departmental indirect taxes are relatively few in number, the principal ones being levies on tobacco products, alcoholic beverages, gasoline, lotteries, and livestock-slaughtering.

The departments have several sources of revenue other than the indirect taxes that they administer. In departments where oil fields are located, the departments share the national government royalties and surface taxes. The department of Cundinamarca obtains revenue from a tax on the pipeline transportation of oil. Also, the departments receive revenue from certain taxes imposed by the national government, as, for example, the tax on lotteries and lottery prizes. Some departments also receive 80 per cent of the revenue from the registry and recording taxes.

For purposes of describing the indirect taxes administered by the departments, they may be grouped into eight categories. Because of the variation in the taxes among departments, the department of Cundinamarca is used in most cases for illustrative purposes:

1) *Tobacco Products.* Domestic tobacco products for consumption within the department of Cundinamarca are taxed at the manufacturer's sale price. The rates are 50 per cent for cigarettes and cigars and 40 per cent for snuff. The tax is collected from the producer or distributor. In addition, the departments and territories share proportionately, according to consumption, the proceeds from a special import tax of $.12 per package of twenty cigarettes levied on imported cigarettes.

2) *Beer Consumption.* The department of Cundinamarca imposes two types of taxes on domestic beer. The first is a consumption tax based on rates that are determined by the size and type of container and the wholesale price of the product. This tax is paid by the producer or by the distributor in the case of beer shipped from other departments. Rates currently in effect are:

Container	Rates
Bottles where the wholesale price is less than $1.40 per dozen exclusive of container	$.01 per 360 grams or fraction
Bottles up to 180 grams	$.0375 per bottle
Bottles over 180 grams	$.075 per 360 grams or fraction
Barrels or similar containers	$.10 per liter

The second tax, a sales tax based on rates applied to the invoice price at the brewery, has a rate of 5 per cent. In computing the invoice price, a deduction is allowed for beer sold outside the department, as well as for such items as bonuses, discounts, the cost of containers, and packing and shipping cost.

3) *Imported Wines and Liquors.* The tax on foreign wines and liquors is assessed either when it enters a department or when it is withdrawn from a licensed warehouse. The rates applicable to imported wines and liquors in the department of Cundinamarca are:

Distilled spirits and sparkling wines	$1.50 per 100 grams
Heavy wines (less than 22 per cent alcoholic content) and table wines (less than 15 per cent alcoholic content)	$1.50 per bottle of up to 360 grams and $3.00 for 375 to 1,000 grams

4) *Domestic Wines.* This tax is imposed on the producer or, in the case of wine produced outside the department, on the distributor upon entry into the department. The rates vary according to the size of the container:

Size of Bottle	Tax Rate
Up to 375 grams	$.20
375 to 500 grams	.30
500 to 750 grams	.40
750 to 1,000 grams	.50
Over 1,000 grams	.05 per 100 grams

5) *Consumption of Distilled Liquors from Other Departments.* This tax is established by means of agreements between departments. For example, the sale of "Ron Bulk 58" manufactured in the department of Santander is taxed in the department of Cundinamarca at the rate of $2.00 per bottle of 720 grams and $1.00 per bottle of 360 grams.

6) *Gasoline.* Traditionally, the tax on gasoline was a national tax, but since 1957 this levy has been transferred to the depart-

ments. At the present time, the tax rate is $.04 per gallon plus a subsidy of $.06 per gallon paid to the departments by the Empresa Colombiana de Petróleos.

7) *Other Departmental Lotteries.* Law 64 of 1923 permits the departments to prohibit the sale of lottery tickets from other departments or to tax them at the rate of 10 per cent of their value. Practically all departments utilize the 10 per cent tax.

8) *Livestock Slaughter.* Two taxes on livestock slaughtering are imposed. One is a tax on butchering, based on the weight of the animal:

Weight of Animal	Steers, Males, Cows	Heifers
Over 200 kilograms	$.01 per kilogram	$.02 per kilogram
Less than 200 kilograms	$2.00 per head	$4.00 per head

The second tax is earmarked for the maintenance of public scales, and has the following rates:

Class of Cattle	Rates Where Public Scales are Available	Rates Elsewhere
Steers, males, cows	$.10 per kilogram	$3.00 per head
Heifers	$.10 per kilogram	$6.00 per head

Comments on Departmental Indirect Taxes

Most of the departmental indirect taxes fall on tobacco and liquor products, and the basic issues involved in taxing these products are much the same. In principle, taxes on these products are undesirable, for they tend to be sharply regressive and they prevent consumers from allocating their expenditures freely. The principle virtue of taxing these products, on the other hand, is that they are productive of revenue, and this is certainly not unimportant in a country that is urgently in need of additional public revenues at all levels of government. In general terms, the desirable policy conclusion is that, despite advantages in terms of sheer expediency, the taxation of tobacco and liquor products should not be emphasized. At any rate, one never needs to encourage politicians to raise taxes on these products.

Two principal reforms may be introduced to rationalize the taxation of both of these products. The first is to reserve their taxation to the departmental level of government. This would mean that the national government would relinquish to the departments the tax on distilled liquor. Second, all taxes should be *ad valorem* instead of specific. *Ad valorem* taxes have two principal advantages: (1) They are neutral with respect to lower and higher priced brands. (2) They prevent a reduction of revenues under inflationary conditions.

Rather than turn to heavier taxes on tobacco and liquor products, the national government would be well advised to permit the departments to exploit the taxation of gasoline more effectively. This product is one of the most undertaxed in Colombia and is immeasurably better as a base of taxation than either tobacco or liquor products. The present tax of only $.04 per gallon (exclusive of the subsidy of $.06 per gallon paid to the departments by the Empresa Colombiana de Petróleos) represents only 3.2 per cent of the retail price of a gallon of regular gasoline in Bogotá.

Another tax that would be appropriate for exclusive use by the departments is the taxation of lottery tickets and prizes. At the present time, this field of taxation is shared by the national and departmental governments, a policy which appears to be particularly undesirable in view of the need for grants from the national government to the departments. Also, since the lotteries are operated by the departments, it is appropriate for them to have lotteries as a base of taxation.

The remaining principal indirect tax at the departmental level on livestock-slaughtering should be eliminated. Meat is a basic consumption item, and, therefore, the incidence of the tax is regressive. The tax is a particular anachronism in view of the fact that all other food products in Colombia are exempt from taxation. To the degree that a charge is necessary for the use of public slaughter-houses or scales, the levy should be not a tax but a fee based on the cost of the service.

MUNICIPAL INDIRECT TAXES

Municipal taxation is circumscribed, first, by the legal requirement that municipalities may tax only properties, activities, and trans-actions not taxed by either the national government or the departments. Second, the departments specify the taxes that may be levied by the municipalities within their juris-dictions. An exception to the latter is Bogotá, which is empowered to assess and collect taxes without the intervention of the depart-ment of Cundinamarca. Capital cities of departments with an annual budget of over $200,000 also have more autonomy in fiscal matters than do smaller municipalities. Because municipal taxes vary a great deal in Colombia, only the taxes levied in Bogotá will be used for illustrative purposes. Five different indirect taxes are levied in Bogotá.

1) *Industry and Commerce.* This tax is imposed on all businesses, with a distinction being made for industrial and commercial enterprises. Industrial firms are taxed on the basis of monthly gross sales and the amount of installed horsepower. For gross sales, the rate rises from $1.10 per $1,000 on the initial $9,000 of sales to $2.00 per $1,000 on sales over $72,000. For installed horse-power, the rate is from $1.50 per horsepower on the initial 3 horsepower to $3.00 per horsepower over 240.

Commercial establishments are taxed on the basis of monthly rent and gross sales. The tax on gross sales is the same as for industrial enterprises, while the tax based on rent rises from 3.5 per cent on the initial $300 of monthly rent to 12.5 per cent on rents above $1,400. No tax is paid on monthly rents of less than $200. Banking institutions and in-surance companies pay a tax of $1,000 for their central office and $100 for each branch. New commercial establishments are given a deduction of 50 per cent of their tax liability for the first twelve months, and new indus-trial establishments are exempt for the same period. Establishments suffering losses may claim a 50 per cent reduction in the tax.

2) *Gambling.* Games that do not involve gambling risks (billiards, etc.) are considered as "permitted" games. In Bogotá, these are taxed at the rate of $10 to $100 per month according to the appraisal of the Municipal Finance Board. For raffles and similar activi-ties, the tax rate is 2 per cent of the value of the tickets. For cock fighting, the tax is from $10 to $50 for each performance plus a tax on the cockpits of up to $120 per annum. A tax of 15 per cent is levied on the receipts from wagers on horse races and football pools, but the receipts of the Techo Racetrack are taxed at 10 per cent. Winnings from wagers are taxed at 12 per cent.

3) *Public Entertainment.* In most munici-palities, public entertainment is taxed by both the national and municipal governments. The reason for this is that the tax was originally a municipal levy, but when the national govern-ment entered the field in 1932, the munici-pal taxes were left in force, but their level was stabilized. Thus, at the present time, the municipal taxes range from 2 to 10 per cent, but these taxes are allowed as a deduction before application of the national tax. As an example, the municipal rates established for boxing matches in Bogotá are 4 per cent on tickets up to $2.00, 6 per cent on tickets from $2.01 to $3.00, and 8 per cent on tickets of $3.01 or more.

4) *Weights and Measures.* As an illustra-tion, the department of Cundinamarca au-thorizes the municipalities within its jurisdic-tion to levy the following taxes: (1) the continued use of rented weight and measure-ment devices owned by the municipality,

$5.00 per month; (2) the use of privately owned equipment, from $1.00 to $2.00 per month; and (3) the use of public equipment, $.05 to $.10 for each use.

5) *Slaughter Tax on Small Animals.* Rates for this tax vary among the departments. In the department of Cundinamarca, the authorized tax is up to $2.00 for each slaughtered head of pigs, sheep, or goats.

Comments on Municipal Indirect Taxes

The tax on industry and commerce, the most important indirect tax at the municipal level, is in the nature of a license measured by rents, sales, and, in the case of industrial firms, installed horsepower. There is no valid reason for using these variable bases, and the use of installed horsepower, in particular, is undesirable. It would be an improvement in terms of equity, neutrality, and administrative convenience to base the tax only on gross sales. Also, industrial and commercial activities should be taxed at the same rate.

A tax on entertainment or public shows appears particularly appropriate for the use of the municipalities in terms of administrative convenience. Therefore, it was probably a mistake for the national government to enter this field in 1932 and for revenues to be split, since that date, between the national and municipal governments. The tax should be returned in its entirety to the municipal governments. A distinction also should be made for entertainment that does not involve gambling (such as billiards and boxing) and other activities such as horse races and football pools. The former should be taxed under an entertainment tax, while the latter should be subject to special gambling taxes.

The other indirect taxes used by municipalities—on weights and measures and the slaughtering of small animals—are essentially archaic and should not be used in a progressive and enlightened tax system. There is justification for a service charge when publicly owned scales are used, but it should be measured by the cost of the service. The tax on slaughtering is really a special sales tax on a basic consumption item and is undoubtedly regressive in its incidence.

INDIRECT TAX REVENUES

National Government Indirect Taxes

The statistics for national government indirect taxes shown in Table 10–1 indicates

TABLE 10–1

Indirect Taxes of the National Government, 1950 to 1962

(Thousands of Pesos)

	Taxes on Foreign Commerce	Percentage of Total Indirect Taxes	Internal Indirect Taxes	Percentage of Total Indirect Taxes	Total Indirect Taxes	Internal Indirect Taxes as a Percentage of Total National Tax Revenues
1950	$140,752	69.3	$ 62,405	30.7	$203,157	15.2
1951	228,129	77.0	68,260	23.0	296,389	12.1
1952	231,451	82.1	50,411	17.9	281,862	9.0
1953	300,611	83.8	58,281	16.2	358,892	9.0
1954	389,906	85.7	65,102	14.3	455,008	7.0
1955	415,217	90.2	45,307	9.8	460,524	4.8
1956	317,462	73.6	113,930	26.4	431,392	12.8
1957	205,437	79.5	53,132	20.5	258,569	5.1
1958	608,564	91.1	59,624	8.9	668,188	4.2
1959	582,122	87.7	82,013	12.3	664,135	5.3
1960	708,645	86.7	108,810	13.3	817,455	5.9
1961	695,219	82.1	152,062	17.9	847,281	8.0

Source: Subdivisión de Recaudación, División de Impuestos Nacionales, Ministerio de Hacienda y Credito Público.

that collections have risen from $62.4 million in 1950 to $152.0 million in 1961, an increase of 144 per cent. But the revenues through this span of years have been very erratic, more than doubling from 1955 to 1956 but then falling precipitously in 1957. However, the trend in revenues has been upward since 1957.

Collections from internal indirect taxes compare unfavorably both with the growth of revenues from foreign commerce and with total national tax revenues. From 1950 to 1961, internal indirect taxes as a percentage of total national government indirect taxes (including taxes on foreign commerce) decreased from 30.7 to 17.9 per cent. During the same span of years, internal indirect taxes as a percentage of total national tax revenues decreased from 15.2 to 8.0 per cent.

Table 10–2 indicates that stamps and stamped paper are by far the most important of the national government's internal indirect taxes, representing 58.1 per cent of collections in 1961. The other indirect taxes, in order of revenue importance, were distilled

TABLE 10–2

Internal Indirect Taxes of the
National Government, 1961

	Collections	Percentage of Total Internal Indirect Taxes
Stock issuance and transfer	$ 783,965	0.50
Matches and playing cards	5,190,092	3.40
Stamps and stamped paper	88,314,471	58.10
Gold production	99,337	0.07
Lotteries	3,545,942	2.30
Gambling	13,939,831	9.20
Public shows	9,208,666	6.10
Insurance premiums	5,421,151	3.60
Oils and greases	2,250,759	1.50
Hotel occupancy	5,487,936	3.60
Distilled liquor	17,787,551	11.70
Classification of motion picture films	33,269	0.02
TOTAL	$152,062,970	100.00[a]

[a] Total does not add due to rounding.
Source: Subdivisión de Recaudación, División de Impuestos Nacionales, Ministerio de Hacienda y Crédito Público.

liquors, 11.7 per cent; gambling, 9.2 per cent; and public shows, 6.1 per cent. The remaining indirect taxes resulted in less than 5 per cent of internal indirect tax collections.

Departmental Indirect Taxes

Table 10–3 shows that indirect tax revenues constitute the overwhelming proportion of revenues derived from taxes at the departmental level. In 1961 total revenues derived from indirect taxes were $395.6 million as compared to $25.3 million from direct taxes. The ratio of indirect to total tax revenues was 93.99 per cent for all of the departments. This ratio is more or less the same in all departments. On the other hand, because the departments have substantial non-tax sources of revenue, the ratio of indirect tax revenues to total revenues is much lower. In 1961 this ratio for all departments was 41.43 per cent. It is also apparent from Table 10–3 that some departments are inordinately more important than others in terms of total departmental indirect tax revenue. The department of Cundinamarca, for example, collected nearly 25 per cent of all indirect taxes collected by the seventeen departments in 1961.

Table 10–4 indicates that revenues from the departmental indirect taxes increased from $220.5 million in 1955 to $395.6 million in 1961, an increase of 79.4 per cent. However, when the 1961 total is expressed in terms of 1955 prices, the increase was only 5.4 per cent, which is, of course, less than the growth in the gross internal product during the intervening years. Table 10–4 shows also that there have been wide differences among the departments in the degree to which departmental indirect tax revenues have increased. In absolute terms, indirect tax revenues have increased. in two departments (Magdalena and Córdoba) by 134.78 and 151.35 per cent respectively, while in two other departments they increased by only 38.77 and 57.79 per cent (Caldas and Valle del Cauca respectively).

Table 10–5 shows the collections derived

TABLE 10–3

Departmental Indirect Taxes Related to Direct Taxes and Total Revenues, 1955 and 1961

(Millions of Pesos)

Departments and Years		Indirect Tax Revenues	Direct Tax Revenues	Total Revenues	Percentage of Indirect Tax Revenues to Total Tax Revenues	Percentage of Indirect Taxes to Total Revenues
Antioquia	1955	$ 33.0	$ 3.1	$ 68.3	91.41	48.32
	1961	68.2	7.8	185.5	89.74	36.77
Atlántico	1955	9.1	0.9	23.7	91.20	38.40
	1961	17.6	2.5	43.7	87.56	40.27
Bolívar	1955	6.9	0.3	20.5	95.83	33.66
	1961	14.9	1.6	70.6	90.30	21.10
Boyacá	1955	12.8	2.1	28.4	85.91	45.07
	1961	21.2	1.9	40.8	91.77	51.96
Caldas	1955	22.7	n.a.	37.9	n.a.	59.89
	1961	31.5	n.a.	71.6	n.a.	43.99
Cauca	1955	3.4	0.2	11.0	94.44	30.91
	1961	6.2	0.4	29.9	93.94	20.74
Córdoba	1955	3.7	0.2	9.9	94.87	37.37
	1961	9.3	0.5	22.8	94.90	40.79
Cundinamarca	1955	55.6	n.a.	76.3	n.a.	72.92
	1961	94.7	1.4	145.4	98.54	65.13
Chocó	1955	1.0	n.a.	3.6	n.a.	27.78
	1961	2.2	n.a.	6.0	n.a.	36.67
Huila	1955	3.8	0.2	11.3	95.00	33.63
	1961	8.0	0.6	25.3	93.02	31.62
Magdalena	1955	6.9	0.3	17.4	95.83	39.66
	1961	16.1	1.1	27.8	93.60	57.91
Nariño	1955	3.7	n.a.	12.7	n.a.	29.13
	1961	7.8	0.6	25.7	92.86	30.35
N. Santander	1955	6.8	n.a.	15.8	n.a.	43.04
	1961	13.8	0.6	44.1	95.83	31.29
Santander	1955	10.7	0.3	18.7	97.27	57.22
	1961	19.6	0.3	55.5	93.49	35.32
Tolima	1955	11.5	0.7	30.4	94.26	37.83
	1961	18.8	1.0	56.2	94.95	33.45
Valle del Cauca	1955	28.9	0.8	73.6	97.31	39.27
	1961	45.7	5.0	104.0	90.14	43.94
TOTALS	1955	$220.5	$ 9.0	$459.5	96.08	47.99
	1961	395.6	25.3	954.9	93.99	41.43

Source: Departamento Administrativo Nacional de Estadística.

from the various individual departmental indirect taxes during the period from 1955 to 1961. Evident from this data is that taxes on tobacco and liquor products dominate the indirect taxes in terms of revenue productivity. These two products accounted for 89.7 per cent of indirect tax collections in 1961, somewhat lower than the same percentage for 1955 of 93.9 per cent. Since 1955, the principal change in departmental indirect taxes has been the receipt of the gasoline tax from the national government. In 1961, how-

ever, this tax resulted in only 6.7 per cent of departmental indirect tax collections.

Municipal Indirect Taxes

Municipal indirect taxes produce less than one-quarter as much in revenue as their counterparts at the departmental level of government. In 1961 total revenues derived from indirect taxes at the municipal level were $90.4 million as compared to $395.6 million at the departmental level. Also, in-

TABLE 10–4
Indirect Taxes by Departments, 1955 to 1961

(Millions of Pesos)

Departments	1955	1956	1957	1958	1959	1960	1961	Percentage Increase, 1955 to 1961	1961 Revenues Expressed in 1955 Prices
Antioquia	$ 33.0	$ 38.4	$ 45.0	$ 49.6	$ 53.4	$ 60.0	$ 68.2	106.67	$ 40.1
Atlántico	9.1	10.3	13.5	13.0	13.8	16.0	17.6	93.41	10.3
Bolívar	6.9	7.7	9.5	10.3	13.2	14.3	14.9	115.94	8.8
Boyacá	12.8	14.0	16.5	16.7	19.5	21.2	21.2	65.63	12.5
Caldas	22.7	25.3	29.9	31.5	30.6	29.6	31.5	38.77	18.5
Cauca	3.4	4.1	4.8	5.1	5.2	5.6	6.2	82.35	3.6
Córdoba	3.7	4.0	5.7	7.3	8.1	9.3	9.3	151.35	5.5
Cundinamarca	55.6	62.1	66.9	74.3	79.0	88.9	94.7	70.32	55.6
Chocó	1.0	1.2	1.4	1.6	1.7	2.1	2.2	120.00	1.3
Huila	3.8	4.5	5.8	6.8	7.4	7.8	8.0	110.53	4.7
Magdalena	6.9	8.8	9.5	11.4	12.1	14.8	16.2	134.78	9.5
Nariño	3.7	4.2	4.8	5.4	6.1	6.7	7.8	110.81	4.6
Norte Santander	6.8	8.2	10.5	13.0	14.1	15.3	13.8	102.94	8.1
Santander	10.7	11.5	14.1	15.8	18.1	18.6	19.6	83.18	11.5
Tolima	11.5	13.1	15.2	17.2	17.5	17.7	18.8	62.61	11.0
Valle del Cauca	28.9	34.2	35.9	38.5	38.9	43.3	45.6	57.79	26.8
TOTALS	$220.5	$251.6	$289.0	$317.5	$338.7	$371.2	$395.6	79.41	$232.4

Source: Departamento Administrativo Nacional de Estadística.

direct taxes are relatively less important as a source of revenue to municipal governments, principally because the municipal governments have the real property tax as a source of revenue. In 1961 municipal indirect taxes were 28.11 per cent of total tax revenues of the municipalities and were only 8.62 per cent of total revenues. Only in a few departments, like Chocó and Huila, are indirect taxes a relatively important source of revenue. (See Table 10–6.)

Collections from indirect taxes at the municipal level have risen from $65.3 million in 1957 to $90.4 million in 1961, an increase of 38.4 per cent. Once again, however, it is apparent that inflation has eliminated nearly all of the real increase, as the implicit price index used in the national accounts has risen from an index of 88.2 in 1957 to 124.4 in 1961.

Nearly two-thirds of municipal indirect tax revenues are raised from the tax on industry and commerce, and this proportion has increased from 59.4 per cent in 1957 to 64.3 per cent in 1961. The remaining indirect

municipal taxes, in order of importance in 1961, are consumption taxes, 13.9 per cent; permitted games, 12.3 per cent; entertainment, 4.9 per cent; weights and measures, 1.0 per cent; and other indirect taxes, 3.6 per cent. (See Table 10–7.)

Table 10–8 shows that the municipalities in a few departments are responsible for a large proportion of municipal indirect tax collections. The municipalities in the departments of Antioquia and Valle del Cauca, plus the city of Bogotá, accounted for 60.7 per cent of municipal indirect taxes in 1961, and Bogotá, alone, collected 25.5 per cent of the total.

ANALYSIS AND RECOMMENDATIONS

Before considering the particular internal indirect taxes at each level of government, some general issues should be discussed. The first of these is the rationale or justification of indirect taxes. For this purpose, it is helpful to classify indirect taxes into several

TABLE 10–5

Individual Departmental Indirect Taxes, 1955 and 1961

(Millions of Pesos)

Departments and Years		Tobacco (Cigars and Cigarettes)	Beer Consumption and Sales	Cattle-Slaughtering	Liquors from Other Departments	Foreign Liquors	Domestic Wines	Gasoline	Other Indirect Taxes
Antioquia	1955	$ 22.2	$ 9.4	$ 1.3	$ —	$ —	$0.2	$ —	$ —
	1961	40.5	16.3	4.5	—	—	0.5	6.5	—
Atlántico	1955	4.0	3.3	0.3	0.6	0.4	—	—	0.5
	1961	6.7	5.9	1.3	1.7	0.3	—	1.7	—
Bolívar	1955	3.7	1.6	0.4	—	0.2	0.6	—	0.4
	1961	7.3	3.0	1.1	1.1	0.2	0.1	1.6	0.5
Boyacá	1955	2.0	9.9	0.5	—	0.5	—	—	—
	1961	4.2	15.3	0.6	—	0.2	0.5	0.5	—
Caldas	1955	14.6	6.3	1.3	—	0.1	0.4	—	—
	1961	21.4	8.5	—	—	—	0.4	1.2	—
Cauca	1955	2.2	1.0	0.2	—	—	—	—	—
	1961	4.1	1.5	—	—	—	0.1	0.5	—
Córdoba	1955	2.4	0.7	0.2	0.3	—	—	—	0.1
	1961	6.0	1.6	0.4	0.6	—	—	0.6	0.1
Cundinamarca	1955	11.7	38.5	0.9	—	4.0	0.6	—	—
	1961	23.0	58.6	0.7	2.7	4.1	2.6	3.0	—
Chocó	1955	0.8	0.1	—	—	—	—	—	0.1
	1961	1.5	0.3	—	0.2	—	—	—	0.2
Huila	1955	2.0	1.4	0.4	—	—	—	—	—
	1961	4.1	2.7	—	0.4	0.1	—	0.7	—
Magdalena	1955	3.8	2.5	0.3	—	—	0.1	—	0.2
	1961	8.6	4.7	0.7	1.1	—	—	1.0	0.1
Nariño	1955	2.6	0.6	0.2	—	—	—	—	0.3
	1961	4.6	1.3	0.3	0.7	—	0.1	0.7	0.1
N. Santander	1955	2.9	2.5	0.5	—	0.4	—	—	0.5
	1961	5.6	6.0	1.0	0.6	0.1	0.1	0.3	0.1
Santander	1955	3.6	5.8	0.5	0.2	0.5	0.1	—	—
	1961	6.6	10.1	1.2	0.3	0.3	0.1	1.2	—
Tolima	1955	5.6	5.0	0.9	—	—	0.2	—	—
	1961	9.1	7.9	—	—	—	0.3	1.5	—
Valle del Cauca	1955	15.0	10.2	1.3	—	—	0.3	—	2.1
	1961	25.1	11.8	1.6	—	1.0	0.4	5.7	—
TOTAL	1955	$ 99.1	$ 98.8	$ 9.2	$1.1	$6.1	$2.5	—	$4.2
	1961	178.4	155.5	13.4	9.4	6.3	5.2	$26.7	1.1
PERCENTAGE OF TOTAL IN:	1955	44.8	44.7	4.2	0.5	2.8	1.1	—	1.9
	1961	45.1	39.3	3.4	2.4	1.6	1.3	6.7	0.3

Source: Departamento Administrativo Nacional de Estadística.

groups. At present, indirect taxes are levied on: (1) services rendered by the government; (2) taxes on particular products or activities like tobacco and alcohol, or gambling, because of their sumptuary nature; (3) consumption and production; and (4) entertainment.

For taxes on services rendered by the state, the policy conclusion is clear. These are not a desirable form of taxation. As taxes, they encumber business, are a nuisance, tend to be regressive, and lack interpersonal equity. On the other hand, the government should recover the cost for those services that are necessary for the conduct of business and public affairs. Thus, the appropriate recommendation is that all charges for services that are made only for purposes of obtaining revenue should be eliminated, while the other charges should be as fees and not

TABLE 10–6
Municipal Indirect Taxes Related to Direct Taxes and Total Revenues, 1957 and 1961

(Millions of Pesos)

Departments and Years		Number of Munici-palities	Direct Taxes	Indirect Taxes	Total Revenues	Percentage of Indirect Tax Revenues to Total Tax Revenues	Percentage of Indirect Taxes to Total Revenues
Antioquia	1957	101	$ 35.4	$ 13.0	$105.7	26.86	12.30
	1961	102	47.9	21.2	246.2	30.68	8.61
Atlántico	1957	20	9.1	4.3	24.3	32.09	17.70
	1961	21	15.8	4.4	41.3	21.78	10.65
Bolívar	1957	43	2.6	2.8	16.3	51.85	17.18
	1961	43	5.6	2.6	33.7	31.71	7.72
Boyacá	1957	115	3.3	1.1	7.1	25.00	15.49
	1961	117	4.6	1.9	15.7	29.23	12.10
Caldas	1957	45	12.2	6.3	44.7	34.05	14.09
	1961	47	19.2	7.9	68.7	29.15	11.50
Cauca	1957	33	1.1	0.4	5.2	26.67	7.69
	1961	33	2.2	0.9	8.2	29.03	10.98
Córdoba	1957	20	2.2	0.9	6.0	29.03	15.00
	1961	21	3.2	1.0	12.3	23.81	8.13
Bogotá, D.E.	1957	1	36.4	20.7	188.3	36.25	10.99
	1961	1	56.3	23.3	343.4	29.27	6.79
Cundinamarca	1957	107	7.8	1.5	20.8	16.13	7.21
	1961	106	10.7	2.3	37.3	17.69	6.17
Chocó	1957	15	0.1	0.2	0.8	66.67	25.00
	1961	16	0.1	0.3	1.0	25.00	30.00
Huila	1957	32	1.5	0.8	5.7	34.78	14.04
	1961	33	1.9	2.2	12.7	53.66	17.32
Magdalena	1957	30	2.2	1.1	7.6	33.33	14.47
	1961	30	3.6	1.8	10.5	33.33	17.14
Nariño	1957	49	1.4	0.7	5.1	33.33	13.73
	1961	49	2.3	0.9	7.5	28.13	12.00
N. Santander	1957	34	3.4	0.8	9.9	19.05	8.08
	1961	35	5.6	1.9	21.5	25.33	8.84
Santander	1957	74	6.9	2.2	14.2	24.18	15.49
	1961	74	10.9	3.4	26.4	23.78	12.88
Tolima	1957	42	6.1	2.1	17.3	25.61	12.14
	1961	43	8.9	3.5	28.8	28.23	12.15
Valle del Cauca	1957	42	21.8	6.4	74.3	22.70	8.61
	1961	42	32.4	10.9	134.0	25.17	8.13
TOTALS	1957		$153.5	$ 65.3	$ 553.3	29.84	11.80
	1961		231.2	90.4	1,049.2	28.11	8.62

Source: Departamento Administrativo Nacional de Estadística.

taxes, with the fees based on the cost of providing the services.

With the other indirect taxes that fall on consumption, sales, and production, the emphasis should be placed on taxes that are genuinely productive of revenue, that are relatively convenient in terms of compliance and enforcement, and that are as progressive as possible in their incidence. To be avoided are trivial taxes that sometimes do not even cover the cost of their administration, taxes that are borne in the most part by low income groups, and taxes that are essentially arbitrary in terms of their rates and bases. In other words, indirect taxes can have considerable respectability if they tax semi-luxury and luxury goods in such a way that they are productive of revenue and relatively easy to administer.

Another general issue concerning indirect taxation in Colombia is the allocation of these taxes among the different levels of govern-

TABLE 10–7

Revenues from Individual Municipal Indirect Taxes, 1957 to 1961

(Millions of Pesos)

	1957	Percentage of Total	1958	Percentage of Total	1959	Percentage of Total	1960	Percentage of Total	1961	Percentage of Total
Industry and commerce	$38.8	59.4	$48.2	72.5	$47.1	60.2	$51.2	62.0	$58.7	64.3
Consumption	9.0	13.8	5.6	8.4	13.3	17.0	11.0	13.3	12.7	13.9
Permitted games	6.4	9.8	4.3	6.5	9.8	12.5	11.6	14.0	11.2	12.3
Entertainment	3.3	5.1	3.3	5.0	3.5	4.5	4.3	5.2	4.5	4.9
Weights and measures	1.1	1.7	1.2	1.8	0.9	1.2	0.8	1.0	0.9	1.0
Other indirect taxes	6.7	10.2	3.9	5.8	3.6	4.6	3.7	4.5	3.3	3.6
TOTALS	$65.3	100.0	$66.5	100.0	$78.2	100.0	$82.6	100.0	$91.3	100.0

Source: Departamento Administrativo Nacional de Estadística.

TABLE 10–8

Municipal Indirect Taxes by Departments, 1961

(Millions of Pesos)

	Industry and Commerce	Consumption	Permitted Games	Entertainment	Weights and Measures	Other Indirect Taxes	Total
Antioquia	$17.5	$ 2.2	$ 0.4	$ 1.0	$ —	$ 0.1	$21.2
Atlántico	3.5	0.2	0.3	0.2	—	0.2	4.4
Bolívar	1.5	0.2	0.1	0.4	—	0.3	2.5
Boyacá	0.8	—	0.1	0.1	0.1	0.8	1.9
Caldas	3.6	2.0	0.9	0.6	0.1	0.6	7.8
Cauca	0.3	0.3	0.1	0.1	—	—	0.8
Córdoba	0.7	0.1	—	0.1	—	—	0.9
Bogotá, D.E.	11.7	3.4	7.9	0.3	—	—	23.3
Cundinamarca	1.2	0.8	0.2	0.1	0.1	—	2.4
Chocó	0.2	—	0.1	—	—	—	0.3
Huila	1.1	0.7	0.2	0.1	0.1	0.1	2.3
Magdalena	1.4	0.1	0.1	0.2	—	0.1	1.9
Meta	0.7	—	—	0.1	—	0.3	1.1
Nariño	0.5	0.1	0.1	—	—	0.1	0.8
Norte Santander	1.4	—	0.2	0.2	0.1	—	1.9
Santander	2.2	0.2	0.1	0.5	0.3	0.1	3.4
Tolima	1.7	1.0	0.2	0.2	0.1	0.3	3.5
Valle del Cauca	8.7	1.4	0.2	0.3	—	0.3	10.9
TOTALS	$58.7	$12.7	$11.2	$ 4.5	$ .9	$ 3.3	$91.3

Source: Departamento Administrativo Nacional de Estadística.

ment. It makes very little sense for two levels of government to be taxing the same base, as in the taxation of lotteries and entertainment. This is especially undesirable since the national government subsidizes by transfer payments both the departments and the municipalities. Therefore, it would be advisable for the national government to relinquish certain indirect taxes to the departments and municipalities. In general, the national government should confine itself to the direct taxes on income and wealth and to broad-based indirect taxes.

Finally, should indirect taxes in general be extended in Colombia? Provided that the taxes are generally progressive in their incidence, a case can be made for their extension. One argument for this is Colombia's unusual dependence on direct taxes, which makes a further development of these levies difficult in terms of compliance and enforcement. Second, is the urgent need for government revenues to contain inflationary pressures. Well-conceived taxes on semi-luxury and luxury goods are immeasurably more equitable than inflation, which rightly has been called the most inequitable of all taxes.

National Government Indirect Taxes

In keeping with the philosophy expressed above, the following activities should be relieved of stamp taxes on the grounds that they are not suitable activities for taxation: appointments of government officials and officers of private companies; payrolls and accounts presented by government employees for payment at government offices; appraisals of property; documentary evidence; and transfers of money. For other activities involving stamps and stamped paper, the charge made should be equated to the cost of providing the service.

The national government should relinquish to the departments and municipalities certain of its indirect taxes in order to eliminate the duplication of two levels of government taxing the same base and to provide additional revenues for the departments and municipalities. National government indirect taxes on distilled liquor, tobacco products, and gambling activities (including the lottery) should be given to the departments, while the tax on public shows (admissions) should be transferred to the municipalities.

The earmarking of revenues should be eliminated. This applies, in particular, to the taxes on hotel occupancy, the classification of motion picture films, the consumption of cotton and cotton yarns, the "Fund for the Blind," and taxes on the registry and recording of documents.

Several taxes should be made *ad valorem* instead of specific, namely: the taxes on liquor and tobacco products, matches, playing cards, oils and greases, and oil and gold production. In the case of oil production, the several royalties and taxes should be consolidated into a single tax.

In addition to this type of rationalization

of the national government's indirect taxes, there is a need for a broad-based indirect tax. There are two ways to justify this tax, both very persuasive. One is the need for additional government revenues in an amount that can be obtained only from a broad-based tax. Second, is that the tax would be consistent with a desirable reorientation of Colombia's development policy. It has been demonstrated in Chapter 9 on Tariffs and Development that Colombia would be better advised to emphasize the development of exports rather than to concentrate on a policy of import substitution. The introduction of a system of internal excises would facilitate this shift in emphasis by increasing the prices of internally manufactured luxury and semi-luxury goods, which would, in turn, reduce their demand and channel investment funds to the production of more essential goods or exports.

During 1963 the government gave serious consideration to the adoption of excise taxes on both domestically produced and imported articles with rates ranging from 3 to 10 per cent. Exempted from the tax would be basic foods, school textbooks, drugs, and exports. Even with these exemptions, however, the tax would be undesirably regressive. It is estimated by the government that this tax would produce about $150 million in revenue annually.

To be preferred is a system of selective excises with emphasis on luxury and semi-luxury goods and with rates varying from 5 to 20 per cent. Table 10–9 has been developed for purposes of suggesting rates and bases for such a tax. A system of selected excises like the one proposed would be much less regressive than the one considered by the government and, at the same time, would result in about $650 million in revenue annually instead of only $150 million.

One further comment should be made with respect to national taxes, although it is entirely unrelated to the previous discussion. This is the issue of social security taxes. Since these are somewhat atypical, and since they are not dealt with in any other section

TABLE 10–9
Proposed System of Selective National Excises

Item	Base	Rate	Approximate Yield (Millions)
Tires and tubes	$145 million	10 per cent	$ 14.5
Gasoline	400 million gallons	50 centavos per gallon	200.0
Diesel oil	150 million gallons	50 centavos per gallon	75.0
Chocolate confections	$100 million	20 per cent	20.0
Soft drinks	$160 million	10 per cent	16.0
Beer	$550 million	20 per cent	110.0
Wines	$15 million	20 per cent	3.0
Alcoholic liquors	$265 million	20 per cent	52.0
Cigarettes	$360 million	20 per cent	72.0
Cigars	$30 million	20 per cent	6.0
Clothing and shoes	$700 million	5 per cent	35.0
Furniture and wood-manufacturing	$80 million	10 per cent	8.0
Rubber shoes	$46 million	5 per cent	2.3
Cosmetics	$40 million	20 per cent	8.0
Electrical consumer products	$200 million	10 per cent	20.0
Jewelry and items of precious metals	$20 million	20 per cent	4.0
Records	$25 million	20 per cent	5.0
		TOTAL	$650.8

of this survey, it is convenient to mention them here. A basic social security system was introduced in Colombia in 1946, with one-half the costs being met by a tax on the employer and the other one-half by equal contributions from the employee and the government. The system is administered by the Colombian Social Security Institute. In addition, there are special social security systems for the armed services, the police force, and the railway workers.

At the present time, the basic social security system covers only maternity benefits and insurance for illness or disability not arising from employment, and it is restricted to certain municipalities in the departments of Cundinamarca, Quindio, Santa Marta, Antioquia, and Valle del Cauca. In the first two of these areas the employee and the national government each pay a tax of 2 per cent of the average wage base, and the employer pays 4 per cent. In the other three areas, the tax is on a sliding scale from approximately 2 per cent in the lowest wage bracket to over 4.5 per cent in the highest for the employer's share, with the government and the employee each paying one-half these rates.

The development of social security systems in Latin America often has been condemned as an undesirable luxury, that creates excessive costs on business and allocates resources from investment to consumption expenditures. These criticisms are certainly not applicable to Colombia, since the social security system has had such a limited development. In fact, if any criticism should be levied in Colombia, it is that an insufficient number of employees is covered. An extension of social security would eliminate the need for the disabled to throw themselves on the mercy of private charity. Moreover, a well-developed social security system would provide a fund of savings that could be used by the government for development purposes.

Departmental Indirect Taxes

Under the reorganization of indirect taxes proposed above, the departments would have the exclusive right to tax tobacco and liquor products, with the exception that these products would also be taxed under the system of selective excises proposed for the national government. All of these taxes should be *ad valorem* rather than specific. The second type of tax that should be used exclusively by the departments is the tax on gambling activities, including that on lotteries. As explained previously, the tax on the slaughtering of animals should be eliminated, since meat is a basic consumption item.

For the extension of departmental indirect taxes, there are two bases of taxation that should be exploited further. One is the tax on gasoline. The present tax is ridiculously low. In Bogotá, the price of a gallon of regular gasoline is $1.248, only $.04 of which represents a tax. This means that the tax is only 3.2 per cent of the retail price, while it could very well be as much as 50 per cent. At the present time, the price of a gallon of gasoline is only the equivalent of U.S. 12.48 cents. If a tax of 50 per cent were levied, the retail price would still be only $1.872 or U.S. 18.72 cents per gallon.

Given the tremendous need for highways, roads, and streets in Colombia, there should be no question that a significantly higher tax on gasoline is warranted. Also, an exception to the general case against the earmarking of revenues is justified with respect to this tax. This is a levy with a unique relationship in terms of payment and benefits received, and, therefore, the revenues should be used for highway purposes.

The second tax that could be exploited more effectively at the departmental level is the tax on vehicle registrations. This levy has not been described previously in this chapter because it is considered to be a direct tax for governmental accounting purposes. Since its inception in 1913, the tax has been a source of revenue for the municipalities, and it is administered entirely by them. Although information is not available on the rate structure of the tax throughout the country, there apparently is considerable variation, for it is a practice of some vehicle owners to "shop around" for a municipality with low rates.[1] In Bogotá, where about one-half of the private vehicles of Colombia are registered, private passenger vehicles are taxed on a basis of their weight as follows:

Weight in Kilograms	Tax per Month
Up to 800	$10.00
801 to 1,000	15.00
1,001 to 1,400	20.00
1,401 to 1,700	25.00
Over 1,700	40.00

According to this schedule, an average size United States passenger vehicle would bear an annual tax of $240 to $300 or U.S. $24 to $30. There are several reasons for objecting to this relatively low tax burden. The first is that the ownership of private vehicles in Colombia is confined to those who are relatively wealthy. Therefore, a higher tax burden would be progressive in its incidence. Second, through the government's import restrictions, vehicles actually appreciate in value rather than depreciate. As a result, a higher tax is justified to remove part of the windfall gains resulting from restrictions of supply. Third, by such a low tax, the highway user is not paying for the facilities necessary for vehicles in the form of highways, roads, and streets.

In giving consideration to higher taxes on vehicle registrations, the government should weigh the advantage of basing the tax on the value of the vehicle rather than its weight, for value is a base that is more consistent with making the tax more progressive and for recouping windfall gains. Assuming that the average market price of a vehicle is $30,000 in Colombia, the rate of the tax should be about 3 per cent of value, or about $900 per annum for the average vehicle. This rate should be standardized throughout Colombia. Since there are about 140,000 private vehicles in the country, at an average value of $30,000 per vehicle, the total tax base would be $4.2 billion. Thus, with a 3 per cent tax, the yield would be approximately $126 million. This amount may be compared to actual collections from vehicle registrations in 1961 of only $15.4 million.

---

[1] It is known, for example, that the rates are only about one-third as high in the departments of Antioquia, Bolívar, and Boyacá as they are in Bogotá.

It would appear, too, that the vehicle registration tax is a more appropriate levy for the departments than for the municipalities. As a departmental tax, there is likely to be more efficiency in its administration, which is an important consideration if a shift is made to vehicle value as a tax base. Also, in the process of evolving a progressive and efficient system of highway-user taxes in Colombia, which has barely been started, it would be advantageous to associate both of the principal highway-user taxes on gasoline and vehicles at the same level of government.

Municipal Indirect Taxes

Under the reorganization of indirect taxes proposed, the municipal governments would receive the exclusive right to tax public shows and any tax levied on entertainment. As explained previously, the taxes on weights and measures and on slaughtering should be eliminated, as they are essentially regressive and arbitrary levies. Municipalities would also lose the vehicle registration tax. On balance, this would reduce municipal revenues from indirect taxes, but the municipalities have two very productive bases of taxation in the real property tax and the tax on industry and commerce. The real property tax will become more productive of revenue as progress is made with the re-assessment project. With respect to the tax on industry and commerce, the base should be gross sales instead of a combination of sales, rent, and horsepower, with a uniform rate applicable to both industry and commerce. This tax also could be made more productive of revenue merely by raising the rate.

SUMMARY OF RECOMMENDATIONS

National Indirect Taxes

1) All stamp taxes and stamped paper should be eliminated for those activities that are merely taxed for revenue purposes, and the other charges should be equated to the cost of the service.

2) National government indirect taxes on distilled liquor, tobacco products, and gambling activities should be transferred to the departments, while taxes on public shows should be given to the municipalities.

3) The earmarking of revenues should be eliminated.

4) All specific excises should be converted to an *ad valorem* basis.

5) All royalties and production taxes on the petroleum industry should be consolidated into a single tax.

6) A broad system of excises on semi-luxury and luxury goods should be adopted with rates varying from 5 to 20 per cent.

7) The coverage of the social security system should be extended.

Departmental Indirect Taxes

1) Taxes on liquor and tobacco products should be *ad valorem* instead of specific.

2) The tax on the slaughtering of animals should be eliminated.

3) The tax on gasoline should be raised by $.50 per gallon and the revenues should be earmarked for highway purposes.

4) The tax on vehicle registrations should be based on the value of the vehicles at a rate of approximately 3 per cent, and the tax should be transferred to the departments. The tax rate should be uniform throughout Colombia.

Municipal Indirect Taxes

1) The taxes on weights and measures and on the slaughtering of small animals should be eliminated.

2) For the tax on industry and commerce, the base should be gross sales instead of a combination of sales, rent, and horsepower, and the same rate should be applicable to both industry and commerce.

CHAPTER 11

The Incidence of the Tax System

THE DISTRIBUTION OF INCOME

As a FIRST STEP in the calculation of the tax burden, it is necessary to determine the distribution of income. In 1962 approximately 1.16 million individual income tax returns were filed out of a total labor force of 5.02 million. In other words, 23.6 per cent of the labor force had incomes of at least $2,500, the level for reporting purposes. Of those who filed returns, only 486,113 paid income taxes. Deductions and exemptions resulted in no taxable income for the remainder. Thus, only 9.7 per cent of the labor force paid income taxes.

A sample of 1962 income tax returns presently being tabulated will reveal detailed information about taxpayers.[1] Until these data are available, one is forced to rely on data collected in 1958, which show the number of taxpayers by brackets of net taxable income.[2] This 1958 distribution is shown in Table 11-1, together with an estimated distribution based on these data for 1962.

As a result of the devaluation in 1957 and increases in the domestic price level, wages, and salaries, a substantial increase in the number of taxpayers has taken place. There were only 202,919 actual taxpayers in 1958, but by 1962 the number had increased to 486,113, or by 140 per cent. Except for the

[1] The sample was developed as part of this fiscal survey, but the results were not available for analysis by the time that the survey was completed.
[2] Louis Shere, "A Tax Program for Colombia," Pan American Union, 1960, p. 103. (Mimeographed.)

TABLE 11-1

Individual Income Taxpayers by Income Classes, Actual 1958 and Estimated 1962

Brackets of Net Taxable Income	Actual Number of Tax-payers, 1958	Percent-age of Total, 1958	Estimated Number of Tax-payers, 1962
$ 0–$ 2,000	73,604	36.40	176,751
2,000– 3,000	24,088	11.91	57,896
3,000– 4,000	16,751	8.28	40,250
4,000– 5,000	12,266	6.06	29,458
5,000– 6,000	10,174	5.03	24,451
6,000– 7,000	8,206	4.06	19,736
7,000– 8,000	6,850	3.39	16,479
8,000– 9,000	5,542	2.74	13,319
9,000– 10,000	4,865	2.40	11,667
10,000– 12,000	7,769	3.84	18,667
12,000– 14,000	5,557	2.75	13,368
14,000– 16,000	4,356	2.15	10,451
16,000– 18,000	3,417	1.69	8,215
18,000– 20,000	2,560	1.26	6,125
20,000– 30,000	7,305	3.61	17,549
30,000– 40,000	3,327	1.64	7,972
40,000– 50,000	1,713	0.85	4,132
50,000– 100,000	2,660	1.32	6,417
100,000– 200,000	870	0.43	2,090
200,000– 400,000	261	0.13	632
400,000– 600,000	45	0.02	351[b]
600,000– 800,000	15	0.01	81[b]
800,000–1,000,000	8	—	29[b]
1,000,000–2,000,000	10	—	23[b]
2,000,000–3,000,000	0	—	4[b]
	202,219[a]	99.97	486,113

[a] The column adds to 202,219, but the table in the original report shows a total of 202,919.
[b] Actual data from 1962 income tax returns and not estimates.
Source: For 1958 data, Louis Shere, "A Tax Program for Colombia," p. 103.

five brackets with the highest taxable income, the 1962 estimated distribution in Table 11-1 was based on the percentage that each bracket bore to the total number

TABLE 11-2
Employment and Remuneration by Sectors of the Economy, 1961

	Total Remuneration[a] (Millions)	Labor Force (Thousands)	Number Employed[a] (Thousands)	Average Wage	Self-Employed[b] (Thousands)
Primary	$ 3,345.0	2,334[b]	$1,710	$1,956[c]	556
Agriculture	3,076.1	2,253[a]			543
Extractive	268.9	50[a]			
Secondary	$ 2,585.1	984[b]			269
Manufacturing	1,683.5	749[a]	276	$6,100[c]	246
Construction	822.4	211[a]			
Utilities	79.2	20[a]			
Tertiary	$ 4,833.9	1,700[b]			306
Commerce and finance	1,124.6	341[a]			171
Transport and communications	886.9	216[a]			32
Services and government	2,822.4	1,245[a]	913	$3,091[c]	103
	$10,764.0	5,018[b]			1,131
		(5,059.6)[a]			

Totals do not sum accurately due to different sources for the data.
[a] National income accounts, Central Bank.
[b] Department of Planning.
[c] Total remuneration divided by employment.

of taxpayers in 1958. For the five brackets with the highest taxable income, an actual count was made to determine the number of taxpayers in 1962.

Since each taxpayer had a personal exemption of $2,500 for himself, $2,500 for his spouse, and $1,000 for each dependent, plus the deductions and exemptions detailed previously in the chapters on income taxation, it may be assumed (in the absence of the data now being collected by the above-mentioned sample) that deductions and exemptions averaged $10,000. On the basis of this assumption, the incomes of the taxpayers shown in Table 11-1 were all above $10,000 by the amounts of taxable income indicated in the table.

Data on the distribution of income for the remaining 90 per cent of the labor force is practically nonexistent. Certain clues, however, enable one to develop a rough estimate of the income distribution. In Table 11-2 are shown wages and salaries for each of the three sectors of the economy, the total labor force, and the average remuneration

of employees in the three sectors. Table 11-2 shows an average annual wage of $1,956 in agriculture, $6,100 in manufacturing, and $3,091 in services and government in 1961. By a weighted average of the wage of $6,100 in manufacturing and the wage of $3,091 in services and government, it may be determined that the average annual earnings in the secondary and tertiary sectors was $3,789.

To obtain an idea of the nature of the income distribution about this average, it was necessary to rely on the distribution of family incomes of urban employees determined in 1953 for the purpose of preparing cost-of-living indices. This 1953 income distribution is shown in Table 11-3. Two open-ended categories are shown in this table, one for wages of over $1,000 per month and the other for salaries of over $2,000.

The distribution pattern shown in Table 11-3 was then applied to the annual average earnings previously determined for the secondary and tertiary sectors of $3,789 in 1961. This made it possible to estimate the income distribution of urban salaried and

TABLE 11-3

Income Distribution of Families of Urban
Salaried and Non-Salaried Employees, 1953

Monthly Income	Number of Employees in the Sample	Percentage of Total	Cumulative Percentage	Total Estimated Income
$ 0-$ 99	13	0.88	0.88	$ 650
100- 199	213	14.46	15.34	31,950
200- 299	318	21.59	36.93	79,500
300- 399	286	19.42	56.35	100,100
400- 499	202	13.71	70.06	90,900
500- 599	116	7.88	77.94	63,800
600- 699	81	5.50	83.44	52,650
700- 799	62	4.21	87.65	46,500
800- 899	51	3.46	91.11	43,350
900- 999	30	2.04	93.15	28,500
Over 1,000	11	0.75	93.90	13,200 [a]
1,000-1,099	19	1.29	95.19	19,950
1,100-1,199	8	0.54	95.73	9,200
1,200-1,299	12	0.81	96.54	15,000
1,300-1,399	13	0.88	97,42	17,550
1,400-1,499	9	0.61	98.03	13,050
1,500-1,599	7	0.48	98.51	10,850
1,600-1,699	3	0.20	98.71	4,950
1,700-1,799	1	0.07	98.78	1,750
1,800-1,899	5	0.34	99.12	9,250
1,900-1,999	2	0.14	99.26	3,900
Over 2,000	11	0.75	100.00	29,700 [a]
	1,473	100.00		$686,250

[a] These two open-end categories were arbitrarily assigned estimated incomes for the purpose of computing the arithmetic mean income of $465.9 ($686,250 divided by 1,473) used for extending the distribution of this table to Table 11-4.
Source: Economía y Estadística, No. 85, 1958.

TABLE 11-4

Estimated Income Distribution of Urban Salaried
and Non-Salaried Employees, 1961

Income Class	Estimated Number of Employees (Thousands)	Percentage of Total [a]
$ 0-$ 813	18.6	0.88
814- 1,627	305.0	14.46
1,628- 2,440	455.3	21.59
2,441- 3,253	409.6	19.42
3,254- 4,066	289.1	13.71
4,067- 4,880	166.2	7.88
4,881- 5,693	116.0	5.50
5,694- 6,506	88.0	4.21
6,507- 7,319	73.0	3.46
7,320- 8,133	43.0	2.04
Over 8,133	15.8	0.75
8,134- 8,946	27.2	1.29
8,947- 9,759	11.4	0.54
9,760-10,572	17.1	0.81
10,573-11,386	18.6	0.88
11,387-12,199	12.9	0.61
12,200-13,012	10.1	0.48
13,013-13,825	4.2	0.20
13,826-14,639	1.5	0.07
14,640-15,452	7.2	0.34
15,453-16,265	3.0	0.14
Over 16,265	15.8	0.75
	2,109.0 [b]	100.00

[a] From Table 11-3.
[b] Total does not add because of rounding.
Source: Table 11-2, utilizing the mean wage in manufacturing and services and government of $3,789 and the total labor force in the secondary and tertiary sectors of 2,109,000 (2,684,000 less the self-employed of 575,000).

non-salaried employees in 1961 shown in Table 11-4. The determination of income classes in Table 11-4 was obtained by dividing the known arithmetic mean of 1961 earnings of $3,789 by the arithmetic mean of the distribution in Table 11-3 of $465.9 and then multiplying by the class boundaries of Table 11-3.

Table 11-5 shows the distribution of daily wages in agriculture during the third quarter of 1962. The arithmetic mean wage of $6.857 per day was estimated by multiplying the number in each category by the amount of earnings that appeared to be close to the average for each class. The open-ended group was not included in the calculation.

The distribution pattern shown in Table 11-5 was then applied to the annual average

TABLE 11-5

Distribution of Daily Wages (without Food)
in Agriculture, Third Quarter, 1962

Daily Wage	Number of Employees in the Sample	Percentage of Total	Estimated Total Income
$ 0-$ 4.00	55	4.7	$ 192.50 (55 × 3.50)
4.01- 5.00	134	11.5	636.50 (134 × 4.75)
5.01- 6.00	183	15.7	1,052.25 (183 × 5.75)
6.01- 7.00	287	24.6	1,937.25 (287 × 6.75)
7.01- 8.00	238	20.4	1,844.50 (238 × 7.75)
8.01- 9.00	64	5.5	560.00 (64 × 8.75)
9.01- 10.00	129	11.0	1,257.75 (129 × 9.75)
Over $10.00	77	6.6	
	1,167	100.0	$7,480.75 [a]

[a] The arithmetic mean wage of $6.857 was determined by dividing $7,480.75 by 1,091 (excluding 77 in the open-ended group earning over $10.00 per day).
Source: Boletín Mensual de Estadística, January, 1963.

earnings of agricultural workers determined in Table 11–2 of $1,956 per annum. Self-employed farmers were included in the distribution, because most of them would not be filing income tax returns and would have incomes comparable to agricultural workers. This procedure made it possible to estimate the income distribution of the agricultural labor force shown in Table 11–6. The de-

TABLE 11–6
Estimated Distribution of Income for
Agricultural Workers and Farmers, 1961

Income Class	Percentage of Total	Estimated Number of Workers and Farmers (Thousands)
$ 0–$1,141	4.7	106
1,142– 1,426	11.5	259
1,427– 1,712	15.7	354
1,713– 1,997	24.6	554
1,998– 2,282	20.4	460
2,283– 2,567	5.5	124
2,568– 2,852	11.0	248
Over 2,852	6.6	150
TOTALS	100.0	2,255

Source: Tables 11–2 and 11–5.

termination of income classes shown in Table 11–6, once again, was obtained by dividing the known arithmetic mean daily wage of agricultural workers determined in Table 11–5 into the average annual wage determined in Table 11–2 and by multiplying by the class boundaries of Table 11–5.

The data from Tables 11–1, 11–4, and 11–6 were then combined in Table 11–7 to develop the income distribution of natural persons in the labor force for 1961. Adjustments were made for the unemployed and the self-employed. The unemployed were assumed to be 10 per cent of the number employed, and adjustments were made accordingly in the income classes up to $5,000. The self-employed, excluding farmers and those already accounted for in Table 11–2, were calculated by taking the difference between the total labor force and the total already accounted for in the second column of Table 11–7.

According to the national income accounts, wages and salaries in 1961 amounted to $10.76 billion, and the proprietory income of natural persons amounted to $12.76 billion, for a total of $23.52 billion. (See Table 11–8.) The total in Table 11–7 for these two types of income is $21.64 billion. Among the factors that may account for this difference, two are apparent: (1) The estimates in Table 11–7 may be low due to errors in estimating. (2) They may be low because of tax evasion, which is considered to be widespread.[3] On the basis of the assumptions made for calculating the income of the lower income groups, the likelihood is that their incomes are overstated. On the other hand, evasion would tend to understate the income of the wealthier individuals, the upper 10 per cent, who are income taxpayers. Therefore, if any bias exists in Table 11–7, it is probably in the direction of understating the income of the wealthy.

Table 11–7 provides very important information on the distribution of income for public policy purposes. At the lower end of the income scale, the table shows that 11.06 per cent of the persons in the labor force in 1961, earning less than $1,000, received only 1.92 per cent of the national income. Going up the scale, the table shows that 64.54 per cent of the labor force received only 26.16 per cent of the income. On the other hand, starting from the top of the scale, .91 per cent of the labor force received 12.44 per cent of the income, and 2.15 per cent received 18.95 per cent. With this type of income distribution, one need hardly belabor the point that everything possible should be done through the tax system to promote a more equitable distribution of income.

THE METHOD OF APPORTIONING TAXES

The basis of apportioning the various taxes to the income groups was as follows:
1) Income taxes on natural persons were allocated entirely to the upper quartile of

[3] For more evidence, see the chapters on income taxation.

TABLE 11–7

Income Distribution of Natural Persons in the Labor Force, 1961

Income Class	Number of Persons (Thousands)	Adjust-ments[a] (Thousands)	Corrected Number of Persons	Percent-age of Total	Cumula-tive Percent-age	Estimated Income (Millions)	Percent-age of Total Income	Cumula-tive Percent-age
$ 0–$ 1,000	181.2	+374	555.2	11.06	11.06	$ 416.4	1.92	1.92
1,000– 2,000	1,626.5	−163	1,463.5	29.16	40.22	2,195.2	10.14	12.06
2,000– 3,000	1,356.4	−136	1,220.4	24.32	64.54	3,051.0	14.10	26.16
3,000– 4,000	542.7	− 54	488.7	9.74	74.28	1,710.4	7.90	34.06
4,000– 5,000	207.0	− 21	186.0	3.71	77.99	837.0	3.87	37.93
5,000– 6,000	132.2	+ 26	158.2	3.15	81.14	870.1	4.02	41.95
6,000– 7,000	99.0	+ 38	137.0	2.73	83.87	890.5	4.11	46.06
7,000– 8,000	64.7	+ 51	115.7	2.31	86.18	867.8	4.01	50.07
8,000– 9,000	42.9	+ 64	106.9	2.13	88.31	908.6	4.20	54.27
9,000– 10,000	23.6	+ 77	100.6	2.00	90.31	955.7	4.42	58.69
10,000– 12,000	176.8		176.8	3.52	93.83	1,944.8	8.99	67.68
12,000– 13,000	57.9		57.9	1.15	94.98	723.8	3.34	71.02
13,000– 14,000	40.2		40.2	0.80	95.78	502.5	2.32	73.34
14,000– 15,000	29.5		29.5	0.59	96.37	427.8	1.98	75.32
15,000– 16,000	24.5		24.5	0.49	96.86	379.8	1.76	77.08
16,000– 17,000	19.7		19.7	0.39	97.25	325.0	1.50	78.58
17,000– 18,000	16.5		16.5	0.33	97.58	288.8	1.33	79.91
18,000– 19,000	13.3		13.3	0.27	97.85	246.0	1.14	81.05
19,000– 20,000	11.7		11.7	0.23	98.08	228.2	1.05	82.10
20,000– 22,000	18.7		18.7	0.37˜	98.45	392.7	1.81	83.91
22,000– 24,000	13.4		13.4	0.27	98.72	308.2	1.42	85.33
24,000– 26,000	10.5		10.5	0.21	98.93	262.5	1.21	86.54
26,000– 28,000	8.2		8.2	0.16	99.09	221.4	1.02	87.56
28,000– 30,000	6.1		6.1	0.12˙	99.21	176.9	0.82	88.38
30,000– 40,000	17.5		17.5	0.35	99.56	612.5	2.83	91.21
40,000– 50,000	8.0		8.0	0.16	99.72	360.0	1.66	92.87
50,000– 60,000	4.1		4.1	0.08⁻	99.80	225.5	1.04	93.91
60,000–110,000	6.4		6.4	0.13 −	99.93	544.0	2.51	96.42
110,000–210,000	2.1		2.1	0.04	99.97	325.5	1.50	97.92
210,000–410,000	.6		.6	0.01	99.98	186.0	0.86	98.78
410,000–610,000	.4		.4	0.01	99.99	—	—	
610,000–810,000	.1		.1	—	—	256.0	1.18	99.96
TOTALS	4,762.4		5,018.4	100.00[b]		$21,640.6		

a Adjustments were made for: (1) unemployment of 10 per cent of total employees of 3,887,000 (total labor of 5,018,000 minus self-employed of 1,131,000) subtracted from the first five categories; and (2) self-employed of 255,400 with incomes of less than $10,000.

b Does not total due to rounding.

TABLE 11–8

Distribution of the National Income, 1961

(Millions)

Total national income	$25,101.9
Wages and salaries	10,764.0
Other income	14,337.9
Families and natural persons	12,763.1
Savings of legal entities	754.6
Taxes on legal entities	569.2
Government proprietary income	331.8
Less interest on the public debt	−80.8

Source: Central Bank.

taxpayers, since only about 10 per cent of the labor force pays income taxes. Total income tax receipts were divided between natural persons and legal entities on the basis of 1962 assessments, which in the most part means 1961 incomes.

2) For income taxes on legal entities, 50 per cent was assumed not to be shifted and was allocated to the upper quartile, while the remaining 50 per cent was considered to be shifted and allocated to the various quartiles, as noted below, for indirect taxes. Some of the large corporations are foreign-

owned, but since it was not possible to determine their number, the income tax burden
on the upper quartile is exaggerated somewhat by these assumptions.

3) Indirect taxes, except for those on tobacco, alcoholic beverages, gasoline, and vehicle registrations, were considered to be
shifted to consumers and were allocated to
the various quartiles on the basis of estimated
total consumption expenditures less food expenditures. The latter were not considered
to be taxed by the indirect tax system. Apart
from the exceptions noted, the allocation of
indirect taxes was 5 per cent to the first
quartile, 14 per cent to the second, 23 per
cent to the third, and 58 per cent to the
fourth.

4) For taxes on gasoline and vehicle registrations, one-third was assumed not to be
shifted, falling on the owners of private
vehicles. These were assigned to the first
quartile. The remaining two-thirds of the
taxes were considered to be shifted and were
assigned on the basis of estimated total
consumption expenditures. This resulted in
an allocation of 7.12 per cent to the first
quartile, 17.63 per cent to the second, 22.56
per cent to the third, and 52.69 per cent to
the fourth.

5) Taxes on tobacco and liquor products
were assumed to be shifted and to be regressive. The allocation was 15 per cent to
the first quartile, 20 per cent to the second,
30 per cent to the third, and 35 per cent
to the fourth.

6) One-fourth of real property taxes was
considered to be not shifted and to be borne
by the upper quartile. One-half of the remainder was assumed to fall on commercial
and industrial properties and was assigned in
the same way as indirect taxes, while the
other one-half was allocated in proportion
to income, since the 1953 study of expenditures by urban families showed that expenditures on housing were nearly proportional
to income.

7) Not allocated were fees, fines, special
assessments, proprietory income of govern-

ment enterprises, and other miscellaneous
government receipts.

THE TAX BURDENS OF THE VARIOUS INCOME GROUPS

The result of these allocations to quartiles
of the population is shown in Table 11–9.
This table indicates that $119.1 million in
taxes were borne by the first quartile, $257.3
million by the second, $409.2 million by the
third, and $1,785.1 million by the fourth.

To relate these tax burdens to the income
of the population by quartiles, the estimates
of income accruing to each quartile of the
population were derived from Table 11–7.
Income classes falling into more than one
quartile were allocated on the basis of the
percentage of the class in each quartile. The
resulting apportionment of income was
$1,089.4 million in the first quartile, $2,749.1
million in the second, $3,696.9 million in
the third, and $14,105.2 million in the fourth.
Thus, the lower quartile received 5 per cent
of the income, and the upper quartile received 65 per cent.

Table 11–10 shows the results of relating
the tax burdens and incomes by quartiles.
This table indicates that the percentage of
taxes to income for the lowest quartile is
10.93 per cent; for the second, 9.36 per cent;
for the third, 11.06 per cent; and for the
fourth, 12.66 per cent. Thus, despite biases
that appear to understate the income of the
fourth quartile, there is only a slight degree
of progression between the first and fourth
quartiles and some regressivity between the
first and second quartiles.

Table 11–10 also shows that the burden
of taxes levied by the national government is
progressive, rising from 4.94 per cent for
the first quartile to 10.24 per cent for the
fourth quartile. The departmental taxes, however, are highly regressive, falling from 5.02
per cent for the first quartile to 1.26 per
cent for the fourth quartile. Municipal taxes,
due to the effect of the real property tax,
were somewhat progressive, rising from .97
per cent for the first quartile to 1.16 per

TABLE 11–9

Calculation of the Burden of Taxation, 1961

(Millions of Pesos)

	Total Taxes	First Quartile	Second Quartile	Third Quartile	Fourth Quartile
National Government					
Income tax, natural persons[a]	$ 538.25	$ 0	$ 0	$ 0	$ 538.25
Income tax, legal entities	451.72	11.29	31.62	51.95	356.86
Indirect taxes	850.14	42.51	119.02	195.53	493.08
Gift and inheritance taxes	55.71	0	0	0	55.71
Totals	1,895.82	53.80	150.64	247.48	1,443.90
Departments					
Indirect	48.52	2.43	6.79	11.16	28.14
Property	.79	.03	.08	.14	.54
Tobacco	180.98	27.15	36.20	54.29	63.34
Beer	158.88	23.83	31.78	47.66	55.61
Foreign liquors	6.47	0	0	0	6.47
Domestic wines	5.26	0	0	0	5.26
Gasoline	26.84	1.27	3.16	4.04	18.37
Totals	427.74	54.71	78.01	117.29	177.73
Municipalities					
Real property	140.29	5.28	14.05	21.09	99.87
Automobiles, trucks, buses	15.49	.74	1.82	2.33	10.60
Other indirect	91.37	4.57	12.79	21.02	52.99
Totals	247.15	10.59	28.66	44.44	163.46
TOTAL TAXES ALLOCATED	$2,570.71	$119.10	$257.31	$409.21	$1,785.09

[a] Income taxes apportioned between natural persons and legal entities on the basis of 1962 assessments.

Source: Table 11–7.

TABLE 11–10

Percentage Distribution of the Tax Burden among Income Groups, 1961

Level of Government	First Quartile (Per Cent)	Second Quartile (Per Cent)	Third Quartile (Per Cent)	Fourth Quartile (Per Cent)
National government	4.94	5.48	6.69	10.24
Departments	5.02	2.84	3.17	1.26
Municipalities	0.97	1.04	1.20	1.16
All governments	10.93	9.36	11.07[a]	12.66

[a] Total does not equal due to rounding.
Source: Tables 11–7 and 11–9.

cent for the fourth quartile, although they were higher for the third quartile with 1.20 per cent.

In addition to allocating part of the income tax paid by foreign-owned corporations to the upper quartile, three other biases should

be mentioned. The first is that these calculations exclude most capital gains, especially those made in real estate, the sale of securities, and of businesses, since these are not taxed effectively under the income tax. The second is that much of the foreign income of Colombians is probably untaxed. Third, there are the retained earnings of corporations. All of the foregoing factors, together with evasion on the part of professionals and businessmen, would tend to exaggerate the burden of taxation on the upper income groups.

It is possible that better income and expenditure data would result in a somewhat different distribution of the tax burden. And, of course, it is evident that the bulk of taxes is borne by the upper quartile, $1,785 million out of a total tax burden of $2,571 million, or 69.4 per cent. Nevertheless, there are other considerations that should dispel any complacency. There are taxes and restrictions that do not yield revenue but nevertheless impose a serious burden in the form of higher prices for consumer goods. These are the protective tariffs. Designed to promote economic development, they place a considerable part of the burden of development on consumers. They affect the prices of everything from raw materials to electrical products and create opportunities for producers to realize monopolistic profits.[4] If the burden of this policy could be measured and included in the calculation of the incidence of the tax system, even less progressivity in the tax system would be apparent.

The distribution of income before taxes is a result of the political and economic organization of societies. In an underdeveloped economy, a disproportionate share of income is received by a small minority of the population. In the United States and other industrial countries, wages and salaries as a share of the national income are as much as 60 to 70 per cent; but in Colombia, wages and salaries are only about 43 per cent of the

[4] See Chapter 9 on Tariffs and Development.

national income. Among the characteristics of the economy that result in this relatively low percentage, are extensive land-holdings, monopoly profits, and insufficient employment opportunities, all of which tend to restrict artifically the demand for labor and, therefore, its wage.

Finally, the burden of taxes on the upper quartile cannot be considered heavy in absolute terms, regardless of its relationship to the other quartiles. The indicated effective rate of 12.66 per cent must be considered low in relation to the massive development needs of the economy. These needs can only be provided, except with foreign assistance, by that part of the economy which produces an available surplus above subsistence levels. The only quartile that has this surplus (except for the corporate sector) is the upper quartile. As shown previously, the upper quartile enjoys 65 per cent of the total income of natural persons, while the lower quartile receives only 5 per cent. Under these circumstances, the upper quartile should provide a greater amount of the vast public investment requirements of Colombia, while the lower quartile, rather than contributing more, probably should have its tax burden reduced.

CHAPTER 12

The Autonomous Agencies

A study of the income and expenditures of the public sector in Colombia should not be limited to regular or formal governmental activities, for the result would be a telescoped view of the real magnitude of the public sector. The reason for this is the existence of a wide number of autonomous agencies, primarily at the national government level but also at the departmental and municipal levels. Because of limitations on research time and resources, this chapter will be concerned only with the autonomous agencies at the national government level.

THE NATURE OF AUTONOMOUS AGENCIES

An autonomous agency is an entity that is established by law or decree and has legal authority, administrative autonomy, and independent financial resources provided directly or indirectly by the government. It is usually created for the purpose of providing a particular public service. Law 151 of 1959 states that "decentralized public agencies, whatever their form of administration, are part of the public administration; their property and income, by reason of their origin, are a division of the public sector, and they are responsible for providing public services, cultural or social, and for the regulation and stimulation of the national economy within the limits set by the Constitution." Therefore, although autonomous agencies enjoy special administrative and fiscal privileges,

they are still viewed as part of the public sector.

Autonomous agencies are managed by a board of directors and a general manager named by the executive branch of the government. The national government usually maintains a representative on the board. In the management of their funds, autonomous agencies are subject to the control of the Comptroller General. These entities are not authorized to establish taxes, since Article 43 of the Constitution states that ". . . in time of peace only Congress, the Assemblies, and the Municipal Councils shall impose contributions." But this does not prevent these entities from receiving contributions or subsidies from the national government or from collecting revenues from taxes for their own use by authority of the national government.

Only recently, by Law 151 of 1959 and Decree 1,016 of 1960, have autonomous agencies been obliged to submit their budgets through the Ministry of Finance to the national Congress as annexations to the general budget. This requirement was established so that the national budget would reflect the government's entire scope of activities. Only in this way can the national government coordinate and integrate all the fiscal resources at its disposal within a general plan of economic development. The fact that this requirement is only of recent origin provides an insight into the relative autonomy that these entities have enjoyed. Some agencies have even alleged that they "do not constitute a division of the public sector" and have rejected the control of the Comptroller General.[1]

Quasi-public financial institutions are a unique case. According to Law 151 of 1959, these entities are not considered to be autonomous agencies and are therefore subject only to an administrative type of control, such as that exercised by the Superintendent of Banking. In this group are such important institutions as the *Banco Central Hipotecario,* the *Caja de Crédito Agrario, Industrial y Minero,* and the *Banco Popular.*

THE HISTORY OF AUTONOMOUS
AGENCIES

Governmental action through autonomous agencies in Colombia assumed importance about 1930 with the creation of various development and credit institutions. These were created for the purpose of promoting certain functions without the bureaucratic restrictions characteristic of the executive branch. The principal activities that the national government sought to promote in this way were agricultural and industrial development, housing, and public works. In the agricultural sector the main organization that was created was the Caja de Crédito Agrario, Industrial y Minero in 1931. Its principal functions were to grant short-, medium-, and long-term agricultural credit, to furnish technical advice, and to undertake agricultural improvements, particularly irrigation. The National Coffee Fund (Fondo Nacional del Café) was created in 1940 under the administration of the National Federation of Coffee Growers (Federación Nacional de Cafeteros) for the purpose of regulating the coffee market by the purchase, storage, and sale of coffee. In 1944 the Corporation for the Defense of Agricultural Products (Corporación de Defensa de Productos Agrícolas)[2] was established for the purpose of guaran-

teeing farmers minimum prices for certain products and regulating their supply through sales and imports according to conditions of the domestic market. The Cotton Institute (Instituto Algodonero), created in 1947 as a private concern, was converted to a semiofficial agency in 1948. Its principal function was to promote the cultivation of cotton.

With respect to industrial development, the first autonomous agency to be established was the Industrial Development Institute, created in 1940 by Decree 1,157. Its main function was to promote the establishment and expansion of firms dedicated to the development of basic industries. In the field of electric power, the most important agency to be created was the National Institute for the Exploitation of Water and Electrical Development (Instituto Nacional de Aprovechamiento de Aguas y Fomento Eléctrico), whose purpose was to study zones that could be irrigated, drained, and electrified and to undertake the necessary projects directly or in co-operation with other agencies.

The Banco Central Hipotecario was founded in 1932 to stimulate housing construction by the granting of medium- and long-term credit. For the same purpose, the Instituto de Crédito Territorial was created in 1939, but this institution directed its efforts to the construction and financing of middle and low income housing in urban and rural areas. In 1940 the Instituto de Fomento Municipal was created for the purpose of constructing school buildings, hospitals, aqueducts, sewer systems, and power plants. This agency gradually concentrated its resources on the construction and financing of aqueducts and sewer systems.

Finally, mention should be made of two credit and financial agencies. The first of these, the Colombian Savings Bank (Caja Colombiana de Ahorros), was established in 1932 for the purpose of mobilizing domestic savings and channeling them into productive forms of investment. By Decree 1,472 of May 27, 1955, the Colombian Savings Bank became part of the Caja de Crédito Agrario. In the last decade the re-

---

[1] Such is the case, for example, of *Acerías Paz del Río, S.A.* and of *Cementos Boyacá, S A.*

[2] The Corporation for the Defense of Agricultural Products was changed to the Instituto Nacional de Abastecimiento (INA) by Legislative Decree 0040 of February 21, 1958.

sources of the Colombian Savings Bank have been used primarily for housing construction.

The second agency, the Stabilization Fund (Fondo de Estabilización), was created as an independent institution by Decree 540 of May 16, 1939. Its principal original function was to regulate the money market, especially the market for government bonds. In 1950 the fund was permitted to invest the deposits which it received as a guarantee of imports. The fund then became a powerful financial organization, which had as its principal credit beneficiaries those public entities or companies in which the government was a stockholder.

In general terms it may be said that approximately ten important decentralized organizations were created between 1930 and 1945. After 1945, however, the number increased so greatly that by 1963 some fifty were in operation.[3]

THE IMPORTANCE OF AUTONOMOUS AGENCIES

The number of autonomous agencies does not indicate much about their importance. For the purpose of this study, an important comparison is the national government's budget with the sum of the individual budgets of the autonomous agencies. These totals for 1962, in current prices, were $3,526.2 million for the national government and $3,309.9 million for the autonomous agencies.[4]

But this comparison is deceptive, for it presupposes a complete separation of the two budgets. This is not the case, since part of the financial resources of the autonomous agencies is obtained from the national government. In other words, the above comparison is defective because it contains some

"double counting." For 1962, the contributions and aids given by the national government to the autonomous agencies totalled $603.2 million, an amount that should be subtracted from the total budget of the agencies. The result of this subtraction is $2,706.7 million. Using this total for comparison, the budget of the autonomous agencies was 81.79 per cent of the government's budget for 1962.[5] It is apparent, then, that from the point of view of budget resources, the autonomous agencies represent a dominant part of public activity. Furthermore, the importance of the agencies is increasing, for in 1961 the percentage of the total budgets of the agencies to the national government's budget was only 67.41 per cent.

Using as a criterion of importance the volume of budgeted investment, it may be determined that $474.3 million or 33.06 per cent of the total direct and indirect investment made by the national government in 1962 was invested by the autonomous agencies. As it may be seen in Table 12–1, the percentage of indirect investment made through autonomous agencies has increased since 1959. The total of indirect investment made through the departments and municipalities has also risen since 1957, although not consistently. From 1957 to 1962, this type of indirect investment reached its lowest point in 1959 and its highest in 1961. One might thus discern a trend on the part of the national government to channel an increasing proportion of its total investment as indirect investment and within this portion, in turn, to invest an increasing percentage through the autonomous agencies.

THE INCOME OF THE AUTONOMOUS AGENCIES

The income of the autonomous agencies may be divided according to origin into two principal categories, ordinary and capital in-

---

[3] It should be mentioned that not all of the agencies represent new activities of the national government, since in some cases they merely undertook activities previously administered by the national government. Such is the case, for example, of the National Railroads and some of the universities.

[4] Dirección Nacional de Presupuesto, *Análisis Económico del Presupuesto de Colombia, 1962.* See Table 1, Rentas e Ingresos Nacionales, and the table entitled "Presupuesto de Ingresos de las Empresas Decentralizadas, 1962."

[5] In a strict sense, it cannot be said that all transfers by the national government to decentralized agencies have been eliminated, for it is possible that the agencies received contributions from the departmental and municipal governments, which in turn received transfers from the national government.

TABLE 12-1

Distribution of Direct and Indirect Investment of the National Government, 1957 to 1962

(Millions of Pesos)

	1957		1959		1961		1962	
	Amount	Per Cent	Amount	Per Cent	Amount	Per Cent	Amount	Per Cent
Direct investment of the national government	$312.3	71.14	$485.7	73.17	$465.2	49.07	$772.9	53.88
Indirect investment of autonomous agencies	126.7	28.86	136.6	20.58	303.7	32.03	474.3	33.06
Indirect investment of departments, municipalities, and others	—	—	41.5	6.25	179.2	18.90	187.4	13.06
Total indirect investment	126.7	28.86	178.1	26.83	482.9	50.93	661.7	46.12
Total direct and indirect investment	439.0	100.00	663.8	100.00	948.1	100.00	1,434.6	100.00

Source: For the period 1957 to 1961, Dirección Nacional de Presupuesto, *Análisis Económico del Presupuesto de Colombia*, 1961, p. 34; and for 1962, Dirección Nacional de Presupuesto, *El Presupuesto de Colombia en Resumen, 1962*, pp. 44–45.

come. Out of total income in 1962 of $3,309.9 million, $2,522.0 million was obtained in the form of ordinary income, and $787.9 million in capital income. Ordinary income may be subdivided into five groups: funds from property, services, contributions, tax collections, and occasional income. Capital income may be subdivided into two groups: funds from previous fiscal years and credit resources.

Ordinary Income

1) *Property.* The most important source of income of the autonomous agencies in 1962 was income from the sale of goods, representing 34.84 per cent of total income.

2) *Services.* The income from the sale of services was 11.97 per cent of total income and was divided between sales to the public sector, 0.12 per cent, and sales to private entities, 11.85 per cent. Sales of goods and services, taken jointly, represented 46.81 per cent of total income.

3) *Contributions.* The total amount of contributions for 1962 was $724.1 million, of which the central government accounted for $558.4 million, or 77.1 per cent of the total. The remainder came from departmental and municipal governments and from other official and private entities. Contributions were of second importance as a source of income of the autonomous agencies.

4) *Tax Collections.* The amount received from tax collections was $101.1 million in 1962, representing 3.06 per cent of total income. Tax collections consist principally of earmarked revenues allocated to some autonomous agencies, such as the steel and electrical development tax, the housing tax, and the surcharge on the real property tax for the Corporación Autónoma Regional de la Sabana de Bogotá.

5) *Occasional Income.* These are funds granted principally by the national government for investment in specific projects. Their total for 1962 was $147.2 million.

Capital Income

Capital income represented 23.80 per cent of the total income of autonomous agencies in 1962. This source of income may be classified into domestic and foreign credit, with a total of $482.8 million, and funds from previous fiscal years, totalling $305.1 million.

In resumé, the principal source of finance for the autonomous agencies in 1962 was the sale of goods and services, representing 46.81 per cent of their total income. Contributions, tax collections, and occasional income accounted for 29.39 per cent. Lastly, capital income represented 23.89 per cent of total income. Table 12-2 provides more detailed information on the derivation of income of the autonomous agencies.

The Sectoral Derivation of Income

The autonomous agencies may be classified into groups to show the derivation of their income according to the sectors of the economy in which they operate. Table 12–3 shows the income received by sectors for the forty agencies that submitted their budgets to the Director of National Budgets in 1962. The first line of Table 12–3 shows that

TABLE 12–2
Income of the Autonomous Agencies, 1962

	Amount (Millions)	Per Cent
Ordinary income	$2,522.0	76.20
Goods	1,153.3	34.84
Sales	1,028.7	31.08
Rents	13.3	0.40
Amortizations	42.0	1.27
Interest	20.8	0.63
Other	48.4	1.46
Services	396.1	11.97
Public sector	3.9	0.12
Private sector	392.2	11.85
Contributions	724.1	21.88
Affiliated organizations	51.9	1.57
National government	558.4	16.87
Departmental governments	25.1	0.76
Municipal governments	30.0	0.91
Other state agencies	21.1	0.64
Private entities	37.5	1.13
Tax collections	101.1	3.06
National government	77.9	2.36
Others	23.2	0.70
Occasional income	147.2	4.45
Aids: 1. National	44.8	1.35
2. Other	1.3	0.05
Reimbursements	91.4	2.76
Other	9.7	0.29
Income from capital	787.9	23.80
Income from previous years	305.1	9.22
Loans	482.8	14.58
TOTAL INCOME	$3,309.9	100.00

Totals do not add because of rounding.
Source: Dirección Nacional de Presupuesto, *Análisis Económico de Colombia, 1962.*

those agencies operating in the agricultural sector received the major part of the total income of all autonomous agencies, or 30.56 per cent. In second place are those agencies classified in the power and fuel group, with 25.12 per cent, and in third place is the transportation and communications group with 19.77 per cent. The groups with minor revenue receipts are community services, with 5.45 per cent of total income; industry, with 1.15 per cent; public health, with 0.11 per cent; and revolving funds, with 0.45 per cent. Between the major and minor groups are housing agencies, with 8.90 per cent of the total income. In brief, the agencies in agriculture, power and fuel, transportation and communications, and housing received 84.44 per cent of the total income of all the autonomous agencies classified in Table 12–3.

Table 12–3 also shows the percentage distribution of ordinary income by sectors. The table shows that the agencies operating in the agricultural sector and the power and fuel sector received 88.22 per cent of the total income derived from the sale of goods by all autonomous agencies. On the other hand, the transportation and communications sector received 88.97 per cent of the total income derived from the sale of services. Of the total contributions received, agencies in agriculture received 34.42 per cent, and those in transportation and communication received 16.54 per cent. The agencies that received the largest percentages from tax collections were those in agriculture (42.59 per cent), power and fuel (30.83 per cent), and community services (21.05 per cent). As for the receipt of credit, the agencies in the housing sector received 32.41 per cent of the total obtained; those in transportation and communications, 25.54 per cent; and those in agriculture, 20.03 per cent.

Table 12–4 presents the sectoral derivation of income of the autonomous agencies in a different way, showing the percentages of different income received relative to the total income of each sector. Appearing below are brief comments on the derivation of income of the autonomous agencies in each sector:

TABLE 12–3

Sectoral Distribution of the Income of Autonomous Agencies, 1962

(Millions of Pesos)

	Total		Agriculture[a]		Power and Fuel[b]		Industry[c]		Transportation and Communications[d]		Education and Culture[e]	
	Amount	Per Cent	Amount	Per Cent	Amount	Per Cent	Amount	Per Cent	Amount	Per Cent	Amount	Per Cent
Total income	$3,309.9	100.00	$1,011.4	30.56	$831.5	25.12	$ 38.2	1.15	$654.4	19.77	$114.5	3.46
Ordinary income	2,522.0	100.00	777.2	30.82	754.3	29.91	25.2	1.00	531.1	21.05	106.1	4.21
Goods	1,153.4	100.00	466.8	40.47	550.7	47.75	8.5	0.74	51.2	4.44	1.8	0.16
Services	396.1	100.00	18.0	4.54	20.4	5.15	—	—	352.1	88.97	0.2	0.05
Contributions	724.1	100.00	249.2	34.42	60.9	8.41	11.0	1.52	119.8	16.54	95.7	13.22
Tax collections	101.2	100.00	43.1	42.59	31.2	30.83	5.6	5.53	—	—	—	—
Occasional income	147.2	100.00	0.1	0.07	91.1	61.89	0.1	0.07	7.7	5.23	8.4	5.71
Income from capital	787.9	100.00	234.2	29.72	77.2	9.80	13.0	1.65	123.3	15.64	8.4	1.07
Income from previous fiscal years	305.1	100.00	137.5	45.07	69.6	22.81	6.5	2.13	—	—	1.7	0.56
Loans	482.8	100.00	96.7	20.03	7.6	1.57	6.5	1.35	123.3	25.54	6.7	1.39

	Public Health and Welfare[f]		Public Health[g]		Housing[h]		Revolving Funds[i]		Community Services[j]	
	Amount	Per Cent	Amount	Per Cent	Amount	Per Cent	Amount	Per Cent	Amount	Per Cent
Total income	$163.7	4.94	$ 3.7	0.11	$297.6	8.99	$ 15.0	0.45	$179.8	5.45
Ordinary income	134.0	5.31	3.7	0.15	89.9	3.56	13.5	0.53	86.9	3.46
Goods	6.9	0.60	0.4	0.03	51.0	4.42	12.5	1.08	3.5	0.31
Services	1.9	0.48	0.3	0.07	2.5	0.63	0.4	0.11	—	—
Contributions	86.6	11.96	3.0	0.41	35.3	4.87	0.6	0.08	62.1	8.58
Tax collections	—	—	—	—	—	—	—	—	21.3	21.05
Occasional income	38.6	26.15	—	—	1.1	0.75	—	—	—	—
Income from capital	29.7	3.77	—	—	207.7	26.36	1.5	0.20	92.9	11.79
Income from previous fiscal years	0.6	0.20	—	—	51.2	16.79	—	—	37.9	12.42
Loans	29.1	6.03	—	—	156.5	32.41	1.5	0.31	55.0	11.37

a Instituto Nacional de Reforma Agraria, Instituto de Fomento Tabacalero, Instituto Nacional de Abastecimientos, Corporación Autónoma de la Sabana, Corporación Autónoma Regional del Cauca, Instituto Zooprofiláctico, Instituto Geográfico "Agustín Codazzi," Instituto de Fomento Algodonero.
b Instituto Electroaguas, Instituto de Asuntos Nucleares, Empresa Colombiana de Petróleos.
c Instituto de Fomento Industrial, Industria Militar, Fondo de Promoción Turística.
d Ferrocarriles Nacionales, Empresa Colombiana de Aeródromos, Empresa Puertos de Colombia, Empresa Nacional de Telecomunicaciones.
e Universidad Nacional, Universidad Pedagógica Femenina, Universidad Pedagógica de Tunja, Servicios Nacional de Aprendizaje, Fondo Universitario Nacional, Instituto Colom-

biana de Especialización Técnica en el Exterior, Instituto Caro y Cuervo, Instituto de Cultura Hispánica.
f Caja Nacional de Previsión, Caja de Sueldos de Retiro de las Fuerzas Militares, Ejército, Caja de Sueldos de Retiro, Fuerzas de Policía, Caja de Previsión Social de Comunicaciones.
g Instituto Nacional de Cancerología.
h Instituto de Crédito Territorial, Caja de Vivienda Militar.
i Fondo Rotatorio Fuerzas Policía, Fondo Rotatorio Armada Nacional, Fondo Rotatorio Fuerza Aérea, Fondo Rotatorio Ejército, Fondo Rotatorio Judicial.
j Instituto de Fomento Municipal.
Source: Dirección Nacional de Presupuesto, *Análisis Económico del Presupuesto de Colombia,* 1962.

TABLE 12–4

Percentage Distribution of the Income of the Autonomous Agencies According to Source for Each Sector, 1962

	Agriculture (Per Cent)	Power and Fuel (Per Cent)	Industry (Per Cent)	Transportation and Communications (Per Cent)	Education and Culture (Per Cent)	Public Health and Welfare (Per Cent)	Public Health (Per Cent)	Housing (Per Cent)	Revolving Funds (Per Cent)	Community Services (Per Cent)
Total income	100.00	100.00	100.00	100.00	100.00	100.00	100.00	100.00	100.00	100.00
Ordinary income	76.84	90.72	65.97	81.15	92.58	81.80	100.00	30.21	90.00	48.33
Goods	46.15	66.22	22.25	7.82	1.57	4.22	10.81	17.14	83.33	1.94
Services	1.78	2.46	—	53.85	0.17	1.16	8.11	0.84	2.67	—
Contributions	24.64	7.34	28.80	18.30	83.51	52.90	81.08	11.86	4.00	34.54
Tax collections	4.26	3.74	14.66	—	—	—	—	—	—	11.85
Occasional income	0.01	10.96	0.26	1.18	7.33	23.52	—	0.37	—	—
Capital income	23.16	9.28	34.03	18.85	7.42	18.20	—	69.79	10.00	51.67
Previous fiscal years	13.60	8.37	17.02	—	1.57	0.43	—	17.20	—	21.08
Loans	9.56	0.91	17.01	18.85	5.85	17.77	—	52.59	10.00	30.59

Source: Dirección Nacional de Presupuesto, Análisis Económico del Presupuesto de Colombia, 1962.

Agriculture. The principal source of income of the autonomous agencies in this sector is the sale of property and the receipt of contributions, representing 46.15 per cent and 24.64 per cent of their income respectively. Capital income represented 23.16 per cent, 13.60 per cent from previous fiscal years and 9.56 per cent from loans.

Power and Fuel. Income from the sale of goods represented 66.22 per cent of the total income of agencies in this sector, while contributions represented 7.34 per cent, tax collections represented 3.74 per cent, and occasional income represented 10.96 per cent. The agencies in this sector provide relatively few services, the income from this source representing only 2.46 per cent of total income.

Industry. The principal source of ordinary income of the agencies in this sector is contributions, representing 28.80 per cent of total income. Of second importance is the sale of goods, accounting for 22.25 per cent of income. The income from tax collections is relatively significant at 14.66 per cent. Capital income accounted for 34.03 per cent of total income, divided almost equally between income from previous years and from loans.

Transportation and Communications. As would be expected, the principal source of income for agencies in this sector was the sale of services, representing 53.85 per cent of total income, while contributions accounted for 18.30 per cent and the sale of goods for 7.82 per cent. Capital income, entirely from loans, accounted for 18.85 per cent of total income.

Education and Culture. More than four-fifths (83.51 per cent) of the income of this sector was derived from contributions, while capital income represented 7.42 per cent.

Public Health and Welfare. The agencies in this sector received a relatively large proportion of their income from contributions, amounting to 52.90 per cent, while capital income accounted for 18.20 per cent.

Public Health. This sector has only three sources of income, the principal one being contributions, accounting for 81.08 per cent of total income.

Housing. Agencies in the housing sector received most of their income (52.59 per cent) from loans. Next in importance were income from previous fiscal years (17.20 per cent) and income from the sale of goods (17.14 per cent).

Revolving Funds. Agencies classified in this sector received 90.00 per cent of their income from the sale of goods, with the remainder derived from loans, contributions, and services.

Community Services. Principal sources of income for the agencies in this sector were contributions (34.54 per cent), tax collections (11.85 per cent), and capital income (51.57 per cent).

In comparing the above derivations of income for the autonomous agencies by sectors, it is apparent that income from the sale of goods is most important in those agencies classified under revolving funds (83.33 per cent), power and fuel (66.22 per cent), and agriculture (46.15 per cent). Service income is most important in transportation and communications, accounting for 53.85 per cent of income in this sector. The highest proportions of income from contributions are received by agencies in education and culture (83.51 per cent) and in public health (81.08 per cent), while the lowest percentages of income from this source are received by agencies in power and fuel and revolving funds. In general, income from tax collections is of minor importance, being relatively high only in industry (14.66 per cent) and community services (11.85 per cent). The autonomous agencies in six sectors receive no income from tax collections. The agencies dependent most on borrowing are those in housing, with 52.59 per cent of their income derived from this source.

It is evident also that the four sectors receiving the largest proportion of agency income (agriculture, power and fuel, transportation and communications, and housing) are also the sectors in which the sale of goods and services as a source of income is the most important. On the other hand, the remaining sectors that received only 15.56 of the total income were dependent on contributions, tax collections, and occasional income (aids).

THE EXPENDITURES OF THE AUTONOMOUS AGENCIES

Economic Classification of Expenditures

The expenditures of the autonomous agencies may be classified into four groups: (1) consumption expenditures, which include those made for wages and salaries and for consumer goods and services; (2) transfer expenditures, which represent payments to individuals that do not involve services; (3) public debt expenditures, including both amortization and interest expenses; and (4) capital expenditures, involving both direct and indirect investment.

Table 12–5 shows the above classification of expenditures for the autonomous agencies during 1962. Consumption expenditures represented 47.93 per cent of total expenditures, and this percentage was divided between 12.37 per cent for wages and salaries and 35.56 per cent for the purchase of goods and services. Transfer expenditures accounted for 6.42 per cent of total expenditures, and these were largely for public health and welfare. Public debt expenditures were the least important, representing only 3.00 per cent of total expenditures. Capital expenditures, on the other hand, accounted for 42.65 per cent of total expenditures, divided between 42.39 per cent in the form of direct investment and 0.26 per cent in indirect investment. In summary, consumption and capital expenditures were dominant, with these two categories being more or less of equal importance.

Sectoral Distribution of Expenditures by Economic Classification

Table 12–6 shows the percentage distribution of the expenditures of autonomous agen-

TABLE 12–5

Classification of the Expenditures of Autonomous Agencies, 1962

(Millions of Pesos)

	Amount	Percentage of Total Expenditures
Consumption expenditures	$1,586.5	47.93
Salaries and wages	409.6	12.37
Purchases of goods and services	1,176.9	35.56
Transfer expenditures	212.1	6.42
Public health and welfare	162.7	4.91
Payments to other public entities that are not investment expenditures	20.4	0.62
Payments to private entities that are not investment expenditures	23.5	0.71
Payments to international organizations	5.5	0.18
Public debt service	99.5	3.00
Foreign	4.2	0.13
Domestic	95.3	2.87
Capital expenditures	1,411.8	42.65
Direct investment	1,403.1	42.39
Indirect investment	8.7	0.26
TOTALS	$3,309.9	

Source: Dirección Nacional de Presupuesto, Análisis Económico del Presupuesto de Colombia, 1962.

TABLE 12–6

Sectoral Distribution of Total Expenditures in Percentages According to Economic Classification of Expenditures[a]

	Consumption (Per Cent)	Transfers (Per Cent)	Public Debt (Per Cent)	Capital (Per Cent)
Agriculture	38.60	4.06	13.24	26.72
Power and fuel	32.43	17.93	—	19.76
Industry	0.49	0.57	0.20	2.05
Transportation and communications	19.10	10.95	50.45	19.68
Education and culture	3.98	5.05	1.10	2.82
Public health and welfare	1.41	61.07	—	0.83
Public health	0.22	0.09	—	—
Housing	1.87	—	27.48	17.03
Revolving funds	0.84	—	—	0.12
Community services	1.05	0.28	7.52	10.98
	100.00	100.00	100.00	100.00

[a] Totals do not add because of rounding.
Sources: Dirección Nacional de Presupuesto, and Análisis Económico del Presupuesto de Colombia, 1962.

TABLE 12-7

Percentage Distribution of Expenditures by Economic Classification within Each Sector, 1962

	Agriculture (Per Cent)	Power and Fuel (Per Cent)	Industry (Per Cent)	Transportation and Communications (Per Cent)	Education and Culture (Per Cent)	Health and Welfare (Per Cent)	Public Health (Per Cent)	Housing (Per Cent)	Revolving Funds (Per Cent)	Community Services (Per Cent)
Consumption expenditures	60.56	61.87	20.42	46.32	55.06	13.69	94.59	9.98	88.67	9.29
Salaries and wages	5.32	6.94	8.38	30.93	41.62	7.33	56.76	6.45	10.67	5.06
Purchases of goods and services	55.24	54.93	12.04	15.39	13.44	6.36	37.83	3.53	78.00	4.23
Transfer expenditures	0.85	4.58	4.14	3.55	9.25	79.09	5.41	—	—	0.33
Public health payments	0.03	2.25	0.26	2.14	2.27	77.63	5.41	—	—	0.05
Payments to other public entities that are not investment	0.02	2.07	1.31	0.14	1.22	0.18	—	—	—	—
Payments to private entities that are not investment	0.50	0.02	1.31	1.27	5.41	1.28	—	—	—	0.28
Payments to international organizations	0.30	0.24	1.26	—	0.35	—	—	—	—	—
Public debt	1.30	—	0.52	7.69	0.96	—	—	9.21	—	4.17
Foreign	0.42	—	—	—	—	—	—	—	—	—
Domestic	0.88	—	0.52	7.69	0.96	—	—	9.21	—	4.17
Capital expenditures	37.29	33.54	75.92	42.45	34.73	7.21	—	80.81	11.33	86.21
Direct investment	37.17	33.54	75.92	42.45	28.36	7.21	—	80.81	11.33	86.21
Indirect investment	0.12	—	—	—	6.37	—	—	—	—	—

Source: Dirección Nacional de Presupuesto, *Análisis Económico del Presupuesto de Colombia, 1962.*

cies by sectors. The autonomous agencies in agriculture, power and fuel, and transportation and communications accounted for 90.13 per cent of total consumption expenditures. Similarly, entities in public health and welfare, power and fuel, and transportation and communications accounted for 89.95 per cent of transfer payments. Agencies in two sectors —transportation and communications and housing—accounted for 77.93 per cent of public debt expenditures. Finally, for capital expenditures, agriculture accounted for 26.72 per cent, power and fuel for 19.76 per cent, transportation and communications for 19.68 per cent, and housing for 17.03 per cent.

The expenditures of the autonomous agencies may now be shown by economic groups within each sector. This is done in Table 12–7. The findings in Table 12–7 may be summarized as follows:

Agriculture. Consumption expenditures were the most important in the agricultural sector, accounting for 60.56 per cent of total expenditures, while capital expenditures were of next importance, accounting for 37.29 per cent of the total.

Power and Fuel. In this sector, consumption expenditures were also dominant, representing 61.87 per cent of the total, with capital expenditures of 33.54 per cent making up most of the remainder.

Industry. Agencies in this sector spend most of their resources (75.92 per cent) on direct investment and only 20.42 per cent on consumption expenditures.

Transportation and Communications. The two principal types of expenditures in this sector were consumption and capital expenditures, accounting for 46.32 per cent and 42.45 per cent, respectively, of total expenditures.

Education and Culture. Similarly, in this sector consumption and capital expenditures were dominant, accounting for 55.06 per cent and 34.73 per cent, respectively, of total expenditures.

Public Health and Welfare. In contrast with the other sectors, transfer expenditures represented 79.09 per cent of total expenditures, most of which were for public health and welfare payments.

Public Health. Practically all (94.59 per cent) of autonomous agency spending in this sector was for consumption expenditures.

Housing. Over 80 per cent of expenditures in this sector represented direct investment, and, consequently, expenditures for public debt service were the highest for any sector, 9.21 per cent of total expenditures.

Revolving Funds. Entities in this sector spent 88.67 per cent of their resources on consumption expenditures, principally for goods and services.

Community Services. This sector was highest in direct investment, with 86.21 per cent of total expenditures allocated to this category. Consumption expenditures were minor, only 9.29 per cent.

In summary, the sectors in which the autonomous agencies spent relatively high percentages of their resources on wages and salaries were public health, education and culture, and transportation and communications. Considering the nature of agency activity in these sectors, this is to be expected. The purchase of goods and services represented an important expenditure in more than one-half of the sectors, being most important in revolving funds. Public debt expenditures were important only in housing and transportation and communications. Capital expenditures were relatively important in community services, housing, industry, and transportation and communications.

Functional Classification of Expenditures

One further classification of the expenditures of autonomous agencies is helpful, and that is a division into functional groups according to the different type of services provided. There are five of these groups: (1) General services include police, justice, defense, and other general services. (2) Economic services represent expenditures for capital formation, conservation, development, and the more effective use of land, forest, animal, and fishing resources. (3) Cultural and social services include expenditures for education, culture, public health, welfare, and housing. (4) Non-classified expenditures include the servicing of the public debt and other expenses involved with tax collection, reimbursements, indemnities, refunds, and reserves. (5) Community services consist of expenditures that are related to community life, such as sanitation and municipal development.

By using this functional classification of expenditures, it is shown in Table 12–8 that 66.63 per cent of the expenditures of autonomous agencies is used in providing economic services, 15.40 per cent for providing social and cultural services, 7.23 per cent for providing general services, 6.07 per cent for non-classified expenditures, and 4.67 per cent for community services.

In a brief summary of the expenditures of the autonomous agencies, it may be said that these entities spent 47.93 per cent of their resources on consumption expenditures and 42.65 per cent on investment. The autonomous agencies operating in agriculture, power and fuel, and transportation and communications accounted for 90.13 per cent of total consumption expenditures. With respect to capital expenditures, entities in agriculture accounted for 26.72 per cent of the total, those in power and fuel for 19.76 per cent, and those in transportation and communica-

TABLE 12–8

Distribution of the Expenditures of the Autonomous Agencies by Functional Classification, 1962

(Millions of Pesos)

	Amount	Percentage
General services	$ 239.5	7.23
Economic services	2,205.7	66.63
Cultural and social services	509.7	15.40
Non-classified expenditures	200.5	6.07
Community services	154.5	4.67
TOTAL	$3,309.9	100.00

Source: Dirección Nacional de Presupuesto, *Análisis Económico del Presupuesto de Colombia, 1962.*

tions and housing for 19.68 per cent and 17.03 per cent respectively.

The percentage of resources spent by the autonomous agencies in investment is relatively high, certainly higher than is characteristic of regular government departments. This is consistent with the basic purpose of establishing most of the agencies—to increase the productive capacity of the country. But this percentage is not high in all sectors. For example, among the agencies operating in the agricultural sector, 38.60 per cent of their expenditures were for consumption purposes.

THE DESIRABILITY OF AUTONOMOUS AGENCIES AND SOME OF THEIR PROBLEMS

It is apparent from the foregoing that the autonomous agencies constitute an important extension of the activities of the national government. Their creation grew out of the objective to execute and subsidize certain specific undertakings. The system of public action through these agencies has been in existence in Colombia for some thirty years, although the present importance of these units has been acquired only during the last ten years. There appears to be a trend toward their increasing importance. In fact, in Colombia these agencies are so important that they are almost like a fourth level of government. In view of these developments, it is appropriate to consider the reasons justifying this type of governmental action, to consider whether the planned objectives have been realized, and to evaluate generally the desirability of the autonomous agencies.

What was sought in the establishment of the autonomous agencies? Fundamentally, an attempt was made to carry out certain activities with relative independence of the regular government. In itself, this implied a recognition that these activities could not be carried out efficiently within the normal governmental structure. It was an attempt, then, to remove the undertaking of these activities from the defects and obstacles of normal public administration and, also, from the uncertainties and inhibitions of political influence.

Has this experiment been successful? Have autonomous agencies actually achieved greater efficiency in public administration, and have they been removed from political influence? Unfortunately, there are no objective standards by which these questions can be answered. Certainly, there is a consensus in Colombia that they have been successful, which is evident from their recent growth. There is also general recognition in Colombia that the level of public administration in the regular government departments has not improved materially in the last thirty years, while the level of efficiency in the autonomous agencies is believed to compare favorably with the private sector.

If these contentions are indeed true, it is probably because the autonomous agencies enjoy several prerogatives that set them apart from the regular government. They are permitted to pay higher salaries for personnel, and they can act with greater autonomy and flexibility than regular government departments. In other words, if good people are the fundamental requirement of good administration, there probably is a presumption that the autonomous agencies have a decided advantage over the regular government departments in the undertaking of public activities.

All of this is not to say, however, that no problems exist as a result of the widespread development of autonomous agencies. Certainly, it is to be decried that the level of efficiency of public administration in general is such that the government must turn to autonomous agencies to undertake a large part of its responsibilities and must do so to an increasing extent. It would seem, too, that the mere fact that the government has this alternative prevents a rationalization of its own public administration performance.

One of the most important problems that results from the creation of autonomous agencies is that of integrating them into the regular public sector. The government has certain objectives with respect to public policy, and it is mandatory for all of the government's resources to be allocated for the attainment of these objectives. There is nothing wrong with a fourth level of government, in itself, if it is not working at cross purposes with the regular government and if its operations and activities are closely integrated with government policies. To this end, the agencies should be subject to the supervision and control of the national government. What is to be avoided is another government acting unto itself.

In Colombia, there appears to be an adequate mechanism that would make co-ordination possible between the national government and the autonomous agencies. A number of the directors of the board, as well as the general manager of each agency, are appointed by the national government. In the majority of cases, the president of the governing board is an appointee of the government. Moreover, the national government may, through the distribution of contributions, aids, and earmarked taxes, channel its resources to meet its policy goals. Another instrument of co-ordination at the government's disposal is that the Administrative Department of Planning and Technical Services (Departamento Administrativo de Planeación y Servicios Técnicos) must approve all applications for foreign credit.

Although it appears that sufficient means of co-ordination exist, there is also some evidence that their utilization has been inadequate. The criticism is often made in Colombia that autonomous agencies operate "on their own," constituting sovereign states over which there exists no effective control. And this criticism is justified in the sense that some autonomous agencies have conducted their activities, if not free of government control, at least without the degree of co-ordination with the national government that would be desirable. In other words, it is not that the autonomous agencies deliberately pursue objectives that are in conflict with those of the national government, but, rather, that on occasion it is either a case that the two parties are not sure of the basic objectives, or, if they are, that inadequate efforts of co-ordination are exercised.

To illustrate the problem, there is the case of the Stabilization Fund, an agency created in 1940 and administered by an autonomous board composed of the Minister of Finance, the manager of the Central Bank, and a member designated by the President of Colombia. The management of the fund was thus, for all practical purposes, in the hands of those persons responsible for the monetary policy of the country. Nevertheless, when the Minister of Finance asked Congress in 1959 for the authority to discontinue the operations of the fund, one of the reasons given was that the agency had contributed to inflationary pressures and that it was advisable, therefore, to "avoid the possibility that by this route that there should be a relapse into similar processes." [6]

How could more adequate co-ordination between the national government and the autonomous agencies be achieved? One possible solution would be through the creation of a Superintendent of Autonomous Agencies, who would have as his principal function the control, co-ordination, and supervision of the agencies. But this would have the danger of creating one more organization, with its own administrative overhead and bureaucracy. (It also might be one more autonomous agency.) Another method is to seek a solution through existing administrative machinery. Such a possibility is offered through the budgetary procedure—the way in which the budgets of the autonomous agencies are prepared, presented, approved, and executed. For this solution, the legislative and administrative machinery already exists.

The objective should be to develop budgets for all of the national public sector (including the autonomous agencies) that would be globally integrated and uniform in their classification and presentation. If the budgets of all of the autonomous agencies were reviewed and approved by the Administrative Department of Planning and Technical Services

and the National Director of the Budget, there would be adequate co-ordination with the activities of the national government. The principal advantage of this procedure is that it would permit co-ordination before, rather than after, the execution of the programs. Co-ordination through budget procedures also has the advantage that the unification of the government's activities would cease to depend solely on the representatives of the national government on governing boards but would be carried out, instead, through executed budgets.

Financial Institutions

A numerically small but very important group of financial institutions actually falls within the category of autonomous agencies, but they are not considered as such in Colombia, even though the government owns a principal proportion of their stock.[7] In this group are such institutions as the Banco Central Hipotecario, the Caja de Crédito Agrario, Industrial y Minero, and the Banco Popular. An indication of the importance of these institutions is the amount of their accounts receivable. As of December 31, 1962, these receivables totaled $820.8 million for the Banco Central Hipotecario, $329.1 million for the Banco Popular, and $1,278.0 million for the Caja de Crédito Agrario.

Because these financial institutions are not construed to be autonomous agencies, they are not under a legal obligation to submit their budgets to the national government. Nor must they submit their accounts to the Contraloría General de la República. Only an *ex post* administrative control is exercised over these institutions by the Banking Superintendent.

The result of this degree of decentralization is that national government control and supervision must be executed through indirect means, and, although some co-ordination of activities is possible in this way, more effec-

---

[6] Hernando Agudelo Villa, *Memoria de Hacienda, Anexo II, 1959*, p. 28.

[7] Law 151 of 1959 notes that "banking establishments that represent state property are not considered for the purpose of this law as autonomous agencies."

tive co-ordination could be established through the budgetary process. Therefore, these agencies also should be brought within the same regulations as other autonomous agencies with respect to the submission and approval of their budgets.

National Federation of Coffee Growers

If any autonomous agency is really autonomous and a world unto itself in Colombia, it is the National Federation of Coffee Growers, a "private" entity similar to a guild. The federation administers the National Coffee Fund, which is financed primarily by taxes on coffee exports. These taxes have been earmarked for the fund by the national government.

It is not possible to determine the total assets of the federation, since this information is not a matter of public record. Up to December 31, 1958, the national government had provided $833.7 million to the National Coffee Fund. As of December 31, 1962, these contributions have probably exceeded $1,000 million. But no one really knows the total amount of contributions made, as the Comptroller General in 1961 observed that "in spite of the efforts made by the *Contraloría,* it was not possible to obtain information concerning the contributions made by the State to the National Coffee Fund." [8] Nor does the federation disclose information on its financial statements or budgets to the public. Instead, it surrounds itself in secrecy as if it were a private organization.

With its ample resources, the federation has made large investments in different activities related to the coffee industry. For example, it owns 80 per cent of the Colombian capital invested in the Colombian Merchant Fleet (Flota Mercante Grancolombiana). It is also the owner of about 45 per cent of the Caja de Crédito Agrario, Industrial y Minero, owns 100 per cent of the stock of the Banco Cafetero, and participates in the operations of the Instituto Nacional de Abastecimientos.[9] In view of this broad involvement in the economy and the fact that the federation is essentially a government-subsidized institution, the National Federation of Coffee Growers should be brought within the control and supervision of the national government.

SUMMARY OF RECOMMENDATIONS

1) With the present standard of efficiency in public administration in the regular government departments, the execution of certain functions by autonomous agencies is probably desirable. On the other hand, rather than continuing to emphasize this trend, which would eventually lead to a point where the autonomous agencies, as a group, would be more important than the government itself, the national government would be well advised to intensify efforts to improve its own administrative organization and effectiveness.

2) To achieve greater co-ordination between the activities of the national government and those of the autonomous agencies, all agencies should submit their budgets for review and approval. These budgets also should follow a standardized procedure.

3) For purposes of budgetary control, autonomous agencies should include all financial institutions in which the national government is a major stockholder as well as the National Federation of Coffee Growers.

4) The National Directorate of the Budget should submit a consolidated national budget that should include all autonomous agencies.

5) The autonomous agencies also should submit their accounts for auditing to the Comptroller General.

6) The government should draw to the attention of its representatives on the boards of the autonomous agencies, continuously and with emphasis, that one of their most important functions is to act as co-ordinators of government and agency activities.

[8] *Informe Financiero, 1961,* p. 184.

[9] For additional information on the organization and scope of operations of the National Federation of Coffee Growers, see Comisión Económica para América Latina, *El Café en América Latina y El Salvador, México, 1958,* p. 94.

APPENDIX

The Taxation of Corporations
and Limited Liability Companies

INTRODUCTION

A PRINCIPAL PURPOSE of this appendix is to examine and evaluate the corporate income tax structure in Colombia in order to shed some light on the effect of the tax on private savings and investment. Attention will also be given to the comparative taxation of the various forms of business organization. In other words, the study is concerned with the effect of the alleged discriminatory fiscal treatment of corporations on the development of the corporate sector, and hence on the corporate ability to save.

The first section, entitled "The Role of the Corporate Sector in Mobilizing Resources," is devoted to the presentation of empirical data on the role of corporate savings in financing private investment, the flow of transferable savings into and from the corporate sector, and the role of private business and personal savings in financing the target growth rates of the development plan. In the next section, entitled "The Monetary Burden of Direct Corporate Taxes," there is a consideration of the impact of the corporate income tax on corporate ability to save and invest. The focus here is on the monetary burden of the tax, in both absolute and relative terms.

Following this is an analysis of the effect of the tax on what might be called the "desire" to save at the corporate level. An attempt is made to determine the variables important in corporate decisions to save in the Colombian environment, the impact of tax policy on these decisions, and the effect of various changes in the tax structure on corporate saving policies. In the next analytical section limited liability companies are examined to determine if there is unneutrality in the tax treatment of this type of business organization. This section analyzes the effect of taxation on the relative growth of corporations and limited liability companies. Finally, at the end of the appendix appear some considerations with respect to the taxation of corporations in an inflationary environment.

A note of caution is warranted both with respect to the methodology and the policy conclusions. This study will emphasize adverse economic effects, something necessarily inherent in all taxation. The government could seek a combination of taxes that minimizes these adverse economic effects. However, there are other very important noneconomic effects of taxation, such as revenue productivity and income redistribution. The public authorities, then, should choose that set of taxes, each with its own effects, that satisfies best the several goals of fiscal policy.

THE ROLE OF THE CORPORATE SECTOR IN MOBILIZING RESOURCES

The positive case for using a tax on the net income of corporations was discussed in Chapter 3 of this study. However, once the use of the tax is justified in principle, there remain problems in formulating the details of the tax. There is the possibility, for example, that the particular structure of the tax may retard the development of the corporate sector. This could result in several possible ways: by discouraging existing corporations from growing, by discouraging other forms of business enterprise from assuming the corporate form, or, possibly, by encouraging existing corporations to liquidate and assume another form.

It would be contrary to desirable developmental policy if the tax system discouraged the growth of corporations, for it is apparent that the share-issuing limited liability company has been a principal vehicle for the rapid and continuing growth of the Western industralized nations. With the growth of the middle class, it is important that government policies do not deter the flow of their savings into the corporate sector. This is especially important if there is some degree of inflation in the development process.

The middle class has participated little in Colombian corporate development, but their participation is increasing. Table A–1 shows that less than 1 per cent of the shareholders held nearly 73 per cent of the total shares in 1959. On the other hand, Table A–1 shows that the number of shareholders owning from one to one thousand shares in seven of the largest manufacturing corporations for which there is comparable data increased by 27 per cent between 1958 and 1961.

There is also the danger that the particular structure of corporate income taxation may stimulate corporate profit distribution as opposed to profit retention. Such an undesirable

TABLE A–1
Ownership of Shares in Colombian Corporations

All Colombian Corporations, 1959				
Holding of Shares	Number of Shareholders	Percentage of Total Shareholders	Number of Shares Held	Percentage of Total Shares
1–100	161,824	63.83	4,690,426	1.21
101–15,000	89,325	35.23	101,375,542	26.08
15,001–100,000	1,963	0.78	65,202,892	16.78
Over 100,000	411	0.16	217,388,933	55.93

The Nine Largest Corporations in the Manufacturing Sector				
Firm	Shareholders June 30, 1947	Shareholders Dec. 31, 1961	Shareholders in 1961 as a Percentage of 1947	Shareholders Holding 1 to 1,000 Shares, 1958	Shareholders Holding 1 to 1,000 Shares, 1961
A	5,321	66,000	1,240.4	38,043	53,466
B	8,157	30,299	371.4	21,186	24,634
C	n.a.	90	n.a.	n.a.	46
D	4,462	10,545	236.3	n.a.	7,951
E	1,822	5,737	314.9	4,663	4,219
F	n.a.	1,031	n.a.	764	741
G	n.a.	3,127	n.a.	2,627	2,641
H	121	1,180	975.2	1,123	922
I	734	2,048	279.0	1,337	1,672

Sources: Various issues of the *Revista de la Superintendencia de Sociedades Anónimas* and of the *Directorio de Compañías Inscritas,* Bolsa de Bogotá.

effect may result from particular attempts to integrate the income tax at the corporate and individual levels. Students of economic development point to the business retention of profits as historically the primary source of capital accumulation in Western industrialized nations.[1]

[1] See, for example, Ragnar Nurske, *Problems of Capital Formation in Underdeveloped Countries* (London, 1958). Professor Nurske, referring to the role of retained business earnings in Western economic growth, points out that "if the pattern can be repeated elsewhere, it would be an effective and almost automatic way of maximizing a country's marginal savings ratio" (p. 155).

As in most of the non-industralized countries, business savings in Colombia are a large component of total private savings, and corporate savings, in turn, represent a strategic element in private savings. Table A–2 shows that gross corporate savings as a percentage of total savings increased from 9.6 per cent in 1953 to 17.5 per cent in 1959. Table A–2 also indicates that gross corporate savings represented 24 per cent of total private savings in 1959. Table A–3, which includes data for domestic corporations only,

TABLE A–2

The Financing of Gross Domestic Investment Expressed in Percentage Terms, 1951 to 1959

	Domestic Savings (Per Cent)	Foreign Finance (Per Cent)	Central Bank (Per Cent)	Government Savings[a] (Per Cent)	Private Savings (Per Cent)	Gross Corporate Savings[b] (Per Cent)	Subscription of Corporate Shares (Per Cent)	Savings by Institutions (Per Cent)
1951	91.7	3.4	4.9	28.2	63.5	n.a.	n.a.	4.0
1952	80.9	10.7	8.4	27.6	53.3	n.a.	n.a.	4.5
1953	94.3	4.6	0.9	25.8	68.5	9.6	1.7	4.0
1954	83.1	7.1	9.7	26.4	56.7	11.3	4.4	4.4
1955	83.4	3.6	13.0	25.5	57.9	6.8	10.3	3.5
1956	79.1	12.3	8.6	23.9	55.2	12.7	6.4	4.0
1957	47.9	25.5	26.6	20.8	27.1	15.9	4.6	3.6
1958	80.8	8.8	10.4	24.3	56.5	16.7	8.9	3.7
1959	98.0	4.2	−2.2	24.9	73.1	17.5	7.0	4.2

[a] Government savings equals total government revenues minus ordinary (non-capital) government expenditures.
[b] Includes non-distributed profits, depreciation, and depletion allowances for Colombian and foreign corporations.

Sources: Banco de la República and Superintendencia de Sociedades Anónimas y Superintendencia Bancaria.

TABLE A–3

Liquid Profits and Gross and Net Savings of Domestic Colombian Corporations, 1953 to 1959

(Millions of Pesos)

	Liquid Profits	Dividends Paid	Retained Earnings[a]	Gross Corporate Savings	Gross Corporate Savings as a Percentage of Gross Private Savings
1953	$253.36	$130.02	$123.34	$109.2	9.9
1954	311.26	147.03	164.23	224.4	18.3
1955	254.53	159.65	98.88	117.7	8.6
1956	359.95	180.26	179.69	274.6	20.0
1957	429.76	203.67	226.09	439.4	42.2
1958	481.99	222.67	259.32	530.1	24.5
1959	581.56	289.53	292.03	576.4	18.1

[a] Retained earnings for each year represent after-tax profits minus the sum of ordinary and extraordinary dividends paid in each year. All these retained earnings cannot be utilized for capital expansion, however, because 10 per cent of profits must be added to legal reserves until these reserves are 50 per cent of paid-in capital. The data on retained earnings in this table are

considerably smaller than those reported by the Superintendencia de Sociedades Anónimas, because the statistics reported by the latter are based on financing from reserves in each year rather than profits actually placed in reserves.

Source: Revista de la Superintendencia de Sociedades Anónimas, various issues.

shows that these firms accounted for an average of 20 per cent of total private savings during the period from 1953 to 1959, and in 1957 they accounted for 42 per cent of total private savings.

In addition, considerable savings have been mobilized through the issuance of corporate equity and debt instruments. Table A–4 shows that the nominal value of these instruments increased by over $1 billion between 1955 and 1959, and that they accounted for over 70 per cent of the value of all securities in circulation in 1959. These securities do not entirely represent a mobilization of private savings in addition to corporate savings, however, since more than 50 per cent of them is held in the corporate sector.[2] Table

[2] A study of 10,000 companies (undertaken for this fiscal survey) showed that they owned 52.8 per cent of corporate shares in 596 corporations in 1958. These data include ownership of *Paz del Río* steel plant shares. This proportion increased in 1959, when 57.2 per cent of all shares was held by legal entities, or 51.3 per cent if *Paz del Río* steel plant shares are excluded.

TABLE A–4

Value of Securities in Circulation in Colombia, 1955 to 1959

(Millions of Pesos)

	1955	1956	1957	1958	1959
Issued by corporations					
Shares	$1,819	$1,984	$2,142	$2,484	$2,971
Bonds	n.a.	n.a.	10	14	30
Issued by banks and other financial institutions					
Mortgage cedulas	238	278	328	411	511
Industrial bonds	27	55	88	86	71
Agrarian bonds	90	105	92	110	121
Issued by governments					
Bonds representing internal public debt	252	382	447	529	501
TOTALS	$2,426	$2,804	$3,107	$3,634	$4,205

Source: Unpublished study by Robert W. Adler, Universidad de los Andes, 1963.

TABLE A–5

Financial Flows to and from the Corporate Sector and
Corporate Ownership of Debt and Equity Instruments, 1953 to 1960

(Thousands of Pesos)

	1953	1954	1955	1956	1957	1958	1959	1960
Domestic loans to corporations[a]	$111,118	$100,687	$ 35,775	$178,817	$447,715	$223,373	$368,084	$527,818
Corporate financial investments[b]	106,843	196,596	23,590	262,094	224,878	497,341	483,646	550,480
Corporate holdings:								
Stocks in corporations	121,734	97,705	131,024	151,932	222,406	282,360	376,175	472,109
Stocks in affiliates	71,620	70,765	171,657	179,979	189,209	224,413	315,753	295,536
Rights in limited liability companies	24,658	23,688	52,512	42,532	62,723	67,498	100,635	127,654
Internal public debt instruments	12,451	9,287	8,600	6,519	7,248	7,005	6,221	7,316
Bonds of corporations and various semi-autonomous public entities	3,985	1,284	6,838	4,641	1,691	4,394	15,725	45,742

[a] Includes loans from banks, financial institutions, and individuals.
[b] Includes savings and time deposits and public debt instruments.

Source: Consolidated accounts of Colombian corporations prepared by the Superintendencia de Sociedades Anónimas.

A–5 shows that corporations in 1961 held almost one billion pesos of shares in other corporations, including affiliates.

Some writers have pointed out that increases in business savings in general and corporate savings in particular are not in themselves unqualified blessings, since a large part of these savings may not be readily transferable.[3] In other words, business savings may be used generally for investment within the firm itself. Thus, stimulating these savings may make it more difficult to obtain savings for other uses where the demand for them may be greater.

However, a significant amount of corporate savings that superficially appears to be "retained," may, in fact, be readily transferable to the non-corporate private sector and to the public sector. Within a firm there need be no correlation at a point of time between the magnitude of depreciation allowances, for example, and the replacement of fixed assets. This is equally true in the aggregate corporate sector in any one year. Savings not immediately required for investment in fixed capital and inventories will be held in

[3] See, for example, "Private Savings Flows and Economic Growth," an unpublished report prepared for the International Bank for Reconstruction and Development by Mervyn L. Weiner, 1954.

various financial instruments. Because of this lack of continuity between savings and planned investments, there can be a continuous flow of funds from corporations into other sectors.

The data in Table A–5 indicate that the corporate sector in 1960 provided $7.3 million to the public sector directly through public debt instruments and loaned an additional $45.7 million to corporations and semigovernmental agencies. And Table A–6 shows, for the same year, that the domestic corporate sector did not obtain any funds from government loans. In fact, the repayment of government loans (including repurchase of corporate bonds) was over $51 million.

What is true for the public sector is also true for all sectors in the aggregate. Table A–5 indicates that corporate financial investments (savings deposits, time deposits, and public and semi-public debt instruments) in 1960 exceeded the total domestic loans to corporations. In other words, an increase in corporate savings not merely claims resources for the corporate sector but also releases resources to other sectors (including the public), and provides the transferable savings necessary for other sectors to finance their investments.

TABLE A–6

Sources and Uses of Finance, Colombian Corporations, Selected Years from 1953 to 1960

(Thousands of Pesos)

	1953		1955		1959		1960	
	Amount	Per Cent	Amount	Per Cent	Amount	Per Cent	Amount	Per Cent
Internal finance	$109,161	41.9	$117,706	36.1	$576,417	44.5	$528,976	33.5
Retained earnings	73,876	28.4	49,712	15.3	410,643	31.7	338,683	21.5
Depreciation and depletion	35,285	13.5	67,994	20.8	165,774	12.8	190,293	12.0
External finance	151,074	58.1	207,965	63.9	717,370	55.5	1,048,410	66.5
Total loans	124,709	47.9	35,775	10.9	410,163	31.7	682,835	43.3
Banks	23,004	8.8	24,859	7.6	159,494	12.3	146,806	9.3
Government	7,986	3.1	471	−0.1	−667	−0.1	−51,510	−0.3
Financial enterprises	−15,624	−6.0	45,044	13.8	−7,678	−0.5	−186,603	11.8
Foreign	13,591	5.1	22,238	6.8	42,709	3.3	155,017	9.8
Individual	208,722	80.2	−109,889	−33.7	198,417	15.3	199,339	12.6
Other	−133,030	−43.3	−17,556	−5.4	16,554	1.3	12,214	0.1
Increases in paid-in capital	26,365	10.2	243,740	74.8	307,207	23.8	365,575	23.2
Fixed capital	174,714	67.1	236,830	72.7	505,277	39.0	711,163	45.1
Inventories	11,898	4.6	65,051	20.0	304,864	23.6	277,946	17.6
Financial assets	106,843	28.3	23,590	7.3	483,646	37.4	550,480	37.3

Source: Revista de la Superintendencia de Sociedades Anónimas, October, 1960, and November, 1961.

The requirements for both corporate savings and investment in the development plan [4] are demanding, but they are probably attainable under favorable conditions. As shown in Table A–7, domestic savings are scheduled to provide the bulk of investment financing for the development plan through 1970. The

TABLE A–7

Gross Investment and Savings as Percentages
of the Gross National Product

	Gross Investment	Total Domestic Savings	Public Savings	Gross Private Savings
1959	18.7	20.5	5.0	15.5
1961	24.8	22.3	5.1	17.1
1964	26.1	23.3	5.6	17.7
1970	25.4	25.1	7.7	17.4

Source: Based on estimates in the Colombian Ten-Year Development Plan.

increase of total domestic savings from 20.5 to 25.1 per cent of the gross national product by 1964 represents a return to the average savings propensity attained during the favorable period of the middle nineteen fifties. The private savings component, expected to increase from 15.5 to 17.7 per cent of the gross national product by 1964, represents a private savings level of over $5 billion. This goal for private savings must be attained if the targets established for private investment are to be reached.

A large part of private savings is expected to originate in depreciation and depletion allowances. Table A–8 indicates that these allowances are expected to attain a level of $2,825 million by 1964, which represents over 50 per cent of projected total private savings for this year. Retained earnings are expected to represent 16 per cent of private savings by 1964, and personal savings 30 per cent. The increase in retained earnings

[4] The development plan refers to a set of published and unpublished documents, particularly the *General Plan of Economic and Social Development*, January, 1962, and a *Four-Year Plan of National Public Investment, 1961–1964*, December, 1960. In addition, there is a series of unpublished provisional documents that complement the *General Plan*.

TABLE A–8

Projected Sources and Uses of Domestic
Private Savings in 1964

(Millions of 1958 Pesos)

Sources of domestic private savings	
Personal savings	$1,493
Retained earnings	811
Depreciation (depletion) allowances	2,825
Total private savings	$5,129
Uses of domestic private savings	
Fixed investment, private sector	$4,461
Inventory changes	847[a]
Net transfers to the public sector	121[b]
Total (gross) private investment	$5,429
Net inflow of capital, private sector	300

[a] Includes about $300 million (1958 pesos) of coffee stocks.
[b] Originally $181 million in net borrowing by the public sector, adjusted for $60 million of financial investments by the public sector in the private sector.
Source: Projections from the *General Plan of Economic and Social Development*, January, 1962.

assumes an average annual increase of 11 per cent. The personal savings component of $1,493 million by 1964 is at a level three times that of 1959 and assumes a marginal savings ratio of about 50 per cent.

Personal savings in the base year 1959 were abnormally low. For this reason, the 1960 reforms of the income and complementary taxes included several measures designed to stimulate personal savings. These included exemptions of: (1) the first $5,000 of dividends for individuals with a taxable income of less than $48,000; (2) interest received from the first $5,000 of savings deposits; (3) interest received on mortgage bonds and government debt instruments; (4) investments in development bonds from both the income and net wealth taxes; (5) up to $20,000 in corporate shares from the net wealth tax; and (6) contributions by employers to mutual funds established for employees.[5]

Notwithstanding the large increases sched-

[5] "The Committee of Nine" of the Alliance for Progress recommended that these incentive measures should be strengthened and supplemented. See *Evaluation of the General Economic and Social Development Program of Colombia*, Report Presented to the Government of Colombia by the Committee, July, 1962, pp. 184–85.

uled for per capita income and the incentive devices noted above, it does not seem prudent to rely on a 50 per cent marginal (personal) savings ratio.[6] The results of the incentive measures listed above may well be to lower the revenue productivity of the income tax while accomplishing little more than a re-arrangement of investments at the margin with no over-all increase in personal savings. Business savings, on the other hand, probably could be raised substantially through meas-ures designed to increase expected rates of return after taxes. To the extent that personal savings are overstated in the development plan, there will, of course, be a greater need to increase business savings in order to imple-ment the plan successfully.

THE MONETARY BURDEN OF DIRECT CORPORATE TAXES

From the point of view of effective tax rates, assuming "reasonable" returns on assets, the monetary burden of taxes on corporations does not appear to be excessive. The effective rate of the basic income tax is 35.74 per cent on $50,000,000 of taxable income, 30.72 per cent on $2,500,000, and only 12 per cent on incomes under $100,000.

Nevertheless, the progression of the income tax structure, together with the excess profits

tax, provides a curious mixture of incentives and disincentives to corporate development. In Table A–9 are shown the income tax liabilities under the present rate structure for firms of various sizes. It is clearly apparent from this table that the basic income tax under the present rate structure discriminates against larger firms. For example, Firms C and E both earn 10 per cent on net assets before taxes, but Firm C, the larger company, earns over 1 per cent less on its assets after taxes than the smaller firm.[7] It is probably de-sirable to apply a lower corporate income tax rate to low incomes to stimulate the develop-ment of small firms, but this should be done in such a way that the effective tax rate becomes proportional very rapidly as income increases. The efficient size for a firm should be determined on economic and not fiscal grounds. A corporate income tax structure with the degree of progressivity of the present one certainly violates the rule of neutrality with respect to the size of firms.

This discrimination against larger firms is reversed when the excess profits tax is taken into account. Since this tax is based on the relationship between income and capital, the tax burden should be related to the rate of re-turn on capital and not to the size of the firm as measured by income. But the present

[7] In the example shown in Table A–9, the other two direct taxes earmarked for housing and steel and elec-trical development were not included. These are regres-sive with respect to size of income so that some of the income tax discrimination is offset. Nevertheless, when these two taxes are included, the above conclusions re-main valid.

[6] In an analysis undertaken for this study based on the marginal personal savings propensity from 1950 to 1960, it was determined that the personal savings goal in the development plan was unlikely to be reached.

TABLE A–9
Comparative Income Tax Burdens on Corporations

	Firm A	Firm B	Firm C	Firm D	Firm E	Firm F	Firm G	Firm H
Net wealth	$250,000,000	$100,000,000	$50,000,000	$25,000,000	$10,000,000	$5,000,000	$2,000,000	$1,000,000
Net profits	25,000,000	10,000,000	5,000,000	2,500,000	1,000,000	500,000	200,000	100,000
Percentage rate of return	10.0	10.0	10.0	10.0	10.0	10.0	10.0	10.0
Basic income tax[a]	8,868,000	3,468,000	1,668,000	588,000	228,000	108,000	36,000	12,000
Effective rate	35.47	34.68	33.76	30.72	22.80	21.60	18.00	12.00
Rate of return after income tax	6.45	6.53	6.62	6.92	7.72	7.84	8.20	8.80

[a] The housing and steel and electric development taxes are not included.

excess profits tax in Colombia, both because of the progressive rates of the basic income tax and because the income tax is allowed as a deduction from the excess profits tax base, is not neutral with respect to the size of firms. The effect of this is to penalize firms because of their size rather than because of their excess profits. In effect, the tax is a penalty for being small rather than large.

Although the present excess profits tax structure superficially appears progressive in relation to rates of return on net assets, Table A–10 shows that Firm F, earning a 25 per cent return on net assets, pays a tax on its excess profits of 22.17 per cent, while two larger firms, D and E, both with the same rate of return on net assets, pay a tax on their excess profits of 20.0 per cent. Similarly, Firm C, a small firm earning a 50 per cent return on net assets, pays a rate of 31.32 per cent on its excess profits as compared to two larger firms with the same rate of return that pay only 27.27 per cent (Firm A) and 27.68 per cent (Firm B). Firm A in Table A–10, which is illustrative of a large company in a strong monopoly position, can earn up to 29.87 per cent on its net assets without those earnings being subject to the excess profits tax, while Firm F, which might represent a new firm in a risky line of activity, pays excess profits tax on that part of its income that represents a return of over 15.60 per cent on its net assets.

From the above discussion it is apparent that the present corporate tax rate structure is not conducive to industrial development. In the range of moderate returns on investment, there is discrimination against larger firms. This encourages them to split into non-economic units. Also, the progressivity of the income tax discourages the growth of small firms. For corporations with relatively large returns on net assets, however, the discrimination is against the smaller firms. The present excess profits tax structure becomes less effective as a monopolist grows stronger, but it has the undesirable feature of taxing rather quickly the excess profits of a small firm. This is likely to deter growth on the part of small firms operating in sectors where the risk factor is substantial.

In general, however, it does not appear that the combined monetary burden of the income and excess profits taxes is particularly burdensome. This is supported by the effective rate of direct taxes on the aggregate corporate sector. Direct taxes on the corporate sector as a function of net corporate income were estimated by the function $Y = 24.8214 + 0.372985965\ X$, where Y is direct corporate taxes plus the estimated income tax on dividends, and X is taxable corporate income. During the period from 1955 to 1959, each peso of taxable corporate income on the average resulted in 37 centavos of direct taxes at the corporate and individual levels. When the same procedure was repeated but

TABLE A–10
Comparative Excess Profits Tax Burdens on Corporations

	Firm A	Firm B	Firm C	Firm D	Firm E	Firm F
Net wealth	$100,000,000	$10,000,000	$500,000	$100,000,000	$10,000,000	$500,000
Net income	50,000,000	5,000,000	250,000	25,000,000	2,500,000	125,000
Percentage rate of return on net assets	50.00	50.00	50.00	25.00	25.00	25.00
Excess profits tax	5,490,160	594,160	44,480	826,400	106,400	10,420
Average tax rate on excess profits	27.27	27.68	31.32	20.00	20.00	22.17
Excess profits tax as a per cent of income	10.98	11.88	17.79	3.30	4.26	8.34
Percentage return not subject to excess profits tax	29.87	28.68	21.60	20.86	19.68	15.60
Excess profits tax as a per cent of total taxes	21.32	23.00	42.50	7.46	10.41	29.14

the estimated individual income tax on dividends was excluded, the marginal tax rate was approximately 30 per cent.

There are no generally accepted rules for determining the amount of income tax (and other direct taxes) that should be obtained at the corporate level as compared to the individual level. One of the more important criteria to be kept in mind, however, is the rate of development of the corporate sector. This criterion is especially important in Colombia because public policy is oriented consciously toward rapid industrialization and the promotion of private as well as public capital formation, and corporations are important savers and are dominant in the manufacturing sector.

Table A–11 summarizes the results obtained from an attempt to assess the relative monetary burden of direct taxes on the domestic corporate sector in Colombia. When estimated taxes on corporate dividends were added to direct corporate taxes, it was found that the corporate sector paid a proportion of the total national direct taxes ranging from 34.34 per cent in 1955 to 37.91 per cent in 1959. In 1957, over 46 per cent of direct national taxes was obtained from the domestic corporate sector. At the same time, the contribution of domestic corporations to the net private product was less than 8 per cent in 1955 and reached 11 per cent in only one year during this period. The estimate of individual taxes on corporate dividends was crude, but even if it is assumed that no taxes were paid on dividends during the period and the possible pyramiding of the 5 per cent tax on intercorporate dividends is ignored, the results are not altogether different. Excluding these two taxes, corporations paid direct taxes ranging from about 30 per cent of total direct taxes in 1955 to about 33 per cent in 1959. During this period, direct taxes on the corporate sector, on the average, were about $20 for every $100 of value added to the net private product.

TABLE A–11

Relative Burden of Direct Taxes on the Domestic Corporate Sector, 1955 to 1959

(Millions of Pesos)

	1955	1956	1957	1958	1959	1960
Net national product	11,342.2	12,813.2	15,107.0	16,874.4	19,402.7	22,077.4
Contribution of the private sector to the national product	10,658.5	12,087.7	14,272.5	15,876.5	18,251.6	20,703.6
Contribution of domestic corporations to the national product	828.0	1,068.0	1,302.0	1,600.0	2,019.0	2,137.0
National income originating in corporations as a percentage of:						
Net national product	7.30	8.33	8.62	9.48	10.40	9.67
Net private product	7.77	8.83	9.12	10.07	11.06	10.32
Direct taxes on corporations	164.67	182.90	247.50	272.21	312.24	n.a.
Direct taxes on corporations as a percentage of total national direct taxes	29.71	30.28	41.20	35.70	32.99	n.a.
Corporate dividends	159.65	180.26	203.67	222.67	289.53	n.a.
Income tax on dividends	25.71	29.03	32.82	35.86	46.63	n.a.
Direct taxes on the corporate sector[a]	190.38	211.93	280.32	308.07	358.87	n.a.
Direct taxes on corporations as a percentage of:						
Total direct taxes	34.34	35.08	46.66	40.40	37.91	n.a.
The contribution of corporations to the net national product	22.99	19.84	21.53	19.25	17.17	n.a.

[a] This figure includes all national direct taxes on corporations plus estimated taxes on dividends. An estimate for the net wealth tax on individual shares was not included, but the 5 per cent tax on intercorporate dividends in effect during the period was included. This results in double-counting, since the intercorporate dividend tax is also included in direct corporate taxes. However, the dividend tax was included to offset both the exclusion of the net wealth tax on individual shares and the possible pyramiding of the 5 per cent tax on intercorporate dividends.

Source: *Cuentas Nacionales 1950-1960*, Banco de la República; *Revista de la Superintendencia de Sociedades Anónimas*, various issues.

An examination of tax rates and the aggregate and marginal tax burdens at the corporate level, however, is not the whole of the issue with respect to the "tax capacity" of corporations. By "tax capacity" is meant the amount that corporate incomes can be reduced by taxation and still leave the sector able to grow and attract capital. Tax capacity, therefore, is a relative as well as absolute consideration; i.e., tax burdens in other sectors have a bearing on the degree to which corporations may be taxed without harmful effects. For this reason, it is appropriate to compare the tax burden on agriculture, where there are relatively few corporations, to the tax burden borne by the corporate sector.

Table A–12 provides an estimate of direct national taxes borne by the agricultural sector in Colombia. This table shows the startling fact that the agricultural sector is estimated to contribute only 14.29 per cent of the national direct taxes in 1959, although this sector in the same year contributed 42.54 per cent of the net private product.

Although the results shown in Table A–12 are based on very generous assumptions for the payment of taxes on agricultural income, the analysis nevertheless shows a severe imbalance between tax burdens on the corporate as compared to agricultural sectors. Even considering that perhaps one-half of agricultural output is of a subsistance nature, the direct tax burden on that sector appears to be extremely low in relation to the tax burden on the industrial sector.

It does not appear that the introduction of national indirect taxes into the analysis would qualify the fiscal discrimination in favor of the agricultural sector, although the incidence of these taxes is uncertain. In 1962, 38.0 per cent of national government tax revenue was derived from indirect tax receipts, and 62.0 per cent was derived from direct taxes. With the exception of taxes on the export of coffee and bananas, few of the other indirect taxes would fall on the agricultural sector. Therefore, the previous conclusion with respect to the bias of the tax system in favor of the agricultural industry as compared to manufacturing appears to be valid.

One final illustration may be offered to demonstrate the unneutralities that have developed because of the tax discriminations against corporations. Corporations are not evenly distributed among sectors of economic activity, most of them being in manufacturing, commerce, and the services. In addition, the larger corporations are concentrated in manufacturing. As a result, 80.51 per cent of direct corporate taxes was paid by corporations in the manufacturing sector in 1961, as compared to only .90 per cent by corporations in agriculture and .81 per cent by those in transport and communications. There is also a wide variation in the effective rates of direct taxes among sectors of economic activity. In 1961 the effective rate of direct taxes on manufacturing firms was 31.1 per cent as compared to 8.6 per cent for those in agriculture and 14.2 per cent for those in transport and communications. (See Table A–13.)

This evidence does not suggest, however, that corporate taxes are too high. In fact,

TABLE A–12

Estimates of the Monetary Burden of Direct Taxes on the Agricultural Sector[a]

(Millions of Pesos)

	1955	1956	1957	1958	1959
Percentage of net private product contributed by agriculture	42.00	42.75	44.75	44.63	42.54
Estimated direct taxes on income derived from the ownership of agricultural property	79.06	101.01	114.74	120.21	135.31
Estimated direct taxes on the agricultural sector as a percentage of total national direct taxes	14.26	16.72	19.10	15.76	14.29

[a] Includes agriculture, stock-raising, and forestry as presented in the *Cuentas Nacionales*, published by *Banco de la República*.

Source: Computed on the basis of data in *Cuentas Nacionales 1950–1960, Banco de la República.*

Effective Rates of Direct Corporate Taxes by Economic Activities, 1961

(Thousands of Pesos)

Sector	Number of Corpo-rations	Gross Assets	Average Gross Assets	Taxable Income	Average Taxable Income	Direct Corporate Taxes[a]	Effective Rates of Direct Taxes (Per Cent)
Agriculture and stock-raising	42	$ 286,151	$ 6,813	$ 32,563	$ 775	$ 2,797	8.6
Mining and petroleum	31	362,110	11,681	60,403	1,948	16,783	27.9
Manufacturing	348	7,807,745	22,566	796,369	2,302	248,015	31.1
Construction	10	33,738	3,374	1,052	105	16	1.5
Transport and communications	83	611,158	7,363	17,619	212	2,499	14.2
Services	138	948,629	6,874	26,974	195	7,210	26.7
Commerce	252	2,179,768	8,650	99,542	395	30,748	30.9

[a] Estimated.

Source: Revista de la Superintendencia de Sociedades Anónimas, August, 1961, p. 137.

the absolute levels of the tax burdens on corporations appear to be moderate. The policy conclusion which should be drawn is that the fiscal authorities should try to lower the *relative* (not absolute) tax burdens on corporations by such measures as strengthening the individual income tax, increasing the tax burdens on the agricultural industry, raising taxes on urban real property, and improving tax administration in general.

CORPORATE TAXES AND PRIVATE SAVINGS

Judging from the tax reforms of 1960, there is a widespread belief in Colombia that the corporate income tax has a deleterious effect on private savings and investment. This section attempts to inquire into the probable effect on private and domestic savings of an increase in direct corporate taxes.

The question is approached from the point of view of the impact of a tax increase on corporate savings policy. It has been argued that corporate tax increases will cut deeply into private savings because the income of individuals with high savings propensities will be reduced through lower dividend distributions. However, in an inflationary environment, especially one accompanied by periodic devaluations, one must take into account the propensity of these individuals

to export their savings. Under these circumstances, it is possible that total domestic savings and investment could be increased considerably through transferring income from the dividend recipients to the public sector, which is, itself, an important saver in Colombia. For this reason, the relevant issue in Colombia is the extent to which an increase in direct corporate taxes would result in a decrease in dividends as compared to a decrease in retained earnings. The more of the increased tax liability that is financed through a reduction of net corporate saving, *ceteris paribus,* the more severe will be the impact of the tax increase on private savings and investment. In the extreme, it might be possible for total domestic savings to decline if the tax increase were to result wholly in a reduction of the retained earnings of corporations.

The Corporate Propensity to Save

Of the myriad factors taken into account when a corporation places part of its annual earnings in reserve, there are probably two principal considerations: (1) the desire for funds for capital expansion without the necessity of recourse to the capital market; and (2) the desire to stabilize dividends from year to year by setting aside reserves in profitable years to pay dividends when earnings are low. The usual hypothesis is that the relative importance of these two factors depends to a large extent on whether a firm is small and growing or large and well established. The small company is generally thought to place a larger share of its profits in reserves for the following reasons: (1) It has difficulty in obtaining external finance. (2) The small corporation tends to be more tightly held, with the result that individual owners use the firm as a vehicle for personal savings. (3) When there is a steeply graduated personal income tax, profits may be retained to avoid individual tax liabilities. Large firms, on the other hand, are generally thought to pay less attention to reserves and more to dividends for two reasons: (1) Large and growing dividends enhance the companies credit position for loan capital. (2) Since the firms actively seek equity capital for expansion, they are likely to sacrifice reserves for dividends, the latter being weighed more heavily in the market valuation of shares.

For the reasons listed above, it is generally thought that an increase in the rate of the corporate income tax would have a more deleterious effect on the growth of small firms. These firms are not likely to be distributing a large proportion of earnings, so that, faced with an increase in tax liabilities, their scope of action is limited. The tax, or a large part of it, will be paid by a reduction in retained earnings, making it increasingly difficult to obtain funds for capital expan-

sion. The large firms have a greater scope of action in the face of a tax increase. They have a choice between reducing reserves or dividends or, in some cases, raising prices to compensate for the tax increase.

Savings Policies of Colombian Corporations

The evidence strongly suggests that the above hypothesis with respect to the savings behavior of small corporations is valid in Colombia. Table A–14 shows the percentage of profits distributed in 1960 by various corporate groups. While all domestic corporations in 1960 distributed 54.25 per cent of their liquid profits, the 98 large corporations listed on the Bogotá stock exchange, with average profits of $4,438,550, distributed 69.72 per cent of 1960 profits. On the other hand, 932 smaller non-listed corporations, with average profits of $252,425, distributed only 25.64 per cent of their total profits in 1960. Since there are some large corporations which are not registered on the Bogotá stock exchange, there are probably some small corporations which are distributing few, if any, dividends.

The corporations listed on the stock exchange in 1960 were classified into two groups: the 54 non-financial corporations registered for ten years or more, and all others. The former group, with 42.4 per cent

TABLE A–14

Net Savings of Colombian Corporations by Corporate Groups, 1960

	Profits (Millions)	Average Profits per Firm	Dividends (Millions)	Retained Earnings (Millions)	Percentage of Total Retained Earnings	Average Percentage of Profits Distributed	Percentage of Total Corporate Profits
All Colombian corporations	$670.24	$ 650,718	$363.60	$306.64	100.00	54.25	100.0
All corporations listed on the Bogotá Stock Exchange	434.98	4,438,550	303.27	131.71	42.95	69.72	64.9
Corporations not listed on the Bogotá Stock Exchange	235.26	252,425	60.33	174.93	57.05	25.64	35.1
Non-financial corporations listed on the Bogotá Stock Exchange	284.25	5,263,948	205.48	78.77	25.69	72.29	42.4
Other corporations listed on the Bogotá Stock Exchange	150.72	3,425,523	97.89	52.83	17.23	64.88	22.5

Source: Superintendencia de Sociedades Anónimas.

of total domestic corporate profits in 1960, distributed 72.3 per cent of their profits. The net savings of this group was only 25.7 per cent of total corporate savings. All corporations listed on the stock exchange accounted for 64.9 per cent of total corporate profits in 1960 but for only 42.9 per cent of total net corporate savings. The smaller corporations not listed on the stock exchange accounted for only 35.1 per cent of total 1960 corporate profits but for 57.0 per cent of total net savings.

But the hypothesis advanced above concerning the savings behavior of small corporations must be modified somewhat for the Colombian institutional environment. Table A–15 shows the percentage of profits distributed by the 54 non-financial corporations listed on the stock exchange. While there is a tendency for the larger firms in this group to distribute a higher proportion of annual earnings than the smaller companies, the proportion distributed by the smaller corporations is also very high. In 1957, 47.4 per cent of all domestic corporate profits was distributed. In the same year, the 10 corporations in Table A–15 with profits under $500,000 distributed (on the average) 52 per cent of their earnings. Over the period 1957 to 1960, listed firms with less than $1 million of profits consistently distributed 50 to 60 per cent of their earnings. It appears,

therefore, that the most meaningful distinction to make in Colombia with respect to corporate savings policies is not between large and small firms, *per se*, but between listed and unlisted firms. The latter group will include a majority of small family corporations, while the former will encompass both small and large firms.

The unlisted corporations accounted for over one-half of total retained corporate earnings in 1960. The average savings propensity of this group was about 75 per cent. Such an emphasis on retained earnings implies that financing from internal resources is given more weight in savings decisions than are dividend distributions. These firms are not seeking equity funds in the organized capital markets, although they undoubtedly attract some equity capital from the unorganized capital markets.

What are the implications of an increase in corporate taxes for this group? First, because of the present income tax discrimination in favor of small firms, the average effective rate of direct corporate taxes will be quite low, assuming a moderate return on capital. A firm with $250,000 of taxable income and no excess profits would pay total direct taxes at a rate of 24.33 per cent. How would the average of such firms react to an increase in tax liabilities of, for example, 20 per cent? If it is assumed, on the average,

TABLE A–15

Percentage of Annual Profits Distributed by Non-Financial Corporations
Listed on the Bogotá Stock Exchange, 1957 to 1960

	1957		1958		1959		1960		Average
Liquid Profits	Percentage of Dividends to Profits	Number of Firms	Percentage of Dividends to Profits	Number of Firms	Percentage of Dividends to Profits	Number of Firms	Percentage of Dividends to Profits	Number of Firms	Percentage of Profits Distributed 1957 to 1960
$ 0–$ 100,000	28.5	1	55.0	2	0.0	1	n.a.	n.a.	n.a.
100,001– 200,000	74.4	2	29.6	2	43.7	3	69.5	—	54.3
200,001– 500,000	54.7	7	42.5	9	55.6	4	55.6	6	52.1
500,001– 1,000,000	67.1	8	76.7	7	47.1	8	67.0	8	64.5
1,000,001– 2,000,000	78.8	9	65.7	11	75.3	16	69.2	9	72.3
2,000,001– 5,000,000	68.4	12	83.4	15	64.3	12	67.4	12	70.9
5,000,001–10,000,000	67.0	7	69.6	7	76.0	9	72.3	12	71.2
over 10,000,000	81.9	4	81.0	3	79.5	3	72.4	3	78.7

Source: Annual and semi-annual reports of the companies made available by the Bogotá Stock Exchange.

that $75 is placed in reserve for each additional $100 in after-tax profits, it would appear that a disproportionate amount of a tax increase would be met by a reduction in savings. That is, if income is reduced by $100 through additional taxes, it would seem that dividends would be reduced by $25 and savings by $75. This is highly speculative, since it is not based on an actual savings function. It might be that dividends would be reduced by more than 25 per cent of the tax increase. But, since such a large proportion of earnings is placed in reserve, it seems likely that a large percentage of the tax increase would be reflected in a reduction of retained earnings.

The reaction to an increase in direct taxes by those firms that are members of the stock exchange and are actively seeking equity capital is somewhat easier to predict. For these, it appears likely that retained earnings will be reduced to a greater extent than dividends if they are faced with an increase in direct tax liabilities. This is based on the assumption that these firms are actively seeking equity capital and would rather reduce savings more than profit distributions in order to maintain dividends at a constant or increasing level. These companies find equity capital a very important source of finance for capital investments. Such capital increases can be timed to coincide with plans for the expansion and replacement of assets. But, if the firms are to be able to attract this capital when it is needed and on reasonable terms, their shares must be attractive. In addition, if dividends can be maintained or increased, a firm's credit standing for loan capital is enhanced.

The foregoing discussion exposes a dilemma. The corporate and government sectors are the two most important savers in Colombia. Also, to the extent that personal savings do not reach required levels for developmental purposes, business or government savings will have to be increased as a compensation. An attempt to increase government savings through increases in corporate taxes may be successful, but it may be offset in part or in full by a reduction in total domestic savings. This places a burden on the government to tax corporations prudently and to use the revenues for investment purposes.

THE RELATIVE TAX TREATMENT OF CORPORATIONS AND LIMITED LIABILITY COMPANIES

The tax discrimination against the corporation and in favor of the limited liability company is apparent from the rate structures applicable to these two forms of business organization. While the corporation has a three-rate schedule of 12 per cent on taxable income up to $100,000, 24 per cent from $100,000 to $1,000,000, and 36 per cent over $1,000,000, the limited liability company has three rates of only 4 per cent on the first $100,000 of taxable income, 8 per cent on income between $100,000 and $300,000, and 12 per cent on income in excess of $300,000. All of the income of a limited liability company after payment of the tax at the business level is construed to be distributed for tax purposes at the individual level, but this provision does not serve to even the tax burden between corporations and limited liability companies.

The tax discrimination against corporations and in favor of limited liability companies also is likely to be greater than it appears from an examination of the rate structures. This is because a larger proportion of taxes is collected from limited liability companies at the individual level, and the higher this proportion, the greater the chances for tax evasion. There is also more likelihood that the limited liability company can evade taxes at the level of the firm, since their accounts, in general, unlike corporations, do not come under the supervision of the Superintendent of Corporations. Corporate owners are favored to the extent that they pay the individual income tax only on profits actually received, but this is less of an advantage than it might appear, since many corporations distribute a relatively high percentage of their earnings, and this portion is taxed twice.

It has been assumed by many tax experts in Colombia that the limited liability company has characteristics of both a partnership and a corporation, so that neutral tax treatment requires tax burdens that are lower than those borne by corporations but higher than those placed on partnerships. This has resulted in limited liability companies being taxed like partnerships but with somewhat higher rates.

It is also argued that the limited liability company is a necessary step in the evolutionary growth of a firm from a partnership to a corporation. But this contention is not supported by the available evidence. The majority of Colombian corporations were never limited liability companies, and there are innumerable cases of companies that have retained the limited liability form throughout their existence even though they are larger today than all but the largest corporations. For example, Table A–16 shows the gross assets of limited liability companies registered with the *Cámara de Comercio* in Bogotá for selected years. Of those companies registered in 1954, there were sixty-four with assets in excess of $1 million, and their average asset size was about $4 million. The two largest of these firms had average assets of about $27 million.

Popular opinion in Colombia holds that the limited liability company is discriminated against with respect to bank credit, but there is no evidence to substantiate this belief. According to many banking officials in Colombia, the only difference between extending credit to a corporation and to a limited liability company is that in some cases one or more owners of a limited liability company may be asked to co-sign a bank note. But even this restriction is apparently quite rare and only applies in cases where a firm has had previous financial difficulties.

The tax unneutrality that exists between corporations and limited liability companies may well retard industrial development. Firms that might otherwise incorporate and seek capital from a broader market may be dissuaded because of the sharp increase in

TABLE A–16

Gross Assets of New Limited Liability Companies, Department of Cundinamarca, 1950, 1954, and 1958

(Thousands of Pesos)

	1950	1954	1958
Companies with less than $1,000,000 in gross assets[a]			
Number of companies	106	338	551
Total gross assets	$29,127	$62,667	$91,013
Average gross assets	274.8	185.4	165.2
Companies with gross assets in excess of $1,000,000 [a]			
Number of companies	17	64	65
Total gross assets	33,987	255,517	160,323
Average gross assets	1,999.2	3,992.5	2,466.5

[a] In each case this is the number of new limited liability companies registered in the *Cámara de Comercio*, Bogotá. However, the gross assets listed are not always the assets corresponding to the year when the firms were registered. For example, the assets listed for some companies registered with the *Cámara de Comercio* in 1950 would be their assets as of 1955. In other words, there is a delay in reporting assets.

Source: Annual records of the *Cámara de Comercio*, Bogotá.

tax liabilities attendant with a change in legal form. On the other hand, the fact that the limited liability company is restricted to the capital provided by twenty persons and that its shares cannot be traded, demonstrates that it is not the proper vehicle for capital expansion and industrial development.

The available evidence indicates that the tax differential between corporations and limited liability companies may have been of considerable importance in the growth of the latter. The 1953 tax reforms resulted in minor adjustments to corporate rates and in the introduction of a proportional tax of 3 per cent on partnerships and limited liability companies. But more important, corporate dividends were taxed for the first time at the individual level. Table A–17 shows that eighty-seven corporations with assets of $96 million liquidated and changed to limited liability companies in the second six months of 1953. This evidence suggests that a tax differential may well be enough (even under the present rate structure) to deter a small firm from taking the corporate form. Concomitant with these corporate liquidations, there was a reduction in the flow of

TABLE A–17

Corporate Organizational Activities after the 1953 Tax Reform

(Thousands of Pesos)

	First Six Months of 1953	Second Six Months of 1953	First Six Months of 1954	First Six Months of 1955
New corporations	49	45	23	26
Paid-in capital	$50,030.1	$23,094.5	$ 9,034.5	$ 8,555.4
Capital increases				
Number of authorizations	46	34	18	36
Capital	74,471.6	37,995.1	18,084.0	49,670.0
Authorizations to place shares				
Number of authorizations	95	n.a.	63	78
Number of shares	7,552,723	n.a.	6,748,337	5,653,428
Value of shares	52,846.9	n.a.	40,383.4	37,131.3
Liquidation of corporations	n.a.	128	n.a.	n.a.
Assets of liquidated companies	n.a.	18,188.6	n.a.	n.a.
Assets of corporations transformed into limited liability companies	n.a.	95,612.2	n.a.	n.a.
Number of liquidations	n.a.	128	n.a.	n.a.
Number of corporations transformed into limited liability companies	n.a.	87	n.a.	n.a.

Source: *Revista de la Superintendencia de Sociedades Anónimas*, various issues.

capital into the corporate sector. While there were forty-nine new incorporations with paid-in capital of $50 million in the first six months of 1953, in the comparable period of the following year there were twenty-three new incorporations with paid-in capital of only $9 million.

The reduction in the growth of new corporations following the 1953 tax reform was not merely a transitory phenomenon. Table A–18 shows the comparative growth of new corporations and selected limited liability companies for the period from 1953 to 1959. In 1953 the paid-in capital of new corporations was $84.5 million, or about 50 per cent of the paid-in capital of new limited liability companies. In 1956 the paid-in capital of new corporations was only $29.2 million, or about 10 per cent of the paid-in capital of new limited liability companies. In 1958, the last year for which there are complete data, the net increase in paid-in capital [8] for domestic corporations was only some 63 per cent of capital increases in those limited liability companies registered with the Superintendent of Corporations.

An examination of the comparative rates of growth of these two forms of business organization for various departments is even more revealing. Table A–19 shows various measures of the growth of corporations and limited liability companies in the department of Valle for selected years from 1945 to 1961. While the number of corporations domiciled in this department decreased by 4 from 1945 to 1961, during the same period the number of limited liability companies increased from 308 to 1,313. Because of the rapid growth of a few large corporations, the total gross assets of corporations grew faster than the total assets of limited liability companies. This growth in size, but not in the number of corporations, may be noted in the changes in the average size of corporations over the period. The average size of corporations as measured by gross assets increased over tenfold between 1945 and 1961.

Table A–20 shows the comparative rates of growth of corporations and limited liability companies in the departments of Valle, Antioquia, and Atlántico. In these three depart-

[8] The net increase in paid-in capital is the sum of capital in new companies and capital increases in other companies minus the capital of liquidated companies.

TABLE A-18

Comparative Growth of Paid-in Capital in Corporations and Selected Limited
Liability Companies, 1953 to 1959

(Millions of Pesos)

	1953	1954	1955	1956	1957	1958	1959[a]
Corporations							
Paid-in capital, new companies	84.48	59.81	79.69	29.16	65.47	112.87	48.62
Capital increases	96.94	216.97	252.46	296.58	149.29	274.58	194.67
Net increase in paid-in capital[b]	159.59	226.11	124.12	301.98	198.34	304.03	231.20
Limited liability companies[c]							
Paid-in capital, new companies	172.67	210.74	269.84	284.29	339.90	353.83	163.23
Capital increases	91.81	264.53	134.74	104.10	179.54	251.50	126.45
Net increase in paid-in capital	189.29	369.11	250.06	287.41	391.84	482.46	226.87
Net increase in corporate paid-in capital as a percentage of the increase in capital of limited liability companies	84.31	61.26	49.64	109.54	50.62	63.02	101.91
Paid-in capital of new corporations as a percentage of capital of new limited liability companies	49.13	28.38	29.53	10.26	19.26	34.72	29.79

[a] January 1 to June 30.
[b] Capital of new companies plus capital increases in other companies minus capital of liquidated firms.

[c] Includes only limited liability companies registered with the Superintendencia de Sociedades Anónimas.
Source: Superintendencia de Sociedades Anónimas.

TABLE A-19

Corporations and Limited Liability Companies in the Department of Valle,
Various Years from 1945 to 1961

(Thousands of Pesos)

	1945	1947	1950	1953	1956	1961
Corporations						
Number	122	113	135	91	79	118
Total gross assets	102,729	132,580	301,560	426,580	548,650	1,038,628
Average gross assets	842.0	1,173.3	2,233.8	4,687.7	6,944.9	8,801.9
Index of average gross assets, 1945 = 100	100	139.3	265.3	556.7	824.8	1,045.4
Limited liability companies						
Number	308	408	628	766	1,002	1,313
Total gross assets	42,206	83,020	169,379	316,086	630,374	1,358,378
Index of total gross assets, 1945 = 100	100	196.7	401.3	748.9	1,943.6	3,218.4
Other forms of business organization						
Number	717	735	936	998	1,058	2,365
Total gross assets	45,063	91,700	154,902	253,539	234,822	903,681
Gross assets as a percentage of assets of limited liability companies	106.8	110.5	91.5	80.2	37.3	66.5
All forms of business organization						
Percentage of total assets in commercial activities	40.17	36.83	41.10	38.92	30.07	39.64
Percentage of total assets in industrial activities	21.74	50.89	49.33	48.30	51.12	45.23

Source: Data on corporations from the *Revista de la Superintendencia de Sociedades Anónimas;* data on limited liability companies compiled from the records of the Cámara de Comercio for the department of Valle.

ments there were 101 fewer corporations in 1956 than in 1950, while there was an increase of 59 per cent in the number of limited liability companies. The gross assets of limited liability companies in these three departments also increased from 33 per cent of gross corporate assets in 1950 to 64 per cent in 1956.

The data on gross assets obscure the fact that it is a few large and mature corporations that have grown rapidly over the last decade. As shown in Table A-21, there were only

TABLE A-20

Corporations and Limited Liability Companies in the Departments of Valle,
Atlántico, and Antioquia, Various Years from 1950 to 1961

(Thousands of Pesos)

	1950	1953	1956	1958	1961
Limited liability companies					
Number	1,806	2,268	2,876	2,283	3,871
Total gross assets	422,807	803,494	1,555,457	2,116,546	3,311,532
Index of total gross assets, 1950 = 100	100	190.04	367.89	500.59	783.23
Average gross assets	234.1	354.3	540.8	927.1	855.5
Index of average gross assets, 1950 = 100	100	151.35	231.01	396.02	365.44
Corporations					
Number	356	281	255	n.a.	n.a.
Total gross assets	1,297,551	1,715,153	2,429,634	n.a.	n.a.
Index of total gross assets, 1950 = 100	100	132.3	187.2	n.a.	n.a.
Average gross assets	3,644.8	6,103.7	9,528.0	n.a.	n.a.
Index of average gross assets, 1950 = 100	100	167.5	261.4	n.a.	n.a.
Gross assets of limited liability companies as a percentage of assets of corporations	32.58	46.85	64.02	n.a.	n.a.

Source: Data on corporations derived from various issues of the *Revista de la Superintendencia de Sociedades Anónimas;* data on limited liability companies compiled from annual records made available by the *Cámara de Comercio* in Cali, Medellín, and Barranquilla.

TABLE A-21

Characteristics of Colombian Corporations, 1940 to 1960

	Number of Corporations	Index 1940=100	Paid-In Capital (Thousands)	Index 1940=100	Total Assets (Thousands)	Index 1940=100	After-Tax Profits (Thousands)	Index 1940=100	Percentage Return on Capital	Percentage Return on Total Assets
1940	710	100	$ 212,927	100	$ 384,741	100	$ 26,300	100	12.35	6.84
1941	805	113	246,680	116	442,275	115	35,789	136	14.50	8.09
1942	842	118	279,114	131	515,599	134	43,700	166	15.66	8.48
1943	846	119	322,581	151	589,268	153	53,443	203	16.57	9.07
1944	910	128	394,693	185	745,278	194	63,867	243	16.18	8.57
1945	949	134	464,062	218	950,960	246	81,099	308	17.48	8.45
1946	998	140	605,550	284	1,190,735	309	110,824	421	18.30	9.31
1947	1,056	149	784,805	369	1,596,709	415	126,305	480	16.09	7.91
1948	1,094	154	989,547	465	1,996,976	519	158,624	603	16.03	7.94
1949	1,192	168	1,160,641	545	2,426,669	631	169,746	645	14.63	7.00
1950	1,212	171	1,259,170	591	2,849,489	741	214,992	817	17.07	7.54
1951	1,260	177	1,363,595	640	3,195,001	830	215,581	820	15.81	6.75
1952	1,217	171	1,454,293	683	3,515,607	914	249,064	947	17.13	7.08
1953	1,226	173	1,480,658	695	3,766,271	979	253,357	963	17.11	6.73
1954	1,024	144	1,575,667	740	4,198,502	1,091	311,263	1,184	19.75	7.41
1955	900	127	1,819,407	854	4,498,704	1,169	251,526	968	13.82	5.59
1956	885	125	1,984,046	932	5,276,709	1,371	359,948	1,369	18.14	6.82
1957	921	130	2,142,369	1,006	6,183,322	1,607	429,757	1,634	20.06	6.95
1958	955	135	2,483,509	1,166	7,314,140	1,901	481,994	1,833	19.41	6.59
1959	981	138	2,790,716	1,311	8,540,592	2,220	581,561	2,211	20.84	6.81
1960	1,033	145	3,156,291	1,482	10,031,265	2,607	670,243	2,548	21.23	6.68

Source: Revista de la Superintendencia de Sociedades Anónimas, various issues.

1,033 domestic corporations in 1960, 193 less than in 1953. Growth in the corporate sector, however, should not be confined to the rapid expansion of existing companies but, rather, also should result in an increasing number of new firms. In Colombia, however, there has been a marked decline in the formation of new corporations, and it is very likely that it has been the differential tax treatment of corporations and limited liability companies that has been responsible for this.

Limited Liability Companies Engaged in Commercial Activities

It might be argued that the much greater growth of limited liability companies as compared to corporations merely reflects a faster rate of growth in commercial as compared to industrial activities; i.e., the limited liability form may be ideal for commercial ventures, and this sector may have been growing faster than the industrial sector. This is a plausible hypothesis, but it appears that it may be rejected on the basis of the evidence available. Table A–22 shows certain financial data for forty-seven medium-size limited liability companies registered with the Superintendent of Corporations in 1957. These data show that 52.0 per cent of the total assets of these firms were in the manufacturing sector as opposed to 29.9 per cent in commerce and 11.0 per cent in services.

TABLE A–22

Financial Data for Forty-Seven Limited Liability Companies Registered with the Superintendent of Corporations, 1957

(Thousands of Pesos)

Type of Activity	Total Assets	Capital	Profits	Percentage of Total Assets
Primary production	$2,154	$1,372	$ 107	1.9
Mining	4,502	4,000	198	4.0
Construction	1,332	550	n.a.	1.2
Manufacturing	58,898	26,672	3,166	52.0
Services	12,521	8,100	490	11.0
Commerce	33,917	7,535	851	29.9

Source: *Revista de la Superintendencia de Sociedades Anónimas*, August, 1958, p. 205.

Table A–19, presented previously, also shows the growth in assets by type of business activity in the department of Valle from 1945 to 1961. These data demonstrate that, as measured by asset values, the commercial sector grew less rapidly than the industrial sector during this seventeen-year period. In 1945, for example, 21.74 per cent of total business assets was in the industrial sector, and 40.17 per cent was in commercial activities. By 1961, 45.23 per cent of total business assets was in the industrial sector, and 39.64 per cent was in commercial activities. It is implicit in the data that much of the growth in assets of limited liability companies was in industrial activities. In the department of Valle, the total growth in assets in the industrial sector during the period from 1945 to 1961 was $1,492.9 million. The growth in corporate assets over the same period was $935.9 million. Even under the extreme assumption that all of the growth in corporate assets was in industrial activities, there remains $557 million of growth in industrial assets to be accounted for by other business forms. If all of these assets are attributed to limited liability companies, it would mean that about 43 per cent of the asset growth for this type of company was in industrial activities.

The most conclusive evidence with respect to the importance of limited liability companies in industrial activities was obtained in the department of Atlántico. During the period from 1955 to 1961, about 50 per cent of the assets of new limited liability companies was in industrial ventures. During the same seven-year period, there were 338 new limited liability companies formed in the industrial sector, with total assets of $49,042,438. On the other hand, there were only 11 new corporations formed in the industrial sector, with total assets of $22,088,-434.[9] The data with respect to the capital increases of existing companies is much the same. Between 1955 and 1961, 7 industrial

[9] One company accounted for $17,700,000, so that the average size of the remaining corporations was only about $439,000.

corporations increased their paid-in capital by $16,310,486. During the same period, 141 limited liability companies engaged in industrial activities increased their capital by $28,073,615.

The above discussion does not imply that there is no role for small- and medium-scale firms in the process of economic development of Colombia. Studies have shown that these firms in Colombia have played an important role in the process of industrialization.[10] The analysis has demonstrated, however, that limited liability companies and corporations are directly competitive in many instances, and the differential tax treatment in favor of limited liability companies has retarded the growth of new share-issuing firms. As a result, a strong case exists for the equalization of direct tax burdens on these two forms of business organization.

In making appropriate tax rate adjustments, two restraints are apparent: (1) The tax burden on limited liability companies will have to be raised, for it is not fiscally prudent to lower tax rates on corporations. (2) Because of tax enforcement problems, the upward adjustments should result in increased collections at the level of the firm rather than at the individual level. In view of these requirements, it would be desirable to tax individual owners of limited liability companies only on profits actually distributed to them and adjust the tax rates of limited liability companies upward at the company level—that is, treat limited liability companies exactly like corporations for income tax purposes. It would also be desirable to subject limited liability companies to the excess profits tax.

SPECIAL PROBLEMS RELATED TO AN INFLATIONARY ENVIRONMENT

The previous observation that the burden of direct corporate taxes does not seem excessive was provisional in the sense that only

[10] See, for example, *Small and Medium Industry in Colombian Development*, Stanford Research Institute, June, 1962.

tax rates were examined and not the determination of taxable income. If accounting profits as defined in the tax laws exceed economic profits, the real tax burden will also exceed the nominal monetary burden. Accounting profits will exceed economic profits if certain costs are not included in the determination of taxable income. Critics of the Colombian income tax system maintain that the principal cost item that is not fully reflected is depreciation allowances.

The arguments that are advanced in Colombia over the relative advantages of depreciation allowances based on historical cost as compared to replacement cost are often misleading. Also, since considerable controversy has arisen on this subject, it is worthwhile to examine the economic and equity considerations involved.

Statements supporting the replacement cost approach are often formulated around the misleading term "taxing away capital." This argument may be presented in the following manner: Assume that a piece of equipment costs $100, has a service life of one year, and cost $150 to replace. Assume, further, that net income (but gross of depreciation) derived from the equipment is $200 and the effective tax rate is 40 per cent. On an historical cost basis, depreciation allowances would be $100, taxable income $100, and taxes $40. If it is assumed that the income net of depreciation and taxes is distributed, there would be insufficient funds to replace the asset. Hence, $50 of capital in the guise of income has been distributed. When the government levies a tax of 40 per cent on the $100 of net income, it has "taxed away" $20 of capital as income.

On the other hand, the opponents of depreciation based on replacement cost often couch their arguments around the equity considerations involved. They argue that other taxpayers also suffer from inflation. Assume that an individual owns a non-depreciable asset in the form of a fixed interest bond with a face value of $100,000, an interest rate of 7.5 per cent, and an annual income of $7,500. With a marginal tax rate of 20 per cent, the personal income tax liability would be $1,500, and the after-tax income would be $6,000. But, if the price level rises by 20 per cent, the investor's after-tax income would have to be $7,500 for him to derive the same real income as he received before the rise in the price level. Conversely, this person would have to invest $120,000 instead of $100,000 to derive the same real income, assuming the same rate of interest. Thus, depreciation based on replacement cost discriminates against persons who own non-depreciable assets and who depend on fixed incomes.

It is implicit in the latter argument that it is undesirable to give tax relief to some and not to others during a period of inflation. Since it is impossible to give relief to everyone, why select any particular group for special treatment? This argument has some merit, but there are other goals of tax policy besides neutrality of treatment and equity. For example, exemptions from tax are granted to some firms although there is little to be said for them on equity grounds. Very high and steeply progressive rates of tax on individual income are justified on equity grounds although their economic justification may be less convincing.

Another possible argument against replacement cost depreciation is the belief that owners of depreciable assets, especially those in the corporate sector, are the "gainers" under inflationary conditions. There is little evidence to support this contention as far as Colombian corporations are concerned. During the inflationary period of 1956 to 1958 (with devaluation in 1957), unit costs in the manufacturing sector rose about 55 per cent, factory prices increased 48 per cent, and industrial profits declined from 14 to 11 per cent of the gross volume of output.[11]

There is no doubt that if the replacement cost of an asset rises over the productive period of the asset and depreciation allowances are based on initial cost, the effective

tax rate on economic profits will exceed the nominal rate. But the lack of available data on depreciation allowances in Colombia makes an adequate assessment of this problem difficult. There are some data on financing from depreciation and depletion allowances for the corporate sector that are summarized in Table A–23. Depreciation and depletion allowances accounted for 8.9 per cent of the total amount of internal corporate financial resources from 1941 to 1945, 20.8 per cent in 1955, but since then have declined steadily, representing only 12.0 per cent of internal financial resources in 1960. In 1956 depreciation financing as a percentage of fixed investment was as high as 42.3 per cent, but by 1960 this ratio had fallen to 26.6 per cent. On the basis of this evidence, even though it is inconclusive, it appears that some adjustment in depreciation allowances is justified.

There are two principal ways in which depreciation policy may be adjusted to give greater tax relief: depreciation allowances based on replacement cost, and more rapid historical cost depreciation. The replacement cost approach involves considerable administrative complexity. The most difficult problems arise with respect to defining the costs involved and allocating them over the period of depreciation and determining the appropriate rate, if any, to tax recognized increases in asset values. The easiest system to administer, an across-the-board increase in the value of the depreciable assets of all taxpayers, tends to distribute the tax relief capriciously, in many cases resulting in little correlation with actual asset values. In a more sophisticated method based on the use of a price index, two difficulties arise: (1) Various economic sectors will be affected differently by price increases. (2) It is almost impossible to determine to what extent the increased cost of equipment reflects price increases as compared to improvements in the quality of the assets. One may question seriously the desirability of burdening the administrative resources with the difficult problems inherent in administering such a program.

---

[11] Data from an unpublished study by the International Bank for Reconstruction and Development on the Colombian Development Plan.

TABLE A–23

Sources and Uses of Finance in Percentage Terms for Colombian Corporations, Selected Years

	Average for 1941 to 1945	Average for 1946 to 1952	1952	1953	1954	1955	1956	1957	1958	1959	1960
Sources of Finance:											
Internal finance	21.7	21.9	28.7	41.9	49.6	36.1	40.0	42.0	43.2	44.5	33.5
Undistributed profits	12.8	11.5	13.9	28.4	33.6	15.3	24.7	31.4	30.8	31.7	21.5
Depreciation and depletion	8.9	10.4	14.8	13.5	16.0	20.8	15.3	10.6	12.4	12.8	12.0
External finance	78.3	79.1	71.3	58.1	50.4	63.8	60.0	58.1	56.8	55.4	66.5
Total loans	33.8	35.4	43.4	47.9	29.4	−11.0	36.2	42.8	29.0	31.6	43.3
Banks				8.8	19.1	7.6	16.6	19.5	9.7	12.3	9.3
Government				3.1	−1.6	−0.1	0.8	0.2	0.6	−0.1	−0.3
Financial institutions				−6.0	1.2	13.8	14.7	13.5	15.0	−0.5	11.8
Exterior				5.1	7.2	6.8	10.1	−0.4	2.6	3.3	9.8
Individuals				80.2	−0.8	−33.7	5.8	9.6	0.1	15.3	12.6
Other				−43.3	4.3	−5.4	−11.8	0.4	1.0	1.3	0.1
Contributions and increases in capital	44.5	43.7	27.9	10.2	21.0	74.8	23.8	15.3	27.8	23.8	23.2
Uses of Finance:											
Fixed capital	41.1	42.2	46.1	62.1	67.1	72.7	36.2	37.5	32.3	39.0	45.1
Inventories	14.7	13.4	15.3	4.6	5.4	20.0	19.4	36.9	27.4	23.6	17.6
Financial investment	44.2	44.4	38.6	28.3	27.5	7.3	44.4	35.6	40.3	37.4	37.3
Depreciation financing as a percentage of fixed investment	21.6	24.6	32.1	20.1	23.8	28.6	42.3	28.3	38.4	32.8	26.6

Source: Analysis and Projections of Economic Development: Part III. The Economic Development of Colombia. United Nations, CEMLA, 1957; and *Revista de la Superintendencia de Sociedades Anónimas,* various issues.

The alternative to replacement cost depreciation is some type of accelerated depreciation policy based on historical cost. The theoretical rationale of accelerated depreciation can be summarized as follows: Faster depreciation allowances mean smaller profits and, thus, a reduction of tax liabilities. Firms that are growing, in the sense of acquiring new fixed capital assets, gain permanent tax relief. Firms that are not growing merely have their tax payments postponed. This postponment of taxes has been likened to a "tax-free loan." [12] Accelerated depreciation is infinitely easier to administer for the tax officials than is replacement cost depreciation.

At any time, there exist four general uses for a firm's financial resources: (1) investment in capital assets, either in replacing old ones or expanding capacity; (2) investment in inventories; (3) investment in land and buildings not directly related to the operations of the firm; and (4) investment in financial assets.

For any firm, there need be no coincidence between the depreciation reserves available and their use for asset replacement and expansion. In the interim, the firm must hold long-term funds for eventual capital investment outlays. Of importance, therefore, is the need to maintain the real value of the funds. This problem is difficult when there is continuous monetary depreciation.

The low nominal interest rates and the legal limitations on amounts that may be held in savings institutions make this type of investment particularly undesirable. [13] Mort-

[12] See E. D. Domar, "The Case for Accelerated Depreciation," *Quarterly Journal of Economics,* Vol. LXVII, No. 4, November, 1953.

[13] Under current legislation, the interest rates vary from 4 to 5 per cent. There is also a legal limit of $15,000 in any one institution, with a total limit of $165,000.

gage cedulas and government development bonds are more acceptable instruments, especially in view of their tax-exempt status and the marginal tax rates at the corporate level. But even with these instruments, there are limits to the amounts that may be invested. A certain amount of mortgage cedulas is, in effect, forced into corporate portfolios under existing tax legislation. To satisfy tax requirements, these cedulas must be purchased at par value through regular channels and held in trusteeship with the Central Mortgage Bank for five years. They may be held longer since such instruments are discounted about 15 per cent by the market. These instruments also can be purchased at a discounted value and yield a substantial return (about 8.5 per cent) plus the advantage of tax exemption. But even this rate of return represents only partial protection from inflation. Government development bonds are approximately equal in rate of return, and are discounted only by about 5 per cent. These instruments provide a reasonably good investment for some internal funds.

There is also the possibility of holding shares of other corporations, although, in the aggregate, there are also limits to this type of investment. Only about 15 per cent of Colombian corporations are listed on the Bogotá stock exchange. Moreover, quoted stock prices are sluggish, and although an adequate index of stock prices does not exist, it appears doubtful that share values accurately reflect the effects of inflation. Even if rates of return (including capital gains) are sufficient to maintain the real value of the financial capital, the opportunity cost of such an investment is high. That is, it does not seem desirable for a firm to hold all of its long-term funds pending outlays on fixed capital in a form in which the real rate of return may be negligible. On the other hand, two of the best possibilities for not only "riding the inflationary wave" but perhaps outpacing it, are not desirable from a social point of view. One is investment in real estate not directly related to the operations of the enterprise, while the other is investment in inventory. The tendency to invest in inventory emphasizes the need to relate tax relief for depreciation directly to capital investments.

In addition to the problem of maintaining the real value of internal funds, inflation results in problems related to external finance, especially the obtaining of equity capital. With the exception of some medium-term bonds issued by the larger corporations, most corporate loan capital is relatively short term. Colombian corporations find it necessary, therefore, to sell shares to provide long-term capital. However, the instruments that corporations sell for this purpose become less desirable during a period of prolonged inflation, expecially when the inflation results in frequent devaluations. Under these circumstances, foreign investments become increasingly more attractive than domestic corporate shares.

An investor can obtain, on the average, a return of about 10 or 11 per cent from stocks listed on the Bogotá stock exchange. But, by comparison to foreign investments, this yield is not competitive. Table A–24 shows the nominal rates of return per annum which could have been obtained from temporary investments made abroad for various lengths of time between 1953 and 1961. The calculations are based on a rate of return

TABLE A–24

Annual Interest Yields on Temporary Foreign Financial Investments for Various Durations of Time, 1953 to 1961[a]

Duration of Foreign Investment	Annual Yield (Per Cent)
Average of seven two-year periods	15.6
Average of six three-year periods	17.4
Average of five four-year periods	15.1
Average of four five-year periods	17.3
Average of three six-year periods	16.2
Average of two seven-year periods	15.8
Average of one eight-year period	15.0

[a] The calculations are based on the assumptions that capital is exported and imported at the free exchange rate and that the funds are invested in the United States at a rate of return of 3 per cent per annum.

Source: Unpublished study by R. W. Adler, CEDE, Universidad de los Andes, Bogotá.

of 3 per cent. Because of frequent devaluations, a Colombian could have invested in a savings account in New York in 1953, allowed the interest to accumulate, and then repatriated the principal and interest in 1961 for a nominal rate of return of 15 per cent per annum. The table shows further that between these years, temporary investments abroad at 3 per cent for various lengths of time, from two years up to eight years, would have yielded a rate of return ranging from 15 to over 17 per cent. These returns are based on speculative investments in the sense that both principal and interest are repatriated after a short period of time. It is clear, however, that if one invested permanently in the United States in an investment that yielded 5 or 6 per cent and merely repatriated the interest every year or two, the rate of return because of devaluations would be 10 to 12 per cent during the period, and the capital could be kept intact. The principal could then be repatriated when desired with a sizable gain due to successive devaluations. Not only is this a problem with respect to corporate financing, but it is an even greater problem from the point of view of retaining private savings in Colombia for the financing of economic development.

SUMMARY OF RELEVANT POLICY CONCLUSIONS

1) Colombian corporations are very closely held, with less than 1 per cent of the shareholders owning nearly 73 per cent of total shares in 1959. This characteristic has relevance with respect to equity considerations and proposals for integrating the corporate and individual income taxes.

2) Business savings in Colombia are an important component of total private savings, and corporate savings, in turn, represent a major part of business savings. A large part of private savings for the fulfillment of the development plan is expected to originate in depreciation and depletion allowances. On the basis of the evidence available, there is a need to encourage higher levels of business savings.

3) The monetary burden of direct taxes on corporations does not appear to be excessive, assuming "reasonable" returns on assets. However, the progressivity of the income tax, together with the excess profits tax, provides a curious mixture of incentives and disincentives to corporate development. The corporate income tax penalizes large firms, while the excess profits tax discriminates against small firms.

4) Although the absolute burden of taxes on corporations does not appear excessive, they are over-taxed in a relative sense. While the corporate sector paid a proportion of the total national direct taxes ranging from 34.34 per cent in 1955 to 37.91 per cent in 1959, the contribution of domestic corporations to the net private product was less than 8 per cent in 1955 and reached 11 per cent in only one year during this period. By comparison, the agricultural sector was estimated to contribute only 14.29 per cent of national direct taxes in 1959, although this sector in the same year contributed 42.54 per cent of the net private product.

5) The larger corporations are concentrated in manufacturing. As a result, 80.51 per cent of direct corporate taxes was paid by corporations in the manufacturing sector in 1961 as compared, for example, to only .90 per cent for corporations in agriculture and .81 per cent for those in transportation and communications.

6) Small corporations (especially those not listed on the stock exchange) retain a higher percentage of their earnings than do large corporations. If these small firms were subjected to an increase in income taxes, corporate savings probably would be reduced to a greater extent than would be the case for large firms. If the net effect of an increase in corporate taxes is to reduce corporate savings, this would place a burden on the government to tax corporations prudently and to use the revenues for developmental purposes.

7) There is serious tax discrimination

against corporations and in favor of limited liability companies. This detracts from the growth of the corporate form of business and should be adjusted by taxing both types of firms neutrally.

8) The evidence points to a need for a liberalization of depreciation allowances, but accelerated depreciation based on historical cost rather than replacement cost depreciation is the preferred policy.

Index

L

Q

R

S

T

FISCAL SURVEY OF COLOMBIA
JOINT TAX PROGRAM OAS/IDB

designer:	Edward D. King
typesetter:	Monotype Composition Company
typefaces:	Bodoni, Times Roman
printer:	Universal Lithographers, Inc.
paper:	Warren's Bookman Offset
binder:	Moore and Company
cover material:	Bancroft Arrestox C